Media Politics

A Citizen's Guide

FIFTH EDITION

Shanto Iyengar

STANFORD UNIVERSITY

W. W. NORTON & COMPANY
Celebrating a Century of Independent Publishing

W. W. NORTON & COMPANY has been independent since its founding in 1923, when William Warder Norton and Mary D. Herter Norton first published lectures delivered at the People's Institute, the adult education division of New York City's Cooper Union. The firm soon expanded its program beyond the Institute, publishing books by celebrated academics from America and abroad. By midcentury, the two major pillars of Norton's publishing program—trade books and college texts—were firmly established. In the 1950s, the Norton family transferred control of the company to its employees, and today—with a staff of five hundred and hundreds of trade, college, and professional titles published each year—W. W. Norton & Company stands as the largest and oldest publishing house owned wholly by its employees.

Copyright © 2023, 2019, 2016, 2011, 2007 by W. W. Norton & Company, Inc.
All rights reserved
Printed in Canada

Editor: Laura Wilk
Project Editor: Maura Gaughan
Assistant Editor: Catherine Lillie
Managing Editor, College: Marian Johnson
Managing Editor, College Digital Media: Kim Yi
Associate Director of Production, College: Benjamin Reynolds
Media Editor: Spencer Richardson-Jones
Media Associate Editor: Lexi Malakhoff
Media Editorial Assistant: Quinn Campbell
Marketing Manager, Political Science: Ashley Sherwood
Design Director: Rubina Yeh
Designer: Margaret M. Wagner/Anna Reich
Photo Editor: Catherine Abelman
Permissions Manager: Megan Schindel
Permissions Clearing: Patricia Wong
Composition: Graphic World / Project Manager: Sunil Kumar
Manufacturing: Transcontinental—Beauceville, Quebec

Permission to use copyrighted material is included in the credits section of this book, which begins on page 373.
Library of Congress Cataloging-in-Publication Data

W. W. Norton & Company, Inc., 500 Fifth Avenue, New York, NY 10110-0017
wwnorton.com
W. W. Norton & Company Ltd., 15 Carlisle Street, London W1D 3BS

1 2 3 4 5 6 7 8 9 0

BRIEF CONTENTS

CONTENTS

9. Going Public: Governing through the Media 289

VIDEO ARCHIVES FOR
MEDIA POLITICS

The Media Politics video archive includes Video Features on the topics listed below. Each Video Feature presents clips that illustrate the discussion in the text. An icon in the margins of the text indicates when a corresponding clip is available. The video archive can be accessed at *mediapolitics.stanford.edu*.

ACKNOWLEDGMENTS

A substantial part of this book derives from a series of collaborative research projects conducted over the past four decades. The author has had the good fortune to cross paths with several distinguished scholars, including Toril Aalberg, Stephen Ansolabehere, Roy Behr, James Curran, Lauren Davenport, Matthew DeBell, James Fishkin, Sharad Goel, Franklin Gilliam Jr., Justin Grimmer, Kyu Hahn, Allison Harrell, Simon Jackman, Donald Kinder, Jon Krosnick, Daniel Lowenstein, Robert Luskin, Helmut Norpoth, John Petrocik, Markus Prior, Adam Simon, Stuart Soroka, Nicholas Valentino, Lynn Vavreck, and Emily West. He thanks them all for their ongoing contributions to the study of media politics.

No less important was the continuous support provided by graduate and undergraduate students at Yale University; the State University of New York—Stony Brook; University of California—Los Angeles; and Stanford. This edition incorporates research by several recent Stanford PhDs including Yphtach Lelkes, Masha Krupenkin, Solomon Messing, Erik Peterson, Gaurav Sood, Matthew Tyler, and Sean Westwood. Jamal Johnson also provided superb research assistance in updating the figures and tables for this edition.

The updated video archive was compiled by John Walker, the technical director of the John S. Knight Journalism Fellowship Program at Stanford University.

Scott Althaus, Matthew Baum, Jamie Druckman, Steven Livingston, Robert Sahr, James Endersby, Russell Neuman, Chris Burnett, Matt Eshbaugh-Soha, Paul Freedman, Phil Habel, Paul Harwood, Danny Hayes, Travis Ridout, John Sides, Jaeho Cho, David Karpf, Rich Shumate, Stuart Soroka, and Nicholas Valentino contributed insightful commentary on individual chapters for previous editions; the end result was a significantly strengthened manuscript. Daniel Lowenstein not only reviewed but also revised the account of campaign finance reform. For this edition, the author is indebted to Nathan Angelo, Nora Baldner, Michael Baranowski, Jeff Gulati, Tom Johnson, Christopher Kelley, Steve Kirchhoff, Matthew Pietryka, and Michael Pickering for their constructive feedback.

Finally, a number of Norton staff, including Laura Wilk, Catherine Lillie, Spencer Richardson-Jones, Lexi Malakoff, Quinn Campbell, Maura Gaughan, and Benjamin Reynolds, helped ensure a smooth transition from the fourth edition to the fifth.

Shanto Iyengar
PALO ALTO
JULY 2022

1

Introduction

January 6, 2021—At noon, thousands of Trump supporters attend a "Save America" rally in Washington, DC. President Trump addresses the crowd and repeats his false assertions of voter fraud, which he had been expressing since he lost the election in November. "We will never concede. . . . You don't concede when there's theft involved. . . . We won this election and we won it by a landslide."[1] Following the rally, hundreds march to the Capitol, overwhelming the police and storming the building. Inside, terrified senators and representatives— meeting in joint session to certify the Electoral College vote—are rushed out of the House chamber to safety. Some report fearing for their life.

After several hours of chaos and multiple requests for assistance from the Capitol Police, National Guard troops arrive on the scene and clear the Capitol and the surrounding area. Congress reconvenes at 9:00 PM. Five people die; hundreds are injured. The Capitol complex is now under 24-hour military protection. The following day, Twitter makes the unprecedented decision to shut off Donald Trump's account, citing the risk of further incitement to violence.

The events of January 6 encapsulate the essence of media-based politics as practiced in the United States. Politicians exploit and manage media platforms to promote partisan political interests and mobilize their supporters, even going so far as to spread falsehoods and deny the legitimacy of a presidential election. For their part, partisan voters are so committed to their cause that they readily accept as reality falsehoods promoted by party leaders. The Trump supporters who came to Washington, DC, on January 6 from across the country were convinced Mr. Trump was the legitimate victor and that elections officials had manipulated vote counts to deny him reelection.

Although the events of January 6, 2021, constitute an extreme case, the use of mass media for personal political ends reverberates throughout political life. The incidents illustrated in Video Archive 1.1 reflect situations at different points of the politician's comfort gradient, ranging from blame or failure avoidance to credit claiming. In 1998, facing questions over his leadership and an impeachment effort by congressional Republicans, President Bill Clinton went on national television to deny emphatically and falsely an inappropriate sexual relationship with White House intern Monica Lewinsky. In 2020, President Trump's advisers carefully staged daily White House press briefings at the height of the COVID-19 pandemic to assure Americans that the Trump administration had the virus under control. Rather than allowing public health experts to speak, Trump monopolized the limelight and dominated the agenda.

▶ **Video Archive 1.1**
Image Is Everything

At the other end of the spectrum, when politicians face more favorable circumstances, they manipulate their media opportunities for purposes of credit claiming and self-congratulation. In the early days of the COVID-19 pandemic, President Trump boasted that by banning travel from China, his administration had minimized the fatality rate: "You have fifteen people, and the fifteen within a couple of days is going to be down to close to zero." Following the 2003 invasion of Iraq and the toppling of the Saddam Hussein regime, President George W. Bush, a trained pilot, flew a fighter jet onto the aircraft carrier USS *Abraham Lincoln* to declare victory in the war against Iraq and take credit for combating international terrorism.

Elected officials' preoccupation with media imagery is hardly surprising given that most Americans' only contact with the world of public affairs is through the media. In fact, from the perspective of the public, events not covered by the news media make no greater impression than the proverbial tree falling in the forest when no one is around to hear it. For the public, what's in the news—be it in the newspaper, on cable television, radio, or social media—is all there is to know.

No longer confined to elections and campaigns, media appeals have become standard fare in the day-to-day conduct of government and are used by private interests as well as by politicians. During legislative debates, as in the case of the contentious 2021 COVID-19 relief bill, known as the American Rescue Plan Act, officials from both sides appeared regularly on television news programs and talk shows as well as social media platforms to cast their individual spin on the policy. Rather than relying solely on old-fashioned lobbying methods, private parties now sponsor ads and social media posts intended to cue officials about issues such as healthcare, immigration, and gun control.

The habit of playing to the public has spread to policy arenas not typically associated with partisan politics. Fifty years ago, congressional debates over the qualifications of Supreme Court nominees would focus on their legal training, experience, and judicial philosophy. The Senate hearings to confirm nominees did not become prolonged media events. Between 1910 and 1968, the confirmation process for all Supreme Court justices averaged 23 days. "The norm for the period was the absence of controversy, little or no committee deliberation, limited media coverage, and a quick confirmation" (Davis, 2014, p. 656). Today, however, the hearings have become major media spectacles often featuring the same tactics and posturing used in political campaigns. In 1991, after President George H. W. Bush nominated Clarence Thomas, the Democrats (who controlled the Senate) decided to hold hearings to investigate allegations of sexual harassment against him brought by Dr. Anita Hill. As described in Chapter 9, these televised hearings became a blockbuster media event, attracting huge audiences. Some 30 years later, an almost identical script played out in the hearings to confirm Brett Kavanaugh, who had to defend himself against allegations of sexual assault by Dr. Christine Blasey Ford. It is striking that since 1991 the average length of a Senate confirmation has been 74 days.

Even natural disasters have become occasions for public posturing. The George W. Bush administration's inexplicably slow response to Hurricane Katrina, which killed 1,833 people in 2005, generated a wave of negative publicity. In an attempt to stem the tide of bad news, the president ended his summer vacation early, dispatched high-profile spokespersons (such as Secretary of State Condoleezza Rice) to the affected areas, and replaced the head of

FEMA (the Federal Emergency Management Agency). In addition, the government announced that news organizations would be prevented from reporting on the recovery of the dead. It was only the threat of a lawsuit by CNN that caused the government to abandon its effort to censor the news.

The lessons of Katrina were not lost on Bush's successors. Immediately after the explosion in the Gulf of Mexico of the BP oil rig *Deepwater Horizon* in 2010, President Barack Obama's top energy adviser appeared on NBC's *Meet the Press* and declared that the Obama administration was in control of the situation. President Obama made several visits to the Gulf Coast to signal his concern. In the aftermath of Hurricanes Irma and Maria and the sluggish delivery of emergency supplies to the people of Puerto Rico, President Trump toured the devastated areas and was filmed distributing paper towels to an appreciative crowd.

Overall, the use and frequent manipulation of the mass media for political purposes has transformed the practice of leadership and governance. Policy makers resort to the very same tactics that are used by candidates running for election. Advertising, credit taking, blame avoidance, finger-pointing, and other forms of political rhetoric air long after the election is over. Campaigns are continuous.

The unceasing use of the media to further partisan and self-serving objectives has a harmful effect on the collective welfare. Electoral victors are those who excel at projecting powerful imagery and symbolism but not necessarily those who offer substantive expertise, political experience, or pragmatism. The flood of misleading claims sows the seeds of misinformation among partisans on both sides. Large numbers of Republicans continue to believe that Trump, not Biden, won the 2020 election. The use of media platforms to attack and counterattack increases animus and ill will toward political opponents. This phenomenon of affective polarization (described at some length in Chapter 8) poses grave risks to the legitimacy and long-term stability of democratic institutions as illustrated by the violence of January 6. The lack of goodwill in Congress and state legislatures makes it more difficult for elected representatives to bargain and compromise. The role of policy maker has devolved from decision making based on bargaining and accommodation to attempts to intimidate and coerce opponents. On more than one occasion, the result has been gridlock and paralysis in government. Thus, the practice of media politics amounts to a tragedy of the commons: individual participants may be able to manipulate the media to their personal advantage, but in the long run both the body politic and the politician are weakened.

OUTLINE OF THE BOOK

In this book we have the following goals:

- To explain the rise of media-based politics
- To describe the media strategies used to contest elections and to govern
- To document the payoffs associated with these strategies: increases in the candidate's share of the vote on election day, higher approval ratings while in office, and assured reelection
- To assess the liabilities of media-based politics, most notably the possibility of intensified party conflict and polarization, which makes it more difficult for leaders to govern
- To consider the importance of direct politician-to-voter communication facilitated by social media platforms as a new arena of media politics
- To raise questions about how media politics and changing forms of mass communication affect the practice and future of democracy in America

We begin, in Chapter 2, by providing a theoretical perspective. In democratic societies, the news media are expected to contribute three important public services. First, they provide an electoral forum in which all candidates can solicit support from voters. In the United States, the forum is a combination of paid and free media appearances but primarily the former. In most European democracies, on the other hand, the mix heavily favors the latter: most countries do not permit paid political advertising and instead award free broadcast time to all major political parties before elections. Second, the news media are expected to create an information environment—sometimes called the public sphere—where voters can encounter a variety of perspectives on the issues that concern them. In effect, news and other forms of public affairs programming are expected to facilitate the expression of informed opinion. Third, the news media are expected to act as an agent of the public by policing the behavior of government officials. Citizens lack the resources to monitor the actions of their leaders on a daily basis; they delegate this watchdog task to the media. In countries with a free press, the fear of transparency (in the form of media publicity) is supposed to deter public officials from engaging in corrupt behavior (Besley & Prat, 2006). In short, democratic theory casts news organizations as multitasking public utilities.

Against the standards of democratic theory, most contemporary media systems fall short of meeting their civic responsibilities, but the American media appear especially inadequate. A distinctive feature of the American media system is that virtually all news outlets are privately owned. Private ownership creates an inherent tension between the profit motive and civic responsibility. The need to survive forces owners to value audience size over news content; they deliver content that sells rather than content that informs. Inevitably, infotainment takes precedence over serious coverage of national and international issues.

Most democratic societies deal with the dilemma of civic shirking by providing public subsidies to news organizations. The BBC in the United Kingdom, CBC in Canada, ARD in Germany, and NHK in Japan are giant television networks, watched by millions of viewers and financed by taxpayers. Freed from market forces, these organizations deliver more news, documentaries, and other forms of public-spirited programming than their privately owned competitors do. In many nations, the public broadcaster is the market leader, suggesting that people do not necessarily tune out serious and substantive news programming.

The United States has adopted a different approach to encouraging the free flow of public affairs information. Rather than advocating for the growth of public broadcasters (PBS and NPR), communications policy has evolved from early regulations requiring media outlets to provide at least some public service programming to a more laissez-faire reliance on the market. Supporters of regulation assume that the existence of multiple media organizations does not necessarily create a flourishing marketplace. In the early years of broadcasting, for instance, the FCC (Federal Communications Commission) required all national networks to provide a minimal amount of daily news programming in exchange for their free use of the airwaves. The anti-regulation argument, on the other hand, rests on the assumption that the sheer number of news outlets—daily newspapers, national television networks, local television stations, cable networks, blogs, and online social networks—provides Americans with ample opportunity to encounter the proverbial marketplace of ideas.

On a more practical level, *media politics*—as exemplified by the American system—requires two conditions. The first is universal access to the media. No matter how independent or civic-minded the press, societies with low levels of literacy or relatively few television sets or limited internet access will be characterized by alternative forms of political communication, simply because mass media will not be the most efficient means for politicians to reach voters. When the news media's reach is restricted, those who seek votes through media strategies are disadvantaged. The case of Howard Dean's internet-based 2004 presidential campaign is revealing. Although he raised vast sums of money over the Web, and in so doing established himself as the early front-runner for the 2004 Democratic nomination, Dean's pioneering use of technology did not translate into a single primary victory. Fifteen years ago, most primary voters (unlike donors) remained on the wrong side of the digital divide.

The second necessary condition for the flourishing of media politics is the diminished role of political parties in selecting candidates. In most democratic societies, political parties recruit and sponsor candidates. Parties offer competing policy bundles; voters choose among parties; and, depending on the party's share of the popular vote, some number of the individual candidates running under the party banner are declared elected. When the party establishment loses control over the selection of candidates, as vividly illustrated by the rise to prominence of "insurgent" candidates such as President Donald Trump, Senator Bernie Sanders, Representative Alexandria Ocasio-Cortez, and Representative Marjorie Taylor Greene, these *free-agent candidates* turn to the media as the most efficient form of communicating with voters and running for office. Media politics becomes a substitute for party politics.

In fact, the rise of media politics in the United States coincides with the increased reach of the broadcast media and the weakening influence of party elites over the selection of candidates. Beginning in the 1960s, candidates became less dependent on their party organizations and migrated to the mass media as the principal means of reaching voters. Because candidates for elective office represent a significant revenue stream during political campaigns (in the form of paid television advertising), media owners have been only too happy to encourage this form of cash-on-the-barrelhead electioneering.

BEHAVIOR AND PERFORMANCE OF THE PRESS

In Chapter 3, we examine the performance of the American media. First, we trace programming decisions to the pull of market forces and to the professional values and aspirations of journalists. Market forces and journalistic values both compromise the public sphere. As already noted, market forces create incentives to produce superficial news. Concurrently, journalistic values have shifted somewhat, with two relevant sets in play. First, a new class of news organizations has emerged, more dedicated to promoting a political point of view than promoting fact-based reporting. Fox News, MSNBC, One America News, and HuffPost illustrate this genre of journalism. While the number of partisan outlets has increased over time, the dominant model of journalism remains committed to balanced, point-counterpoint reporting. Somewhat paradoxically, the independence that is so valued by nonpartisan news organizations also exacts a toll on press performance. Professional journalists seek autonomy and control over their work product. They are unwilling to act as mere stenographers for politicians and instead go out of their way to resist candidates' efforts to use them as mouthpieces. The role of the campaign reporter today is not to describe but to provide independent analysis of the candidates' actions. Presidential candidates still tour the country making as many public appearances as possible, but their voices are rarely encountered in news presentations. Instead of the candidates, whose speeches represent bias, nonpartisan journalists have turned to a coterie of expert commentators for objective analysis of the campaign. Interpretive or analytic journalism has largely supplanted the earlier standard of descriptive reporting.

Professional norms are but one element of a broader organizational model of journalism. In this view, the news is shaped by the culture of the newsroom and the routines of the workplace. The importance of authoritative sources makes journalists especially reliant on government officials. The Pentagon, State Department, and White House together account for the great majority of news reports on a daily basis. In the aftermath of the deadly terrorist attack in 2016 at the Pulse nightclub in Orlando, Florida, the Federal Bureau of Investigation (FBI) took control of all media releases about the ongoing investigation. A further element of the organizational model is journalistic prestige. The pecking order within journalism creates a strong copycat mentality: what is reported in this morning's *New York Times* and *Washington Post* is inevitably repeated in television newscasts and on internet news sites.

In Chapter 4, we extend the analysis of press performance to the question of adversarial journalism. We show that the stylized account of a watchdog press does not fit well with the facts, particularly reporters' heavy reliance on government officials as news sources. On a regular basis, the Washington press corps converges on the White House press office for the official briefing from the presidential press secretary. In the aftermath of the American invasion of Iraq, daily briefings took place at the Pentagon and also, although only briefly, at the Iraqi Ministry of Information in Baghdad.

The dependence on government sources does not necessarily compromise nonpartisan reporting; after all, Democratic sources can easily be neutralized by Republicans and vice versa. But the preoccupation of the press with official sources means that incumbents have a sizable advantage over their challengers in gaining access to the press. Some official sources are more newsworthy than others. The president is the prime official source; any White House event—no matter how trivial or stage-managed—elicits considerable news coverage.

Even though coverage of government policy can be *indexed* or designed to reflect the degree of diversity among the opinions of elected officials, sometimes elite disagreement is quashed and one particular perspective achieves dominance. The prototypical case of elite consensus occurs during times of military tension or imminent conflict, when opponents of the incumbent administration tend to fall silent as the nation prepares for war. During these periods, the news becomes dominated by official accounts of events, and the press is generally in no position to scrutinize, discount, or otherwise cast doubt on these accounts.

In the aftermath of the invasion of Iraq in 2003, news reports from American journalists embedded with the American invading force were overwhelmingly celebratory in tone and devoid of references to the pain and suffering inflicted on Iraqi civilians. Given the one-sided presentation, it was inevitable that a significant number of Americans would come to believe that Iraq did in fact possess weapons of mass destruction and that Saddam Hussein's regime was implicated in the September 11 attacks on the United States, despite the fact this would turn out to be false. When opposition sources fall silent, the news becomes a conduit for the official version of events. This is a far cry from watchdog journalism.

In our final look at the behavior of the press, Chapter 5 addresses whether the civic capacity of the media has been strengthened or weakened by the massive revolution in information technology. Paradoxically, public affairs information may flow even less freely in the aftermath of the technology-induced transformation of the media marketplace. In 1968, most Americans got their news from one of the three national network newscasts because they had no other choice. Today, the same newscasts compete with cable and satellite networks, local news programming, a variety of soft news programs, millions of websites the world over, and gigantic online social networks. This bewildering array of media choices makes it almost certain that exposure to the news will be more selective; like consumers of goods and services, people will seek out news from preferred providers or programs and tune out others. In addition, social media enable any individual to become a "journalist" by posting information and commentary on a daily basis. The information conveyed through social networks is more likely to attract the receiver's attention since it typically comes from a friend or an acquaintance.

Because people prefer being entertained to being informed, the enhanced media environment has substantially reduced the audience for public affairs programs. In 1960, some 60 million Americans—representing 55 percent of the voting-age population—tuned in to the presidential debates between Richard Nixon and John Kennedy. In 2020, the audience for the Biden–Trump debates averaged around 68 million viewers, representing less than 27 percent of the voting-age population.

The increased fragmentation of media audiences raises important questions about the motives underlying consumer behavior. Some have suggested that the explosion of online news and the increased availability of partisan news encourages consumers to seek out news providers on the basis of whether they expect to agree with the message being presented, thus reducing chance encounters with unknown or disagreeable voices. No longer will all Americans be subject to the same media messages and believe in the same set of facts; instead, they will encounter their preferred party's or candidate's point of view. Immersion in such "echo chambers" leads people to believe in diverging accounts of the political world. The people who stormed the Capitol on January 6 were convinced their cause was just; their social media feeds regularly conveyed claims of a "stolen" election. Thus, when a person's exposure to public affairs information is limited to one perspective, political discord and division are inevitable.

Others have suggested, more optimistically, that the increasing use of the internet will transform the nature of social interaction; people will use online encounters as a substitute for in-person encounters with friends and neighbors. These scholars cite the amount of time people spend immersed in their online social networks and the vast amounts of money raised online by charitable organizations as symptoms of the revival of community and public spirited-ness. By this account, the increased use of information technology strengthens *social capital* and allows individuals to belong to multiple communities and obtain information on demand rather than be limited by the availability of news programming.

Academic investigations into the effects of new-media use (which we summarize in Chapter 5) suggest conclusions somewhere between the pessimistic and optimistic accounts. The fact that Americans can choose from multiple news outlets does not necessarily mean that they tune in only to sources that share their own values. In addition to participating in gated communities to nurture their partisan preferences, consumers can resort to a more utilitarian form of screening by seeking out information on matters that affect their daily life, such as the weather forecast and details about the daily commute. By this logic, local news will trump partisan commentary as a source of information. However, the emergence of huge online social networks has increasingly placed individuals in the path of messages from like-minded "friends," thus inserting considerable partisan bias into the flow of information.

More ominously, because social media platforms know no geographical boundaries, it is now possible for foreign actors to deliver biased messages in the hope of swaying Americans' points view. In 2016 and again in 2020, the Russian government sponsored a series of information campaigns on social media designed to advantage candidate Donald Trump. In Chapter 5, we explain how the "weaponization" of social media occurred and the belated steps taken by Facebook and Twitter to prevent inaccurate and misleading information from entering their networks.

SHAPING THE NEWS

Having dealt with the theory and practice of press performance, we turn next to the second set of players in media politics: the candidates and advocacy groups that seek to shape the news. A candidate's overriding goal is to attract more votes than the opponent. Interest groups and political activists, for their part, seek to promote or prevent the passage of particular policies. Ever since the onset of media politics in the 1960s, political campaigns have become increasingly professionalized with cadres of media consultants, campaign managers, and strategists, all of whom are well aware of the norms and values of journalists and who hope to capitalize on this expertise to achieve the most favorable media treatment of their clients.

From the perspective of the candidate, there are two sets of media opportunities. *Free media* refers to news coverage, even though it is hardly cost free. Typically, campaigns hire well-known media consultants and public relations firms to maximize their client's visibility in the news. In some instances, media strategy centers on damage control and limited visibility when candidates become ensnared in controversy or scandal. Candidates also rely heavily on *paid media*, typically in the form of political advertisements broadcast over television and social media platforms. Candidate Trump attracted so much news coverage in 2016 and 2020 that his team could afford to invest only token amounts on advertising. The content of the ads, their timing, their geographical location, and even their appearance during specific time slots are all a matter of careful calibration and analysis.

The ability of campaigns to inject their spin into the media varies across different platforms. In the case of social media, since there are no editorial "gatekeepers," candidates are free to speak their mind. Trump's regular use of Twitter not only enabled him to reach an audience of millions; it also shaped the agenda of news organizations since most recirculated his tweets in their daily news reports. When candidates attempt to shape the content of news to their advantage, they first turn to news providers aligned with their cause. In the immediate aftermath of the multiple controversies triggered by President

Trump, he would appear on *Fox and Friends* or *Hannity* (both aired by the Fox network) to debunk news reports critical of his actions.

Social media and partisan outlets prove amenable to candidates' efforts to control the flow of news. Achieving one-sided favorable coverage is more difficult in the case of the mainstream media, which are committed to journalistic independence. Campaigns have had to adapt to the more adversarial posture of mainstream journalists. Following the 1988 presidential campaign between incumbent vice president George H. W. Bush and Massachusetts governor Michael Dukakis, when reporters for the first time decided to take off the gloves and publish hard-hitting ad-watch reports challenging the veracity of campaign advertisements, consultants responded by producing ads with a veneer of objectivity (by citing newspaper reports in the ads, for instance). More interesting, campaigns began to produce ads that were designed as bait to elicit ad-watch coverage, with the aim of generating more free media coverage for their candidates. Because they take a strategic approach to adapting their game to the prevailing actions of the press, campaign consultants generally succeed in getting coverage that is beneficial to their clients.

The continuing struggle between journalists and campaign operatives to control the news provides a classic instance of a collective action dilemma. Society benefits when journalists and campaigners cooperate: the news focuses on what the candidates say, the candidates focus on the issues, and voters learn about matters of substance rather than strategy. Because presidential campaigns typically feature two evenly matched sides, old-fashioned descriptive reporting guaranteed that the electorate would be exposed to equal amounts of opposing (and offsetting) spin. Today, in contrast, journalists prefer to inject their voices into the news to tear away the façade of the campaign and reveal the candidates' vote-seeking strategies. The end result is that voters come away with a cynical sense of the process.

Dealing with the press is but one element of campaign strategy. Candidates also have access to the paid element of media—namely, advertisements. In the most general terms, all advertising campaigns are idiosyncratic. Advertising strategy varies depending on the stage of the campaign, the persona and reputation of the sponsoring candidate, and the overall state of the political race. Even allowing for these contextual variations, however, there are several tried-and-true tactics in campaign advertising, including setting the campaign agenda, focusing attention on the candidate's strengths, and attacking the opponent relentlessly. We outline these strategies in Chapter 6 using a series of illustrations from recent presidential and statewide campaigns.

Advertising is the largest expenditure incurred by candidates. No account of advertising strategy is complete without reference to the complex rules governing campaign finance. We close Chapter 6 with a brief survey of federal lawmaking on the subject—from the 1974 amendments made to the Federal Election Campaign Act of 1971, which established the system of public financing of presidential campaigns (and associated expenditures and contribution limits); to the Bipartisan Campaign Reform Act of 2002, which eliminated *soft money* (money raised by political parties rather than by specific candidate organizations) and which banned the airing of *issue ads* (ads advocating the passage or defeat of particular legislation) in the weeks preceding the election; to the 2013 decision of the US Supreme Court in *McCutcheon v. Federal Election Commission*, striking down the cap on the total amount individuals could donate to multiple campaigns.

MEDIA EFFECTS

Having considered how journalists craft their coverage of politicians and how candidates in turn make use of the media, we turn next to assessing the consequences of their actions. How do the content and form of news coverage influence audiences, and do candidates and elected officials who wage more sophisticated media campaigns secure more votes and influence as a result?

We present the evidence in two separate chapters, beginning in Chapter 7, where we take up the question of campaign effects. Despite the enormous investments in advertising and the scrupulously choreographed nature of every campaign event and utterance, there remains considerable doubt about the capacity of campaigns to sway voters. Political scientists can forecast presidential election outcomes quite precisely (although with the notable exceptions of the 2000 and 2016 elections) using indicators that seem to have little bearing on the candidates' media strategies. The state of the economy and the approval level of the incumbent administration, for instance, are among the factors used to forecast the vote. If the annual rate of growth in per capita GDP (gross domestic product) in 2019 yields an accurate prediction of the vote count in 2020, surely the time and effort committed to changing voters' opinions is of secondary importance!

In fact, we show that the forecasting models are consistent with the arguments that campaigns matter. The so-called fundamental forces used by forecasters—the state of the economy, the approval level of the incumbent president, public concern over some problem—are precisely the issues on which the candidates campaign. "It's the economy, stupid!" became the slogan for the 1992 Clinton campaign because voters expressed pessimism over the national economy. In 2020, "It's the pandemic, stupid!" became the narrative, as Joe Biden capitalized on the rising death toll from the COVID-19 pandemic to critique the competence of the Trump administration. In short, presidential campaigns are debates about the fundamentals; over time, as more voters encounter the candidates' messages, their opinions on the fundamentals become more closely aligned with their candidate preference.

Campaigns do more than activate voters' positions on the state of the economy or the performance of the incumbent. Voters acquire considerable information about the candidates' personal qualities as well as their positions on the issues. Campaigns also shift the salience of particular issues in the minds of voters. Finally, campaigns can also affect the level of election turnout. On the positive side, get-out-the-vote efforts and facilitating absentee or mail-in voting (as in 2020) can mobilize large numbers of voters. Simultaneously, negative campaigning can be used to demobilize voters whose partisan attachments are weak and who might find the spectacle of attacks and counterattacks sufficiently distasteful for them to forgo voting. In the current era of intense party polarization, there is evidence that campaigns get more bang for the buck from attempts at mobilization than from efforts to persuade voters to switch sides.

Next, in Chapter 8, we provide a panoramic view of the entire field of media effects research. Following an initial preoccupation with political propaganda campaigns, researchers gradually adopted a more encompassing definition of *media effects* that ranged from influencing what Americans see as the important problems facing the country (*agenda setting*), to shifting citizens' take on public issues (*framing*), to altering the criteria by which voters make their choices (*priming*). And when conditions were ripe—namely, during periods of one-sided news coverage favoring a particular candidate or policy position—the evidence demonstrated considerable change in public sentiment (*persuasion*). Thus, the initial expectation of wholesale changes in public sentiment was replaced by a more cautious definition of the effects of political communication. Against this more realistic baseline, study after study demonstrated that the news media exercise considerable leverage over public opinion. We summarize this evidence in Chapter 8, which includes discussion of a set of recent studies documenting the intensified state of partisan polarization in American society.

GOING PUBLIC

The same media revolution that swept through the arena of campaigns has similarly transformed the nature of governance and leadership. In the premedia era, the campaign ended on election day. The president-elect (or governor-elect) would assemble a broad-based coalition consisting of legislative allies and supportive interest groups who would work together to implement the administration's policy initiatives. The process typically involved bargaining and accommodation between rival camps.

As described in Chapter 9, bargaining with the opposition has fallen out of fashion in Washington and state capitals. Elected officials now prefer to go public. They resort to public relations tactics designed to cultivate the appearance of responsive, effective leadership—through rhetorical posturing, credit claiming, and avoidance of blame. President Trump, for example, took to Twitter on a daily basis to berate and demean his critics. Key behind-the-scenes confidants are no longer senior party leaders but the legions of spokespersons, commentators, and media consultants who make their daily rounds on television news shows and social media.

The acceleration of going public can be traced to the gradual encroachment of election campaigns on the policy process. Elected officials and interest groups have accumulated considerable expertise in the use of public relations strategies while attempting to win elections, and it is only to be expected that they seek to capitalize on this expertise when formulating and debating legislation. Campaign techniques such as television advertising are now used long after Election Day. While Congress was considering the landmark Affordable Care Act in 2010, the US Chamber of Commerce launched a significant ad campaign (at a cost of nearly $200 million) in an unsuccessful attempt to derail passage of the bill.

Going public is designed to maintain elected officials' popularity. A president who attracts high marks from the American public can use that personal popularity as leverage to get policy agendas passed. The premium on popularity has led chief executives to avoid putting themselves on the media firing line. They avoid televised press conferences, where they may be asked tough questions, in favor of the more scripted opportunity of the presidential speech. President Obama held only 20 press conferences a year during his tenure. President Trump, during his four years in office, held fewer than one press conference each month, but he held more than 80 rallies over the course of his presidency. Of course, the great majority of a president's domestic speeches and appearances occur in states that are in play in the next election.

In theory, popular leaders are more able to persuade their opponents. Congresspersons may defer to a popular president's legislative proposals, fearing that opposition could jeopardize their reelection. Conversely, when the president's opponents sense that majority opinion is on their side, they seize the opportunity to push their own policy agenda. President Trump's weak standing in the polls may have emboldened Republican senators Susan Collins and Lisa Murkowski to occasionally vote against his stated position on bills. But judging a president's popularity can be tricky. In the aftermath of the Monica Lewinsky scandal, congressional Republicans mistakenly assumed that the public would approve of their efforts to remove President Clinton from office. In fact, the scandal did little to weaken public approval of Clinton's performance as president, the impeachment effort failed, and the Republican Party suffered unprecedented losses in the 1998 midterm elections.[2]

Does the strategy of going public help elected leaders get things accomplished? We end Chapter 9 by considering competing theories of popularity. One theory proposes that political leaders are relatively powerless to shape public opinion on their own. In this view, Donald Trump's level of popularity has less to do with his communication skills and social media activity and more to do with the fact that he is disliked by almost everyone who voted for his opponent. Presidential popularity has become caught up in the vortex of polarization; no matter what presidents say or do, voters evaluate them based on their partisanship. A related theory, which also discounts the role of media strategies, holds that popularity derives mainly from the course of events. Peace and prosperity lead to strong approval, whereas prolonged pandemics, economic downturns, and involvement in military campaigns increase disapproval of the president's performance. Finally, there are those who believe that the considerable investment in media appearances does have payoffs and that leaders can use the media to insulate themselves from any rising tide of public discontent or even to improve their standing in the aftermath of policy failures. In this view, events do not speak for themselves. In many instances, political events are ambiguous (representing neither a major success nor a debacle), and how the public views an event and the actions of a president or governor very much depends on media presentations of that event and those actions. In 1983, President Ronald Reagan was able to justify the American invasion of the tiny island of Grenada as a response to a communist threat. Ten years later, President Clinton convinced Congress and the American people that there were several compelling reasons to send American troops to Somalia. In both cases, the president's ability to command media attention, coupled with the willingness of administration critics to remain silent, created a one-sided flow of news in favor of the administration.

We consider all these arguments concerning the dynamics of presidential popularity—polarization, events and conditions, and media management—in the context of recent presidencies. We conclude that while polarization has weakened the capacity of US presidents to shape their public image, media management remains a significant resource; all else being equal, the ability to direct and shape news coverage can make a difference to a president's political fortunes.

CONCLUSION

To close the discussion, in Chapter 10 we consider the implications of media politics for the democratic process. On the bright side, there is the real possibility that media politics has made policy makers more responsive to public opinion. Democracy presumes the consent of the governed, and in the era of going public, elected officials are preoccupied with gaining the approval of their constituents. In this sense, media-based politics approximates policy making by referendum. Other beneficial outcomes include the development of new forms of politician-to-voter communication that not only enable elected representatives to reach their constituents without going through the media, but also lower the costs of mobilizing citizens and potentially reducing age and wealth-related biases in the rate of political participation. In this sense, media politics facilitates democratic politics.

Critics of media politics point to more ominous prospects. The preoccupation with imagery leads elected officials to propose cosmetic over genuine problem-solving actions. American society faces any number of deep-seated, structural problems: massive budget deficits, persistent racial biases in policing and law enforcement, degradation of the environment, a never-ending epidemic of mass shootings, and increasing economic inequality, to name but a few. Solving any of these festering problems will require actions that carry significant short-term political costs (such as increased taxes) or that arouse the wrath of entrenched interests (such as the National Rifle Association in the case of firearms control). In this era of media politics, elected officials generally cannot afford to bear these costs. Rather than formulating policy on the basis of a coherent theory or systematic evidence-based analysis, officials pander to public opinion. We describe the consequences of pandering in the case of crime, where policy makers have rushed to adopt punitive policies that make them look tough on criminals.

A different but no less threatening scenario concerns the growth of polarization. The primal sense of "us against them" makes partisans fixate on the goal of defeating and even humiliating the opposition at all costs. This bias in voting behavior undermines traditional theories of electoral accountability that rest on incumbents' abilities to deliver policy and performance benefits. When animosity toward the opposing party becomes the primary motive underlying vote choice, candidates are less likely to be sanctioned for demonstrating incompetence, dishonesty, and unethical behavior. In the words of Donald Trump, "I could stand in the middle of Fifth Avenue and shoot somebody and I wouldn't lose voters."

Media politics takes on added significance when we factor in the interplay between polarization and the increased availability of news and commentary with a clear partisan slant. As documented in Chapter 8, partisans prefer to hold beliefs that sustain rather than challenge their strong sense of dislike for the opposition. This has created incentives for news providers to offer biased reporting, catering to only one side of the partisan divide. For the majority of news organizations that remain dedicated to the practice of dispassionate, point-counterpoint journalism, as described in Chapter 3, they face an increasingly hostile audience, as partisans dismiss their reporting as biased. The declining credibility of the news media, coupled with the lingering effects of the all-out assault by the Trump administration on the integrity and competence of reporters, has created the potential for voter manipulation. Elected officials can put out disinformation, knowing that it will be circulated without challenge by sympathetic media outlets. President Trump persuaded millions of Republicans that he was the legitimate victor of the 2020 presidential election. They were sufficiently angered to take action on January 6, 2021.

The growing disconnect between the tribalism of partisan discourse and evidence-based reasoning will inevitably undermine fundamental tenets of democratic governance and the rule of law. When media reports are routinely rejected as biased, it becomes easier to undermine press freedoms. It is no accident that dictators around the globe, from Russia to Venezuela to Myanmar, have taken up the Trump slogan of fake news. Meanwhile, here in the United States, Republican leaders and commentators are increasingly calling into question the legitimacy of the 2020 election. Despite the lack of compelling evidence of voter fraud, Arizona commissioned a little-known firm affiliated with conspiracy theorists (Cyber Ninjas) to "investigate" voting irregularities in areas won by Joe Biden. Several state legislatures (all controlled by Republicans) have passed laws that weaken voting rights by restricting access to absentee and mail ballots and by imposing new voter identification requirements.

American politics stands at a critical crossroads. For decades, candidates and elected officials depended on the news media to get out their message—with predictable consequences. Journalists took advantage of their gatekeeping influence to develop new forms of reporting that weakened candidates' control over the news while enhancing the voices of journalists. In the process, voters were left confused and cynical. The development of new forms of candidate-to-voter communication has unquestionably strengthened the hand of the politician in the ongoing struggle between politicians and reporters to control the message. But in the era of polarized politics, politicians have no reason to moderate their views and propose legislation that might elicit bipartisan support. Their supporters' strong hostility toward the opposition sends a clear signal to party leaders. Not only are they to avoid cooperating with the opposition (seen as appeasement), but they must also take every opportunity to reinforce their supporters' fears and prejudices. The dominance of negative advertising in political campaigns and the proclivity of incumbent congresspersons to "taunt" the "out" party in their press releases (Grimmer & King, 2011) provide stark testimony to the rhetorical responsiveness of leaders to their voters' sense of team identity. This tactic of demeaning opponents was fundamental to the Trump administration's daily messaging via social media. The spiral of mass and elite negativity can only lead to gridlock and policy dysfunction (Mann & Ornstein, 2016).

Does the intensified level of polarization represent a new and permanent—if not already calcified—"equilibrium" founded largely on modern media realities? What other factors may still play a role? American politics has witnessed significant periods of polarization before (during the Civil War, for example, and the early twentieth century) as well as periods of relative harmony (typically during international crises and in the aftermath of major wars). Other societies have undergone similar changes, from periods of convulsive and violent conflict to eras of peace and stability. Will the country's gradual recovery from the devastating COVID-19 pandemic help restore a more general commitment to tolerance and open democratic processes? Are there other ways to promote greater mutual respect among all of the identity groups making up our polity? For anybody concerned about the future trajectory of American politics, it is important to reflect on these issues and to identify the circumstances and actions that have the potential to move us toward a period of greater civility and partisan collegiality.

NOTES

1. Associated Press. (2021, January 13). Transcript of Trump's speech at rally before US Capitol riot. Retrieved August 24, 2021, from AP News website: https://apnews.com/article/election-2020-joe-biden-donald-trump-capitol-siege-media-e79eb5164613d6718e9f4502eb471f27.

2. The Republicans lost only a handful of House seats. However, it is quite remarkable for the party of the incumbent president to pick up House seats in a midterm election—a circumstance that has, in fact, arisen only three times since the Civil War, most recently in 2002.

2

The Press and the Democratic Process

The American System in Comparative Perspective

The news media can—and arguably should—contribute to the democratic process in several important ways. First, the media can provide a forum for candidates and political parties to debate their qualifications for office before a national audience. Second, even when there is no forthcoming election, news outlets can contribute to an informed citizenry by providing a variety of perspectives on the important issues of the day. Third, acting as agents of citizens, the media can monitor the acts of public officials, thus helping deter them from violating the public trust.

In modern industrialized democracies, the broadcast media reach virtually all adults and provide a national forum for politicians and political parties. From country to country, however, politicians' practical ability to access this forum varies significantly. In the United States, entry costs are significant barriers; there is no guaranteed minimum level of free access. In most European democracies, access is provided at no cost, and broadcasters typically are obligated to provide an equal (or proportionate) amount of free airtime to major political parties shortly before the election.

In the delivery of the electoral forum, the extent to which candidates' messages are *unmediated* or *mediated* also varies across countries. American parties and candidates must reach voters through news media that interpret and scrutinize the candidates' rhetoric and actions. In performing this function, the media have become increasingly hostile and unwilling to permit candidates to speak for themselves. In European countries, by contrast, in part because of free access, party spokespersons have greater ability to reach voters without going through the filter of news organizations; their messages are delivered without accompanying analysis or commentary.

As social media expands its reach on a global scale, a phenomenon we take up in Chapter 5, we can anticipate greater use of direct politician-to-voter communication.

A closely related civic responsibility of the media is to keep the citizenry abreast of public affairs. The news media are expected—again, to a greater or lesser extent, depending on the country—to supply programming that encompasses a broad range of political perspectives and to provide citizens with opportunities for expressing their own viewpoints. This dialogue is viewed as necessary if citizens are to make informed decisions about public issues. This idea has been eloquently stated by Peter Goldmark (2001, p. 9):

> News is for the citizen. The citizen is that dimension of each one of us that is responsible for, contributes to, and benefits from the cooperative endeavor of self-government. The citizen is the basic constituent element of the public dimension of human activity. Without the citizen, there is no self-government, no individual basis for responsibility, choice and values; there is only the state in all its fearful, unchecked power and unaccountability. And without the independent news function, the citizen is starved, paralyzed, neutered, rendered insensate, ineffective, and robotic.

Of course, the democratic ideal of fully informed citizens is rarely realized. Ordinary people are preoccupied with their personal affairs and have little time for keeping abreast of public issues. Indeed, most television viewers prefer sitcoms or sports over news. At the other extreme, there are people whose political preferences are so intense that they refuse to accept information that challenges their views. Naturally, the ability of the media to perform the function of keeping the public informed is compromised when citizens are uninterested or fanatically partisan. In the final analysis, as we show in Chapter 3, privately owned news media cannot be expected to deliver a steady stream of in-depth public affairs programming that no one will watch.

Over time, the idealized notion of attentive citizens who scour the media for political information has given way to a more realistic argument that democracy can function through "efficient" citizens who either pay attention only to issues of personal importance or rely on a variety of psychological cues, such as a candidate's party affiliation, to compensate for a lack of in-depth factual information. A related alternative to the classic ideal of informed citizenship is that of citizens who pay attention, but only when the media sound a sufficiently loud alarm alerting them to issues that threaten the well-being of society or the nation.

Even when judged by these weaker standards, however, the performance of the American media can be questioned. Widespread famine in Ethiopia in the early 1980s went unnoticed until a BBC television report caught the attention of an NBC News producer based in London. The collapse of the American savings and loan industry in the late 1980s was similarly ignored and ultimately cost taxpayers $175 billion in the form of a government bailout. The widespread sexual harassment of women in the entertainment industry was generally disregarded until the issue implicated major figures in the industry, including Bill Cosby and Harvey Weinstein. Until the murder of George Floyd and the subsequent mass protests, the media gave little attention to police killings of non-Whites. No matter how low one sets the bar for the delivery of public affairs information, the American media do not rate a high grade.

A third important function of the media is to serve as a watchdog on behalf of citizens, scrutinizing the actions of government officials and blowing the whistle when those officials cross the bounds of political propriety. Individual citizens do not have the means to keep abreast of the actions and beliefs of their numerous elected representatives; they delegate this task to the media. Maintaining an adversarial posture toward government is one of the core principles of modern journalism.

The best evidence of the successful exercise of the watchdog function comes from studies of corruption. Countries with a free press are characterized by lower levels of corruption. And more generally, the presence of a free press makes government officials more responsive to the needs of ordinary citizens (Besley & Prat, 2006).

The ability of the news media to deliver on the electoral forum, public sphere, and watchdog functions (or, more broadly, civic performance) varies considerably across societies and media systems. Two key factors affect media performance: regulatory policy and market forces. Regulatory policy derives from a society's position on the "free market" versus "social welfare" ideological continuum. In the United States, a country that has lagged behind the rest of the world in accepting a social welfare role for government, the agency charged with regulating the media (the Federal Communications Commission, or FCC) has taken an increasingly laissez-faire approach, arguing that free market competition is sufficient to ensure the delivery of diverse perspectives on public affairs issues. The FCC has gradually weakened the rules governing ownership of media companies and, most recently, has abandoned regulation of internet service providers ("net neutrality"). Most other advanced industrialized democracies, on the other hand, while also moving in the direction of deregulation, have maintained much tighter control over media owners and programming, with the aim of ensuring the delivery of welfare-enhancing public goods.

⊚ IN FOCUS

Three Important Functions of Media in Democratic Societies

- To provide a forum for candidates and political parties to debate their qualifications for office before a national audience
- To contribute to informed citizenship by providing a variety of perspectives on the important issues of the day
- To serve as a watchdog, scrutinizing the actions of government officials on behalf of citizens—most of whom do not have the opportunity to closely follow the actions of politicians and the government

Market forces have a significant effect on levels of civic performance. In societies where the media are predominantly privately owned (as in the United States), competitive market pressures compel media owners to shirk their civic responsibilities. To be profitable, the media must deliver more entertainment than news, and when they do deliver news, they must use formats that are designed to be entertaining rather than informative on substantive issues. The alternative to exclusively private ownership is a mixed model consisting of both privately owned and publicly subsidized media. In most European democracies, at least one television network is financed with government revenues. Public subsidies offer broadcasters significant protection from market forces, enhancing their ability to deliver serious (rather than entertaining) news programming. Thus, societies in which media ownership is mixed rather than entirely private are more likely to support informed citizenship.

Both regulatory policy and market forces influence the production of news. The political significance of media programming, however, ultimately depends on the strength of political parties. Countries with strong political parties are less dependent on the news media to provide an electoral forum and guide voters' choices. Parties control the selection of their candidates and can rely on their supporters to cast informed (party-line) votes. In these systems, accordingly, what the media might offer by way of public affairs presentations is likely to be of little consequence to the outcome of elections.

Compared with most other democracies, the United States is characterized by weak political parties. Most notably, party leaders have little say over the selection of candidates. For American voters, candidate and issue considerations compete with party affiliation as important voting cues. Although some Americans lack strong ties to a party, the sense of party identification has intensified among partisans (as discussed in Chapters 7 and 8), making them completely reliable party-line voters. We'll outline the effects of news coverage on voter attitudes and behavior in later chapters; in the rest of this chapter, we'll put the American system in perspective by comparing the role of political parties and the media in the United States and Europe. Regarding political parties, we'll focus on American reforms that have undermined the influence of party organization and contrast the weakened party system of the United States with the strong party systems that predominate in Europe. Regarding media systems, we'll contrast the American and European models in terms of the extent of government regulation and the structure of media ownership.

MEDIA POLITICS AS THE SUCCESSOR TO PARTY POLITICS

How and why did the mass media become so central to political life in the United States? Certainly the sheer size of the country contributed to the situation. It would be difficult for any presidential candidate to traverse all 50 states to meet and greet each eligible voter in person. Congressional candidates, too, would have a hard time connecting with all their constituents in person; most US senators represent many millions of citizens (over 25 million in California, for example), and the average population of a US House of Representatives district is 710,000 (the US Constitution originally suggested one representative for every 30,000 citizens).

However, the reliance on the mass media is not simply a result of population growth, as candidates relied more on personal campaigning than media until recently despite the country's size. In the 1896 presidential campaign, for instance, the candidates relied on "retail" politics, "crisscrossing the country to deliver hundreds of public speeches to a total audience estimated to exceed 5 million people" (Iyengar, 1997, p. 143). Certainly the population at that time was smaller and the media options were fewer, but even as late as the 1960s, when radio and television were widely available, campaigns relied more heavily on teams of volunteers who organized local appearances for the candidate, canvassed neighborhoods, knocked on doors, distributed campaign flyers, and transported people to the polls on Election Day. What was it, then, that precipitated the switch to media-based campaigns?

The explanation is rooted in the candidate nomination process. As documented by Nelson Polsby (1983), rule changes adopted in the late 1960s weakened the influence of party elites on the selection of candidates and created a void that was filled by the news media. Before 1968, the selection of delegates to the national party conventions, and therefore the nomination of the party's presidential candidate, was controlled by state and local party organizations. Although some states did hold primary elections, the great majority of the convention delegates were selected by the party leadership.

The turmoil that engulfed the 1968 presidential campaign—the protests over the Vietnam War, the unexpected withdrawal of President Lyndon Johnson as a candidate for nomination, the assassination of Robert Kennedy, the ensuing clashes between supporters of the two Democratic candidates Eugene McCarthy and Hubert Humphrey, and the climactic suppression of the protests outside the convention hall—led the Democratic Party to establish a commission to reform the delegate selection process (for a detailed account, see Polsby, 1983). This commission recommended primary elections as the means of democratizing the selection of candidates. The widespread adoption of primaries, along with changes in campaign finance regulations after the 1972 Watergate scandal, fundamentally altered the incentives of presidential hopefuls in such a way as to diminish the role of party organizations and increase the importance of the media. By 1972, as Figure 2.1 shows, a majority

FIGURE 2.1
National Convention Delegates Selected in Primary Elections

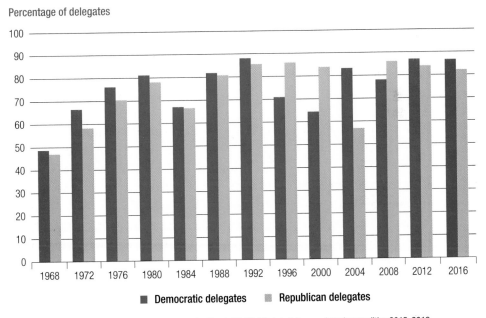

Source: 1968–2012 data from H. W. Stanley & R. G. Niemi. (2015). *Vital statistics on American politics 2015–2016*. Los Angeles: Sage. 2016 data compiled August 31, 2021, from the Real Clear Politics website: https://www.realclearpolitics .com/epolls/2016/president/republican_delegate_count.html.

of the delegates to both party conventions were selected on the basis of primary elections.

The adoption of primaries meant that instead of cultivating party activists and leaders, candidates had to appeal directly to the public. At the same time, technological developments—in particular, the widespread proliferation of television—made it possible for candidates to reach statewide and national audiences. By 1963, 91 percent of American households had at least one television set, up from only 45 percent just 10 years earlier (see Figure 2.2).

Although radio had been almost as widespread (more than 80 percent of American households had a radio set in 1940) and had also commanded huge audiences, it was no match for television's visual imagery. This new medium allowed its audiences to experience major events (such as the Army–McCarthy hearings involving allegations of communists serving in the military and the aftermath of the assassination of President John F. Kennedy, including the on-air shooting of his assassin) in real time, almost as though they were at the scene. It wasn't long before television supplanted radio and newspapers as the public's principal source of information. Politicians could not ignore this

FIGURE 2.2
TV Ownership, 1950–1978

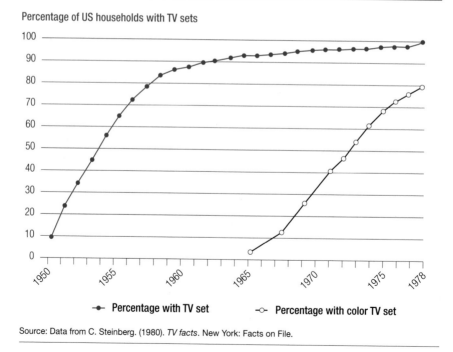

Percentage of US households with TV sets

Source: Data from C. Steinberg. (1980). *TV facts*. New York: Facts on File.

new mass medium even if they were inclined to do so, particularly in light of the weakening of political parties and the fact that other social institutions (clubs, newspapers, and so on) that had been important in grassroots-type politics were declining at the same time.

The end result of party reform and the rapid spread of television was a shift from party-based campaigns to candidate-based campaigns waged on television. Those who seek elective office covet exposure to large audiences; increasingly it was television that delivered the goods. As the public became entirely dependent on television for political information, candidates altered their campaign strategies to maximize their television exposure.

The most fundamental consequence of party reform was a transformed relationship between candidates and party leaders. Today, after meeting only the most perfunctory requirements, any American citizen can seek a party's nomination for president, senator, or other public office. To qualify for the primary ballot in California, for example, a would-be Republican candidate for president must gather signatures from only 1 percent of the state's registered Republicans (for the Democratic Party, the California signature requirement is 1 percent of registered Democrats or 500—whichever is fewer—in each of the state's congressional districts). In Vermont, a prospective nominee needs the signatures of only 1,000 voters of any partisan affiliation. In the primary election system, moreover, any voter who has simply checked a box on a registration form to claim affiliation with a party has a say in selecting the party nominee. In states that have *open* primaries—in which any registered voter can vote in the primary for any party—voters don't even have to be registered with the party to participate in candidate selection. In addition, some states hold *modified open* primaries, in which registered partisans can vote only in their own party's primary, but independents can vote in any primary (in all of these systems, each voter may vote in only one party's primary). Another primary system, long in use in state elections in Louisiana and recently put in place by ballot initiatives for elections in Washington state and California, is the nonpartisan blanket primary, which consolidates all party primaries onto one ballot. In this system, only the top two vote-getters move on to a general election, regardless of political party, which opens the possibility that candidates of the same political party will face off in the general election. Since the adoption of the "top two" method, several primaries have resulted in two candidates from the same party contesting the general election.

Although candidates who are not established party figures (and who may lack support from party leaders) may be at some disadvantage when seeking election, they have proved quite capable of winning—or at least seriously competing for—statewide and national office. A total of seven presidential candidates qualified for the televised primary debates in 2016 and 2020 despite having no prior elective experience. Of course, one of them, businessman and reality television host Donald Trump stunned the entire world by winning the Republican nomination and then defeating seasoned politician Hillary Clinton.

Moreover, parties now realize that if they want to win in the general election, they are well advised to embrace candidates who are capable of funding and operating an effective media campaign. Thus, some party elites may choose to support and endorse candidates who have not played much of a role in the party or whose ideology is inconsistent with that of the party if they have more resources with which to fight a media battle against their general election opponent. It is not surprising, therefore, that the median net worth of US senators in 2018 was $18 million, while the comparable figure for the median House member was close to $6 million, according to the OpenSecrets, a nonpartisan think tank based in Washington, DC, that tracks the effect of money on elections and public policy.

In contrast with the American model, party organizations in most other industrialized democracies exercise decisive control over candidate selection. As a result, campaigns are run primarily on the level of the party rather than on the level of the individual candidate. In many cases, candidates are prohibited from making individual appeals separate from the party message and can be sanctioned (or expelled from the party) for doing so.

To maintain rigid control over candidate selection, parties in other democracies impose strict eligibility requirements. In general, only party members can be potential candidates. In most countries, party membership represents a much greater political commitment than in the United States. At a minimum, members are required to pay monthly dues to the party organization, but expectations are typically more comprehensive, including representing the party in the community and campaigning for the party.[1]

Merely meeting the eligibility requirements in no way guarantees selection by the party; would-be candidates still have to survive the selection process. In most democracies, the procedure for selecting candidates is adopted at the discretion of political parties, and the *selectorate* (the group that actually selects the candidate) is much more restrictive than in the United States. In their most inclusive form, selectorates include all registered members of a party (defined, again, in the strict sense and not in the loose American sense); a slight variation on this model requires an additional condition to be met by members—such as a minimum length of party membership—before they become eligible to participate in the selection of party candidates. However, cases of even more exclusive selectorates—consisting of small party committees—are common, as are *multistage* systems, in which a small body either preselects a group of candidates (from which a broader selectorate, consisting of all party members, selects one) or selects from candidates nominated by a broader selectorate. In many countries (including Australia, Canada, France, Germany, Italy, Japan, and the United Kingdom), some political parties give their national leaders the power to veto or otherwise alter the roster of candidates selected by a broader selectorate.

The degree of party control over candidate selection also depends on the electoral system. Whereas the United States employs a single-member-district plurality voting system,[2] in which whoever wins the most votes in a district wins the office, many other countries use multimember-district and proportional representation systems, in which parties compete for multiple seats within a single district and the number of seats each party wins is allocated in proportion to its share of the vote. In the common *closed party list* version of proportional representation, parties determine the order in which the candidates are listed on the ballot, but the voter simply casts a vote for the party. For most major parties, candidates appearing at the top of the list are assured election, and those at the bottom have little chance of winning. Candidates who lose favor with the party leadership may find themselves consigned to the bottom of the candidate list.

Thus, in countries with strong parties, it is important for candidates to defer to party leaders. Accordingly, political campaigns in European and other democracies—and media coverage thereof—are more party oriented than are campaigns in the United States. It is true that the media are becoming increasingly important in campaigns around the world, that there is a growing global cadre of political professionals, and that political parties in more and more countries are adopting American-style campaign techniques. Indeed, there is mounting concern in many European countries about the mediatization or Americanization of political campaigns—the increasing emphasis on party leaders rather than on party policies, for example. Nonetheless, traditional methods of campaigning—such as door-to-door canvassing by candidates and party activists—still play a significant role in other industrialized democracies. And perhaps more important, party-centered campaigns are more likely to generate issue-focused news coverage by the media, because campaign events are themselves more issue oriented (such as the release of a party manifesto in Ireland as opposed to the release of a new attack ad in the United States).

Although weak political parties and universal access to media were both necessary to the development of media-based politics in the United States, they do not alone explain the civic performance of American news organizations.

In Chapters 3 and 4, we will describe how a combination of professional norms and economic pressures have severely limited candidates' access to media audiences, constrained both the sheer amount and the range of perspectives represented in news programs, and contributed to the weakening of watchdog journalism. But before we examine the supply and content of news programming, let's take a moment to put the American media system in some comparative perspective.

PATTERNS OF MEDIA OWNERSHIP AND REGULATION

American media differ from most other media systems in two fundamental respects: they are much less subject to government regulation and are almost entirely privately owned. These differences hold the key to explaining why American media are less likely to make good on their civic obligations.

The structure of the media industry—in particular, whether media are owned and operated by government organizations or by private enterprises—has a major impact on the supply of news because government-subsidized media outlets are typically required (by statute) to provide minimal levels of public affairs content, whereas privately owned outlets are generally free to do as they please. Although the issue of public versus private ownership generally applies only to broadcast media, other regulations governing aspects of ownership apply to all forms of media. In the case of election coverage, for example, explicit regulations may directly spell out the subject matter to be covered, as well as when and where the coverage is to occur.

⊚ IN FOCUS

What's Different about American Media?

- **More private ownership.** Media entities in the United States, including broadcast media, are almost entirely privately owned and operated; most other democracies have at least one government-funded broadcast network.
- **Less regulation.** The regulatory structure governing the behavior of American media is considerably more lax than that in most other democracies.

PUBLIC VERSUS COMMERCIAL
OWNERSHIP OF BROADCAST MEDIA

There are three models of ownership of broadcast media: purely public, mixed, and purely commercial. The rationale for publicly owned television (and radio) is that the electromagnetic spectrum, as a scarce public resource, must be utilized for the public good.[3] The concept of public service broadcasting was first put into practice in the United Kingdom with the establishment of the British Broadcasting Corporation (BBC) in 1927 and was soon emulated in some form by most democracies in Western Europe and beyond. In most cases, this entailed the creation of a state-owned broadcasting system that functioned either as a monopoly or as a dominant broadcaster. Typically, the public broadcasting network was financed from radio or television license fees or taxes.

Although these publicly owned media entities are generally free from political interference, they are expected to follow certain principles (the exact details of which vary by country), such as providing universal service and informative, educational, and diverse programming.

In 1979, all but three countries in Europe had monopolistic public television channels, and two of the three that did not (Great Britain and Italy) had mixed systems, with both publicly owned and commercial television channels. By 1997, however, as a result of significant deregulation across Europe, only three countries had exclusively public-sector television markets. Still, even in the now-dominant mixed model, public television channels enjoy large audience shares. In 15 of the 17 European Union countries with mixed-ownership television markets, the public television channels hold the number one market spot and capture larger audience shares than would be expected based on the number of commercial channels with which they compete. The audience share enjoyed by public television in Europe ranges from a low of 17 percent for Portugal to a high of 76 percent in Denmark (see Figure 2.3).

In return for government financing, public broadcasters are required to provide sustained levels of public affairs programming and to represent a diversity of regions, cultures, and viewpoints. Sweden's STV (Sveriges Television), for example, is "obliged to carry cultural and quality programming, and 55 percent of its programming must be produced regionally outside Stockholm" (Williams, 2003, p. 39). Thus, public broadcasters in Europe tend to produce higher quantities of public affairs programs (which, as we'll discuss, are of higher quality than most programs found on commercial television worldwide). These programs reach large audiences; the early localized evening newscast on BBC One

FIGURE 2.3

Public Broadcasters' Audience Share by Country

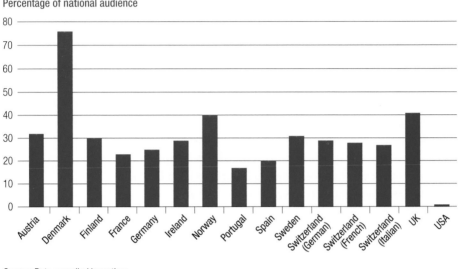

Percentage of national audience

Source: Data compiled by author.

in the United Kingdom, for instance, attracts approximately 30 percent of the television audience. In contrast with audiences in the United States, European audiences are not disinclined to watch serious news.

Unlike the European model, the American television market is dominated by commercial broadcasters. Instead of adopting public ownership, US telecommunications policy has followed a trusteeship approach, by which access to the public resource of the spectrum was granted to those who pledged to act in the "public interest, convenience, and necessity."[4] The FCC is the agency responsible for setting and enforcing the requirements that broadcasters must follow to meet that public interest standard.

Initially, the FCC set fairly high standards for broadcasters' public interest obligations, requiring them, for example, to "promote the discussion of public issues, serve minority interests, and eliminate superfluous advertising" (Zechowski, 2013). These standards quickly fell by the wayside, however, because broadcasters considered them an undue economic burden. The regulations that followed were less stringent and not strictly enforced, and most have since been abandoned.

Contrary to appearances, the United States does not fit a purely commercial model. Congress established the Public Broadcasting Service (PBS) in 1967. However, most PBS funding comes from private corporations

and individual donors, and even the small portion of its funding that
does come from the government is frequently under threat for political reasons (most often from Republicans in Congress who accuse PBS
of displaying a liberal bias). In stark contrast to European public broadcasters, PBS reaches only 1 percent of the American television audience
(see Figure 2.3).

In 2007, the public service networks in Belgium, the Netherlands, the United
Kingdom, Norway, and Sweden aired an average of 78 minutes a day of news
and current affairs during prime time (7:00 PM to 10:00 PM), whereas PBS
in the United States aired just 47 minutes, opting instead to broadcast shows
like *Masterpiece Theatre* or fine arts performances (see Figure 2.4). Even commercial television networks in European countries broadcast nearly 5 times as
much public affairs programming during prime time as their US counterparts,
with an average of 29 minutes per day during prime time in Belgium, the
Netherlands, the United Kingdom, Norway, and Sweden and only 6 minutes
per day during prime time in the United States. Notice, however, that the
average public TV–commercial TV gap in the amount of time devoted to public
affairs programming has increased in many of these countries, with commercial
television devoting fewer minutes to such programming in the Netherlands,
the United Kingdom, Norway, and the United States in 2007 than in 1997

FIGURE 2.4

Public Affairs Programming during Prime Time

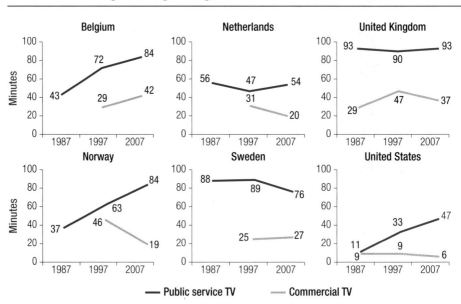

Source: Data from T. Aalberg, P. van Aelst, and J. Curran. (2010). Media systems and the political information environment: A cross-national comparison. *The International Journal of Press/Politics*, 15(3), 255–271.

Note: Average minutes per day devoted to news and current affairs during prime time, 7:00 PM to 10:00 PM, among public service TV and commercial TV, 1987–2007.

and public service television devoting more time to public affairs programming during prime time in Belgium, the Netherlands, the United Kingdom, Norway, and the United States. This increasing gap between private and commercial broadcasters in the level of attention to public affairs is at odds with the so-called "virtuous circle" hypothesis, which posits that in countries with strong public broadcasters, commercial broadcasters will emulate the programming provided by the public broadcaster.

Not only do public broadcasting systems supply a greater quantity of news programming, but they also produce more substantive, issue-oriented programming than commercial stations do. For example, Udo Krüger (1996) found that 37 percent of the news reports broadcast on the three commercial television channels in Germany could be categorized as *infotainment* compared with just 7 percent on the two public channels. Similarly, a study found that news items on commercial television news in the Netherlands and Belgium were shorter than those on public channels (Canninga 1994, as cited in Brants, 1998).

Another difference between news programming on public and commercial television concerns the more limited geographical reach of the latter. In his analysis of the proportion of national versus international news in the news broadcasts of 16 channels across 8 countries, François Heinderyckx (1993) focused mainly on public television channels. However, the two commercial channels that he examined (French TF1 and Belgian VTM) had slightly lower proportions of international news (39 and 44 percent, respectively) than the average (47 percent) for the public channels.

The restricted reach of international news in the offerings of commercial networks is also evident when we compare the level of attention accorded African nations on CNN and the BBC during 2017 (see Figure 2.5). Focusing on the three largest African nations (in terms of population), it is clear that the BBC delivers considerably more coverage of these countries than CNN. In the case of Ethiopia, BBC's coverage is more than twice that provided by CNN.

The differences in the availability of news between the United States and most European countries have important implications for democracy. Most normative models of democracy depend on an informed citizenry, and it is the news media's responsibility to provide cost-free information. Rather than upholding their civic duty, owners of American media value ratings and the bottom line first.

FIGURE 2.5

Coverage of African Nations: BBC versus CNN

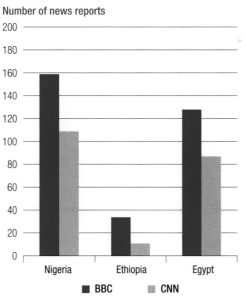

Source: Data from www.bbc.co.uk and www.cnn.com, January 1–December 31, 2017.

The connection between a media system's priorities and levels of public knowledge become apparent when average knowledge levels between countries are compared. As seen in Figure 2.6, Americans compete on level terms with their European counterparts only when it comes to domestic *soft news*—for example, facts about American celebrities. When it comes to knowing about both international and domestic *hard news* as well as international soft news, Americans lag well behind.

An egalitarian society is another important benchmark for democracy, and disparate levels of public knowledge between advantaged and disadvantaged groups translate into disparate levels of political power. In general, differences in hard news knowledge associated with education, income, and ethnicity are much greater in the United States than in European countries. Shanto Iyengar and James Curran (2009) explain:

> In those societies where the media provide ample coverage of hard news and
> where the schedule of news programming is adjusted so as to capture the

FIGURE 2.6

Knowledge of Hard and Soft News in Domestic and International Domains

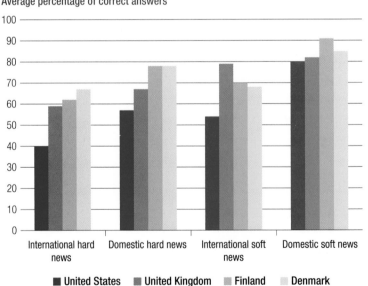

Average percentage of correct answers

International hard news   Domestic hard news   International soft news   Domestic soft news

■ United States   ■ United Kingdom   ■ Finland   Denmark

Source: Data from J. Curran, S. Iyengar, A. B. Lund, and I. Salovaara-Moring. (2009). Media system, public knowledge and democracy. *European Journal of Communication*, 24(1), 5–26.

attention of even relatively inattentive citizens, easy access to information can compensate for inadequate motivation. In the Scandinavian countries of Denmark and Finland, for instance, where news bulletins air regularly during the peak television viewing periods (such as just before a nationally televised sporting event), a sufficient number of citizens who are not especially interested in politics nonetheless find themselves in the path of news reports, thus allowing them to acquire information. Thus, in countries where news programming is more substantive and the delivery of news is scheduled to capture a substantial "inadvertent" audience, we observe a significant narrowing of the traditional knowledge gap. It is in this sense that the supply of news can contribute to civic competence.

Although the evidence is compelling that public television delivers more substantive and global programming than commercial television does, there are shortcomings to the mixed-ownership broadcasting systems common in European industrialized democracies. For example, many Britons object to the mandatory license fee that is imposed on all owners of television sets in the United Kingdom to fund the BBC. Furthermore, the share of the audience reached by public broadcasters in mixed-ownership systems—though still respectable, as noted already—has dropped in response to increased commercial offerings and the proliferation of satellite and cable programming. Some evidence suggests, moreover, that programming quality on public television channels is declining because of the increased competition from commercial channels.

In summary, the structure of media ownership affects news programming. In industrialized democracies where public ownership of at least some television channels is the norm, public affairs programming is more extensive than is the case in the almost purely privately held American media market.

ALTERNATIVE APPROACHES TO MEDIA REGULATION

In addition to the ownership question, different regulatory frameworks have important consequences for the delivery of news programming generally and for the diversity of political perspectives represented in program content specifically. This is true for broadcast media as well as print media, and we will deal with each in turn.

BROADCAST MEDIA

Although the FCC in its early years issued strict (though not always strictly enforced) requirements for public affairs programming by its licensees, most of these no longer apply. From the beginning, broadcasters regularly challenged the FCC regulations as a violation of their First Amendment guarantees of free speech, but the courts generally ruled in favor of the public trustee basis of broadcast regulations. Eventually, ideological change at the FCC—not any judicial mandate—led to a weakening of the public service requirements. Under pressure from President Reagan, the FCC adopted a marketplace approach to the media. In essence, the FCC held that the mere existence of competitive media outlets was sufficient to serve the public interest, making it unnecessary to regulate programming.

The scope of the policy shift was substantial. In 1960, the FCC had published a list of the 14 major elements necessary to serve the public interest. The list included community-oriented programming, political broadcasts, and public affairs and news programs. In 1976, the FCC issued more precise standards: stations were required to air at least 5 percent local programming, 5 percent informational programming (defined as news and public affairs), and an additional 10 percent non-entertainment programming. In 1984, the FCC abandoned these requirements in favor of looser guidelines, which stated that it was sufficient for stations to "air some programming that meets the community's needs" (Bishop & Hakanen, 2002, p. 264).

In the aftermath of deregulation, television stations increased their amount of local news programming both because local news attracted large audiences (see Chapter 3) and because this sort of programming proved inexpensive to produce. The typical local newscast, however, lacks meaningful public affairs content. Moreover, local news replaced other forms of public affairs programming. For example, the number of hours per week devoted to non-news public affairs programming across all TV channels in the Philadelphia market dropped from 57.5 in 1976 (before deregulation) to 28.2 in 1985 (after deregulation), and that number fell even further, to 24, in 1997. Nevertheless, the provision of local news has become increasingly important in the FCC's definition of the public interest standard.

One of the most important shifts in FCC policy eased the restrictions on concentration of ownership. The national TV and local radio ownership rules, established in 1941, limited the number of television stations that could be owned by a single entity to 7 nationwide, only 5 of which could be VHF stations (the most common commercial format), and set a similar limit on the number of radio stations. The dual TV network rule, issued in 1946, prohibited any major network from buying another major network, and the local TV multiple ownership rule (adopted in 1964) limited a broadcaster to just one local station per market unless there were more than 8 stations in that market. Further regulations were implemented in the 1970s limiting cross-ownership of TV stations, radio stations, and newspapers in the same market.

Over time, the multiple-ownership restrictions have been removed. In 1985, the FCC raised the maximum number of TV stations that could be owned by any single entity from 7 to 12. The Telecommunications Act of 1996 further eased the rules by allowing ownership of multiple TV stations, as long as the combined audience of the stations amounted to less than 39 percent of the population. In 2003, the FCC proposed to eliminate all restrictions on cross-ownership within a single market, as long as that market had 9 or more TV stations, and to further raise the TV ownership cap from 39 percent to 45 percent, eventually phasing out TV ownership restrictions altogether. However, this FCC proposal was overturned by a series of court rulings that reinstated the previous ownership limitations. The FCC weakened the media ownership rules again in 2007 by eliminating a cross-ownership statute that prohibited a single company from owning both a newspaper and a television or radio station in the same market. And following the election of Donald Trump, the FCC took further action to relax restrictions on ownership of television stations. Specifically, in 2017 the FCC reinstated a formula (that had been abolished by the Obama administration) by which the estimated reach of VHF stations is cut in half. By this method of calculating broadcast audiences, therefore, individual owners can acquire additional stations while staying below the cap of a 39 percent market share.

Quite predictably, the relaxation of ownership restrictions has increased the holdings of the largest owners. The five largest owners of local television stations—Sinclair, Nexstar, Gray, Tegna, and Tribune—owned 179 local stations in 2004. Ten years later, the holdings of the "Big Five" had more than doubled to 378 stations, according to data compiled by Pew Research (Pew Research Center, 2017).

The concentration of media ownership in the United States extends well beyond television stations. At various times, large multinational corporations have purchased all categories of media. In its heyday, Rupert Murdoch's News Corporation owned a large number of US cable networks as well as the terrestrial Fox network, 34 Fox-affiliated stations, three movie studios, the Fox Sports Radio network, the *Wall Street Journal* and *New York Post* newspapers, and several magazines and major publishing houses. Univision, a relative newcomer to the scene, already holds a virtual monopoly on Spanish-language television, owning 65 local television stations and a similar number of cable affiliates in the United States. Comcast, the nation's largest internet service provider, owns the NBC television network. As noted in the Project for Excellence in Journalism (2004) report,

> In radio, the top twenty companies operate more than 20 percent of all the radio stations in the country; one, Clear Channel, dominates, operating stations in 191 of the 289 Arbitron-rated markets. In local television, the ten biggest companies own 30 percent of all television stations reaching 85 percent of all television households in the United States. In network television, the owners are all giant corporations.

With so much of the industry controlled by so few, there is good reason for concern about the supply and quality of news and about the diversity of voices represented in media programming. Local news is a case in point. Sinclair Broadcasting—the largest owner of TV stations—subscribes to a partisan model of journalism and requires its stations to provide coverage that tilts in a conservative direction. There is evidence that the stations have complied. A 2019 study that tracked changes in news coverage offered by stations purchased by Sinclair in 2017 found that these stations increased the number of national (relative to local) stories and that the coverage became more conservative in slant (Martin and McCrain, 2019).

More generally, research into the effects of ownership on news programming confirms the suspicion that company size is inversely related to quality journalism—that is, the larger the company, the lower the quality. In a comprehensive five-year study of broadcast news quality, the Project for Excellence in Journalism (2003) report found that stations owned by small companies (with holdings of three or fewer stations) were 2.5 times more likely to earn an A grade for news quality than were stations owned by the 25 largest companies.[6]

In addition to relaxing ownership rules, the FCC has weakened directives that aim to increase the diversity of perspectives in news content. The Fairness Doctrine, which required broadcasters to present opposing sides on controversial issues, was repealed in 1987 after broadcasters mounted legal challenges against it. (Other changes in regulation of content, specifically those that deal with candidate access to the airwaves, will be discussed in more detail later in the chapter.)

With the elimination of the Fairness Doctrine, broadcasts with a partisan slant have increased in frequency and scope. Corporate interests have begun to exert influence over news programming in a number of subtle ways, such

⦿ IN FOCUS

The Rise of Comcast

Comcast was founded in 1963 as a cable television provider with 1,200 subscribers. In 1988, the company acquired Storer Communications and became the fifth-largest cable provider in the United States. Through further acquisitions in the 1990s, the company became a major provider of broadband internet. By 2002, Comcast had more than 20 million cable subscribers and 6 million high-speed internet customers.

In 2011, the company acquired NBC Universal from General Electric (along with the cable networks controlled by NBC, including Bravo, CNBC, MSNBC, and Telemundo), making it the single largest source of television programming in the country. The FCC and Justice Department agreed to the merger but imposed several conditions, including that Comcast give up its management of Hulu, a major video-sharing site. Comcast also committed to providing greater local news coverage and expanded Spanish-language programming.

In 2014, the company announced plans to acquire Time Warner. The proposed merger would have created a single telecommunications giant with more than 30 percent of the cable market (33 million subscribers) and nearly as many broadband users. On the grounds that the sheer size of the company would grant it considerable leverage over television production companies in determining which programs are streamed on mobile devices and laptops, the Justice Department opposed the merger and initiated antitrust action against Comcast. Comcast eventually abandoned the planned merger, turning its attention to other acquisitions. In 2018, Comcast announced that it would make a $65 billion bid to purchase 21st Century Fox, only to be outbid by the Walt Disney Company.

as by encouraging journalists not to pursue stories that reflect poorly on their parent corporations or by imposing programming in keeping with their political preferences. In early 2018, Sinclair Broadcasting, whose owners and top executives are major donors to conservative causes, ordered news anchors on their television stations (which have a combined reach of nearly 40 percent of the national audience) to read the same script condemning the spread of "fake news" as dangerous to US democracy. Sinclair's parroting of President Trump's rhetoric came as no surprise; the company signed an exclusive agreement with the Trump campaign in 2016 to air interviews with the candidate over all their affiliated stations. They offered the same opportunity to Hillary Clinton, but she declined. In similar incidents, the Walt Disney Company refused to distribute Michael Moore's *Fahrenheit 9/11*, and CBS refused to air an ad criticizing George W. Bush made by MoveOn.org during the 2004 Super Bowl. Thus, media owners increasingly feel free to base programming decisions on their political interests.

Overall, it appears that concern about the impact of deregulation on the quantity and quality of public affairs programming made available to the American public is not misplaced. Clearly, the FCC has transformed American telecommunications policy in ways that significantly decrease the number of voices that have access to the market.

The American experience is hardly unique in this regard; the trend toward broadcast deregulation is global. In Europe, too, ownership rules have been considerably relaxed in recent years, although in most European countries the relaxed regulations are still stronger than those in the United States. In Germany, for example, ownership of television stations is capped at a combined 30 percent of the national audience. In France, no single entity can exercise more than 49 percent control in a company that owns a national television network, with ownership being limited to 15 percent in a second such company and 5 percent in a third. Furthermore, the presence of public television and radio stations in these countries to some extent counteracts the overall effects of ownership deregulation.

Unlike the American model, the regulatory frameworks of most European countries (and other democracies) take the public service obligations of the media seriously. These countries impose strict programming requirements that apply even to their commercial broadcasters. All European Union countries, for example, have "right-of-reply" laws, which require broadcasters to give people criticized in the media "a right of access to answer criticisms against them" (Hallin & Mancini, 2004, p. 122). In Germany, an internal agreement among all the German states requires any television broadcaster with at least a 10 percent market share to allocate a minimum of 260 minutes of airtime per week to minor political parties. Even in the United Kingdom—which has been criticized for following the US model and dismantling its media regulations in recent years—both the publicly funded BBC and the commercial television stations operate under formal requirements for impartiality and balance in news programming.

Thus, despite the privatization of their broadcast markets, European governments continue to see broadcasting "not simply as a private commercial enterprise but as a social institution for which the state has an important responsibility" (Hallin & Mancini, 2004, p. 161). That responsibility is to ensure that privately owned broadcast outlets, in response to powerful market forces, do not underproduce public affairs programming. This same logic, as we'll see next, is largely mirrored in the regulation of print media.

PRINT MEDIA

In the United States and elsewhere, the print media have never been subject to the same level of regulation as the broadcast media, because the principal rationale for government regulation of broadcasting—that the airwaves are a scarce and publicly owned resource—does not apply to print. Beyond libel laws, regulation of newspaper content has been close to nonexistent. In fact, regulation of American print media has been almost entirely limited to the area of ownership, where the government has applied antitrust laws to promote competition.

Antitrust legislation has been invoked to block the acquisition of one newspaper by another in cases where such mergers or acquisitions would lead to a decrease in competition in the media market, thus potentially harming consumers. In the 1967 *United States v. Times Mirror Co.*, for example, the court blocked the acquisition of the *San Bernardino County Sun* by the larger *Los Angeles Times* on the basis of the government's argument that the deal would harm competition. Antitrust laws have also been used to prevent newspaper companies from using anticompetitive tactics, such as predatory pricing, in which a company prices its product "below cost, usually to run another firm out of business, with the plan of making up the losses later through higher prices" (Lacy & Simon, 1993, p. 200).

The occasional application of antitrust laws has had little impact on the general trend toward concentration of ownership. The lack of effect is partly because the laws have not been rigorously enforced and partly because Congress has exempted newspapers from antitrust provisions in certain situations.[7] Over the years, the newspaper industry has become one of the most monopolistic markets in the American economy.

Historically, American newspaper markets developed on a local level, while those in other Western democracies (most of which are considerably smaller than the United States) developed on a national scale. Only a handful of American newspapers—such as *USA Today* and the *Wall Street Journal*—reach a level of distribution that might be described as national; the vast majority are distributed locally. Because the total readership in local markets is small, American newspapers cannot subdivide the market into narrower segments. The importance of advertising to the newspaper industry adds further impetus to reduced competition. Local advertisers, the major source of revenue for newspaper owners, benefit from monopolistic newspaper markets because they reduce the cost of advertising per reader. Thus, economic pressures push toward a single newspaper per local market with a captive audience.

The combination of the inherent tendency toward monopoly in newspaper markets and the lack of a strict regulatory framework, along with the development of the internet (a factor we discuss in Chapter 5), has had predictable consequences—namely, a significant drop in competition. Between 1910 and 2020, the number of daily newspapers fell from 2,202 to 1,260. As Figure 2.7 shows, the percentage of cities with competing daily newspapers dropped sharply, from 43 percent in 1920 to just 2 percent in 1986. Recent technological changes and the growth of online news consumption have sounded the death knell for many major newspapers, including the *Seattle Post-Intelligencer, Rocky Mountain News,* and *Albuquerque Tribune.* Other economically challenged newspapers have eliminated their weekend editions.

Only limited research has investigated the effects of ownership concentration on the content of newspapers, and the pattern of results to date is inconsistent.

FIGURE 2.7

The Decline of Competition among Daily Newspapers in US Cities, 1880–1986

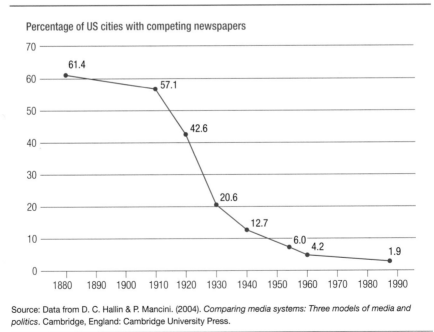

Source: Data from D. C. Hallin & P. Mancini. (2004). *Comparing media systems: Three models of media and politics.* Cambridge, England: Cambridge University Press.

However, the prima facie evidence suggests that the sheer number of voices being represented in the newspaper marketplace has been reduced.

In general, regulation of the print media in Europe has not been as strong as that of the broadcast media. However, some European countries have ownership requirements substantially stricter than those in the United States. In France, for example, a company may not acquire a new publication if the acquisition will push the total daily circulation of all its publications over the 30 percent mark.

An even starker difference between the American and European approaches to print media regulation is the proactive support for diversity in the newspaper market that is provided by European governments, many of which grant direct subsidies to newspapers with the specific aim of increasing diversity. These subsidies seem to have slowed anticompetitive pressures in the European newspaper market.

Another explanation for the greater competitiveness of European print media markets is the willingness of European newspapers to adopt *self-regulation* practices. In many European countries, there exist strong, institutionalized, self-regulatory bodies that monitor content and investigate and respond to complaints. These agencies have the power to develop and enforce codes of press ethics. Although some US newspapers have appointed public editors or ombudspersons, there is no formalized interorganizational agency to regulate behavior or serve as a public forum for concerns about the press. To date, American news organizations have proved reluctant to submit their content to outside review.

In sum, although newspapers are generally subject to less regulation than broadcast media in both the United States and Europe, the same pattern that holds for broadcasting—stronger regulatory frameworks in Europe aimed at promoting the public good—also applies to the print media. As we'll discuss in the next section, this pattern is repeated in the rules governing media coverage of campaigns and elections.

REGULATING THE NEWS MEDIA'S COVERAGE OF CAMPAIGNS

As is the case with public affairs programming more generally, the regulatory treatment of the news media has a significant impact on their ability to fulfill the function of providing an electoral forum. And once again, the United States falls short of other industrialized democracies in establishing a regulatory framework that ensures candidate and voter access to the electoral forum.

The equal-time and equal-access rule, which was intended to ensure that the public would have roughly equal opportunity to encounter the perspectives of opposing political candidates (by requiring radio and television stations to treat candidates equally when providing them airtime), have been rendered meaningless because the FCC now interprets the rule as requiring broadcasters only to make available time to candidates on equal terms, whatever those terms may be.[8] Thus, whenever a candidate cannot afford to buy the same amount of ad time on a given station as the opponent can (as is often the case for challengers running against congressional incumbents), the rule does not require the station to broadcast the lesser-funded candidate's advertisements for free. The public is effectively denied the opportunity to learn about underfinanced candidates.

In other industrialized democracies, by contrast, access to the electoral forum is not contingent on ability to pay. In every industrialized member nation of the Organisation for Economic Co-operation and Development (OECD) *other than the United States*, political parties are granted blocks of free airtime for "party political broadcasts" during campaigns. The allocation of airtime is based on an objective formula that differs depending on the country. In the United Kingdom, for instance, the amount of airtime is based on the number of candidates being fielded by each party; in France, broadcasters are obliged to grant equal airtime to candidates regardless of their prominence or electoral strength. This means that in other democracies, smaller parties, which typically do not have the financial resources available to major parties, are not disadvantaged and still have the opportunity to reach a wide audience through the mass media.

In some instances (such as in the United Kingdom), the party election broadcasts are required to be carried not just by public channels but also by commercial stations. Moreover, all five British television networks are required to air the party election broadcasts on the same day (although not at the same time), thus increasing the size of the audience. In 2001, 58 percent of the respondents in a British panel survey reported that they had seen at least one party election broadcast, and 37 percent said they had seen one from each of the three major parties. The numbers dropped in 2010, however: 50 percent of the British public said they saw at least one party broadcast, and 19 percent said they saw broadcasts from all three parties.

Political parties are not only guaranteed free airtime; many countries (including the United Kingdom, France, Ireland, Belgium, Denmark, Spain, and Switzerland) also prohibit candidates and parties from advertising on television. However, the European Court of Human Rights recently ruled that the ban on political advertising in Norway is a violation of the European Union Charter of Fundamental Rights, and legal experts question whether bans in other countries will withstand court challenges as well. There is a stark contrast between American-style media campaigning and the campaigning in countries with free party broadcasts. Setting aside candidates' attempts to influence the content of news in their favor, broadcast campaigning in the United States consists almost entirely of 30-second paid television ads. In countries with free election broadcasts, in contrast, the blocks of time for campaign messages tend to be considerably longer.

In the United Kingdom in 2001, for example, parties could choose between time slots of 2 minutes and 40 seconds, 3 minutes and 40 seconds, or 4 minutes and 40 seconds. Indeed, British party election broadcasts would seem quite strange to an American audience. They range from plain, straightforward, no-frills presentations—typically featuring the party leader speaking directly into the camera—to more amusing, offbeat presentations from well-known comedians such as John Cleese. Over time, however, as illustrated in Video Archive 2.1, the parties have increasingly resorted to American-style campaign commercials that focus on image and style rather than on the issues.

> ▶
>
> **Video Archive 2.1**
> The Americanization
> of British Party
> Election Broadcasts

It is worth noting that election-time media regulations in other democracies apply to more than just broadcast advertising. Many countries regulate the balance of content within television newscasts and election-related special programs. In France, for example, news programs are required to ensure equality between the amount of airtime allocated to members of the government and the amount allocated to opposition parties. In the United Kingdom, all broadcasters (commercial and public) are required to be impartial in their election coverage and to provide for "balance in viewpoints" (McNicholas & Ward, 2004, p. 156). These regulations contrast sharply with the situation in the United States, where "all news outlets, whatever their means of distribution, may cover elections in any way they deem appropriate" (Kaid & Jones, 2004, p. 33).

Candidates and parties in European democracies are thus guaranteed access to the public, and the public, in turn, is guaranteed the opportunity to learn about the full range of available choices. Furthermore, by eliminating the need for candidates to raise money to purchase airtime, the European model allows candidates to focus on more traditional, grassroots forms of campaigning that strengthen rather than weaken the role of political parties. And even in the case of broadcast campaigning, the length of the party political broadcasts provides a greater opportunity for candidates to provide important and substantive information to the public, at least in comparison with what is made available in the average 30-second American political advertisement.

The case of the internet provides yet another instance of the profound differences in the regulatory approaches of the US and European governments. Since its inception, the US internet has operated under the framework of "net neutrality." This means that internet service providers (ISPs) cannot discriminate against sites, applications, and software. In 2017, the FCC voted (by a 3-to-2 margin) to repeal this rule. As a result, ISPs can now charge sites and services differential rates and create broadband fast lanes that only corporations and the wealthy can afford. The Biden administration, however, has appointed new FCC commissioners and it is expected that the agency will restore the net neutrality guidelines.

In Europe, not only is the net neutrality framework enforced across the European Union, but ISPs must now also comply with regulations designed to protect an individual's privacy. In 2016, the European Parliament passed a law requiring search engines to delete outdated information about an individual's personal background (for instance, a criminal act committed as a juvenile). Companies that did not implement this "right to be forgotten" would face stiff penalties of up to 4 percent of their global revenue. The law has been ratified by the legislatures of all European Union nations.

In direct contrast, the United States continues to treat online data as a form of corporate "freedom of expression" that is protected by the First Amendment. In early 2017, the FCC rejected proposed regulations on ISPs that would have prohibited them from selling individuals' financial and personal information without first obtaining consent. Although President Biden's appointments have tilted the FCC in a pro-consumer direction, it remains unclear whether the agency will revive regulations banning the sale of personal information.

CONCLUSION

It is clear that there are two conditions under which news media in democratic societies are more likely to make good on their civic responsibilities. The first is a more stringent regulatory framework that requires the media to provide a certain level of public affairs programming. This is the approach adopted in most European democracies, and the evidence shows that European media typically deliver a more robust version of the public forum than that realized in the American market-based approach. Although the laissez-faire approach to media regulation is gaining traction around the world, most industrialized democracies persist in viewing the media in general and broadcasting in particular as "an institution whose influence on society is too great to be left under the control of private interests and that must be run under the authority of the state as a representative of the general interest" (Hallin & Mancini, 2004).

The second key condition for helping to ensure that the media meet their civic responsibilities is to afford broadcasters some protection from the ravages of the market. Publicly funded television networks have the necessary cushion to deliver a steady flow of substantive, hard news; they need not constantly look at their market share when making programming decisions. Societies in which public television reaches a significant share of the audience are thus more likely to have relatively well-informed and engaged electorates.

Neither the regulatory framework nor market protection conditions hold in the United States. It is not surprising, then, that American media tend to fall short of expectations; they generally deliver programming that is more entertaining than informative, and instead of acting as a restraint on the actions of government, they frequently toe the official line. The next two chapters will address the weaknesses of contemporary American journalism. In Chapter 3, we'll show how market forces and the norms of professional journalism have combined to undermine the quality of news programming. In Chapter 4, we'll analyze the factors that have undermined the media's ability to play the role of watchdog.

Summary

1. Mass media in democratic societies serve three important functions:
   - Providing an electoral forum for candidates and political parties to debate their qualifications for office before a national audience
   - Contributing to informed citizenship by providing a variety of perspectives on the important issues of the day (the public sphere function)
   - Serving as a watchdog, scrutinizing the actions of government officials on behalf of citizens
2. The centrality of the media's role in the political process depends on universal access to media and on the relative strength of other political institutions—political parties in particular.
3. The media became central to US politics in the 1960s, at a time when major changes in the candidate nomination process were weakening political parties. These changes were made possible by the almost universal spread of television occurring at the same time.

4. The American media system (particularly with respect to broadcast media) differs from that of most other industrialized democracies in two respects:
   - It is almost entirely privately owned.
   - Its regulation is relatively weak.
5. Print media, in the United States and elsewhere, have never been subject to the same level of government control as broadcast media.
6. The United States also has weaker regulatory standards governing the coverage of elections. Whereas politicians in the United States must purchase access to the broadcast media (usually in the form of 30-second campaign commercials), many other democracies grant free airtime to candidates in the run-up to elections. Some also have rules governing the balance of viewpoints presented in news during political campaigns.

FURTHER READINGS

Aalberg, T., van Aelst, P., & Curran, J. (2010). Media systems and the political information environment: A cross-national comparison. *The International Journal of Press/Politics, 15*(3), 255–271.

Besley, T., & Prat, A. (2006). Handcuffs for the grabbing hand? Media capture and government accountability. *American Economic Review, 96*, 720–736.

Curran, J., Iyengar, S., Lund, A. B., & Salovaara-Moring, I. (2009). Media system, public knowledge and democracy. *European Journal of Communication, 24*(1), 5–26.

Dalton, R. J., & Wattenberg, M. P. (2001). *Parties without partisans: Political change in advanced industrial democracies.* New York: Oxford University Press.

Djankov, S., McLiesh, C., Nenova, T., & Shleifer, A. (2001, June). *Who owns the media?* (Working Paper No. 2620). Washington, DC: World Bank, Office of the Senior Vice President, Development Economics. Retrieved February 9, 2022, from https://papers.ssrn.com/sol3/papers.cfm?abstract_id=267386.

Hallin, D. C., & Mancini, P. (2004). *Comparing media systems: Three models of media and politics.* Cambridge, England: Cambridge University Press.

Iyengar, S., & Curran, J. (2009). *Media systems, news delivery and citizens' knowledge of current affairs.* Retrieved October 1, 2010, from http://publicsphere.ssrc.org/.

Martin, G. J., & McCrain, J. (2019). Local news and national politics. *American Political Science Review, 113*, 372–384.

O'Hagan, J., & Jennings, M. (2003). Public broadcasting in Europe: Rationale, licence fee, and other issues. *Journal of Cultural Economics, 27*, 31–56.

Polsby, N. W. (1983). *Consequences of party reform.* New York: Oxford University Press.

Schudson, M. (1998). *The good citizen: A history of American civic life.* New York: Free Press.

Zaller, J. R. (2003). A new standard of news quality: Burglar alarms for the monitorial citizen. *Political Communication, 20*, 109–130.

NOTES

1. Note, however, that several studies have found that levels of party membership and levels of activity by party members are declining all across Europe.

2. The United Kingdom uses the same system. In a handful of cases in the United States, alternative electoral systems are used. For example, San Francisco voters approved a ballot measure in 2002 to bring in the use of instant runoff voting (where voters can specify second preferences that are distributed if no candidate wins a majority) in city elections. Many other cities, including Minneapolis and St. Paul, Minnesota, and Aspen, Colorado, have adopted similar systems since then.

3. The rationale for the regulation of broadcast media lies in the very technology of broadcasting. Operation of a newspaper printing press does not interfere with any other press. Radio and television, by contrast, are broadcast through signals of a specific frequency and power. Televisions and radios receive these signals on a fixed number of channels, each of which corresponds to the frequency of the signal. The channels have to be sufficiently far apart to avoid interference among the signals. Unlike newspapers, the production of which is not exclusive, with broadcast media, "one person's transmission is another's interference" (Krasnow, 1997).

4. The public interest stipulation was built into the Communications Act of 1934, enacted in response to the increasing congestion of the radio airwaves. Any person who wished to build and operate a transmitter needed to get a license first. The act also created a new agency, the Federal Communications Commission, to regulate all interstate broadcast communication. The agency was to grant licenses free of charge either on a one-year provisional basis or for a three-year term. At the end of the term the station could apply for renewal. The FCC could deny or modify a license if the station failed to live up to the commission's standards of the public interest. However, the act said little about what constitutes the public interest.

5. It is estimated that approximately 5 percent of televisions in the United Kingdom are unlicensed. Licenses are enforced, on behalf of the government, by private companies, who maintain a database of all addresses in the United Kingdom. It is assumed that there is a television at every address, so any address that does not have a television license is likely to be visited by enforcement agents. In addition to the address database, enforcement agents use electronic detectors to search for unlicensed TVs (by picking up the small amount of energy radiated by traditional television sets), and electronics retailers can be fined if they do not report the addresses of people buying televisions.

6. The quality measure was based on performance on a number of criteria: "Cover the whole community; be significant and informative; demonstrate enterprise and

courage; be fair, balanced, and accurate; be authoritative; be highly local; presentation; sensationalism" (Project for Excellence in Journalism, 2003).

7. The Newspaper Preservation Act of 1970 permitted two or more newspapers publishing in the same area (at least one of which is failing) to combine advertising, business, circulation, and printing operations, as long as the news operations (meaning both staff and editorial policy) remained separate.

8. In one example of equal terms, the lowest unit rate rule requires that stations offer advertising time to candidates at the lowest rate that they have charged other commercial advertisers during the preceding 45 days (Kaid & Jones, 2004).

3

The Media Marketplace

Where Americans Get the News

Historically, where Americans get their news has depended on the development of new technologies for transmitting information. Today, most of us use a news app, go online to visit our favorite news websites, or are referred to a news story through our social media news feed. Forty years ago, Americans gathered around their television sets at dinnertime to watch the network news. And before 1950, the news arrived each morning in the form of the daily newspaper.

The earliest newspapers were affiliated with political parties. Their news offerings were unabashedly slanted in the direction of their partisan sympathies. During the latter part of the nineteenth century, however, major improvements in the technology of printing lowered the costs of production. Publishers could reach mass rather than niche or localized audiences, and revenues from advertising far surpassed the subsidies provided by political parties, thus spelling the doom of the partisan press. In 1870, nearly 90 percent of all dailies were affiliated with one of the two major parties. Thirty years later, the figure had been cut in half.

As newspapers began to demonstrate both profitability and political independence, civic-minded publishers and editors began to push for the formal training of journalists. They subsidized the establishment of journalism schools at major universities. By the 1930s, journalism had become professionalized, with appropriate "canons of conduct," including the pronouncement that "news reports should be free from opinion or bias of any kind" (Stephens, 1994).

The continued success of large-circulation daily newspapers led to gradual consolidation of the industry as local newspapers were acquired by regional and national newspaper chains. Today, most American newspapers are owned by a chain. In 2018, the six largest newspaper chains accounted for more than 60 percent of the total circulation of 30 million (see Figure 3.1). In 2019, the top two companies in Figure 3.1 merged (under the Gannett name), creating a giant chain that accounts for 40 percent of all US newspapers.

FIGURE 3.1

Print Circulation of the Top US Newspaper Companies, 2018

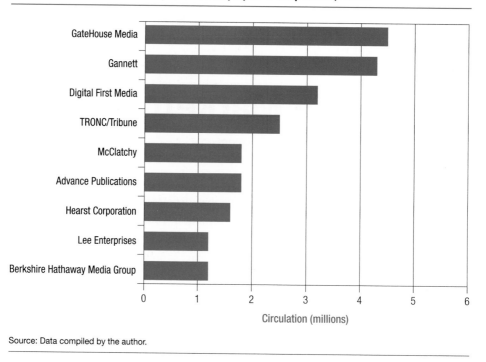

Source: Data compiled by the author.

With the development of radio in the 1920s and the immediate popularity of radio news (spawned by radio's relatively fast-breaking coverage of World War II), newspapers began to surrender their position as the major source of news. The arrival of television in the 1950s accentuated this trend, and broadcast news gradually replaced print outlets as the major carriers of news. The national newscasts aired by the three major television networks (ABC, CBS, NBC) soon emerged as the dominant source of daily news. In 1969, at the height of their dominance, the combined audience for the three newscasts accounted for three-fourths of all American households. More people (approximately 25 million) tuned in to any one of the network newscasts in the late 1960s than subscribed to the top 20 daily newspapers combined.

The development of cable broadcasting in the early 1980s weakened the major networks' monopoly hold on the television audience. CNN, the first all-news cable network, was formed in 1980 and was soon followed by Fox, CNBC, and MSNBC. By 2009, 90 percent of American households had access to cable news channels.

A more significant threat to the dominance of network news was the increasing proliferation of local and soft news programming. Responding to the low cost of producing local news and the substantial audience demand, station owners began to air multiple local newscasts and hybrid entertainment-news programs each day. In the 1960s, most stations broadcast a single evening local newscast; today, the ratio of local to national news programming on television is tilted overwhelmingly in favor of the former. In the San Francisco area, for instance, the five commercial television stations air a total of 10.5 hours of local news each day between 4:00 PM and 7:00 PM (see Figure 3.2).

Most recently, breakthroughs in digital technology have further transformed how we get our news. With the widespread adoption of mobile devices and the personal computer as gateways to the outside world, the competition for news audiences has intensified. Today, all news organizations—big and small—provide their news offerings online, giving consumers instant, on-demand access to the news. We will discuss the implications of information technology for the consumption of news in Chapter 5. For the moment, it is important to note that the content of online news derives primarily from "old," conventional outlets (newspaper, magazines, or television news). Exclusively online sources such as blogs and a handful of news organizations (for example, HuffPost, Vox, and Axios) have yet to match the market share of the established providers of news content (such as CNN).

In the rest of this chapter, we will describe the evolution of the national audience for news and the changing patterns of news consumption. We will

FIGURE 3.2
San Francisco Afternoon TV Listings for July 10, 2021

San Francisco

	4:00 PM	4:30 PM	5:00 PM	5:30 PM	6:00 PM	6:30 PM
KPIX (CBS)	Judge Judy	Judge Judy	KPIX5 News	KPIX5 News	KPIX5 News	CBS Evening News
KNTV (NBC)	The Ellen DeGeneres Show		NBC Bay Area News	NBC Bay Area News	NBC Bay Area News	NBC News
KABC	ABC7 News		ABC7 News	ABC World News	ABC7 News	
KRON	Dr. Phil		KRON 4 News	KRON 4 News	KRON 4 News	KRON 4 News
KTVU (FOX)	KTVU FOX 2 News		KTVU FOX 2 News		KTVU FOX 2 News	

■ National news　■ Local news　■ Entertainment

Source: Data from "TV listings" (2021). Retrieved July 10, 2021, from www.sfgate.com/tv.

also track changes in the public's evaluation of news; for example, do people believe what they read? During the presidency of Donald Trump, the relationship between the White House and the press became more conflictual. President Trump's "fake news" mantra polarized the public's evaluations of news organizations with Republicans overwhelmingly viewing the mainstream news as biased in a liberal direction. Next we'll address the major factors that shape the news. First and foremost are market forces. In a competitive market, audience size is paramount, and all news organizations are in a race to increase their market share. The result is news that is produced to entertain rather than inform. Second, the professional norms and values of journalists shape the content of news. The desire to maintain autonomy, for example, has led journalists to cover campaigns and politicians from a more interpretive perspective. Rather than simply summarizing the candidates' speeches and advertisements, reporters now focus on the state of the horse race and the candidates' strategies and tactics for winning over voters. Third, the news is inevitably a reflection of organizational processes and routines; the beat system, for instance, by which reporters are assigned to particular subjects, ensures a regular supply of news reports from major government agencies.

AUDIENCES

Audience size is everything in the world of news. Because all news outlets (with the exception of National Public Radio and the Public Broadcasting Service) are privately owned, their survival depends on maintaining a loyal audience. Advertising represents the principal source of revenue for publishers and broadcasters. The price of advertising depends on the number of people reached by any given newspaper, television news program, or website. Statistics on newspaper circulation are compiled by the Audit Bureau of Circulations; television news audiences are measured by the Nielsen Company; web metrics are tracked by several companies, including Alexa and ComScore.

Unlike the situation in Europe, where individual newspapers often command a large share of the national audience, American newspapers circulate on a more modest scale. Today, the most widely read American newspaper is the *New York Times,* with a combined print and digital circulation of 7.8 million daily readers (as of 2021), followed by the *Wall Street Journal,* with a combined print and digital circulation of 3.5 million readers. *USA Today,* the only truly national newspaper, is in third place with a combined circulation of just over 1 million. To boost revenue, most newspapers have put in place online "paywalls" and digital subscriptions. Unlike most nations, where newspapers reach a national audience, American dailies are limited to local or regional audiences.

The historical trend in newspaper circulation is not promising. Unlike broadcast media, newspapers require the audience's undivided attention. Americans' lifestyle and use of time changed dramatically in the latter part of the twentieth century. The marked increase in dual-worker households and the increasing amount of time devoted to work-related activities led to significant declines in newspaper circulation. Between 1990 and 2016, newspaper print circulation numbers dropped by about 27 million, and several newspapers went out of business, partly due to declines in advertising revenue (see Figure 3.3). Readers are turning away from reading classified ads, once a major source of revenue for newspapers, and using online sites such as Craigslist and LinkedIn instead. Major corporations and local businesses are also increasingly opting to advertise online. Today, the audience (print only) for the 10 largest newspapers is approximately 3 million. This figure is less than one-sixth the combined daily audience for the syndicated television shows *Wheel of Fortune* and *Jeopardy!* (approximately 18.5 million for the week of January 20, 2021).

Unlike newspapers, network television has a nationwide presence. Television programming produced by a network is transmitted across the country by local stations affiliated with that network. Measuring just how many people watch a particular program is the mission of the Nielsen Company. Nielsen developed the concept of television *gross rating points* (GRPs). One rating point generally translates to 1 percent of the viewing audience. Nielsen compiles information from two sources: television diaries maintained by a large and representative sample of households (more than 5,000) and 24-hour metering of television sets (among a smaller subset of households). Each television program broadcast in the United States is identifiable by a unique digital fingerprint. Nielsen's metering system captures this identifying information, making it possible to estimate precisely the number of television sets tuned in to any particular program.[1]

The audience for broadcast news exists on two levels: local and national. The broadcasting industry consists of hundreds of local outlets, many of which are affiliated with a national network, thus enabling them to relay network programming. In exchange, station owners must pay the networks a subscription fee for access to their programming. The three major television networks (and their corporate parents) are ABC (Disney), CBS (Viacom), and NBC (Comcast). Congress granted Fox a network license in 1986. Initially part of Rupert Murdoch's News Corporation, Fox is now a separate entity (still under the control of the Murdoch family) and has aggressively purchased local stations across the country.

FIGURE 3.3
Status of US Newspapers

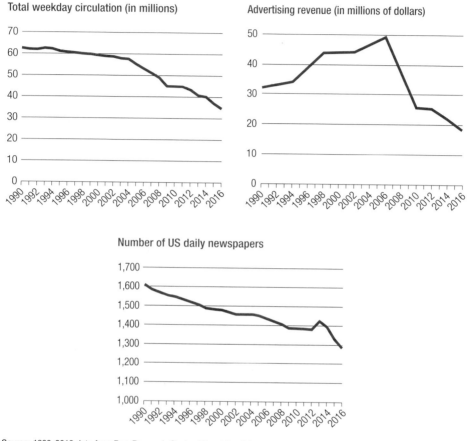

Total weekday circulation (in millions)

Advertising revenue (in millions of dollars)

Number of US daily newspapers

Source: 1990–2012 data from Pew Research Center, *The state of the news media 2013: An annual report on American journalism* (2013). Retrieved September 7, 2021, from the Pew Research Center website: http://assets.pewresearch .org.s3.amazonaws.com/files/journalism/State-of-the-News-Media-Report-2013-FINAL.pdf; 2013–2016 data from Pew Research Center, "Newspaper fact sheet" (2021, June 29). Retrieved September 7, 2021, from the Pew Research Center website: www.journalism.org/fact-sheet/newspapers/; 2012–2016 US Newspaper data from Statista, "Number of daily newspapers in the United States from 1970 to 2018." Retrieved November 17, 2021, from the Statista website: https://www .statista.com/statistics/183408/number-of-us-daily-newspapers-since-1975/.

On a smaller level, the country is divided into 210 local television markets known as *designated media areas,* or DMAs. In many cases, the DMA corresponds to a metropolitan area, but in less urban parts of the country, a DMA may include multiple counties. Whereas California has 12 DMAs, the entire state of Montana has only one. Each DMA consists of a set of antenna-based local television stations licensed by the FCC and assigned to a specific channel.

By the late 1960s, the 30-minute evening newscasts produced by the major networks had emerged as the industry leader. At the height of their popularity, the three network newscasts attracted a combined daily audience in excess of 60 million viewers. The introduction of cable television, however, launched a period of greater competition within the world of broadcasting. CNN emerged as a reputable supplier of news in the 1980s, employing well-known journalists (many of whom had been let go by the networks) and reaching viewers around the globe.[2]

Although the American audience for CNN (and the other cable networks) is typically less than 4 GRPs, the market share of cable news providers increases during periods of international tension or domestic crises. Immediately after the start of Operation Desert Storm in January 1991, CNN reporters Bernard Shaw, John Holliman, and Peter Arnett found themselves the only American television correspondents in Baghdad. Their dramatic reports of the bombing raids were watched by a worldwide audience of more than a billion people. In 2020, the combination of the COVID-19 pandemic and the protests surrounding police shootings created a surge in viewership; all three cable networks recorded their largest audiences ever.

Since the institutionalization of cable television, the audience share of network news has gradually declined. Since their heyday, the three nightly newscasts have experienced a ratings decline of nearly 60 percent. The network television audience share fell from 85 percent of households in 1969 to under 30 percent in 2016. The most dramatic declines occurred in the 1990s, considerably after cable television had come of age. Between 1980 and 2021, for instance, the combined audience for the three evening newscasts was cut in half from 42 million to 21 million (see Figure 3.4). It was precisely during this period that the production of local television news surged.

Despite the increasing competition from cable providers, network news remains the single most watched national news source in the United States. In 2016, the combined audience for the three evening newscasts (23 million) exceeded the combined circulation of the top 40 newspapers.

For decades, CBS was considered the premier network newscast. Under the leadership of Edward R. Murrow, the network recruited a stable of distinguished correspondents, including Walter Cronkite, Howard K. Smith, and Eric Sevareid. During much of Cronkite's long tenure as anchorman, the *CBS Evening News* emerged as the perennial ratings winner. Cronkite's retirement in 1981, however, created a more competitive environment, and by the early 1990s,

FIGURE 3.4

Evening News Household Ratings for ABC, CBS, and NBC, 1980–2020

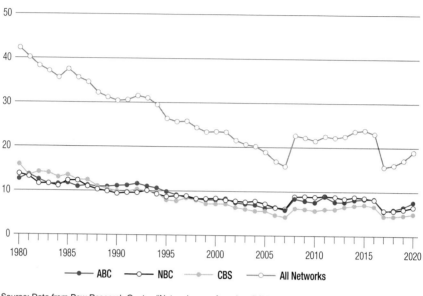

Household TV ratings (in millions)

Source: Data from Pew Research Center, "Network news fact sheet" (2021, July 13). Retrieved September 7, 2021, from the Pew Research Center website: https://www.pewresearch.org/journalism/fact-sheet/network-news/.

the network had fallen to third place in the ratings, trailing both ABC and NBC by a substantial margin. In 2004 and 2005, the long-standing anchors for NBC and CBS (Tom Brokaw and Dan Rather, respectively) both retired, and ABC's Peter Jennings died (having retired several months earlier), prompting speculation that the network news audience would once again be up for grabs.

Since then, the leadership of the evening news has been in relative flux. Brian Williams anchored the *NBC Nightly News* from 2004 to 2014; Lester Holt took over in 2015. Bob Schieffer anchored the *CBS Nightly News* after Rather's retirement and was replaced by Katie Couric shortly thereafter. Couric was replaced by Scott Pelley in 2011; the current anchor is Norah O'Donnell. Charles Gibson replaced Peter Jennings on ABC, and then Diane Sawyer took over in 2009 after Gibson retired. Sawyer announced her retirement in 2014 and was replaced by David Muir.

It is important to place the audience for network news in context. Although millions of people watch the evening news, the newscasts are small fry when compared with reality programming, sports, or prime-time drama. *American*

Idol, CSI, or *Monday Night Football* outdraws any of the nightly newscasts by a substantial margin. In comparison with entertainment, the demand for public affairs programming is weak. The 10 most popular regularly scheduled television broadcasts ever (see Table 3.1) do not include a single news or public affairs program (although soft news events such as the O. J. Simpson low-speed chase through Los Angeles and the funerals of Princess Diana and Michael Jackson attract very large audiences).

The most serious threat to network news today is local news. Station owners have discovered that local news programming can be delivered more or less continuously and at relatively low cost. Moreover, millions of people tune in because local news provides information that is closer to home, more usable (such as the weather forecast), and more entertaining (such as the latest sports results). In market after market, stations have increased the number of programming slots devoted to local news. As we saw in Figure 3.2, local news runs on a continuous basis during the late afternoon–early evening time slots in big-city markets. Across the country, the audience for evening local news aired by the network local affiliates generally equals or exceeds the audience for the network's own national newscast. In fact, as we'll describe later in the chapter, the rise of local television news is a compelling case study of how media economics determines media programming.

TABLE 3.1

Top 10 TV Programs Ranked by Number of Viewing Households, 1961–2020

Program	Episode	Network	Date	Nielsen Rating	Share (%)	Number of Households
Superbowl XLIX	Patriots vs. Seahawks	NBC	2/5/2012	47.5	71	55,341,000
Superbowl L	Broncos vs. Panthers	CBS	2/7/2016	46.6	72	54,310,000
Superbowl XLVIII	Broncos vs. Seahawks	Fox	2/2/2014	46.4	69	53,727,000
Superbowl XLIV	Saints vs. Colts	CBS	2/7/2010	45.0	68	53,600,000
*M*A*S*H* (series)	Final episode	CBS	2/28/1983	60.2	77	50,150,000
XVII Winter Olympics	Women's figure skating	CBS	2/23/1994	48.5	64	45,690,000
Superbowl XX	Bears vs. Patriots	NBC	1/26/1986	48.3	70	41,490,000
Dallas (series)	"Who Shot J. R.?"	CBS	11/21/1980	53.3	76	41,470,000
Superbowl XVI	49ers vs. Bengals	CBS	1/24/1982	49.1	73	40,020,000
Roots (miniseries)	Part 8	ABC	1/30/1977	51.1	71	36,380,000

Source: Data from Nielsen Media Research, unpublished data. Retrieved July 21, 2021, from the Nielsen Media Research website: www.nielsenmedia.com.

Ratings are the lifeblood of the broadcasting industry. Advertising revenues for specific television programs fluctuate on the basis of how many people they reach. Nielsen conducts quarterly ratings "sweeps" during the months of February, May, July, and November. The size of the audience during each sweeps period locks in advertising rates for individual programs and stations until the next period. Programs that suffer a decline in their ratings thus stand to lose significant revenue, so broadcast news providers do their utmost to maintain or improve their ratings.

Efforts to monitor online audiences are still in their infancy. The analytics firm Comscore has emerged as the market leader for online metrics. The company maintains a global sample of Web users whose computers are equipped with monitoring software that enables the company to track online behavior. The panelists also complete surveys on a regular basis, allowing the company to combine consumers' online behavior with their attitude and demographic profiles. Internet traffic is dominated by social networking sites (such as Facebook), online search engines (such as Google), and major portals (such as MSN and Yahoo). As we will discuss in greater detail in Chapter 5, the emerging audience for public affairs information online is not nearly as large as the number of people who engage in online shopping, interpersonal communication (e-mail), pornography, and other browsing activities.

One final point about the supply of news concerns the gradual increase in joint ventures, or *cross-media sources*. Many of these feature partnerships between online services and "old" content providers, as in the case of Hulu, which streams video on demand and is now owned by Disney. Similar cross-platform partnerships have been initiated within conventional media because the FCC has relaxed its cross-ownership limits—that is, the limits on the number of different news outlets operating within a media market that can be owned by a single entity. In many media markets, for instance, the same owner operates both the major newspaper and the top-rated local television station.[3]

The most recent challenge to the broadcasting industry has been mounted by companies that deliver streaming video to audiences watching not on their television sets but on laptop computers, tablets, and even smartphones. Netflix, once a distributor of DVDs, has emerged as the leading producer of digital content, with several popular series, including *House of Cards* and *Squid Game*. With 75 million subscribers in the United States alone, the company can afford a large investment in content production ($17 billion for 2021). Netflix's main competitors are Amazon Prime Video (owned by billionaire Jeff Bezos), with 56 million subscribers, and Hulu, with 39 million subscribers.

Despite the apparent success of video streaming, at the present time there is no reliable data on the market share enjoyed by Netflix, Amazon, or Hulu. The companies refuse to release the metrics on the size of their audiences. In 2017, the Nielsen Company began to track the audience for video streaming services using "total minutes watched" as their barometer of audience size.

CREDIBILITY

Audience size is one measure of the demand for news. But does size also imply credibility? Source credibility (believability) is an important indicator of media status and influence; when people perceive news reports to be unbiased and trustworthy, they are more likely to take them seriously (see Chapter 8). Media scholars have tracked the American public's evaluation of media credibility for several decades.

Given the freedom of the American press from government controls and journalists' commitment to objective reporting, we would expect consumers to view the news as generally unbiased. An approximate indicator of media credibility is the level of overall public confidence in the press. The General Social Survey, conducted annually by the National Opinion Research Center at the University of Chicago, asks a representative sample of Americans for their level of confidence in the media. In 1973, the first year the question was asked, only 10 percent of the public responded "hardly any." By 2008, however, this group had grown to 45 percent of the sample. Although it is true that public confidence in just about every public institution has declined substantially since 1973, in comparison with other institutions the press has taken a much bigger hit. As shown in Figure 3.5, today there are considerably more Americans who say they have "hardly any confidence in the press" than who say they have "a great deal of confidence in the press." In contrast, confidence in education shows a much slower decline over time, with a plurality of Americans expressing great confidence. The audience may be listening, but it is also increasingly skeptical.

The declining level of public confidence in the press coincides with a dramatic increase in party polarization (a topic we cover at some length in Chapter 8). As conflict and ill will across the partisan divide has ratcheted up, trust and confidence in the media have become entangled with the audience's partisan loyalties. Beginning in the 1990s, the General Social Survey showed that Republicans were increasingly more skeptical of the news than Democrats (by a margin of more than 10 percentage points). A similar partisan gap began to appear in evaluations of individual news

FIGURE 3.5

Confidence in the Press versus Confidence in Education

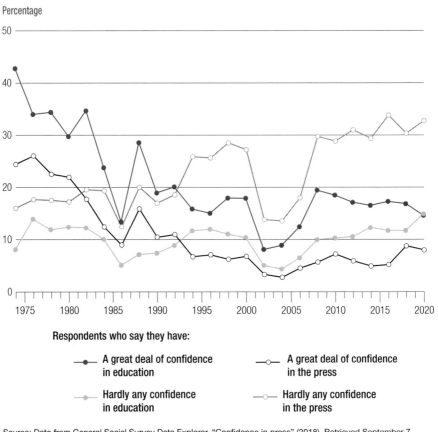

Percentage

Respondents who say they have:

—●— A great deal of confidence in education

—○— A great deal of confidence in the press

—●— Hardly any confidence in education

—○— Hardly any confidence in the press

Source: Data from General Social Survey Data Explorer, "Confidence in press" (2018). Retrieved September 7, 2021, from GSS Data Explorer, NORC at the University of Chicago, website: https://gssdataexplorer.norc.org/variables/454/vshow; General Social Survey Data Explorer, "Confidence in Education" (2018). Retrieved September 7, 2021, from GSS Data Explorer website: https://gssdataexplorer.norc.org/variables/451/vshow.

organizations. In 1998, for instance, 44 percent of Democrats and 39 percent of Republicans gave CNN high marks for believability. Six years later, the gap was considerably larger, as only 29 percent of Republicans were inclined to trust CNN.

Studies of media credibility show one consistent pattern: people who tend to hold strong political views, such as those with a strong sense of political party affiliation, are especially likely to view the news as biased. Enthusiasm for the party line makes partisans suspicious of news presentations that strive to present a balanced perspective on the day's events, the journalistic paradigm that applies to the vast majority of American news organizations. The tendency to attribute bias to objective coverage is directly proportional to the intensity of one's political commitments. In fact, research has shown that people with opposing viewpoints, when shown the exact same news report, will each believe that the report is biased in favor of the other side! This is called the *hostile media phenomenon.* Research by Seth Goldman and Diana Mutz (2011), however, demonstrates that most people view the media they use most often as favoring their own views. This *friendly media phenomenon* highlights the difference between a person's beliefs about the media in general and the media that he or she uses regularly, and it puts a new twist on the hostile media phenomenon.

As the political process has become more acrimonious and divisive, the number of Americans who view mainstream news organizations as biased has increased. Less than a year after the 2016 election, a national poll showed that more than 40 percent of voters agreed that the media sometimes "fabricated" reports about President Trump. Among Republicans, the number was nearly 70 percent. In a 2018 survey, respondents rated several news sources on a scale ranging from "not at all trustworthy" (coded as 1) to "totally trustworthy" (coded as 5). As shown in Figure 3.6, Republicans are less trusting of most mainstream news organizations (such as CNN, *New York Times*, Yahoo News), including those with minimal political content (such as ESPN and the Weather Channel). For their part, Democrats continue to believe that mainstream media outlets are trustworthy. Not surprisingly, the only instance of agreement across the party divide concerns news outlets that have staked out a clear partisan affiliation. The vast majority of Republicans trust Fox a great deal and distrust MSNBC, while almost by the same margins, Democrats distrust Fox and trust MSNBC. Clearly, the American news media have been caught up in the maelstrom of party polarization; today, source credibility is very much a matter of partisan affiliation.

◎ IN FOCUS

The Hostile Media Phenomenon

Research has consistently shown that people who are highly committed to a point of view—strong Democrats or Republicans, for example, or those who are strongly pro-Israeli or pro-Palestinian—generally perceive impartial news stories to be biased in favor of their opponents.

FIGURE 3.6

The Party Divide on Trust in the Media

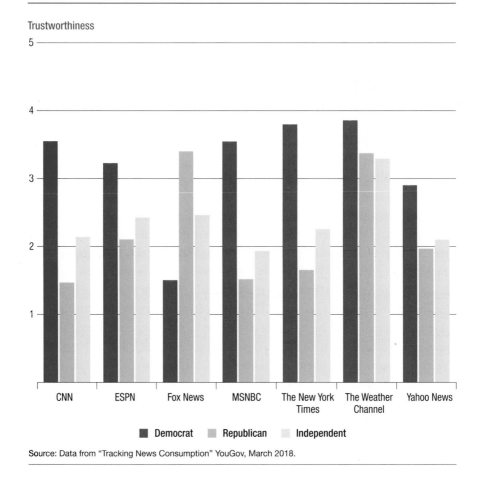

Trustworthiness

Source: Data from "Tracking News Consumption" YouGov, March 2018.

WHAT GETS REPORTED?

News is meant to be a reflection of reality. The major events and issues occurring in the world are the events and issues we expect to encounter in the news. This mirror-image definition of news stipulates close correspondence between the state of the real world and the content of news coverage. During times of rising joblessness, the news focuses on unemployment; when the country is in the grip of a deadly pandemic, the spotlight shifts to public health.

Implicit in the mirror-image definition of news is the well-known asymmetry between newsworthiness and the normal course of events. Events are judged newsworthy only when they deviate from anticipated (everyday) outcomes. Planes that land safely are not news, but planes that land safely on rivers are front-page news. In general, negative events or outcomes tend to attract greater coverage for the simple reason that they indicate a deviation from normalcy. News coverage of the economy is sparse during periods of prosperity but abundant during stock market crashes and recessions. Politicians who behave as law-abiding citizens attract little attention; the few who break the law elicit volumes of coverage. As in economics, where Gresham's law stipulates that bad money drives out good money, negative information always drives out positive information.

The expectation that news organizations behave as mirrors of real-world events is unrealistic on a variety of grounds. Practical considerations make it impossible to cover events at every remote location around the globe, and many issues (such as climate change) do not manifest themselves in the form of observable, concrete events. In other policy areas, indicators of reality (such as the level of threat to US national security) are simply unavailable.[4] In these cases, it is impossible to assess the level of correspondence between reality on the one hand and *mediality* (the "reality" portrayed by the media) on the other.

In the final analysis, the mirror-image definition of news is unrealistic because the practice of journalism rests on fallible and culturally determined human judgments. On any given day, thousands of potentially important events occur. It is physically impossible to cover all of them. Editorial selection (gatekeeping) is the hallmark of news: events are granted coverage in proportion to their newsworthiness. Judgments of newsworthiness are inherently subjective; what's newsworthy to CBS News may be of little interest to All India Radio or, for that matter, to the *New York Times*.

Explaining the content of news, therefore, is very much an exercise in understanding journalists' professional values, career incentives, and decision-making processes, all of which affect their behavior and work product. This perspective is generally referred to as the *organizational process* account of news, meaning that the standard operating procedures of news organizations influence what's reported and what's ignored. Thus, to the degree that news reports deviate from reality, the discrepancy is attributable more to organizational procedures and news-gathering routines and less to deliberate bias on the part of journalists. As we note in the closing section of this chapter, the increasing popularity of online news sources, many of which are not wedded to the norms of professional journalism, has increased the availability of news with a distinct political slant.

The major competitor of the organizational process account of news is the standard market-based account of profit-maximizing behavior. As we have noted repeatedly, the media industry in the United States is privately owned. Consumers are free to choose from a wide array of news providers. Facing competition, rational owners prefer to further their own interests rather than to provide public service to the community. The content and form of news coverage are subject to the same logic that drives all other economic activity: minimize costs and maximize revenues.

MARKET PRESSURES

Consider the following facts from the world of broadcast journalism. The award-winning television news program that delivers the most detailed, substantive, and wide-ranging discussion of policy issues is the hour-long newscast produced by the Public Broadcasting Service. This newscast is watched by approximately 1.5 million Americans each evening. *Entertainment Tonight,* the 30-minute program focusing on Hollywood celebrity news, attracts a daily audience in excess of 5 million viewers. Soft news and reality television programs attract much larger audiences than does serious news.

The message for news organizations is obvious: make news reports more interesting. No matter what the medium, the public affairs content of news has been substantially diluted over time. In an early study, Slattery and Hakanen (1994) found that news about government and policy fell from 54 percent to 15 percent in a sample of Philadelphia local newscasts between 1976 and 1992. Between 2007 and 2015, when US newspapers slashed employment by 40 percent, coverage of government and politics dropped substantially, by as much as 400 stories annually (Peterson, 2021). Even the *New York Times,* with its motto of "All the News That's Fit to Print," has had to chart a similar course, offering entire sections on food, fashion, travel, and other topics with little relevance to current events.

Market pressures are especially intense in the world of broadcast news, where survival must take precedence over informative news reports. Substantive news content and audience size are inversely related. Obviously, news producers have to adapt to the competition from soft news, sitcoms, and cable talk shows. They do so by making their own news programs more entertaining and less serious. Between 1980 and 2000, stories with some policy content fell from 70 to 50 percent in national newscasts. News reports defined as sensationalized increased from 25 to 40 percent (Patterson, 2000). In one of the few tests of the demand for soft news, scholars at the University of California, Los Angeles, tracked network news coverage of the murder trial of NFL superstar O. J. Simpson—an iconic soft news saga. They found that increased attention to the trial in fact increased audience size (Kernell, Lamberson, & Zaller, 2017). The lesson for news organizations is clear: coverage of sensationalized events is more profitable than substance.

This can be seen most clearly when the content of the news from coun-tries where media are driven primarily by market pressures is compared with the content of the news in countries where financial considerations are less important. James Curran and his coauthors (2009) found that 37 percent of television news content from the bottom line–oriented US media is soft compared with only 17 percent for the public service–oriented Finnish media. From a demand-side perspective, a focus on soft news also makes sense. Thomas Patterson (2007) found that Americans were more likely to recall soft news stories than hard news stories, and a study of news interest between 1986 and 2006 (Pew Research Center, 2007) found that people were almost as likely to closely follow soft news stories (18 percent) as they were to closely follow political news (22 percent) and foreign news (17 percent).

Journalism was not always so sensitive to the bottom line. In the early days of television news, most senior managers were themselves journalists, with the view that their news programs were to be the very best rather than the most profitable. All three network news divisions operated in the red during the 1970s, yet they employed large staffs, maintained bureaus in several countries, and provided what was considered top-notch reporting. In effect, the networks used the vast profits generated by their entertainment programs to subsi-dize their news divisions. William Paley, the founder of CBS, is said to have remarked to a journalist concerned about the rising costs of the *CBS Evening News*, "You guys cover the news; I've got Jack Benny [a famous entertainer at the time] to make money for me."

As the networks were acquired by conglomerates, the corporate culture changed. The news divisions were expected to make a profit and sink or swim within the parent company. The amount of time reserved for news in the 30-minute newscast was cut by 10 percent, from 21 minutes in 1990 to 19 minutes in 2009. All three networks were forced to reduce the number of correspondents and close most of their international bureaus. With the end of the Cold War, foreign affairs no longer had a compelling story line ("Can we get along with the Russians?"), and news organizations felt free to scale back their overseas coverage. These measures have created a seri-ous lack of access to international events. In the case of breaking overseas events, American networks typically purchase footage from freelancers or from European network correspondents, with voice-over from the near-est network correspondent. Cost-cutting also ushered in the end of serious documentary programming. Hard-hitting investigative documentaries on matters of national importance were transformed into superficial conversa-tions with celebrities.

Accentuating the new economic logic was the gradual breakdown of the rigid boundaries in the daily television programming schedule, which until the onset of deregulation in the 1980s restricted local news programs to one 30-minute slot in the early- and late-evening schedules. Once stations began airing local and soft news programs in multiple time slots, the pressure on network news only intensified.

When the networks were created, their rationale for airing news programs was hardly selfless. Rather, they were required by the FCC to provide a minimal level of public affairs programming in exchange for free use of the broadcasting spectrum. As we documented in Chapter 2, these public service obligations have long since been weakened or altogether ignored, making it possible for networks to exist as all-entertainment entities. A first-rate news division was once a symbol of a network's commitment to public service; today it is a mere cog in the entertainment machine. News now focuses on what sells. Several of the most basic principles of serious journalism—worldwide news coverage, multiple correspondents working the same story, and the commitment to getting the story right—have become victims of the new economic logic.

Further compromising the quality of journalism was the acceleration of the news cycle. In the current 24-hour cycle, news organizations face intense pressures to deliver the news faster than their competitors do. The race to be first often requires loosening the standards of journalism; rather than confirming a story with multiple sources, editors routinely accept reports that are poorly substantiated. In a recent instance of the risks of beating competitors to a story, the *New York Times*, *Washington Post*, and NBC News all reported (in April 2021) that FBI officials had warned Rudy Giuliani—President Trump's personal attorney—that he was the target of a Russian disinformation campaign. A few days later, all three outlets retracted the story, acknowledging that the FBI had not in fact contacted Giuliani.

Although the conflict between cost-driven journalism and the delivery of hard news is especially pronounced in the world of broadcast journalism, where the financial stakes are much higher, print media have been no less affected. Newspapers have reduced the size of the daily "news hole"—space allocated to current events—in favor of features. On any given day, a reader of the *New York Times* is presented with sections on technology, food, entertainment, real estate, travel, and more. Newspaper design has been visually enhanced with the use of color photography, graphics, and other eye-catching devices. The very same economizing measures implemented at the networks—staff cuts, bureau closings, and softening of news content—have been adopted at leading newspapers across the country. The editors of the *New York Times*, for instance, did not notice any conflict between their motto, "All the News That's Fit to Print," and their assigning a full-time correspondent to cover the O. J. Simpson case in 1995. All news organizations, no matter what their prestige or rank in the world of journalism, converged on the O. J. story because it attracted readers. The *New York Times* simply had no choice; it could either provide intensive coverage of the event or lose readers.

In short, the economic realities of the media business create strong pressures on journalists to cater to the tastes of the median viewer or reader. News programs that are heavy in policy content or in-depth expert analysis will find that their audience has migrated within minutes to ESPN, the Food Network, or *Action News at 6 PM.* The proliferation of broadcast outlets and the resulting competition for the attention of the viewing audience spelled doom for the previously held standards of serious journalism. A new genre of news programs, focusing on the lives of the wealthy and famous and dwelling incessantly on the mayhem and violence on local streets, created the appropriate fit (for owners and publishers) between economic interests and the delivery of public affairs information.

A CASE STUDY OF LOCAL TELEVISION NEWS

The rapid emergence of local news programming during the 1980s provides a compelling case study of the responsiveness of news programming to economic constraints. In the 1960s, station owners typically aired old episodes of popular sitcoms (such as *Hogan's Heroes* and *The Beverly Hillbillies)* in the programming slots just before or after the national newscast.[5] Naturally, they paid a significant fee to the syndication company holding the rights to these programs, and the programs tended to attract only modest audiences; so the resulting profit margin was less than station owners hoped it would be.

In the more competitive media markets (Los Angeles and New York), owners noticed that the 30-minute local newscast proved quite popular with the audience, often drawing in more viewers than the national news. Moreover, the local newscast was inexpensive to produce. The typical local newscast can be staffed by four or five all-purpose correspondents, an anchor or two, a weather forecaster, and a sports correspondent. Local news correspondents, in contrast to their network news counterparts, do not command extravagant salaries. Infrastructure costs for local news programming are similarly limited; for the typical news station, the single most expensive budget item is the monthly lease of a helicopter (to provide immediate access to breaking news). All told, the cost of putting together a local newscast is trivial.

Cost is only half of the programming equation, however. Local news is especially enticing to station owners because they can present the program in ways that bring in large audiences. Not only is local news close to home and the source of both useful (weather forecast, traffic reports) and personally engaging (latest baseball scores) information, but even the public affairs content can be structured to appeal to viewers. It is no accident that the signature issue of local news coverage is violent crime. From armed bank robberies to homicides, home invasions, carjackings, police chases, and gang wars, violence occurs continually in local newscasts. Conversely, little time is devoted to nonviolent crimes such as embezzlement, fraud, or tax evasion, because they lack the action to command the attention of the viewing audience. Thus, local news is essentially a televised police blotter: "If it bleeds, it leads" is the motto of local news directors.

Stories about crime focus on concrete events with powerful impacts on ordinary people, convey drama and emotion, and, above all, provide attention-getting visuals. The power of this formula is apparent to station owners and news directors in media markets across the country. English-language commercial television stations operating in the Los Angeles market aired a total of 3,014 news stories on crime during 1996 and 1997, of which 2,492 (83 percent) focused on violent crime. The crime of murder, which accounted for less than 1 percent of all crime in Los Angeles County during this period, was the focus of 17 percent of crime stories. In fact, the number of murder stories (510) was equal to the total number of nonviolent crime stories (522) during the period sampled (all figures are taken from Gilliam & Iyengar, 2000).

Although brutal acts of violence are understandably newsworthy, this level of overrepresentation of violent crime is extraordinary. Overall, the Los Angeles study found that the typical 30-minute local news segment included three distinct reports on crime, totaling approximately 4 minutes of coverage (out of 12 minutes devoted to news). The results were identical across all six television stations whose offerings were examined. Moreover, violent crime was equally newsworthy in late-afternoon, early-evening, prime-time, and late-night newscasts.

In their preoccupation with violent crime, Los Angeles television stations were not especially distinctive. A study of 56 different cities found that crime was the most prominently featured subject in the local news, accounting for more than 75 percent of all news coverage in some cities (Klite, Bardwell, & Salzman, 1997).

Local news generates significant advertising for the typical television station, well in excess of production costs. The strong profitability of local news

FIGURE 3.7

Revenue from Local News, 2004–2020

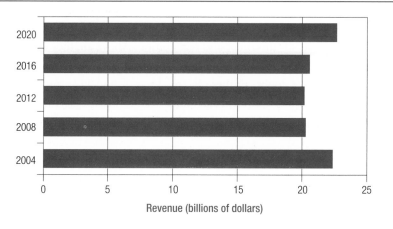

Source: Data from Pew Research Center, "Local TV news fact sheet" (2021, July 13). Retrieved September 7, 2021, from the Pew Research Center website: https://www.pewresearch.org/journalism/fact-sheet/local-tv-news/.

accounts for the steady increase in the number of programming hours. On average, local stations aired nearly 6 hours of local news per day in 2018, representing an increase of 2 hours a day from 2007. As shown in Figure 3.7, the considerable revenue that station owners derive from local programming has held steady in excess of $20 billion since 2004.

In sum, low costs and high interest value make local news a winning combination. More generally, the law of supply and demand has shifted the content of news programming away from relatively serious subjects. Publishers cannot eat Pulitzer Prizes and Peabody Awards; to maintain their competitiveness, they must provide news offerings that attract an audience. Hard news about government and political issues made up 14 percent of all local news programming in 2012, while crime, accidents, traffic, or weather-related reports and other human-interest subjects accounted for 76 percent of the coverage (Pew Research Center, 2013).

ORGANIZATIONAL PROCESSES AND ROUTINES

Although the brutal logic of the bottom line goes a long way toward explaining recent trends in the practice of journalism, a fuller understanding of the production of news entails more than a simple exercise in economic determinism. Although news organizations must make ends meet, journalists continue to have considerable leeway to exercise choice, discretion, and control over their work product. Like other professions, journalism has a culture that guides everyday practice. There is a right way and a wrong way. Journalists also pursue professional advancement and recognition. Above all, they rely on a set of conventions, or standard operating procedures, for uncovering and reporting the news. Without a doubt, all these factors leave an indelible imprint on the content and form of news coverage. Note, however, that the norms and values described below apply primarily to news organizations committed to nonpartisan journalism.

AUTONOMY AND OBJECTIVITY AS DOMINANT VALUES

Modern professional journalism rests on two dominant values: objectivity and autonomy. In the particular case of political news, as elected officials and their handlers have become more choreographed and expert at using the press to get their messages across and boost their standing, autonomy has upstaged objectivity as the guiding principle of journalists' behavior. In the era before media politics, the press defined objectivity primarily in terms of equal time; *both* candidates (or office holders from each party) received regular opportunities to reach their audience. Equal exposure meant that the candidates' partisan rhetoric canceled each other out.

In the aftermath of the 1988 presidential campaign between George H. W. Bush and Michael Dukakis, however, the press decided that merely reprinting both candidates' words seriously compromised journalistic autonomy. In that election, the Bush campaign's use of racial imagery in a television commercial (the "Willie Horton" ad) to attack Governor Dukakis's record on crime was so controversial that it enticed the press into making the ad and its subject matter (crime) the major story line of the campaign. The coverage met the standard definition of objectivity: the Bush and Dukakis campaigns were both quoted extensively on the subject of crime and prison furloughs. By their actions, however, journalists elevated the importance of crime as a campaign issue, thus handing Bush (who, as a Republican, was seen as tougher on crime) a significant edge.

The events of the 1988 campaign led reporters to the conclusion that recycling the candidates' message of the day was an inappropriate form of campaign journalism because it made reporters captive to the agenda of campaign consultants. To protect their autonomy, reporters turned to a more analytic form of news coverage that centered on interpretations and analysis of the candidates' actions. Not only was this more aggressive scrutiny of the candidates designed to reduce the likelihood that reporters would be manipulated by campaign spin, but it also amplified the voice of the journalist. The campaign correspondent was now a solo author of the news, whose voice and own analysis were more newsworthy than what the candidates had to say.

INTERPRETIVE JOURNALISM

The manifestations of the switch from descriptive to interpretive reporting of elections were many. In the first place, reporters became more apt to debunk the candidates' pronouncements. Ads and speeches at campaign events were no longer described exactly as they were; instead, journalists adopted a new genre of reporting—the ad watch or fact-check—in which they dissected and enumerated the specific errors, exaggerations, or undocumented allegations contained in ads or speeches (see Video Archive 3.1). Ad watches soon became a staple of election coverage, with all major news outlets dedicating a full-time correspondent to the task of analyzing the candidates' rhetoric and ads. As we note in Chapter 6, ad watches also changed the behavior of advertisers, but sometimes in a counterintuitive direction.

▶

Video Archive 3.1
Policing
Campaign Ads

Today, the fact-checking of political rhetoric has become a staple feature of news coverage. PolitiFact, a major fact-checking website, has entered into partnerships with news organizations in some 15 states by which they analyze the accuracy of the statements made by state and local officials. Other well-funded fact-checkers include Snopes and the *Washington Post*'s Fact Checker. For the past several years, PolitiFact has published a running tally of the incumbent president's veracity; in the case of President Trump, during his four years in office, they rated 73 percent of his pronouncements as factually inaccurate.

To a great extent, the older, descriptive mode of coverage consisted of reporting the events of the day, often including verbatim reports of significant amounts of candidate speech. The newer, interpretive journalism also reports on daily events but in a much different way. Journalists are generally less interested in describing the event and more inclined to use the event as a means of divining the candidates' motives and tactics. Because the focus is no longer on the candidates' positions, reporters today bypass the candidates and turn to a coterie of experts. The task of the expert is to act as an agent of the reporter and provide the necessary analysis of such questions as whether Hillary Clinton's "basket of deplorables" comment would weaken her standing among blue-collar voters or the extent to which the increased use of mail ballots in the 2020 election would benefit the candidacy of Joe Biden.

Thus, the *strategy frame*—analysis of the rationale and strategy underlying the candidates' rhetoric and positions—has emerged as the single most frequent theme in coverage of the political campaign. News is no longer limited to what the candidates say; it also reports *why* they say it. The staging of campaign events (for example, Trump's joint press conference with the women who accused former president Bill Clinton of sexual harassment), fund-raising tactics, the tone of the candidates' rhetoric and whether going negative will be a plus or minus—all become the stuff of election reports.

The most popular element of interpretive reporting is the state of the horse race. Reporters invariably frame the election not as a contest of ideas or policy platforms but as a race between two teams, each bent on securing more votes than the other. The question at the end of the day is "Who's ahead?" or "Who's scoring more points with the electorate?" Reports on the latest polls or the size of the crowd at campaign events far outnumber reports on the candidates' worldviews, policy pledges, or previous records of decision making. In fact, the state of the horse race now accounts for more news reports than any other category of news. During the 2020 presidential campaign, a study of CBS and Fox News coverage found that reports on the horse race outnumbered reports on the candidates' policy positions by a factor greater than 3 to 1 (Patterson, 2020).

This represented a slight improvement from 2016 when the imbalance was more than 4 to 1 (Patterson, 2017).

What is especially revealing of the new genre of campaign journalism is the synergy between the professional aspirations of journalists and the competitive pressures of the market. Horse-race coverage appears to be a dominant strategy because it satisfies the journalist's need for autonomy and objectivity: it's easy to report, and it sells! All major news organizations now administer their own surveys of public opinion, often once or twice a month. Poll-based coverage is entirely objective; after all, reporters are relaying the results of their own (rather than the candidates') polling, the results are based on representative samples of likely voters, and the journalist or someone in the news bureau with survey and statistical expertise is responsible both for determining the questions to be asked and for tabulating the results. (Most major news organizations employ a full-time survey researcher to design and interpret their election polls.) From the perspective of the reporter, examining the latest poll results on a computer and then telephoning a pair of competing experts to get their take on what the results mean for the eventual outcome is much less labor intensive and less expensive than following the candidate across the country to extract the message of the day.

Polling also helps make the election more interesting to the audience. The idea that the election is a close race with each side making momentary gains, essentially keeping the race deadlocked, capitalizes on voters' curiosity and uncertainty over the outcome. People abhor uncertainty; the less clear-cut the eventual result of the election is, the more often they will tune in to news about the race. In fact, some critics have alleged that during the closing stages of the campaign, media organizations deliberately frame their survey results so as to tighten the race and increase the interest value of their election news.

As the horse race has come to dominate news of the election, coverage of issues has receded into the background. Conventional wisdom holds that issues do not interest the audience. News-reporting organizations cannot protect their market share by covering the candidates' positions on tax cuts or defense. More compellingly, issue information is typically old news. Early in the campaign, once a candidate has announced an economic plan, there may be some ripple of news coverage, but as the campaign progresses, the plan is no longer of interest. A candidate's policy stances are never a fresh news item unless there is some discrepancy between the candidate's stated position and the rhetoric or unless the candidate suddenly reverses position.

Finally, issue-based coverage also weakens the journalist's autonomy from the campaign. Issues are difficult to cover objectively and often leave the reporter open to charges of biased coverage. A spokesperson for President Biden is likely to complain about a story on the Democrats' proposal to rebuild infrastructure on the grounds that the story cited a higher cost estimate than the figures put forward by the White House. Given the ambiguity inherent in most policy proposals, virtually anything the reporter says may be disputed as inaccurate or biased. For these reasons, issues are not high-priority items for reporters on the campaign trail.

There is good evidence that the horse race plays well with the audience, while issues do not. Using a multimedia CD as the medium, Stanford University researchers gave a representative sample of online American voters a large number of typical news reports (from broadcast and print-based sources) about the 2000 presidential campaign three weeks before the election. The CD was programmed to enable usage tracking—that is, recording the specific pages that participants accessed, the number of times they used the CD, and the length of their CD sessions.

The CD usage data revealed that news stories focusing on the horse race were the most popular. After adjusting for the location or placement of the news story within the CD (stories that appeared first or second received much more attention than stories that appeared in the hundredth position), the section on the horse race was found to be the most visited section (with an average of 19 page visits per respondent). Polling-related stories even attracted more attention from CD users than stories focusing on the candidates' personal attributes. In contrast, issue-based stories attracted virtually no attention; the average number of visits to reports covering the candidates' positions on the issues could not be distinguished (with statistical reliability) from zero (see Iyengar, Norpoth, & Hahn, 2004).

The inevitable consequence of interpretive reporting and the associated fixation on the horse race is a reduced role for the candidates themselves in daily news reports. The candidates still crisscross the country making four or five campaign speeches each day, but their appearances on network television amount to a bit role. The disappearance of candidates' voices from the daily news coverage of the campaign is striking. In 1968, a viewer of network news could listen to the opposing candidates for over a minute each day; by 2004, the average duration of a candidate's sound bite was 7.7 seconds; and over the same period, the size of the journalist's sound bite has steadily increased (see Video Archive 3.2).

(▶)

Video Archive 3.2
Candidates' Own Voices
in the News

COMBAT STORIES

Interpretive journalism demands that reporters do their utmost to keep campaigns off message—to cut through the spin cycle and expose the unrehearsed candidate, warts and all. The 2016 tape recording of Donald Trump's lewd comments describing his willingness to force himself on women provided journalists ample opportunity to engage in nonstop analysis of the potential impact of the tape on Trump's candidacy. Because the material was so salacious and explosive, the immediate response from news organizations was to play the tape repeatedly over the next several days. Journalists then devoted their efforts to finding "scoops" in the form of interviews with women who had been victimized by Trump. Only later did journalists turn to legal experts and campaign consultants for analysis of the possibility of lawsuits against Mr. Trump and whether his comments would lead Republican leaders to disown their candidate.

Other opportunities to keep campaigns on the defensive include publicizing inconsistencies between a candidate's record and rhetoric. During the 2008 Democratic presidential primary campaign, Hillary Clinton described landing in Bosnia in 1996 under sniper fire. Her image was severely tarnished when a video of the trip was released that showed her calmly walking down the tarmac, stopping on the runway to shake hands and to listen to a young girl read a poem. Eight years later, Clinton's use of a private e-mail server to send classified State Department messages and the ensuing FBI investigation gave reporters (and Donald Trump) regular opportunities to raise the question of whether the candidate might be subject to criminal prosecution. In today's media environment, to use former presidential candidate Ross Perot's apt characterization, "gotcha" journalism is the order of the day.

A candidate can neutralize a feeding frenzy by mounting a strong counter response. During the 2008 campaign, Barack Obama initially denied ever hearing incendiary comments by his former pastor, the Reverend Jeremiah Wright, but then backtracked. To deal with the media storm that ensued, Obama severed all ties with Reverend Wright and delivered a major speech on racism in America. These actions proved sufficient to distance the candidate from the controversy. In 2016, the release of the *Access Hollywood* tape proved so explosive that Donald Trump was forced to release a 90-second televised statement in which he apologized for his lewd language. But toward the end of his statement, Trump went on the attack, comparing his actions favorably with the behavior of his opponent's husband, former president Bill Clinton: "I've said some foolish things, but there's a big difference between the words and actions of other people. Bill Clinton has actually abused women, and Hillary has bullied, attacked, shamed, and intimidated his victims." The following day, Trump invited the women who had filed charges of harassment against Bill Clinton to be his guests at the upcoming presidential debate.

The one area where the press typically achieves total control over the story line (and in many cases inflicts terminal harm to a campaign) concerns allegations of personal misconduct or other signs of unsuitability for office. From 1988, when Colorado senator Gary Hart was exposed as an adulterer; to 1992, when Bill Clinton faced multiple news reports about his womanizing; to 2012, when allegations of sexual harassment forced Herman Cain to withdraw from the presidential race; to 2016, when Donald Trump faced a firestorm of criticism for his fondling of women, the press has attempted to hold candidates and elected officials responsible for their personal behavior (see Video Archive 3.3). President Bill Clinton faced months of intensive coverage over his relationship with a young White House intern, while New York governor Andrew Cuomo managed to remain in office for several months despite multiple allegations of sexual harassment that surfaced in 2020, before finally resigning in August of 2021. While almost all cases of sexual misconduct involve male offenders, in 2019 freshman US representative Katie Hill (Democrat–California) was forced to resign after media outlets detailed inappropriate relationships with staffers in her office.

▶ **Video Archive 3.3**
Feeding Frenzies

As in the case of horse-race news, sex and scandal meet both the economic and the professional aspirations of journalists. Ratings go up, the journalist makes the front page, and the candidate is weakened. Unlike inconsistencies in a candidate's voting record or policy preferences, which might conveniently be attributed to changed circumstances or other complex excuses, it is impossible for candidates to evade responsibility for their personal misconduct. News coverage of the character issue is especially damning because the personal responsibility is unavoidable. All these ingredients, as Howard Kurtz, media critic for the *Washington Post,* pointed out, made Monica Lewinsky the perfect subject for news coverage when it emerged that President Bill Clinton had an affair with her:

> And then along came Monica. When Monica Lewinsky first burst into public view on January 21, 1998, the journalists were presented with more than a juicy scandal. It was a chance to convince the public at long last that Clinton was a liar. Whitewater was too arcane? Fundraising too complicated? Here at long last was a plot everyone could understand—a president having a tawdry affair with an intern half his age. And the journalists were right on one fundamental point. The president was lying. It was a legitimate story. The president was under criminal investigation by the independent counsel. But the press went

crazy, bonkers, totally over the top. All Monica on the nighttime cable shows with the same cast of characters, all Monica on the Sunday shows, all Monica on the front pages and the magazine covers. And yes, pretty close to all Monica on my CNN program, *Reliable Sources,* where we would critique the all Monica coverage of the other all Monica outlets. (Kurtz, 1999)

The prominence of the character issue in recent history raises an important historical question: why were reports about the candidates' personal lives missing from the news coverage of campaigns in the 1950s and 1960s? It is implausible that the nomination process in those decades produced candidates of such impeccable moral strength that there was simply no basis for questions over their character and integrity. The legendary *New York Times* correspondent R. W. (Johnny) Apple described his first assignment for the paper as watching the elevators going up to President Kennedy's suite in a New York City hotel. Among the president's visitors was a well-known Hollywood actress. Apple dutifully informed his editor, who showed little interest. By 1980, it would have been impossible to keep this story off the front page!

The character issue was not big news in 1960 because the all-male press corps did not deem womanizing as especially unethical or immoral. The values of the newsroom led journalists to believe that they had better things to do than investigate the bedroom. The media began to consider marital infidelity unacceptable behavior only after journalism opened its doors to women. Once the culture of the newsroom had changed, candidates' bad treatment of a spouse could be thought to reflect poorly on their candidacy.

The fact that journalists are trained to suppress their own values when covering elections does not guarantee that these values will not eventually creep into news reports. It is well known that journalists are more likely to identify as Democrats than as Republicans, and critics from the right have long attacked the mainstream media for providing a liberal slant on the news. In fact, however, as we note in the conclusion to this chapter, these fears are misplaced. Most careful analyses of campaign news find few traces of one-sided coverage. Not only are partisan values easy to suppress (by providing candidates equal time), but reporters are especially eager to debunk the liberal-media hypothesis.

If campaign coverage in the 1950s and 1960s reflected the culture of an all-male press corps, more recently the effects of an all-White newsroom were clearer still. In 2001, a survey by the American Society of Newspaper Editors reported that African Americans made up only 8 percent of newsroom staff nationwide; 16 years later, the number was no different (Arana, 2018). Journalism remains a field that underrepresents people of color.

Overall, minorities make up around 17 percent of all journalists (compared with 40 percent of the national population), meaning that few media outlets can match the populations they serve in racial or ethnic background. Tellingly, the absence of diversity is clearest where it matters most, at top management. A recent American Society of Newspaper Editors survey reports that 87 percent of "newsroom leaders" (editors and news directors) are White (Arana, 2018).

The insensitivity of reporters to issues of racial bias is especially clear in local television news coverage of crime. We have already noted that local TV stations converge on crime as a means of strengthening their audience appeal. In doing so, they emphasize particular episodes of violent crime while ignoring violence committed by police officers (until only recently). The focus on specific instances means that more often than not, the audience is given information about a suspect. In the previously cited Los Angeles study of local news, crime stories provided footage of the suspect—in the form of either a live arrest or a photograph or police sketch of the suspect at large—in more than half the instances. Usually, the suspect was either Hispanic or African American.

Even in the absence of a debate about racial profiling by local newscasts, the daily association of criminal activity with the minority community constitutes strong evidence of racial bias. As community advocates have noted, often vehemently, there is much more to the minority community than violence and crime, but these more positive elements are not news. The all-consuming focus on crime to the exclusion of other activities is equivalent to university administrators' informing the news media only about minority dropout rates while ignoring the awards and distinctions achieved by minority students. Why, then, have local news stations persisted in presenting a clearly one-sided view of racial minorities? The answer is simple: the television newsroom across the country is disproportionately White. The lack of diversity in the newsroom translates into habitual acceptance of news reports that stereotype minorities.

ACCESSIBILITY AND APPROPRIATENESS

As for the more mundane elements of the organizational process model, the news must often be tailored to the specific needs of news organizations. Accessibility generally refers to the ability to cover stories in a timely fashion. In terms of everyday news, it is not surprising that Washington, DC, is the center of the universe for most major news organizations. This is where they station most of their correspondents. The *Los Angeles Times* and *New York Times* both assign more correspondents to Washington, DC, than to their respective state capitals. As national news organizations, both newspapers have more interest in the US Congress than in the New York or California legislatures. National news most frequently emanates from the seat of the national government, and news organizations allocate their resources accordingly.

The need for accessibility works as a disincentive for news organizations to cover international news. Most news organizations are hard-pressed to cover developments in Outer Mongolia. In the case of television, the share of international news in the national newscasts has fallen significantly since the end of the Cold War. The likelihood of a newsworthy event occurring in Bangladesh is insufficiently high for the *New York Times* to station a correspondent in that country.

The importance of accessibility to news organizations is a particularly compelling argument against the news-as-mirror-image argument. If the news were indexed to an objective indicator of importance, we would expect that in the case of natural disasters, coverage would be proportional to the number of people who die. Traditionally, the level of coverage of international disasters by the American press was less responsive to the scope of the disaster and more dependent on the distance of the event from Washington, DC: the closer the disaster to the United States, the greater the coverage. But more recently, the development of portable communication devices (most notably the smartphone) has reduced the costs of overseas coverage. Much of the live coverage of the ongoing civil war in Yemen, for instance, is in the form of Twitter messages and videos posted on Facebook and YouTube.

Potential news stories vary not only in their accessibility but also in their appropriateness, or fit, to the particular mission of news organizations. Developments in the stock market are of greater interest to outlets with a focus on the economy; stories involving immigration are especially newsworthy to news audiences in close proximity to the US–Mexico border. Many news outlets are, in fact, targeting niche audiences; these outlets necessarily rely on different criteria for judging the newsworthiness of stories. And, as noted already, news organizations treat international, national, regional, and local events differently. A traffic accident is not news for the *New York Times* but may be a candidate for the lead story on New York City local newscasts.

An alternative definition of appropriateness is independent of subject matter or geography. Some news stories are more likely to be covered to a greater or lesser extent, simply depending on the medium. Broadcast outlets emphasize certain issues and ignore others, and print media reveal a different set of preferences. In the case of broadcast news, issues that generate compelling visual images are especially appropriate. From the perspective of a television reporter, the presence of a clear story line and the ability to convey the report within 2 minutes are additional pluses. Conversely, issues that have fewer concrete referents, or episodes, and that require talking heads are unlikely to be judged broadcast-worthy. Dueling mathematical models of budget deficits and economists' views on macroeconomics may be covered by PBS's *NewsHour* but will almost certainly be ignored by network television.

The particular needs of television create a demand for action news. Well before the current preoccupation with terrorism—during the 1980s and 1990s—the three networks covered the issue extensively because the images of downed airliners and other victims of terrorist attacks were visually compelling. Terrorist incidents provided a steady supply of dramatic visuals, a story line consisting of the forces of good and evil, and an ample supply of individual victims for gut-wrenching interviews. Although the networks aired hundreds of stories on crime and terrorism, they broadcast only a handful of reports on the subject of climate change. The more complex the subject matter is, the less likely it is that the issue will be sufficiently telegenic.

ROUTINES AND PROCEDURES

News organizations rely on well-developed routines as a means of anticipating the location of newsworthy events and facilitating their reporters' ability to cover the stories in a timely manner. These routines include establishing deadlines, assigning reporters to news beats, and relying on authoritative sources.

News reports require considerable editing and revision before they see the light of day. Before the internet, the daily news cycle made it imperative that reporters finalize their stories in time for the publishing deadline. In the case of the evening news, the report had to be filmed, edited, and transmitted to New York well in advance of the 5:30 PM broadcast. In practice, events occurring in the late afternoon were necessarily ignored. Today, as news organizations have replicated themselves online, the news cycle has become compressed. Critics argue this acceleration of the news cycle has contributed to sloppier journalism. The rush to print or broadcast is often accompanied by an inadequate level of background research and fact-checking, as evidenced by the multiple news organizations that retracted the story on the FBI investigation of Rudy Giuliani.

The beat system developed as a way of acclimatizing reporters, allowing them to gain expertise with a particular area or subject matter, and giving them the opportunity to schmooze and develop good relations with key newsmakers. Beats could be defined geographically (such as the West Coast) or topically (for example, healthcare). In some cases, beats reflect career trajectories; the prestige beats are those that guarantee the occupant a regular presence in a newspaper or broadcast. For national organizations, the three premier beats are the White House, State Department, and Pentagon (sometimes referred to as the Golden Triangle); given the newsworthiness of their location, these reporters become household names in a hurry.

Another standard operating procedure of news organizations is to examine and mimic the offerings of the competition. A fixture in any broadcast newsroom is the panel of television monitors playing the newscasts of other stations. As in any other profession, there are leaders and followers. On any typical day, the stories printed on the front page of the *New York Times* invariably appear in the network newscasts. The term *pack journalism* refers to the tendency of high-prestige news organizations to define the daily agenda. Traces of pack journalism are especially visible during the early stages of primary campaigns, when uncertainty over the outcome is the greatest, and inexperienced journalists often follow the lead of well-known veterans. In 1968, for instance, in the aftermath of a chaotic Iowa caucus, the scene in the Des Moines newsroom was this:

> Johnny Apple of the *New York Times* sat in a corner and everyone peered over his shoulder to find out what he was writing. The AP guy was looking over one shoulder, the UPI guy over the other, and CBS, ABC, NBC, and the Baltimore *Sun* were all crowding in behind. . . . No one knew how to interpret these figures, what was good and what was bad, and they were taking it off Apple. He would sit down and write a lead, and they would go write leads. . . . When he wanted quiet to hear the guy announce the latest returns, he'd shout for quiet and they'd all shut up. (Crouse, 1972, p. 84)

Although *pack journalism* generally refers to a top-down process of influence, at times the logic is reversed and the prestige press chases after purveyors of soft news. Dominick Dunne, who covered the trial of O. J. Simpson for *Vanity Fair,* emerged as an authoritative source and was quoted extensively in major print and broadcast national outlets. The *New York Times*, in its coverage of the case, saw fit to cite information published in the *National Enquirer.*

As we will discuss in Chapter 5, the emergence of online media has led, at times, to a reversal of conventional pack journalism. Online sources can be the first to break a story. The very first instance occurred when the Drudge Report ran the story on Monica Lewinsky's dress in 1998, and it occurred on a bigger scale during the 2016 presidential campaign when BuzzFeed News broke the story of the young Macedonian programmers who posted a series of controversial and false reports about Hillary Clinton on Facebook. This story became headline news and forced the major social media companies to take steps to protect their users from malicious propaganda attacks. (We describe this episode in greater detail in Chapter 5.)

SOURCES

Sources are perhaps the most critical elements of the news-gathering process. A basic principle of modern journalism is that news is whatever public officials say it is. As Leon Sigal (1973) states, "Even when the journalist is in a position to observe an event directly, he remains reluctant to offer interpretations of his own, preferring instead to rely on his news sources. . . . In short, most news is not what has happened but what someone says has happened" (p. 69).

Where do reporters go to get the news? In most cases, they do not assemble at the scene of an event but gravitate instead to sources that can provide authoritative accounts of the event. This practice translates into a dependence on government officials. Most newsworthy issues are the province of government agencies or departments. An exodus of refugees fleeing the civil war in Syria sends reporters straight to the State Department; the latest figures on the US trade deficit make the Department of Commerce the news hub; and so on. Even by a conservative count, the overwhelming majority of news stories each day emanates from official sources. In the case of the White House, virtually anything the president does (or fails to do) is news.

Reporters are well aware that official sources often have a vested interest in shaping the news. In the case of obviously partisan sources (such as House Speaker Nancy Pelosi), reporters maintain their objectivity by relying on sources from the opposing side of the partisan divide to ensure that the bias is canceled out. However, objective and balanced coverage requires dissent and conflict among official sources. When official sources all speak with one voice, then the press becomes a tool of government. As we will describe in the next chapter, periods of international tension and impending or actual military conflict are typically devoid of open partisan dissent. As a result, at such times reporters become spokespersons for the administration.

The relationship between reporters and sources is complex, often subject to elaborate rituals. In some cases, a government official provides information but does not wish to be identified (so the journalist cites "a highly placed source"). In other cases, officials seek out reporters to provide information in an attempt either to weaken their political opponents (the typical case of a leak) or to shift course within an agency or administration. In the first several months of the Trump presidency, infighting among the White House staff led to a torrent of leaked information, often describing the president in unflattering terms that landed on the front pages of the *New York Times* and *Washington Post*. In one instance, the leaker provided the full transcript of the president's conversations with the leaders of Mexico and Australia. In the aftermath of these stories, the Justice Department secretly obtained the phone records of journalists who were thought to have been contacted by the leakers and justified the action on the grounds that the journalists were illegally receiving classified information. Eventually, President Trump fired several senior advisers (including his chief of staff) in an effort to stem the flow of newsworthy information from within his inner circle.

In still other cases, the reporter–source relationship becomes a matter of litigation, as in disclosures of information that may threaten national security. The revelation by the syndicated conservative columnist Robert Novak in 2003 that Valerie Plame, the wife of a well-known critic of the George W. Bush administration was a CIA agent prompted a grand jury investigation into Novak's source, the conviction of Lewis Libby (an adviser to President Bush) on perjury and obstruction of justice charges related to the case, and considerable public speculation about the identity of Novak's highly placed source. (Mr. Libby was pardoned by President Trump in 2018.) We defer further discussion of the ways in which official sources attempt to manipulate reporters to Chapter 4.

CONCLUSION

Contrary to the assertion that the news is simply a mirror-image reflection of what happens, we have shown that news content reflects a complex set of interactions between the dictates of the marketplace and the professional aspirations of journalists. The economic model is by far the more parsimonious: the news is simply what sells. Although there is considerable evidence that economic pressures leave their imprint on the news, there is more to news than the desire to protect the bottom line. No matter what journalists might say to the contrary, they have an agenda; they strive to cover campaigns in ways that maximize their autonomy and, happily for them, increase their own professional visibility.

No one who watches cable television political talk shows will be surprised at the revolving door between regularly invited guests and the list of reporters covering a campaign. Interpretive coverage is defended on the grounds that journalists have a responsibility to protect the public from the machinations of campaign strategists, but it provides considerable side benefits as well.

Campaign journalists who project their voices into the news every day not only appear on *Washington Week* or *The Situation Room*; they also command significant book advances from publishers.

One factor conspicuously absent from the commercial account of news is partisan intent. In recent years, however, the number of news outlets aligning themselves with a liberal or conservative point of view has mushroomed. For these outlets, partisan slant is built into their coverage. Fox News regularly promoted the Trump White House perspective during the COVID-19 pandemic, often providing accounts at odds with the scientific consensus (e.g., reports casting doubt on the efficacy of masks). Over time, these outlets have developed a recognizable brand as illustrated by the evidence presented earlier showing that a large majority of the public views Fox News as an ally of conservatives.

More interestingly, perceptions of partisan bias increasingly apply to the ostensibly nonpartisan press. Politicians, interest groups, and commentators on both sides of the partisan divide regularly allege that there is ideological bias in news coverage. Conservatives claim that the mainstream media are staffed by Democrats whose reporting reflects their personal politics. For their part, liberals claim that corporate ownership of news outlets leads to conservative pro-business bias. The overriding financial interests of corporate owners, in this account, act as disincentives for journalists to write stories exposing questionable business practices, even when these practices harm consumers. In 2017, when NBC News did not publish an exposé detailing the extent of Harvey Weinstein's harassment of women, critics claimed the network was responding to corporate pressure. The investigative journalist who wrote the report suggested that NBC killed the story because of Weinstein's political and legal clout. NBC's claims that "the story wasn't ready to go" were undermined when the *New Yorker* published it with no changes, resulting in a tidal wave of negative publicity and the downfall of Mr. Weinstein.

The media's relentless pursuit of the Watergate scandal led many Republicans to suggest that journalists were motivated by their hostility to the Nixon administration. Nixon's vice president (Spiro Agnew), for instance, attacked broadcast journalists as "nattering nabobs of negativity" who were out of touch with the "silent majority." Twenty-five years later, when journalists pursued President Clinton with equal vigor in the course of the Lewinsky scandal, Democrats made much the same argument. In 2017, as the Robert Mueller investigation into possible collusion between the Russian government and the Trump campaign dragged on, increasing numbers of

Republicans began to complain about not only media bias but also anti-Trump bias at the FBI.

Notwithstanding the hue and cry over allegations of ideological or self-interested bias in the news, the fact remains that political motives are less important determinants of news content than are commercial and organizational pressures. The evidence indicates that the American media have performed quite well according to the criterion of balanced political coverage. Issues and events are typically covered in point-counterpoint fashion so that the audience invariably gains exposure to the Democratic and Republican perspective on any given story (see D'Alessio & Allen, 2000). Newspaper coverage of American governors, for example, treats incumbents of both parties similarly, providing favorable coverage during periods of falling unemployment and crime rates but turning critical when real-world conditions deteriorate.

In the current era of polarized politics, however, no matter how hard journalists strive for objectivity, they find it increasingly difficult to avoid allegations of partisan bias. As we showed in Figure 3.6, President Trump's crusade against "fake news" has persuaded most Republicans to view the mainstream media with suspicion; they overwhelmingly view CNN, the *New York Times*, and other nonpartisan outlets as anti-Republican.

The one area where partisan slant is glaringly apparent is cable television. Despite the steady stream of controversies and infighting from within the White House during the initial phase of the Trump presidency (including leaks of the president's less than civil conversations with foreign leaders), Fox News coverage presented equal numbers of reports reflecting favorably and unfavorably on the president. In contrast, the mainstream news outlets responded to the apparent chaos within the White House with coverage that was more unfavorable than favorable (Patterson, 2017). During the 2020 campaign, Fox News coverage of the Trump campaign was eight times more favorable (in terms of the number of positive news reports) than the coverage provided by CBS News (Patterson, 2020).

The ratings for cable news suggest that providing news with a partisan slant is an effective strategy for getting ahead in a competitive market. Fox News consistently ranks as the most-watched cable news channel, and liberal-oriented programs on MSNBC (such as *The Rachel Maddow Show*) dramatically increased the network's ratings during the presidency of Donald Trump.

In addition to the growth of partisan commentary on cable TV, online news sources offer similarly biased offerings. The liberal Huffington Post is among the most popular online news sites. The Drudge Report and Breitbart News offer commentary with a distinctly conservative slant. As we discuss in Chapter 5, the growing reach of cable and online sources that deliver partisan news is testimony to the importance of consumers' political views as a determinant of who they turn to for information. Given their increased ability to select from multiple providers, consumers with strong partisan preferences will form "echo chambers" by gravitating to the news source that provides coverage and commentary they find agreeable rather than disagreeable.

Despite the controversies surrounding questions of media bias, the fact remains that the real problem facing mainstream American journalism today is less the intrusion of political motives into editorial decisions and more the clash between economic pressures and the ability to deliver serious public affairs programming. There is no shortage of compelling factoids on the extent to which the media shirk their public service obligations. Nationwide, broadcast media offerings in 2020 included less than 1 percent that could be considered (even by a generous definition) public affairs programming. In the case of local news—admittedly the most deficient outlet—the results are crystal clear. A large-scale analysis of local news coverage of the 2010 and 2014 congressional elections showed that the largest newspaper in any given congressional district failed to provide daily coverage of the 2010 campaign (Hayes & Lawless, 2015, 2018). Instead, they averaged one story on the congressional contest every other day. In 2014, the coverage diminished further to one story every third day. And while both Trump and Biden focused their efforts on debating the issues before the American people, horse-race news of the 2020 campaign exceeded issue-oriented news by a factor of more than 3 to 1 (Patterson, 2020).

The fixation on the horse race and strategy catches the attention of the audience while simultaneously providing journalists an edge in their continuing clash with the campaigns to shape the content of the news. In the end, the new style of reporting presents the campaign as theatrics rather than as a genuine clash of ideas. When candidates make major speeches on policy issues, they find themselves ignored altogether by major news organizations. Thus, by any stretch of the imagination, modern journalism does not deliver the marketplace of ideas that is so vital to the exercise of informed and engaged citizenship. Unfortunately, the verdict is equally pessimistic when we turn to journalism's second potential contribution to the democratic process—namely, serving as a watchdog over the actions of government officials.

Summary

1. Historically, where Americans get their news has depended on the development of new technologies for transmitting information. In the 1920s, radio began to supplant newspapers as the main source of news for most Americans, and radio was itself supplanted by television in the 1950s.

2. The spread of cable television—and more recently the internet—has transformed the news landscape, but the most serious threat to network news today is local news.

3. The credibility of the media in the eyes of the American public has declined sharply in recent decades, especially in the aftermath of party polarization.

4. Market forces influence the form and content of news. Market pressures are especially intense in the world of broadcast news, where soft news, sitcoms, and reality television shows attract much larger audiences than serious news does. News producers adapt to the competition from soft news, sitcoms, and cable talk shows by making their own news programs more entertaining and less serious. The current 24-hour news cycle has also increased pressure, as news organizations strive to deliver the news faster than their competitors do.

5. Organizational processes and the professional principles of journalists also influence what is reported. Modern political journalism rests on two dominant values: objectivity and autonomy. In attempting to protect their autonomy, reporters tend toward a more analytic form of news coverage centered on interpretation and analysis. Ad watches, candidate strategy, the horse race, and scandal stories feature prominently in this kind of coverage.

6. Accessibility and appropriateness also shape news coverage. In terms of everyday news, Washington, DC, is the center of the universe for most major news organizations, and that's where most of their correspondents are stationed (and hence have access to stories). The appropriateness of a story for a particular news outlet also determines whether it will receive coverage; a car crash in Dallas is not news for the *New York Times,* for example. In addition, a story is more likely to be covered by a television news outlet if it generates compelling visual imagery.

7. Finally, the routines and procedures followed by news organizations have substantial impact on the content and form of the news. The pace of the news cycle means that events are more likely to be covered if they occur at certain times of the day. Assigning reporters to news beats ensures a steady flow of stories on those beats. And in covering an event, reporters gravitate to sources that can provide authoritative accounts of the event, which means that they rely on government officials for their information.

FURTHER READINGS

Curran, J., Iyengar, S., Lund, A. B., & Salovaara-Moring, I. (2009). Media system, public knowledge, and democracy: A comparative study. *European Journal of Communication, 24,* 5–26.

D'Alessio, D., & Allen, M. (2000). Media bias in presidential elections: A meta-analysis. *Journal of Communication, 50,* 133–156.

Hayes, D., and Lawless, J. L. (2015). As local news goes, so goes citizen engagement: Media, knowledge, and participation in US House Elections. *Journal of Politics, 77,* 447–462.

Hayes, D., and Lawless, J. L. (2018). The decline of local news and its effects: New evidence from longitudinal data. *Journal of Politics, 80,* 332–336.

Gilliam, F. D., Jr., & Iyengar, S. (2000). Prime suspects: The influence of local television news on the viewing public. *American Journal of Political Science, 44,* 560–573.

Goldman, S. K., & Mutz, D. C. (2011). The friendly media phenomenon: A comparative study of media environments and news consumption gaps in Europe. *Political Communication, 28,* 22–46.

Hamilton, J. T. (2003). *All the news that's fit to sell: How the market transforms information into news.* Princeton, NJ: Princeton University Press.

Iyengar, S. (1991). *Is anyone responsible?* Chicago: University of Chicago Press.

Kernell, G., Lamberson, P. J., & Zaller, J. (2017). Market demand for civic affairs news. *Political Communication, 35,* 239–260.

McChesney, R. W. (1999). *Rich media, poor democracy: Communication politics in dubious times.* Urbana: University of Illinois Press.

Patterson, T. E. (2016, December 7). News coverage of the 2016 general election: How the press failed the voters. Shorenstein Center on Media, Politics and Public Policy, Kennedy School of Government, Harvard University, Cambridge, MA. https://shorensteincenter.org/news-coverage-2016-general-election/.

Patterson, T. E. (2020, December 17). A tale of two elections: CBS and Fox News' coverage of the 2020 presidential campaign. Shorenstein Center on Media, Politics and Public Policy, Kennedy School of Government, Harvard University, Cambridge, MA. https://shorensteincenter.org/patterson-2020-election-coverage/.

Peterson, E. (2021). Paper cuts: How reporting resources affect political news coverage. *American Journal of Political Science, 65,* 443–459.

Pew Research Center. (2008, October 22). *Winning the media campaign: How the press reported the 2008 general election.* http://www.journalism.org/2008/10/22/winning-media-campaign/.

Sigal, L. (1973). *Reporters and officials.* Lexington, MA: Heath.

NOTES

1. Nielsen has had to defend itself against charges of racial bias in audience counts. African American and Hispanic activists have complained that their communities are underrepresented by Nielsen's metering system, thus resulting in an undercount of the audience size of minority-oriented programs. The controversy is symptomatic of a more widespread debate provoked by Nielsen data showing that network audiences are diminishing. Naturally, the networks would prefer to see data suggesting the opposite.

2. CNN maintains news bureaus in 36 countries and can be seen in more than 200 countries.

3. Most media markets resemble oligopolies, with small numbers of news providers controlling the vast share of the market (Baker, 2002; McChesney, 1999).

4. In the post-9/11 environment, the US Department of State has attempted to compile statistics on the number of terrorist attacks and casualties on a worldwide basis. As noted in the next chapter, the State Department's 2004 report (published in advance of the election) had to be retracted because it was found to underestimate the true level of terrorist activity by a substantial margin.

5. As some scholars have noted, the huge audiences for network news in the 1970s included a nontrivial inadvertent component: people who watched the *CBS Evening News* only because they were waiting for their favorite sitcom, which followed.

4

Reporters, Official Sources, and the Decline of Adversarial Journalism

In 1974, Bob Woodward and Carl Bernstein, two enterprising reporters at the *Washington Post,* brought about the resignation of President Nixon. Their systematic exposure of the Watergate cover-up represented the epitome of investigative journalism: a newspaper had single-handedly enforced the standard of honesty in government.

Twenty-four years later, President Clinton emphatically denied allegations that he had had a sexual relationship with a White House intern. His denials were met by an increasingly skeptical press corps, who proceeded to dig deeper into the story and whose efforts ultimately led Congress to initiate impeachment proceedings against Clinton.

In 2003, the Bush administration decided to invade Iraq, even without the support of key allies and the United Nations. The rationale for American unilateral action rested on two key premises: first, that the regime of Saddam Hussein had the capacity to develop and deliver chemical and biological weapons "in ways that can cause massive death and destruction" (in the words of Secretary of State Colin Powell, speaking at the United Nations in 2003); and second, that the regime was an active collaborator with the Al Qaeda terrorist organization.

What the Bush administration asserted, the press dutifully reported. American journalists accepted the guilty-as-charged claims against Saddam Hussein with little hesitation, despite the opinions of credible international experts to the contrary. One of the country's leading newspapers, the *New York Times,* published a series of reports that supported the administration's position and used Iraqi expatriates as corroborating sources. These same sources were in fact either working as American intelligence agents or Iraqi politicians who harbored aspirations of political power in a post–Saddam Hussein Iraq.

The successful invasion of Iraq and overthrow of the Saddam Hussein regime was followed by several months of frenzied American efforts to find the Iraqi weapons of mass destruction. Gradually, it became apparent that the weapons did not exist. As for the second alleged threat posed by Iraq—the close relationship with Al Qaeda—the 9/11 Commission and other experts ultimately concluded that although there were isolated contacts, these did not amount to a collaborative relationship. Thus, both key premises of the policy of unilateral intervention proved erroneous. Two leading American daily newspapers—the *New York Times* and the *Washington Post*—issued public apologies for their failure to investigate the Bush administration's case against Iraq.

More recently, the clandestine surveillance of foreign leaders and officials of international organizations and the tracking of the electronic communications of millions of American citizens by the National Security Agency (NSA) was exposed by former NSA employee Edward Snowden. As an NSA contractor, Snowden had access to the relevant documents and leaked them to the British newspaper the *Guardian.* Had Snowden not acted, the press (and the public) would have remained in the dark about NSA's widespread violations of fundamental privacy rights protected by the American Bill of Rights.

What accounts for the striking contrast between the performance of the press during the Watergate and Lewinsky scandals and the performance of the press during the Bush administration? Why was the press instinctively skeptical when Nixon and Clinton denied wrongdoing but passively willing to accept the Bush administration's misleading claims concerning the necessity of war with Iraq? The explanation, as outlined in this chapter, is that in matters of national security, the press has been stripped of its ability to act as an adversary of government. When national security issues impinge on domestic politics, as in the current debates over the extent of Russian interference in the 2016 and 2020 presidential elections, the presence of outspoken and authoritative election experts grants journalists the necessary leverage to question official accounts. On matters that fall entirely within the realm of foreign policy and national security, however, critics of government policy tend to fall silent, and the relevant experts lack up-to-date information; as a result the press is left with only official sources.

INDEXING THE NEWS

Inevitably, reporters depend on official sources. Nevertheless, they seek to maintain objectivity in coverage. High-ranking officials, for their part, have a strong political stake in eliciting coverage that reflects favorably on their performance. During political campaigns, these sometimes divergent interests create a basic tension between candidates and journalists that profoundly shapes not only the news coverage of campaigns but also the content of everyday news, as officials seek to promote their policies while reporters attempt to provide objective and balanced news.

For the press to act as a fourth branch of government, journalists must necessarily treat official pronouncements with skepticism. This tension between reporters and officials boiled over in the early days of the Trump administration regarding conflicting estimates of the size of the crowd at Trump's inauguration. Forced to defend the administration's exaggerated claims, Press Secretary Sean Spicer noted, "I think sometimes we can disagree with the facts" (Grynbaum, 2017). A few days later, senior Trump adviser Kellyanne Conway claimed that the administration had provided "alternative facts" (Rutenberg, 2017).

Because journalists are typically trained as generalists, they lack the substantive policy expertise to question or rebut government sources on their own. For critical analysis, they turn to experts and other authoritative sources who may provide a fresh perspective on official policies. If the supply of opposition sources dries up, journalists have no real choice but to defer to official accounts. The availability of opposition sources generally dwindles in the arenas of foreign policy and national security, especially during periods of national crisis or international conflict. During the heat of crisis, journalists tend to cover the story exactly as it is given to them.

In a news system based on official sources, the reality of public policy is the state of official opinion. Reporters attempt to mirror this reality by adjusting their coverage to be in line with the level and intensity of debate among the elites. The higher the level of elite dissent, the easier it is for reporters to pit competing sources against each other.

In practical terms, indexing the news means that the press can represent an adversarial posture only when opponents of government policy outnumber (or prove more vocal than) proponents. On occasions when opponents with stature are not to be found and the government speaks with one voice, the watchdog role falls entirely on reporters. Because reporters have neither the time nor the expertise to critique the views of their sources, elite consensus

Press Briefing on Niger Operation

inevitably slants the news in favor of government policy. When four US soldiers were killed during a special operations mission in Niger in 2017, the Pentagon claimed they were on a reconnaissance operation, while the Niger government offered a different account—that the soldiers were assisting in an operation to capture a jihadist. When reporters pressed for more information, the Pentagon responded by announcing an official investigation into the failed mission. Several months later, in a summary of the official report made available to the press, the investigators attributed the failure of the operation to inadequate planning by junior officers commanding the mission.

In practice, the indexing system works well for domestic issues (in the sense of allowing reporters to maintain their autonomy from any particular source), but in the domain of foreign policy and national security, it results in near-total official control over the news. For most domestic issues, there exists a variety of politically viable policy alternatives and a corresponding network of competing official sources. Arguments over affirmative action, for instance, range from the complete elimination of race-based preferences to government-funded compensation for the victims of discrimination (such as reparations). Any Republican initiative on affirmative action will be met by a chorus of Democratic dissents. Economic issues provide an equally competitive set of sources; as soon as President Biden takes credit for the latest decline in unemployment, the media immediately turn to Republican officials for the appropriate antidote,

IN FOCUS

Indexing the News

Indexing is the process of adjusting coverage of an issue according to the level of disagreement and debate about that issue among policy elites. Indexing is due in large part to the journalistic norms of using official sources and of seeking objectivity by reporting different sides of a debate. If there is conflict among officials, there are opposing viewpoints on which journalists can report and which they can use as a starting point for open debate of the policy in the news. If there is consensus among officials—as there tends to be in foreign policy issues, particularly during national security crises—there is no reportable conflict, and coverage, when it happens, tends to be deferential.

namely, that the recovery took hold well before the arrival of Biden on the political scene and that falling unemployment is more a result of decisive actions taken by the Trump administration to fast-track the development of vaccines that halted the spread of COVID, thus enabling economic activity to resume.

Moreover, the press can call on a second team of sources drawn from various think tanks, with their stables of former officials, policy entrepreneurs, and academic researchers with special expertise. On September 28, 2017, addressing reporters at the White House on the recovery efforts in Puerto Rico following Hurricane Maria, acting Homeland Security secretary Elaine Duke stated that she was satisfied by the efforts to date and that she knew it was "a really good news story" (Diamond, 2017). Not surprisingly, the pushback from the press was swift, with rebuttals from Puerto Rican officials, while experts at the Brookings Institution weighed in on the costs (in the billions) of the required infrastructure investment. In the case of domestic politics, therefore, journalists have no difficulty resisting official spin. The level of elite disagreement and availability of competing authoritative sources are sufficient to ensure balanced, objective reporting.

When foreign policy and national security are the issues of the day, the indexing system breaks down, and officials attain substantial control over the flow of news. Traditionally, foreign affairs have not excited partisan divisions; the executive branch enjoys wide latitude to formulate and implement American foreign policy. During the era of the Cold War, for example, there was general bipartisan support for policies designed to contain the spread of international communism. The president exercises tight control over the foreign policy process with only limited congressional oversight; White House, State Department, and Pentagon officials offer up a coordinated, uniform take on the events of the day. Even on matters of spending, where Congress has exclusive powers, the president can intervene to suit his interests. After Congress authorized millions of dollars of military aid to Ukraine in 2018, the Trump administration held up the funds as a means of influencing the Ukrainian government to release damaging information about Joe Biden. (This controversy became the centerpiece of the first impeachment of President Trump.) Further contributing to executive prerogative on matters of foreign policy, the events in question typically occur beyond the geographical reach of most news organizations since foreign correspondents are few and far between.

In 2011, President Obama made front-page news when he announced to the nation that US Special Forces had found and killed Osama bin Laden in Pakistan. President Trump made a similar announcement in 2020, revealing that a US drone had killed General Qasem Suleimani, who headed the Iranian-backed militia fighting in Iraq. Both these examples illustrate how incumbent officials are typically able to orchestrate the news coverage of foreign affairs.

Although American officials are the principal sources of information in the foreign policy and national security arenas, journalists can introduce a semblance of balance into their reporting by seeking out foreign leaders—especially those who disagree with US policy—to offset White House or Pentagon accounts. In the weeks leading up to the Iraq War, for instance, prominent European critics of the Bush administration policies were frequently quoted in major American newspapers (see Hayes & Guardino, 2013). When President Trump announced in 2018 that the United States was pulling out of the Iran nuclear agreement, originally approved in 2015 by the United States, Iran, Russia, Germany, France, the European Union, and China, European leaders immediately pointed out that Iran was living up to the deal, with no recorded violations.

The state of play between the American press and the foreign policy establishment is exemplified by the treatment accorded the State Department's annual *Patterns of Global Terrorism* report. This report purports to document both the frequency and the severity of terrorist incidents. At the press briefing to announce the release of the 2003 report, Deputy Secretary of State Richard Armitage was on hand to declare, "You will find in these pages clear evidence that we are prevailing in the fight" (US Department of State, 2004). The data revealed a stunning 40 percent decline in the frequency of terrorist incidents since 2001. According to the numbers, 2003 was the safest year on record since

1969. This rosy assessment of the war against terrorism made big news across the country. On April 29, 2004, CNN reported that the Bush administration was winning the war on terrorism. The following month, in a *Washington Post* op-ed column, two scholars, Alan B. Krueger and David Laitin (2004), identified numerous flaws in the State Department's report. All the observed decrease in terrorist activity had occurred within the category of nonsignificant events. Significant terrorist attacks (defined as those causing injury and loss of life) had in fact *increased* by about a third—from 124 incidents in 2001 to 169 in 2003. This revised scorecard obviously reflected less favorably on the administration.

NATIONAL SECURITY NEWS: THE TRIUMPH OF OFFICIAL JOURNALISM

In comparison with foreign policy, national security matters provide officials with even more control over the press. When the United States resorts to military force, politicians from across the political spectrum generally close ranks behind the president. For fear of appearing unpatriotic, leaders of the out party choose not to criticize the administration's actions. The nation—at least as far as the media are concerned—stands united behind the men and women in uniform. Because potential opponents of the use of military force fall silent, the press becomes completely dependent on official spokespersons. In the aftermath of the September 11 attacks, nobody in Washington was willing to question the decision to overthrow the Taliban regime in Afghanistan. And when the Bush administration proposed the USA PATRIOT Act, a measure that would significantly erode Americans' civil liberties, it passed the US Senate by a vote of 99 to 1.

NEWS COVERAGE OF THE VIETNAM WAR: A CASE STUDY OF INDEXING

During the early period of media politics in the 1960s, the first real test of the media's ability to challenge official accounts was the war in Vietnam. In August 1964, the Johnson administration claimed that American navy vessels cruising in the Gulf of Tonkin had been deliberately attacked by North Vietnamese gunboats in two distinct incidents. The president ordered retaliatory air strikes and requested a joint resolution of Congress granting him the power to "take all necessary measures to repel any armed attack against the forces of the United States and to prevent further aggression." The Gulf of Tonkin Resolution, passed in 1964 by overwhelming majorities in the House and Senate, became the principal legal basis for expanding US military involvement in South Vietnam.

The news media did little to question the administration's account of the North Vietnamese attacks, instead deferring entirely to the Pentagon. The major American news magazines, for instance, described the attacks as follows:

> As the "night glowed eerily," wrote *Time,* the Communist "intruders boldly sped" toward the destroyers, firing with "automatic weapons," while *Life* had the American ships "under continuous torpedo attack" as they "weaved through the night sea, evading more torpedoes." Not to be outdone, *Newsweek* described "US jets diving, strafing, flattening out . . . and diving again" at the enemy boats, one of which "burst into flames and sank." (Karnow, 1997, pp. 386–387)

Later it was revealed that there was only one torpedo attack and that the Vietnamese gunboats had, in fact, been provoked.

As American military involvement in South Vietnam increased, news organizations assigned reporters to file stories from the immediate vicinity of the conflict. These reporters found themselves relatively free to roam the country in search of news stories. Despite firsthand access to events, press accounts of the war in the early and mid-1960s proved entirely consistent with official US policy. Reporters suggested that the strategy of training the South Vietnamese to defend themselves (Vietnamization) was working effectively, that heavy losses were being inflicted each day on the communist Vietcong, and that American bombing of North Vietnam was necessary to disrupt the flow of supplies and personnel down the Ho Chi Minh trail.

Not only was the coverage supportive of stated American policy, but in a harbinger of what would occur later, news reports also avoided details and depiction of military combat. According to Peter Braestrup's (1977) systematic compilation of network news coverage of the Vietnam War, less than 5 percent of all stories that aired on the evening news showed images of battle or American casualties. As described by media critic Michael Arlen (1969), the nightly news provided a

> generally distanced overview of a disjointed conflict which was composed mainly of scenes of helicopters landing, tall grasses blowing in the helicopter wind, American soldiers fanning out across a hillside on foot, rifles at the ready, with now and then [on the soundtrack] a far-off ping or two, and now and then [as the grand visual finale] a column of dark billowing smoke a half mile away invariably described as a burning Viet Cong ammo dump. (p. 113)

Thus, the viewing audience had little reason to be concerned.

As the war continued and the American death toll mounted, the Washington consensus over Vietnam unraveled. Senator Eugene McCarthy, the most vocal critic of the war, challenged President Johnson for the 1968 Democratic presidential nomination. McCarthy's surprisingly competitive showing in the New Hampshire primary (he received 41 percent of the vote) signaled unambiguously that his antiwar message was politically viable. In mid-March, Senator Robert Kennedy entered the presidential race. On March 31, realizing that the unpopularity of the war had made it increasingly difficult for him to wage a winning campaign, President Johnson announced that he would not seek reelection (see Video Archive 4.1). Suddenly, Vietnam had transformed the American political landscape.

Video Archive 4.1
LBJ Announcement

The emergence of multiple critics of the war was prompted not merely by the reading of the New Hampshire "tea leaves." There was also high drama in Vietnam. In January 1968, with apparent impunity, the Vietcong launched a full-scale military offensive, including a major assault on the US embassy in Saigon and coordinated attacks on major American military bases across Vietnam. The Tet Offensive and the American counteroffensive became huge news stories; images of napalmed villages, dead and maimed civilians, and American troops under intense enemy fire began to air regularly on television news, as illustrated in Video Archive 4.2.

Video Archive 4.2
Vietnam Coverage, 1968–1970

The Tet Offensive and resulting images on the television screen cast serious doubt on the official accounts of the war. Reporters began to question Pentagon officials more aggressively in an effort to contrast the clinical tone of the daily Pentagon briefings with the bloody chaos on the ground. An increasing number of elected officials from both political parties defected to the antiwar position. Mirroring the shift in elite opinion, news reports from Vietnam became less dependent on information provided by the US mission in Saigon (whose daily briefings came to be ridiculed as the "Five O'Clock Follies") and more focused on communist successes on the battlefield and the rapidly growing antiwar movement in the United States. By late 1968, the indexing process had kicked in and was producing full-fledged adversarial news.

In summary, news coverage of the Vietnam War provides a clear case of elite opinion leading the news in situations of both consensus and dissent. When presidents Johnson and Nixon encountered minimal political resistance to their military policies, press coverage toed the official line. As soon as well-known Americans made public their opposition to the war and the course of events on the battlefield began to clash with statements from Washington, deferential reliance on official sources gave way to coverage that was more aggressively critical of official policy.

THE LESSONS OF VIETNAM: RESTRICTED PRESS ACCESS

To policy planners in the Department of Defense, the lessons of Vietnam were clear: unrestrained battlefield coverage by the media—and especially by television news—could hamstring US strategy, primarily by weakening public support for military conflict. In the future, military officials would need to orchestrate the news more carefully.[1] The first step was to deny reporters access to the war zone, thereby forcing them to rely on official briefings. This more controlled approach was first exercised in 1983 with the American invasion of Grenada.

In October 1983, the elected government of the tiny Caribbean island of Grenada was overthrown by a group of leftist rebels. The former prime minister and several of his associates were killed. The new leaders declared themselves Marxists and appealed to Fidel Castro for assistance. American reaction to the coup was swift and predictable. Washington condemned the developments and declared that the installation of a communist government within the Americas was a violation of the Monroe Doctrine and incompatible with US national security interests. The administration cited the presence of Cuban military advisers and their efforts to expand the runways at Point Salines Airport (now known as Maurice Bishop International Airport) as evidence of the new regime's hostile intent.

The fact that the leaders of the Grenada coup were communists was not the sole basis for intervention. A more urgent concern was the presence of American civilians on the island. St. George's University School of Medicine in Grenada, although unaccredited in the United States, attracted a substantial enrollment of American students. With lingering memories of the 1979 hostage crisis in Iran, the Reagan administration decided to preempt a potential hostage situation by invading Grenada (see Video Archive 4.3). American Marines landed on October 25, 1983 (accompanied by a small contingent of soldiers from neighboring Caribbean nations), and arrested the rebel leaders with minimal loss of American life. The original constitution was reinstated.

▶

Video Archive 4.3
Reagan Speech on Grenada

Major news organizations reacted to the events in Grenada by hurriedly assembling news crews to report from the scene. Hundreds of American reporters attempted to make their way to Grenada. The Pentagon refused to give them access, citing national security concerns. Some newspapers then chartered their own boats in a last-ditch effort to get reporters to the front line. Most of these boats were intercepted and turned back by the American navy. The four American reporters who were based in Grenada accepted an offer from military commanders to file their reports from the USS *Guam*, anchored off the coast of Grenada, only to find that the offer was a hoax. The reporters were prevented from leaving the ship for two days.

In response to mounting media pressure, the Pentagon granted access to 15 reporters, but they were not permitted to file reports from the immediate area of the fighting. Thus, in the first few days of the conflict, the only information delivered to the American public consisted of official briefings and film clips produced by the military. Finally, five days after the invasion, the military granted general press access to all locations in Grenada.[2]

By preventing the press from covering the invasion and then spoon-feeding images and information that depicted American actions in the most favorable light (such as video of rescued American students kissing American soil on their return), the Reagan administration maintained complete control over the story. For the entire period before the president announced on national television that the threat to American security had been removed, American news organizations had been kept in the dark, unable to file independent reports on the situation in Grenada. The president appeared on national television accompanied by the prime minister of one of the neighboring islands, who enthusiastically commended the decisive action taken by the United States. In the days that followed, President Reagan's popularity increased by some 5 percentage points.

Some months after the invasion, several elements of the administration's story line came into question. The airport development was in fact funded by a consortium of European and American companies, as well as by the Cubans. The runway expansion was designed to permit the landing of jumbo jets, thus increasing the volume of tourist traffic. It turned out that the number of Cuban troops in Grenada was less than half that claimed by the administration. The urgent request for US intervention from Grenada's neighbors was solicited rather than spontaneous. Several of the American medical students came forward to state that they had never been at risk. By the time these discrepancies came to light, however, the press had turned its attention to other matters and no real harm was done to President Reagan's credibility. From the perspective of the White House, the strategy of restricting press access had its intended effect; the Reagan administration's account of daily events held sway. In the words of former ABC Pentagon correspondent John McWethy,

> When you are in a situation where your primary source of information is the United States government and where, for three days, basically your only source of information except Radio Cuba is the Pentagon, you are totally at their mercy and you have to make an assumption that the US government is telling the truth. You report that Caspar Weinberger, then the secretary of defense, says "the fighting was heaviest here," or Weinberger says "the barracks are under siege." Well, you believe it. What are you going to do? You report what he says. (Ansolabehere, Behr, & Iyengar, 1993, p. 197)

THE LESSONS OF GRENADA: MEDIA POOLS

In the aftermath of Grenada and the venting of considerable outrage over censorship of the press, the Pentagon was asked to undertake a review of its policies regarding press access. The government appointed a blue-ribbon commission consisting of military and press representatives to study the issue of press access to military combat. The panel recommended a pool system for covering future military operations. The press would be granted access, but only in the form of closely supervised *media pools*—small groups of reporters representing several print and broadcast news organizations who would work under the close supervision of the Department of Defense. One camera crew, for instance, would provide all the video footage for the major networks.

Initially used in the 1989 American invasion of Panama, the pool system became fully institutionalized in 1991 with the onset of Operation Desert Storm, the campaign to liberate Kuwait from Iraqi occupation. Pool reporters were allowed to cover events in Kuwait, but because they were not permitted to stray from Kuwait City, their independent news-gathering ability was limited to question-and-answer sessions after the daily military briefings. Pooled reports were subject to military approval; in several cases (for example, a story about American pilots watching pornographic videos before their missions), stories were censored or altered. In a telling acknowledgment of the power of visual imagery, photographs and footage of body bags and coffins were prohibited.

In addition to rationing access, the Pentagon gave more careful attention to its choreographed daily presentations for the press. The military officers responsible for briefing the press put on a multimedia performance each day. Not only did film of American smart bombs or missiles hitting their intended targets with unerring accuracy demonstrate the military's concern for

Media Pools

In an effort to limit media access without incurring charges of censorship, the Pentagon revised its policy about media access to war zones in 1989. The press would be granted access but only in the form of closely supervised media pools—small groups of reporters representing several print and broadcast news organizations who would work under close supervision of the Department of Defense. The pool reporters' coverage is made available for use by all recognized news organizations.

minimizing Iraqi civilian casualties, but the images also provided compelling material for television newscasts. By relaying the official videos as news, television news spread the message of a clinical and sanitized war effort, devoid of all civilian suffering. In the words of one media critic, "The emphasis was on the nuts and bolts of a sophisticated war machine, but the consequences were never made plain. In other words, television portrayed the war as a war without victims. . . . Indeed, the press as a whole bought into the notion that this was somehow a kinder and gentler war" (Dorman, 1997, p. 121).

Another objective of the Pentagon media managers was to elicit news coverage that followed the official story line of Iraq as the transgressor, Kuwait as the victim, and the United States as the law enforcer. Saddam Hussein was depicted as a modern-day Hitler whose occupying forces had engaged in wanton destruction of Kuwaiti natural resources (such as setting oil fields ablaze) and brutal atrocities against Kuwaiti civilians. Adding to the Pentagon's media management efforts, the exiled rulers of Kuwait retained the well-known public relations firm of Hill and Knowlton to spread the word of numerous Iraqi violations of international law during the occupation. In one particularly vicious case, Iraqi soldiers were alleged to have looted a pediatric hospital in Kuwait City and disconnected hundreds of infants from life support equipment. Hill and Knowlton even produced an eyewitness who described the incident in detail to a congressional committee. In contrast to the Iraqis, who were depicted as demonstrating minimal concern for civilian life, the American and coalition forces were portrayed as minimizing collateral damage in their bombing of Iraq. Thus, on all fronts, news coverage of the war accentuated the positive (see Video Archive 4.4).

Video Archive 4.4
Coverage of Operation Desert Storm

Once again, official accounts of the war went unchallenged. It was not until several months later that reports surfaced of the failure of several smart-weapons systems. During the war, the administration claimed that its Patriot missiles had intercepted and destroyed 41 of 42 airborne Iraqi Scud missiles. But an independent study by MIT professors Theodore Postol and George Lewis concluded that the missiles had failed to disable the Scud warhead in every instance (Postol & Lewis, 1993). Moreover, contrary to what the videos that were played at the press briefings implied, the coalition bombing campaign had inflicted significant damage to civilian areas of Baghdad, killing an estimated 3,500 Iraqi civilians (Conetta, 2003). In addition, the story of Saddam Hussein's alleged mass murder of Kuwaiti children was retracted; instead of the 300 alleged victims, only one could be confirmed.

The various "corrections" to the official record were reported by the press, but only long after the war had receded from national attention. The 1992 presidential campaign was under way, and stories about the failing American economy and the surprisingly strong candidacy of an unknown governor from Arkansas took precedence over revised claims of American military and technological prowess or fabricated eyewitness testimony concerning the behavior of Iraqi soldiers.

A REFINEMENT OF MEDIA POOLS: EMBEDDED JOURNALISTS

In the most recent iteration of the national security media script, the Pentagon decided that it was no longer politically feasible to deny American reporters firsthand access to the 2003 invasion of Iraq. In a modernized version of pooled coverage, a select group of American and international correspondents were to be embedded with the invading forces. While accompanying the coalition forces into battle, the embedded reporters would be subject to strict limitations on the content of their reports; they could not, for instance, discuss operational details, nor could they make any slight reference to information that might be of strategic value. These guidelines were enforced; Geraldo Rivera, one of the embedded correspondents for Fox News, was expelled from Iraq for drawing a map of the mission in the sand.

As anticipated by the Pentagon, news reports filed by the embedded correspondents provided close-up and often dramatic footage of American troops in action. The public was given a live progress report of the invasion from the perspective of American soldiers but without coverage of Americans killed in action or of civilians caught up in the fighting. The Project for Excellence in Journalism (cited in Entman, 2004, p. 116) studied embedded correspondents' reports on the major networks; not a single report

Video Archive 4.5
Coverage of the Iraq War

showed images of people being killed by American soldiers (see Video Archive 4.5).

Once hostilities began, the inability of the press to counter official accounts of daily events was understandable: the Pentagon exercised its monopoly control over information. Briefings by the secretary of defense and other high-ranking military officials were the major sources of news. In the case of American television newscasts, the coverage was thoroughly dominated by current and former government officials. The media watchdog group Fairness and Accuracy in Reporting (FAIR) tracked all references to Iraq in four daily network newscasts (aired by ABC, CBS, NBC, and PBS) over a two-week period that ended one week after Secretary of State Colin Powell's speech at the United Nations in which he insisted that Iraq possessed weapons of mass destruction. During this period, broadcast news reports made reference to 393 sources. As expected, the great majority (68 percent) of the sources were Americans. Even more striking, three-fourths of the Americans interviewed in these programs were current or former government officials. Only one official (Senator Edward Kennedy) was opposed to the war. Even when the networks invited non-Americans, they were drawn overwhelmingly (75 percent) from countries that supported the Bush administration's position on Iraq. Only 4 percent of the foreign sources expressed opposition to the war.[3]

In short, during the period when many Americans were uncertain of their position on the Iraq war, network news coverage was skewed in the direction of official policy. Even PBS, the network typically lampooned by conservatives as a leftist news source, featured a 4-to-1 ratio of war proponents to opponents in their coverage of Iraq. Given the daily exposure to such one-sided coverage, it's no wonder that American public opinion became increasingly supportive of the administration's war plans.

Still more glaring press failures occurred before the onset of hostilities. The Bush administration's policy of unilateral intervention rested on the premise that the regime of Saddam Hussein represented a significant military threat to the international community. According to American intelligence accounts, Iraq possessed significant stockpiles of chemical and biological weapons. As Secretary of State Powell stated in his February 2003 address to the UN General Assembly, "There can be no doubt that Saddam Hussein has biological weapons and the capability to rapidly produce more, many more. And he has the ability to dispense these lethal poisons and diseases in ways that can cause massive death and destruction."[4] Powell's remarks were part of a pattern. A 2008 report by the Center for Public Integrity found that the Bush administration issued 935 false statements about the threats posed by Saddam Hussein between September 11, 2001, and a few months after the invasion of Iraq (Center for Public Integrity, 2008).

What is especially troubling is that these claims went unchallenged by the mainstream press, despite vociferous challenges from credible, international experts. For instance, on the very same day that President Bush referred to Iraqi efforts to obtain uranium for use in the production of nuclear weapons (a claim that was later acknowledged to be false), the deputy head of the UN inspections program held a press conference to debunk the alleged evidence of a renewed Iraqi nuclear program. More generally, months of sustained UN inspections had turned up no traces of the Iraqi weapons of mass destruction. David Kay, one of the UN inspectors later recruited to head the post-war American detection effort (euphemistically titled the Iraq Study Group), resigned in January 2004, stating that he did not believe Iraq had stockpiles of chemical or biological weapons.

In short, in the period leading up to war and continuing thereafter, the press had several opportunities to subject the administration's rationale for war to greater scrutiny. For the most part, these opportunities were squandered. Later, as the true extent of the discrepancies between the facts and official accounts became transparent, the *New York Times* and the *Washington Post* issued hard-hitting apologies for their generally one-sided coverage. In indicting their own judgment, the *Times* editors were brutally honest: "Editors at several levels who should have been challenging reporters and pressing for more skepticism were perhaps too intent on rushing scoops into the paper" (From the Editors, 2004).

CONCLUSION

The outcome of the indexing system of calibrating the news to represent the state of elite debate depends on several circumstances. Clearly, when the focus is on the imminent use of American military force, the president's views are especially likely to dominate. Reporters feel free to ignore congressional leaders or foreign officials as sources because they know that the relevant decision makers are located at the White House and Pentagon. But when war is not imminent, when there is no clear security threat, or when American military power is used to facilitate humanitarian aid (as was the case when a US Navy hospital ship arrived in New York to help ease overcrowding in the city hospitals during the COVID pandemic in 2020), reporters are able to spread their news nets more widely, and the coverage is less biased in favor of the administration. In the case of the navy hospital ship, for instance, multiple news reports noted that most of the hospital beds remained empty, despite the overcrowding in local hospitals.

The outcome of the indexing process also depends on elites' political calculations. When the country is on the verge of war and the conflict has been broadly portrayed as involving the national interest, critics of the president risk being seen as unpatriotic. A study by John Zaller (1994) shows that congressional Democrats were reluctant to openly question the George H. W. Bush administration's aggressive response to the Iraqi invasion of Kuwait because they feared reinforcing the stereotype of their party as soft on national defense. However, when the president undertakes actions that do not fit the standard script of good versus evil or when the president's actions meet with strong international opposition from our traditional allies, as was the case with the Reagan administration's decision to bomb targets in Libya, press accounts tend to be more critical, both because opposing elites are more willing to speak out in opposition and because the press can cite the views of disgruntled American allies.

At other times, despite the prevalence of indexing, the press is able to express muted criticism of official policy. Despite elite consensus on the need for American military action, the press can resort to horse race–type handicapping of the impending hostilities. In the case of the 1991 Persian Gulf conflict, for example, news reports were rife with accounts suggesting that President Bush's political standing and reelection prospects might be seriously jeopardized if Iraqi forces offered stiff resistance or if Kuwait became a quagmire. Similarly, journalists offered a variety of contextual critiques focusing on possible unintended outcomes of war in the Middle East (such as the elevation of Saddam Hussein to martyr status). However, these manifestations of press objectivity did not venture so far as to question the basic premises of US policy. As Scott Althaus (2003) notes, "No journalist ever questioned the demonization of Saddam Hussein. No journalist ever hinted that the United States had taken an inappropriately aggressive posture toward a regional conflict.... At no time did a journalist question whether Iraq's chemical, biological or nuclear capability presented a real threat to the Western world in the foreseeable future" (p. 396).

Finally, there is the possibility that the emergence of new media platforms may compromise political elites' ability to manage the news. We noted in Chapter 3 that widespread use of smartphones has provided reporters with immediate access to breaking events in far-flung locales. And the equally widespread use of digital photography has increased the number of eyewitnesses who may serve as news sources or "citizen journalists." The graphic photographs of Iraqi prisoners abused at Abu Ghraib prison were taken by American service personnel, who transmitted them via their phones. Once the photographs had been obtained by the press, the Department of Defense was forced to acknowledge the atrocities and begin an official investigation. More generally, immediate access to the scene of an event strengthens journalists' ability to resist the official story line. If event-driven reporting becomes more common, the indexing process will no longer produce a one-sided pattern of international and defense-related news.

No matter how balanced the outcome of the indexing process, news coverage that is pegged to official sources threatens the ability of the press to maintain an adversarial stance toward government. During periods of military conflict, the silence of opposition sources inevitably results in a "journalism of deference to the national security state" (Dorman, 1997, p. 124). Even worse, "journalism that indexes debate in Washington violates not just the watchdog ideal, but also the mirror ideal. For under the indexing rule, the journalistic mirror is held up not to reality, but to official interpretations of reality" (Mermin, 1999, p. 145).

We began this chapter by contrasting Watergate with the war against Iraq. The differences between domestic politics and foreign policy are undeniably responsible for the wide gap in press performance in these two instances. International issues have generally proved to be of little interest to Americans, thus encouraging editors to place more emphasis on stories that sell. But the diminished adversarial capacity of the press can also be attributed to the general development of media politics: that is, the relationship between reporters and government sources has changed substantially since Watergate. Officials in all branches of government are now well aware of the importance of the media to their ability to govern. Press secretaries, media liaisons, and public relations specialists are now ensconced in every government agency or office. Officials seize every opportunity to claim credit and present their actions in the most favorable light possible. When news coverage or the course of events is not to their liking, they resort to various strategies (such as leaking information or staging events) for regaining control over the message. These strategies are the subject of Chapter 9.

Before we take up media strategy, however, we must first examine a huge change in the media landscape: the proliferation of media sources and platforms brought on by the rapid spread of information technology. Chapter 5 will examine the consequences of the revolution in information technology for the practice of media politics. How does the availability of more media choices affect the public's exposure to public affairs programming, and does the rapid spread of the internet and new forms of mass communication change the way in which political organizations and campaigns mobilize their supporters for political action?

Summary

1. As coverage of the 2003 invasion of Iraq illustrates, the media tend to be less adversarial in dealing with national security and foreign policy than in dealing with domestic issues.

2. One explanation for the media's less adversarial stance is indexing. In a news system based on official sources, reporters' coverage of issues mirrors the level and intensity of elite debate. The higher the level of elite dissent, the easier it is for reporters to pit competing sources against each other. Where domestic political events are concerned, the presence of vocal and authoritative critics grants journalists the necessary leverage to question official accounts. On matters of foreign policy, however, critics of government policy tend to fall silent, and the press is left with only official sources.

3. National security matters provide officials with even more control over the press. When the United States resorts to military force, opposing elites generally close ranks behind the president for fear of appearing unpatriotic. Because potential opponents of the use of military force fall silent, the press becomes completely dependent on official spokespersons.

4. After the Vietnam War, the Pentagon and the Department of Defense strove to restrict media access to areas of US military action. There was considerable outrage over censorship of the press after it was discovered that the Reagan administration had misled the media and the public about the invasion of Grenada. As a result, the Pentagon revised its policy about media access to war zones; the press would be granted access but only in the form of closely supervised media pools.

5. In contrast to its approach during the 1991 Gulf War, the Pentagon decided that it was no longer politically feasible to deny American reporters firsthand access to the 2003 invasion of Iraq. In a modernized version of pooled coverage, a select group of American and international correspondents were to be embedded with the invading forces. The embedded reporters, however, were still subject to severe restrictions on the content of their reports.

FURTHER READINGS

Aday, S., Livingston, S., & Maeve, H. (2005). Embedding the truth: A cross-cultural analysis of objectivity and television coverage of the Iraq War. *International Journal of Press/Politics, 10,* 3–21.

Althaus, S. (2003). When news norms collide, follow the lead: New evidence for press independence. *Political Communication, 20,* 381–414.

Bennett, W. L. (1990). Toward a theory of press-state relations. *Journal of Communication, 40,* 103–125.

Cook, T. E. (1994). Domesticating a crisis: Washington newsbeats and the network news after the Iraq invasion of Kuwait. In W. L. Bennett & D. L. Paletz (Eds.), *Taken by storm: The media, public opinion, and U.S. foreign policy in the Gulf War* (pp. 105–130). Chicago: University of Chicago Press.

Dorman, W. A. (1997). Press theory and journalistic practice: The case of the Gulf War. In S. Iyengar & R. Reeves (Eds.), *Do the media govern? Politicians, voters and reporters in America* (pp. 118–125). Thousand Oaks, CA: Sage.

Frenznick, D. A. (1992). The First Amendment on the battlefield: A constitutional analysis of press access to military operations in Grenada, Panama and the Persian Gulf. *Pacific Law Journal, 23,* 315–359.

Hayes, D., & Guardino, M. (2013). *Influence from abroad: Foreign voices, the media, and U.S. public opinion.* New York: Cambridge University Press.

Mermin, J. (1999). *Debating war and peace: Media coverage of U.S. intervention in the post-Vietnam era.* Princeton, NJ: Princeton University Press.

Sigal, L. (1973). *Reporters and officials.* Lexington, MA: Heath.

Zaller, J. R. (1994). Elite leadership of mass opinion: New evidence from the Gulf War. In W. L. Bennett & D. L. Paletz (Eds.), *Taken by storm: The media, public opinion, and U.S. foreign policy in the Gulf War* (pp. 186–209). Chicago: University of Chicago Press.

Zaller, J. R., & Chiu, D. (2000). Government's little helper: U.S. press coverage of foreign policy crises, 1946–1999. In B. L. Nacos, R. Y. Shapiro, & P. Isernia (Eds.), *Decisionmaking in a glass house: Mass media, public opinion, and American and European foreign policy in the 21st century* (pp. 61–84). Lanham, MD: Rowman & Littlefield.

NOTES

1. In fact, conclusions about the pivotal role of television news in turning public opinion against the Vietnam War are mistaken. In the first place, as described earlier, coverage faithfully reflected the state of American elite opinion. Second, as John Mueller (1973) has documented, trends in public support for war were no different for Vietnam and Korea, despite the lack of television coverage during the Korean War.

2. This account rests on David Frenznick's (1992) authoritative history of military-press relations in the United States.

3. The sheer number of sources may underestimate the degree of pro-administration slant in the news. For instance, a study by Scott Althaus, Jill Edy, Robert Entman, and Patricia Phalen (1996) of *New York Times* coverage of the 1986 US air strikes against Libya found that foreign sources and American government sources were equally represented in the news. However, the same study documented a more subtle indicator of pro-administration coverage: opposition sources were consistently positioned *after* administration sources within the same news report.

4. Reproduced at "A Policy of Evasion and Deception," *Washington Post*, February 5, 2003, transcript, http://www.washingtonpost.com/wp-srv/nation/transcripts /powelltext_020503.html.

5

New Media, New Forms of Communication

The frenetic pace of technological innovation over the past two decades has revolutionized the transmission of information, with dramatic consequences for news organizations, politicians, interest groups, and anybody trying to influence the political process. For owners of news outlets, the internet has increased competition by bringing a host of online information providers to prominence. Vox, Axios, and Politico—now established online news companies—did not exist 15 years ago. The increased number of sources has resulted in a reduced market share for individual providers, thus adding to the economic pressures facing owners. The array of programming choices now available bears little resemblance to the television-dominated environment of the 1980s.

For politicians, the development of huge online networks such as Facebook and Twitter has made it possible to reach the public without going through intermediaries or gatekeepers, such as journalists. President Trump boasted (rightfully) of his huge Twitter following, and the daily barrage of tweets from the White House—usually from @realdonaldtrump but sometimes from the more official @potus—demonstrates how social media have emerged as a major platform for exercising the "bully pulpit."

For activists and others engaged in advocacy, the ability to send a message that can "go viral" and reach millions via social media represents empowerment on an unimaginable scale. On October 24, 2017, the novelist Saladin Ahmed noticed a striking illustration on the back of his cereal box that depicted many Corn Pops characters frolicking through a shopping mall. The solitary brown corn pop in the crowd was cleaning the floor. Ahmed fired off a tweet to the cereal maker: "hey @kellogsus why is literally the only brown corn pop on the whole cereal box the janitor? This is teaching kids racism." That very same day, Kellogg responded: "Kellogg is committed to diversity and inclusion. The artwork is updated and will be in stores soon. We did not intend to offend, we apologize."

The Power of Social Media

As these examples make clear, the revolution in information technology has altered not only the form of the media landscape but also the very concept of communication. The traditional forms of communication were either *point-to-point* (between a single sender and recipient) or *broadcast* (between a single sender and multiple recipients). Most senders did not have ready access to broadcast forms of communication and could not reach a significant audience. Traditional media were also limited to a single form (print, audio, or video).

The development of the internet permitted simultaneous point-to-point and broadcast forms of communication for the first time and provided individual users with easy access to a huge audience. Every individual on the network of computers making up the World Wide Web is both a sender and a receiver. Any user of the internet can direct messages to individual recipients and at the same time harness the power of worldwide online networks to reach millions. Because messages now reach a global audience, their impact on the behavior of those in power is greater, as illustrated by the case of Kellogg's apology. In addition, unlike conventional media, internet-based communication is multi-channel, allowing the transmission of text, voice, still images, and video.

Our goal in this chapter is to describe how information technology and the proliferation of new media have transformed both the behavior of individual information seekers and the strategies used by politicians and political organizations to reach and mobilize their supporters. At the level of the individual, the age of digital media is the age of information overload, with hundreds of thousands of information sources, ranging from venerable news organizations to little-known bloggers, competing for consumers' attention. The sheer volume of information available forces individuals to rely on a handful of preferred providers. We will explain how individuals choose among providers and program offerings, sometimes limiting their options and giving rise to "echo chambers" where people encounter only one point of view.

At the level of candidates and political organizations, the big story about new technologies is the reduced cost of reaching potential supporters. The explosive growth of social networking sites (Facebook now has more than 2.7 billion active users worldwide) and the development of instantaneous forms of communication (such as Twitter) have given politicians brand-new platforms. Social media make it possible for news reports, campaign videos, and other forms of political messaging to be recirculated on a vast scale. The size of the audience sometimes serves as a deterrent to unethical behavior; politicians know that their transgressions will be out in the open more quickly and more widely than in the past. The news that New York attorney general Eric Schneiderman had physically abused women he dated appeared on the *New Yorker*'s website at 7:00 PM on May 7, 2018. Less than 3 hours later, at 9:50 PM, Schneiderman announced his resignation.

Importantly, candidates and groups can now communicate directly with potential supporters, bypassing the news media entirely. Politicians can speak directly to potential voters when and where they please and on subjects of their own choosing. It is no wonder, as we describe later in this chapter, that candidates and political activists are enthusiastically embracing new forms of campaigning.

THE DIFFUSION OF TECHNOLOGY

The rapid proliferation of information technology has astonished all observers. The Pew Research Center has regularly tracked Americans' use of the internet since 1995. Over the years, survey respondents have been asked some form of the original question, "Do you ever go online to access the Internet or World Wide Web or to send and receive e-mail?" Even allowing for some inflation in self-reported results, the increase over time in the percentage of Americans who say they go online is striking. In 1995, a mere 14 percent of adult Americans said they used the internet. By the turn of the century, the figure had more than tripled to half the population. Continuing on this trajectory, between 1999 and 2016, the share of the online population reached 87 percent. In the span of two decades, self-reported internet use increased by a stunning 621 percent.

Since the early 1990s, when the internet became accessible to the larger public, the percentage of Americans who get their news online has exploded. In 2001, only 13 percent of Americans named the internet as their main source for news, while 74 percent cited television (Pew Research Center, 2011). By 2017, the gap between television and online news was only 7 percentage points (50 for television, 43 for online; Pew Research Center, 2017). Among those under the age of 30, the internet is the primary news source, outstripping television by a wide margin. The rise of internet news and the simultaneous decline of traditional news platforms, such as radio and newspapers, suggest a gradual pattern of product substitution. That's not to say that online news has totally replaced other forms of news. Rather, online news supplements consumers' use of other platforms: overall, across both internet and traditional media, Americans these days are spending more time listening, reading, or watching news than they were 20 years ago.

Technology has also brought about a subtle change in the composition of the news audience. During the era of traditional media, exposure to news presentations required some level of motivation. The people who turned on their televisions at a scheduled time in the evening or subscribed to a newspaper were sufficiently interested in current events to do so. Today, the motivational threshold has been lowered; millions of Americans encounter the news unintentionally when their friends and contacts on social media insert news reports into their news feeds. People more interested in hearing about the exploits of their infant grandchildren find themselves in the path of news reports about President Biden's White House meeting with the family of George Floyd. In the case of Facebook and Twitter, this "inadvertent" audience for news is in the tens of millions and certainly exceeds the circulation of the news organization whose report makes the social media rounds. We will return to this distinction shortly when we introduce the concept of selective exposure to news.

In an attempt to get accurate estimates of media use, the Pew Research Center used to ask respondents to gauge how much time they spent on various activities "yesterday." Figure 5.1 displays the total time respondents reported spending with various forms of news media. Pew stopped posing this question in 2010, but we have comparable 2016 data from eMarketer. The graph reveals two important trends. First, self-reported media use across all "old" media has declined steadily over the past two decades; print newspaper use has declined from 19 minutes per day to just 6, while television news viewing has dropped from 38 minutes to 29. Second, use of online news sites is up; by 2016, people were spending nearly the same amount of time getting the news online as by watching television.

The use of new media platforms isn't constant across demographic groups. In general, younger people are more fluent in the use of technology. For instance, they are the most likely to access news through their cell phones and also the most likely to encounter news reports on social media. Figure 5.2 shows the news sources frequently used by Americans in four different age groups ranging from those under 29 to those over 65. Nearly three-fourths of Americans between the ages of 18 and 29 say they get news from a smartphone or tablet; this figure falls to 48 percent for the oldest group. Conversely,

FIGURE 5.1

How Much Time Americans Spent Following the News, 1994–2016

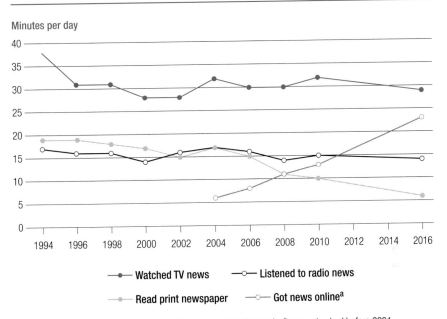

ª Online news includes newspapers read online. Online news "yesterday" was not asked before 2004.
Source: Data for 1994–2010 from Pew Research Center. (2010, September 12). Americans spending more time following the news. Retrieved September 3, 2021, from https://www.pewresearch.org/politics/2010/09/12/americans-spending-more-time-following-the-news/; 2016 data from eMarketer. (2017, October 9). eMarketer updates time spent with media figures. Retrieved September 3, 2021, from https://www.emarketer.com/Article/eMarketer-Updates-US-Time-Spent-with-Media-Figures/1016587.

Americans in their 60s rely heavily on television news (68 percent), a medium used rarely (16 percent) by the young.

News represents a tiny sliver of the information available online. The internet provides access to everything from vital health information (for example, the location of COVID vaccination sites) to job listings. Internet access has become so important in today's world that it's now labeled a "fundamental human right" in several countries, and these countries have passed legislation to ensure internet access for all. A related issue concerns access to bandwidth. Those with regular access to broadband internet have a tremendous advantage over those with a slower, less stable connection. In the United States, there are wide gaps in broadband access between the young and the old, the less and the more educated, and the rich and the poor, as well as between urban and rural dwellers.

The availability of information technology to a majority of the population has created a booming internet economy. In the case of media organizations,

FIGURE 5.2

Sources of News for Americans by Age

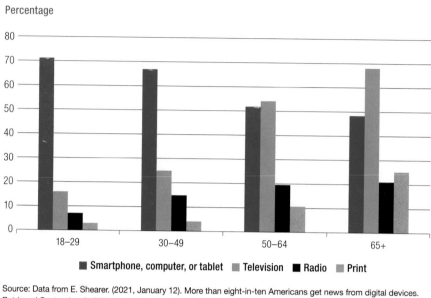

Percentage

Source: Data from E. Shearer. (2021, January 12). More than eight-in-ten Americans get news from digital devices. Retrieved September 3, 2021, from Pew Research Center website: https://www.pewresearch.org/fact-tank/2021/01/12/more-than-eight-in-ten-americans-get-news-from-digital-devices.

thousands of news sites now compete with each other and with the offerings of political parties, candidates, interest groups, think tanks, and virtually anybody with anything to say about politics. Figure 5.3 lists some of the news sites maintained by individual news organizations with the largest weekly traffic, as measured by Alexa.com and Quantcast.com. The list is dominated by the major news aggregators, which feature news from multiple news sources, but it also includes well-known newspapers, cable television networks, and at least one purely online news source (HuffPost).

The proliferation of internet technology and use is not, of course, confined to the dissemination of news. Any of the major internet search engines, for instance, records weekly traffic that far exceeds the online audience for CNN or the *New York Times*. The amount of time allocated to staying abreast of the news in relation to other online activities shows the same pattern. According to data from Comscore, while visitors to nytimes.com spend about 2 hours a month on the site, Facebook users spend nearly 30 hours a month on Facebook.

Given the speed with which information technology has spread, research into the effects of new-media use on individuals, markets, and institutions is still in its infancy. For scholars of media politics, there are three central questions.

FIGURE 5.3
Top Ten Online US News Sites, 2021

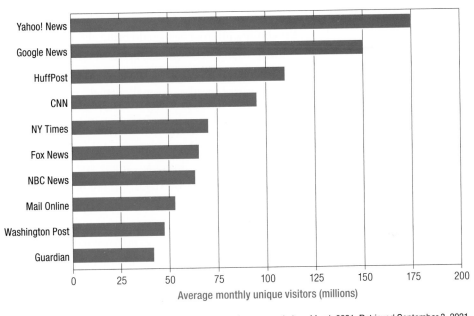

Average monthly unique visitors (millions)

Source: Data from eBiz MBA Guide. (2021). Top 15 most popular news websites, March 2021. Retrieved September 3, 2021, from http://www.ebizmba.com/articles/news-websites.

First, how has increased access to the internet affected the behavior of consumers of news? Second, what is the potential impact of the vast online social networks such as Facebook on the recirculation of news or commentary and individuals' exposure to diverse points of view? Third, how have political candidates and organizations (and, more recently, non-US players such as Vladimir Putin) attempted to harness technology to mobilize and influence individuals and elections? In the discussion that follows, we will address each of these questions in turn, focusing in some detail on the efforts by Russian operatives to spread false and misleading information through Facebook and Twitter to strengthen Donald Trump's candidacy in 2016 and again in 2020.

EFFECTS OF NEW MEDIA ON CONSUMERS

There are two schools of thought concerning the potential impact of new media on the end user. *Optimists* see technology as a means of revitalizing the public sphere. By providing direct and immediate access to diverse political perspectives, the internet should enhance the ability of ordinary people to follow events and to participate in the political process. The hope is that easy online access to public affairs information will build civic awareness and engagement. Former vice president Al Gore epitomized this view when he predicted (in a 1994 speech) that the coming internet age would bring about "robust and sustainable economic progress, strong democracies, better solutions to global and local environmental challenges, improved health care, and—ultimately— a greater sense of shared stewardship of our small planet" (International Telecommunications Union, 1994).

Skeptics, on the other hand, warn that information technology is no panacea for the limitations of conventional news programming and the weak demand for political information. If serious news coverage cannot attract television viewers, why should it draw people online? If Americans are not inclined to read newspapers or watch foreign media, is there any reason to suppose that they will suddenly access the BBC or Xinhua News just because it's possible to do so? Skeptics think not. They believe that the internet will in fact discourage consumers from pursuing news (whether via internet or conventional platforms) in favor of more engaging online pursuits, such as shopping, dating, streaming movies, or keeping in touch. As people become more fluent in the ways of the Web, they may become more personally isolated, preferring surfing alone over community involvement or face-to-face social interaction. Quite possibly, on balance, technology may weaken community and civic engagement.

There is no doubt that the internet makes available an ample supply of news that is not screened for accuracy or objectivity. Journalistic standards are not as stringent for online news providers, and information is often published before there is time to provide corroboration. As we will see later in this chapter, the absence of gatekeeping procedures also makes it possible for individuals (especially political leaders) and groups to intentionally spread misinformation and propaganda online, taking advantage of social media practices that permit and promote the distribution of controversial, often misleading, or frequently inaccurate posts.

Quite apart from the question of whether internet technology will increase or decrease the average American's exposure to public affairs content is the question of whether the internet will, in practice, be used to broaden users' political horizons. Although an infinite variety of information is available, individuals may well sample selectively, limiting their exposure to news or sources that they expect to find agreeable. By turning to biased but favored providers, consumers may be able to "wall themselves off from topics and opinions that they would prefer to avoid" (Sunstein, 2001, pp. 201–202). The end result could be exposure to one-sided news and a less informed and more polarized electorate.

INTERNET USE AND CIVIC ENGAGEMENT

Representing the optimists, some scholars believe that the internet will expand the universe of political participation by reducing costs. Rather than having to write a check, address an envelope, find a stamp, and mail in a political donation, one can simply go online and pay with a credit card. And it's not only making a financial contribution that is easier; creating membership rosters, sending out announcements of upcoming meetings, and signing petitions are all simplified.

Optimists also cite the potential of the internet to draw in individuals who hold a wide variety of ideas and perspectives. Unlike the mainstream news media, which is constrained by the norms of professional journalism and consumer demand, websites can target smaller audiences with more specialized interests, making it possible to create niche networks and discussion groups.

Technology not only facilitates conventional forms of participation but has also spawned new forms of civic engagement. People can contribute to blogs, view and post YouTube videos, and reach out to like-minded others on Facebook and Twitter. These innovations are already influencing the conduct of campaigns. During the 2016 and 2020 presidential primaries, news organizations (including CNN, MSNBC, and Fox News) sponsored candidate debates in which internet users across the country submitted questions to the candidates through Facebook and Twitter.

The increased popularity of online networking and messaging sites may also contribute to unconventional forms of political action. Parler (with 11.1 million users at its peak), CloutHub, and BitChute are all sites that have permitted the expression of extreme political views with no content moderation. Use of these sites has enabled a variety of conspiracy-oriented activist groups on both sides of the ideological divide to raise money and coordinate the actions of their members. Several of these groups (Proud Boys, Oath Keepers, Boogaloo) were active in the storming of the Capitol on January 6, 2021. Extremist groups promoting the cause of White supremacy are especially active online. In early 2021, the FBI released a report on domestic terrorism that identified "racially or ethnically motivated violent extremists" as posing the most significant threat to national security.

Despite the potential of the internet to foster new forms of political engagement, the skeptics claim that the internet has had little impact on the actual level of conventional political participation. In fact, the initial research literature on civic engagement suggested that internet access has exerted little positive effect overall (Boulianne, 2009). More recent work, however, shows a strengthening of this relationship, attributable partly to the growth in the use of social media sites (Boulianne, 2018).

A parallel debate concerns the potential impact of technology on inequality in civic participation. Optimists assume that the internet will draw in hitherto inactive groups and level the playing field. Pessimists, however, argue that the costs of going online, in terms of both money and skills, will only exacerbate existing disparities in participation. Because technology use is significantly correlated with social class, it is unlikely that the voices of the poor and less educated will be heard online. In fact, as shown in Figure 5.4, there is evidence

FIGURE 5.4

Group Differences in Participation in Civic Engagement

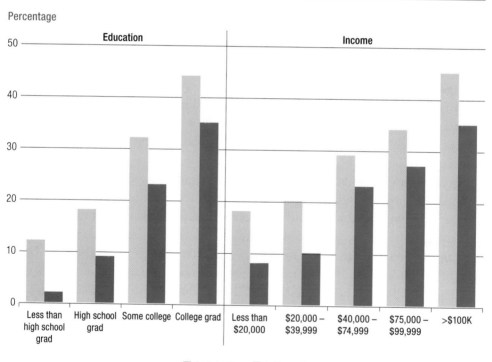

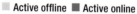

Source: Data from A. Smith, K. Lehman Schlozman, S. Verba, & H. Brady. (2009, September 1). *The internet and civic engagement.* Retrieved September 3, 2021, from the Pew Research Center website: https://www.pewresearch.org/internet/2009/09/01/the-internet-and-civic-engagement/.

that online activists, like their offline counterparts, are drawn disproportionately from high-status groups. For instance, the participation gap between college and high school graduates is almost identical (around 25 percent higher for college graduates) for offline and online participation (Bimber & Davis, 2003; Smith, Schlozman, Verba, & Brady, 2009).

The overrepresentation of higher-status groups as online activists suggests that new forms of participation simply replicate the old. But some skeptics go even further and argue that internet use can displace conventional forms of civic life and lower the overall level of participation. These scholars argue that just as the advent of television sounded the death knell for visually oriented magazines such as *Life*, time spent surfing the Web will gradually diminish face-to-face social interaction. We might become sufficiently preoccupied with our private online spaces to have few opportunities to visit with the neighbors, write letters to the editor, or even converse with anybody on a face-to-face basis. Because technology use is an inherently isolated rather than social experience, it has the potential to weaken the bonds between the individual and the community.

To date, the scholarly verdict on the question of displacement is inconclusive. An early study (Kraut, Lundmark, Patterson, Kiesler, Mukopadhyay, & Scherlis, 1998) focused on a group of Pittsburgh-area residents who were given computers and internet access. Over a two-year period, the researchers found that study participants became less involved in social activities and expressed a higher level of loneliness. More recent studies seem to contradict these findings, especially among youth. Adolescents who use social media frequently, for instance, also report closer friendships and other beneficial psychological outcomes (Valkenburg & Peter, 2007, 2009). However, none of these studies can disentangle selection effects: Do people who are already sociable and well-adjusted choose to spend more time online, or does using the internet make users less anxious or depressed?

Thus, at the level of individuals' self-reported exposure to conventional media and other discretionary activities, the consequences of increased internet use are unclear. For some, internet use may free up time for other pursuits; for others, the effect may be the opposite.

For one group in particular, however, it is clear that the internet has dramatically increased participation. Young adults are the least likely to engage in traditional forms of political activity but the most likely to take advantage of technologically enhanced forms of participation. The young, for instance, are more likely to post comments on blogs and organize for political causes through social networking sites. As shown in Figure 5.5,

FIGURE 5.5

Online Political Engagement by Age and Education

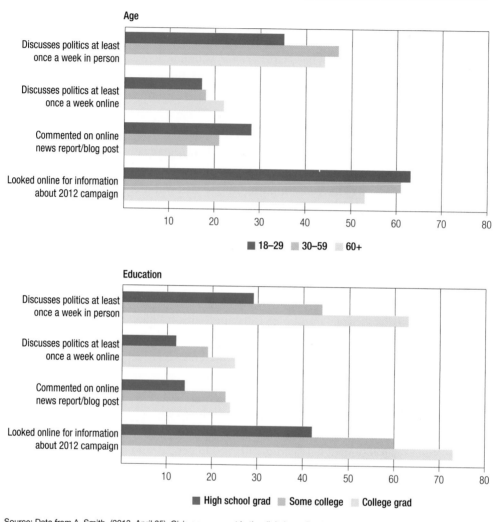

Source: Data from A. Smith. (2013, April 25). *Civic engagement in the digital age*. Retrieved September 3, 2021, from the Pew Research Center website: http://www.pewinternet.org/2013/04/25/civic-engagement-in-the-digital-age/.

the age gap in the use of social networking sites for political purposes and posting political content online favors those between the ages of 18 and 34 by a substantial margin. College students are especially likely to engage in online political activity.

With the notable exception of the young, the advent of new technologies has done little to raise the overall level of involvement in civic or community affairs. Civic participation requires motivation, and the motivated are more likely to take advantage of both new and old forms of participation.

SELECTIVE EXPOSURE TO ONLINE NEWS?

The single most important feature of the current media environment is the increased flow of information. In a world dominated by conventional news sources, the supply of public affairs information hardly burdens the typical voter's attention span. The average presidential candidate sound bite in the networks' evening newscasts runs for less than 10 seconds. Today, however, consumers face information overload—hundreds of information providers all capable of delivering much larger chunks of campaign information. Individuals can cope with the overload because new media also provide greater user control, thus facilitating consumers' ability to attend to information selectively. The audiences for conventional news programs are hard-pressed to avoid coverage of the candidate they dislike, because news reports typically assign equal coverage to each candidate. When browsing the news online, on the other hand, users can filter or search through masses of content more easily than with conventional media. Rather than examining the complete collection of speeches found at donaldjtrump.com, users can instead seek out his references to issues of special concern. In short, as candidates, interest groups, news organizations, and voters all converge on the internet, the possibility of selective exposure to political information increases dramatically. Given the availability of so much information and so many news providers, the audience must make choices or be overwhelmed. Exactly how do news consumers decide whether the information they encounter is worth considering or to be passed over?

Research suggests three main possibilities. First, as we have just seen with the question of political engagement, exposure to political information online may be simply a matter of generic political interest (the *attentive public hypothesis*). Political junkies will seek out news and political commentary, whereas the apolitical majority simply tune out all things political, except when major events generate a torrent of coverage that is impossible to ignore. From this perspective, multiplying the number of information sources only widens the information gap between the more and the less interested.[1] Second, among those with some level of political interest, people with a partisan affiliation may prefer to encounter information that they find supportive or consistent with their political beliefs (the *partisan polarization hypothesis*). For example, Republicans may visit drudgereport.com, while Democrats go to dailykos.com. The blogosphere provides an exemplary case of a polarized information space; the great majority of bloggers participate in completely homogeneous (in-party) discussion networks. Increasingly, there is evidence that news-gathering also fits the partisan selectivity model. Third, people may seek information not on the basis of their anticipated agreement with the message but because of their interest in particular issues (the *issue public hypothesis*). For example, the elderly seek out information bearing on COVID-19 simply because they are more at risk.

The Attentive Public Hypothesis

According to the attentive public hypothesis, the act of seeking out political information, online as elsewhere, is simply a matter of generic political interest. People captivated by politics tune in to all forms of news, whereas the apolitical majority tune out politics in favor of online bargain hunting or keeping up with friends. The increased availability of media channels and sources makes it possible for people who care little about political debates to evade the reach of news programming altogether. As a result, this group is likely to possess very little information about political issues and events. From this perspective, therefore, the internet will simply widen the information gap between the more and less interested.

In the case of conventional media use, a classic study by Vincent Price and John Zaller (1993) reported evidence consistent with the rich-get-richer pattern. They found that respondents with a higher level of education (education is an indicator of political attentiveness—that is, people who are more educated tend to be more interested in politics) remembered all news stories better. These investigators concluded that "someone who is generally well-informed about

⊚ IN FOCUS

Theories of Selective Exposure

- **Attentive public.** People interested in politics tune in to all forms of news, whereas the apolitical majority pay very little attention to news in any medium.
- **Partisan polarization.** People prefer to encounter information that supports their beliefs and avoid information that is inconsistent with those beliefs.
- **Issue public.** People seek out information about subjects that are particularly important or interesting to them and tune out information about other subjects.

politics will tend to be well-informed about whatever the news media also cover, whether the trials of Hollywood celebrities or the latest arms control proposals" (p. 157). Other studies reached similar conclusions, suggesting that people who attend to political information are generalists, soaking up whatever is available, rather than ideologues looking for ammunition to strengthen their arguments or specialists interested in particular issues (Delli Carpini & Keeter, 1996).

In the case of new-media use, we would expect the more educated to be especially overrepresented. Virtually every study of internet use has documented that educated and affluent Americans enjoy greater online access than do their less advantaged counterparts. Because the educated and affluent also tend to be more interested in politics, they will be especially likely to pursue political activities online (such as signing a petition, contacting a government official, or posting news links). Table 5.1 shows that in 2013, the voters most likely to report engaging in such online political activities were college graduates and the young. In fact, the education advantage in online political participation shown here is almost identical to the parallel advantages in offline participation.

There is one group of Americans, however, for whom the "rich-get-richer" maxim may not hold. Young people are generally less interested in politics than the middle-aged and seniors but are experts with technology. Using data from the 2014 General Social Survey, Russell Dalton showed that millennials were the least active age group across a variety of measures of political activity (Dalton, 2016). In the Pew survey reported in Table 5.1, respondents were asked questions about a variety of online civic activities, including signing a petition, contacting a government official, and expressing their political views. People in the 18-to-34 age group registered the highest level of online civic involvement. In the case of the exact same set of civic activities, but this time carried out offline, older Americans were considerably more engaged than the young.

TABLE 5.1

Civic Engagement Online and Offline (in percentages)

	High school	Some college	College graduate	Age 18–34	Age 35–54	Age 55+
Online civic engagement	25	40	51	41	33	27
Offline civic engagement	29	44	50	35	39	42

Source: Data from A. Smith. (2013). *Civic engagement in the digital age.* Retrieved September 3, 2021, from the Pew Research Center website: http://www.pewinternet.org/2013/04/25/civic-engagement -in-the-digital-age/.

The Partisan Polarization Hypothesis

Before the advent of television, campaigns were conducted primarily through partisan channels. Candidates would travel across the country delivering their stump speeches and greeting voters in person. Voters were thought to simplify their choices by relying on the candidates and positions of their preferred political party. Selective exposure on a partisan basis was considered the principal means by which candidates reached the public; voters were motivated to seek out information that supported rather than challenged their political beliefs.

The notion that an individual's partisan affiliation motivates exposure to news is grounded in the theory of cognitive dissonance, which posits that the acquisition of information at odds with one's preexisting beliefs is uncomfortable and therefore to be avoided. Instead, people are thought to prefer acquiring information that reinforces their beliefs and attitudes. By this theory, for example, Republicans would be expected to avoid news stories supportive of President Biden and seek out stories presenting him in an unfavorable light.

Early studies of political campaigns documented the tendency of partisan voters to report greater exposure to appeals from the candidate or party they preferred. This pattern of motivated exposure to congenial information sources was thought to explain the surprising finding that campaigns reinforced rather than changed the attitudes of voters. (We will address this finding in greater detail in Chapter 7.) In what would prove to be an early incarnation of concern over the "*Daily Me*" (a concept we'll discuss in a moment), researchers condemned the preference for congenial information as antithetical to the democratic ideal of informed choice:

> In recent years there has been a good deal of talk by men of good will about
> the desirability and necessity of guaranteeing the free exchange of ideas in the
> market place of public opinion. Such talk has centered upon the problem of
> keeping free the channels of expression and communication. Now we find that
> the consumers of ideas, if they have made a decision on the issue, themselves
> erect high tariff walls against alien notions. (Lazarsfeld, Berelson, & Gaudet,
> 1948, p. 89)

As party-based campaigns were replaced by media-based campaigns, the opportunities for encountering partisan sources gradually disappeared. Television news became the dominant source of public affairs information. The norms of objective journalism meant that no matter which network voters tuned in to, they encountered the very same set of news reports, according balanced attention to parties, candidates, or points of view (see Robinson & Sheehan, 1983). In the era of old media, accordingly, it made little difference where voters obtained their news. The flow of news amounted to an information commons. Americans of all walks of life and political inclination, wherever they turned, encountered the same stream of fact and information.

Given the difficulty of seeking out politically congenial news, research on selective exposure during the era of old media yielded equivocal results. In several instances, what seemed to be motivated or deliberate selective exposure turned out to occur on a de facto (by-product) basis instead: for instance, Republicans were more likely to encounter pro-Republican information as a result of their homogeneous social milieu rather than through any active choices to avoid information that seemed to favor Democrats (see Sears & Freedman, 1967). Today, the very same homogeneity in the composition of online social networks means that people more often than not are prompted to pay attention to news stories sent to them by friends with whom they are likely to agree.

It is not a coincidence that the revolution in information technology and the increased availability of news sources have been accompanied by increasing political polarization. When defined in terms of political ideology, polarization appears to have spread from the elite level to the level of mass public opinion (Abramowitz & Saunders, 2006; Jacobson, 2006; for a dissenting view, see Fiorina, 2017). When defined in terms of partisans' feelings toward their opponents—a phenomenon known as *affective* polarization—the evidence of increased polarization is unequivocal. As we will document in Chapters 7 and 8, Democrats' and Republicans' hostility toward their opponents has steadily intensified to the point that polarized assessments of presidential performance are higher today than at any other time in the history of polling. According to an average of Gallup polls taken during the Trump presidency, Republicans were more likely than Democrats to approve of Trump by an average margin of 81 percent.

The increased level of interparty animus may reflect increasingly segregated streams of political communication and news audiences that are ever more polarized. People who feel strongly about the correctness of their cause or policy preferences are more likely to seek out information they believe is consistent with their preferences. But while as recently as 25 years ago these partisans would have been hard-pressed to find overtly partisan sources of information, today the task has been simplified. In the case of Republicans, all they need to do is tune in to Fox News or access Breitbart.com. For their part, viewers on the left can seek out credible yet sympathetic news programming on MSNBC or the HuffPost.

There is a growing body of evidence suggesting that consumers with a strong partisan preference are motivated to exercise selectivity in their news choices. In the first place, in keeping with what is known as the hostile media phenomenon, partisans of either side have become more likely to impute bias to mainstream news sources (Smith, Lichter, & Harris, 1997). As we noted in Chapter 3, skeptical assessments of the media are most widespread among Republicans, who are twice as likely as Democrats to rate major news outlets committed to the norms of point-counterpoint journalism (such as the three network newscasts, the weekly news magazines, and major newspapers) as biased in favor of liberals (Pew Research Center, 2017). Republicans' hostility toward the mainstream media is sufficiently intense that sustained press criticism of Republican candidates actually boosts their standing among Republican voters. In the aftermath of the widespread media criticism of Republican congresswoman Marjorie Greene's incendiary comments concerning school shootings (she claimed they never occurred) and California wildfires (she claimed they were started by Jewish bankers), she raised $3.2 million in the first quarter of 2021, setting a fund-raising record for a first-term representative. In recent years, but especially after the election of Barack Obama, Democrats have also begun to express perceptions of media bias against their point of view (Pew Research Center, 2011).

Experimental studies of online news consumption confirm the tendency of partisans to self-select into distinct audiences. In an early study administered on a national sample in 2006, the researchers manipulated the source of online news stories in five different subject matter areas ranging from national politics and the Iraq War to vacation destinations and sports (Iyengar & Hahn, 2009). Depending on the category to which participants were assigned, the very same news headline was attributed either to Fox News, NPR, CNN, or BBC. Participants were asked which of the four different headlines they would prefer to read, if any. The results were unequivocal: Republicans and conservatives were much more likely to select news stories from Fox, while Democrats and liberals avoided Fox in favor of NPR and CNN. Especially striking was the finding that the conservatives' preference for Fox applied not only to hard news (such as national politics, the war in Iraq, and healthcare) but also to soft news stories about travel and sports. The polarization of the news audience extends even to nonpolitical subject matter.

These results from the 2006 study stand in sharp contrast to work from the pre-internet era showing very little evidence of politically motivated news selection. In a similar study of exposure to campaign rhetoric, carried out over the course of the 2000 campaign, researchers detected only modest traces of partisan selectivity (see Iyengar, Hahn, Krosnick, & Walker, 2008).

In this earlier study, the investigators compiled a large selection of campaign speeches by the two major presidential candidates (Al Gore and George W. Bush) along with a full set of the candidates' television advertisements. This material was assembled on an interactive, multimedia CD and distributed a few weeks before the election to a representative sample of registered voters with internet access.[2] The CD tracking data in this study showed only weak traces of a preference for information from the in-party candidate. Although Republicans and conservatives were somewhat more likely to seek out information from the Bush campaign, liberals and Democrats showed no preference for speeches or advertisements for Gore over those for Bush. These findings suggest either that the intensity of partisan identity was higher among Republicans in 2000 or that selective exposure had already become habituated among Republicans because they were provided earlier opportunities than Democrats (with the launch of Fox News in 1996) to engage in biased information seeking. The data from both the 2006 news selection study and a 2012 follow-up suggest that Democrats are now keeping pace. In 2000, very few Democrats in the CD study showed an aversion to speeches from then-Governor Bush, but by 2012, virtually no Democrats selected Fox News, and a plurality opted for MSNBC or Huffington Post as their preferred providers (see Lelkes, Sood, & Iyengar, 2017). This pattern of "equal opportunity" selectivity also appears in the Web-browsing literature we describe next.

The experimental research on selective exposure is compelling because it demonstrates that partisan preferences are a major cause of news outlet preferences. But do the findings on selective exposure generalize to the news audience at large and to the world of online news, where partisan sources are the most available? Large-scale studies of Web-browsing behavior initially did not corroborate the experimental research. In their pioneering analysis of Americans' Web-browsing behavior (conducted in 2008), Matthew Gentzkow and Jesse Shapiro (2011) found that online audiences were only slightly more segregated than audiences for network or cable news. They concluded that "Internet news consumers with homogeneous news diets are rare. These findings may mitigate concerns . . . that the Internet will increase ideological polarization and threaten democracy" (p. 1,831).

More recent work, however, suggests that online audiences are becoming more segregated. A 2013 study (also tracking Web-browsing behavior) showed that although most people relied on ideologically diverse online sources such as Web aggregators (Flaxman, Goel, & Rao, 2016), audience segregation tended to increase among individuals who used search engines to locate news stories and among social media users who encountered links in their news feed. Both these pathways to news exposure feature personalized algorithms that make it more likely that individuals encounter information consistent with their political loyalties.

The Web-browsing literature to date has not focused on news consumption during political campaigns, when partisans are especially motivated to support their "team." But in a pair of recent studies, Stanford researchers tracked exposure to online news among a national sample between August and December 2016, the closing stages of an extremely divisive presidential campaign (Peterson, Goel, & Iyengar, 2017; Tyler, Grimmer, & Iyengar, 2021). Their results showed a substantial divide in the browsing behavior of Democrats and Republicans, more so than in previous studies. Republicans, on average, visited news websites with an average audience share that was 57 percent Republican, while Democrats visited domains with an audience share of 68 percent Democrat. This difference, although substantial, represents less than a complete partisan divide in online news consumption. However, the dominance of a few heavily trafficked portal websites (for example, Yahoo News, AOL, and MSN) that provide news and a variety of other products (for example, e-mail accounts) contributes to the finding of overlap in the browsing behavior of partisans. When these portal sites are excluded from consideration and the analysis of selective exposure is limited to dedicated news sites (for example, CNN.com), the level of selectivity increases significantly. In their recent analysis, Matthew Tyler and colleagues (2021) showed that during the 2016 campaign Democrats and Republicans relied heavily on distinct sets of news providers with very little partisan overlap in the audience. This study provided further evidence of selective exposure in the form of increased news consumption by partisans immediately following events seen as favorable to their candidate. For instance, in the days following the release of the infamous *Access Hollywood* tape in which Trump bragged about his sexual exploits, Democrats but not Republicans increased their visits to news sites.

Finally, there is evidence that the diffusion of high-speed internet in and of itself has contributed to partisans' ability to exercise selective exposure. In those parts of the country where broadband is more available, exposure to partisan news sites is greater (Lelkes, Sood, & Iyengar, 2017), suggesting that as the time and effort needed to locate information has fallen, partisans have become more likely to express their political identity in their Web-browsing activity. This study also demonstrates that the availability of broadband contributes to polarization by facilitating exposure to partisan news; partisans without access to broadband were far less likely to access partisan sites.

The Issue Public Hypothesis

The third and final account of selective exposure to information is based on differing levels of interest in particular political issues. In their original review of selective exposure research, David Sears and Jonathan Freedman (1967) identified *utility-based selectivity* as a viable alternative to partisan consistency as a motive for seeking political information. They argued that what individuals paid attention to would depend on how useful they perceived the different pieces of information to be rather than on how much they anticipated agreeing with the implications of the information. In this view, people who derive special benefits from particular government policies are expected to be more inclined to prick up their ears when news programs mention developments concerning these policies (such as senior citizens or those nearing retirement in response to mention of Social Security).

A considerable body of evidence suggests that people do, in fact, allocate their attention according to the personal relevance or utility of information. For instance, Jon Krosnick (1990) found that people express greater interest in policy issues that touch them directly and toward which they have developed attitudes of great personal importance. To attach importance to a particular policy attitude is to become a member of that policy's issue public. For instance, the issues of gay rights and abortion motivate evangelical Christians to become active in political campaigns (Han, 2009).

The role of issue publics in the consumption of conventional news was examined in the previously cited study by Price and Zaller (1993), who carried out several tests of the hypothesis that people whose personal background suggested they might belong to an issue public were more likely to recall news stories bearing on their issue of importance. The results indicated only limited support for the hypothesis: in only about half of the tests, the group identified as the issue public had higher recall of stories bearing on that issue.[3]

In a related investigation of issue publics by Shanto Iyengar (1990), recall of television news reports about Social Security and racial discrimination was significantly higher among older and minority viewers, respectively, than among younger and White viewers. In addition to recalling more stories about race, African Americans proved more informed about matters of civil rights than Whites were, despite the latter group's significantly greater knowledge of overall political information. Other scholars have uncovered a similar pattern with gender: on women's issues, women tend to be better informed than men.

The importance of issue public membership to the use of new media was one of the main lessons of the 2000 CD tracking study. The researchers identified eight different issue publics. The "defense issue public," for instance, was identified as all study participants who had served in the military, and the "Social Security issue public" consisted of all retired participants. In six of the eight tests, members of the issue public visited greater numbers of CD pages concerning the issue of interest. When compared with nonmembers, members of issue publics registered more page visits on an order of magnitude ranging from 50 percent (for the "education issue public") to 80 percent (for the "abortion issue public").

In a recent test of the issue public hypothesis, Jonathan Mummolo (2017) found that, on average, people affected by particular issues were more likely to click on news reports addressing these issues than reports addressing other issues by more than 10 percent. The effects of issue relevance on interest in news reports far exceeded the effects of the ideological affiliation of the source, providing the relevance served to weaken or neutralize the effects of source cues. In general, he found that the two manipulations operated independently of each other. Issue relevance did not weaken the effects of source cues, nor did the partisan affiliation of the source reduce receivers' interest in personally relevant subjects. This study, however, did not consider news coverage of campaigns or individual politicians, subjects that are especially relevant to partisans.

To sum up, the evidence suggests that exposure to political information is determined by multiple factors: the desire to keep up with politics generally, to acquire information that is consistent with existing political preferences, and to learn about issues of personal interest. In the case of online news, the evidence suggests that party identification is increasingly becoming an important determinant of consumers' source preferences. Online news organizations now have some incentive to cater to their viewers' political preferences (Mullainathan & Schleifer, 2005). The very same partisanship seen in media behavior also applies to the world of cable television news. The emergence of Fox News as the leading cable provider is testimony to the viability of partisan news. Between 2000 and 2010, Fox News increased the size of its regular audience by some 50 percent, while CNN, which remains committed to point-counterpoint journalism, found itself mired in last place. MSNBC, after deciding to position itself as the network of the left, has used programming that features the liberal commentators Rachel Maddow and Lawrence O'Donnell to overtake CNN in the ratings. The competition between Fox and MSNBC for the top cable spot has recently heated up. Following the election of Donald Trump, the ratings for most of the prime-time programs offered by MSNBC dramatically increased. Apparently, disappointment and discontent with the surprise result prompted many Democrats to seek "solace" in the form of anti-Trump commentary available only from MSNBC. Once

Trump left office in 2021, MSNBC's ratings dropped and Fox regained its market dominance.

SOCIAL MEDIA AS A NEWS SOURCE: IMPLICATIONS FOR SELECTIVE EXPOSURE

Perhaps the most transforming aspect of technology has been the creation of huge online social networks. Facebook, which was founded in 2004, now has more than 225 million users in the United States alone. Seventy percent of American adults have a Facebook account, and according to a 2017 Pew survey, two-thirds of them say they encounter news there (36 percent say they do so on a regular basis). This translates to a large chunk of the adult population, 39 percent to be precise. For our purposes, what is especially important is that Facebook users not only exchange personal information but also share news and other forms of media, with 50 percent of Facebook users reporting having reposted a news story, video, or image (Pew Research Center, 2017). In fact, there is so much recirculation of media reports that Facebook has emerged as a major source of traffic to the websites of news organizations. For years, the major news sites depended on the big search engines (such as Google and Yahoo) for a major share of their internet traffic. Since 2010, however, Facebook users make up an increasing share of the visitors to news sites, by some estimates providing as much as 40 percent of the referral traffic by 2016 (VanNest, 2016; Ingram, 2015). A 2019 Pew survey showed that 18 percent of Americans say they get most of their political news on social media (Pew Research Center, 2020); thus, for many Americans, Facebook has become a significant source of political information (see Messing, 2013).[4]

Similar to interpersonal networks, online social networks are politically homogeneous; a study of the composition of friendship groups on Facebook found striking levels of ideological agreement. Liberals have few conservative friends (around 20 percent of their network), and the level of agreement is even greater—around 82 percent—for conservatives (Bakshy, Messing, & Adamic, 2015). Since Facebook users' encounters with political information reflect the content that is shared by their friends, there is a clear partisan bias to information exposure. Democrats tend to be exposed to more left-leaning content, while Republicans encounter more right-leaning content. In many respects, this process of news recirculation matches the classic concept of de facto selectivity, the idea that people encounter congenial information not because they actively seek it out but because the people they interact with most often share their political views. Facebook users do not deliberately seek out information that conforms to their political preferences. Instead, they find themselves in the path of news stories that their friends choose to circulate. Furthermore, the data from Facebook suggest that news reports from partisan sources are more likely to be circulated. In fact, the two news organizations with the highest recirculation rates in 2013 on Facebook were Fox News and HuffPost, both offering a distinct partisan slant on events (see Messing, 2013).

While the political composition of online social networks facilitates exposure to agreeable information, news exposure via social media is also shaped by powerful nonpartisan cues. One such indicator is related to topics or subject matter considered trendy or momentarily popular. Research on Facebook news consumption suggests that popularity cues (the number of people who "like" a particular story) are just as powerful determinants of attention, if not more so, than ideological agreement (Messing & Westwood, 2014). Other experiments show that in the context of the Facebook News Feed, individuals are more likely to share news they receive from strong rather than weak ties (Bakshy, Rosenn, Marlow, & Adamic, 2012).

The widespread use of social media and the ease with which "producers" of information can gain access to millions of people has made online networks an especially attractive platform for propaganda campaigns. Not only is there a vast audience; campaigns can also target their messages appropriately to match the political profile of their audience because the interests and tastes of individual users (their social media history) are known. Moreover, it is relatively costless to establish "fake" accounts on Facebook and Twitter and to deliver messages that are misleading or false. In fact, the economic incentives driving social media companies are no different from the standard business model; the more eyeballs one attracts, the more money goes in the pockets of the information provider. The more sensationalized the post, the more likely people are to share and comment on the information, thus elevating the post's "ranking" and its capacity to generate revenue. Further contributing to the spread of misinformation (a phenomenon we address in greater detail in Chapter 8), Facebook applies a double standard to the accuracy of posts from ordinary citizens as opposed to political figures. Unlike the former, whose posts can be flagged as inaccurate or taken down, political figures are free to post misleading and inflammatory comments on the grounds these posts are "newsworthy." (According to the *Washington Post*, Facebook implemented this exemption in response to Trump's social media behavior during the 2016 campaign.) Not surprisingly, Trump and other leaders around the globe have taken advantage of this freedom to spread lies and misinformation. Together, these features of the social media platform created a perfect storm in 2016 as operatives associated with the regime of Vladimir Putin attempted to use Facebook and Twitter to strengthen the candidacy of Donald Trump at Hillary Clinton's expense.

The Russian social media ad campaign was part of a broader effort to circulate information damaging to Hillary Clinton's candidacy. Unlike conventional news organizations that have strict editorial standards and procedures for verifying the accuracy of information, social media venues initially did not discriminate against posts that are inaccurate. (As we will see, they did take steps to remove inaccurate posts following the 2016 election.) On more than one occasion, Mark Zuckerberg has insisted that Facebook is not a news organization but a technology company. The absence of editorial control makes it possible for purveyors of rumor and falsehoods to reach a vast audience. Teenagers in Albania seeking to make quick money, proponents of conspiracy theories, and agents of the Kremlin all circulated false reports about the presidential election (see Subramaniam, 2017; Townsend, 2016). Russian operatives created a number of websites that disseminated election-related information. DCLeaks.com, a site linked to the Russian intelligence agency GRU, posted embarrassing e-mails from senior members of the Clinton team that had been hacked from the Democratic National Committee server. Another site, End-theFed.com, posted a number of false news stories, including one that Pope Francis had endorsed Donald Trump and another that FBI director James Comey was paid millions by the Clinton Foundation. The fake news story that gained the most notoriety linked Hillary Clinton with an alleged child sex ring operated out of a Washington, DC, pizzeria. The story originated on an internet message board; was picked up by conservative-oriented bloggers, such as InfoWars; spread to Reddit; and eventually landed on Facebook, where it quickly went viral. Following the election, a man from North Carolina, armed with an assault rifle, stormed into the pizzeria to "rescue" the children.

Developments on Twitter were no less ominous. As many as 2,700 accounts could be traced to the Internet Research Agency, the propaganda arm of the Kremlin. These accounts delivered 131,000 tweets on matters concerning the election. The vast majority of these messages came from networks of "bots," interconnected accounts programmed to spew out automated content and hashtags—for instance, #WarAgainstDemocrats—several times a minute. Not surprisingly, these mass-produced messages favored Donald Trump over Hillary Clinton by a wide margin (Bessi & Ferrara, 2016; see also Kollanyi, Howard, & Wooley, 2016). The typical bot message featured unflattering images of Clinton, made multiple references to her use of a private e-mail server, or posted blatantly false news reports (for example, that she was about to be arrested).

CASE STUDY:

The "Weaponizing" of Social Media in the 2016 Presidential Campaign

Testifying before the Senate Intelligence Committee in October 2017, the general counsel for Facebook revealed that in the period leading up to the 2016 election, messages posted from Russian accounts had reached 150 million Americans. Russians also invested $150,000 in Facebook ads during the 2016 campaign, many of them depicting Hillary Clinton in unflattering terms. Executives from Twitter and Google provided estimates of equally heavy traffic on their platforms (YouTube in the case of Google) from Russian accounts. At the conclusion of the hearing, when it was clear that the senior management of the social media giants had been caught unaware by the systematic efforts of a foreign government to sway American voters, Senator Richard Burr— chairman of the Intelligence Committee— noted that the testimony documented "the deliberate and multi-faceted manipulation of the American people by agents of a hostile power" (Timberg, Shaban, & Dwoskin, 2017).

In the aftermath of the 2016 election, there was bipartisan agreement—based on the expert judgment of every national security agency in the United States—that the Russians had used social media in a brazen attempt to influence the American election from abroad and that their goal was to weaken Hillary Clinton and strengthen Donald Trump. The Russian social media campaign

was sophisticated and multipronged. In addition to advertising, Russian sources posted controversial messages designed to attract comment and attention. Many of their posts featured racially charged themes—police shootings and rallies by the Black Lives Matter movement—as well as other issues on which Americans were deeply divided, such as immigration and gun control. One Russian-sponsored Facebook page urged readers to attend a rally opposing the "Islamization of Texas." A Russian account formed the Facebook group Defend the Second, which took out Facebook ads opposing gun control and targeting Facebook users whose interests included the National Rifle Association, Second Amendment Sisters, and Gun Owners of America. In his testimony before Congress in 2018, Facebook CEO Mark Zuckerberg reversed himself, acknowledging not only the sophistication of the Russian propaganda campaign but also that the company had been slow to recognize the Russian efforts to sway public opinion (Kang, Hsu, Roose, Singer, & Rosenberg, 2018).

According to the official analysis of the 2020 election carried out by the National Intelligence Council (2021), the Kremlin attempted to replicate its interference by coordinating a social media campaign aimed at discrediting Joe Biden. Russian accounts circulated misinformation about Biden's alleged corrupt involvement with Ukrainian officials and highlighted US domestic conflicts, including the Black Lives Matter protests. Most of the Russian social media activity originated at the same Internet Research Agency (renamed as Lakhta Internet Research in 2018).

Interestingly, the Russians were not the only foreign actors attempting to sow disinformation during the 2020 campaign. The Iranians mounted a cyber campaign designed to discredit President Trump.

Iranian posts on Facebook criticized Trump's response to the pandemic, and, in a highly sophisticated e-mail operation aimed at discrediting supporters of Trump, Iranian agents sent threatening messages purporting to be from the Proud Boys to thousands of Democratic voters in battleground states demanding that they change their party registration. In comparison with the Russian efforts, however, the Iranian disinformation campaign occurred on a smaller scale.

What was the level of exposure on social media to these patently false reports? An analysis by BuzzFeed News found that Facebook users certainly noticed them. Using a measure of "audience share" (based on the number of users who shared, liked, or commented on a fake story), BuzzFeed reported that interest in the fake stories exceeded interest in genuine news stories produced by mainstream news organizations in the months immediately preceding the election (see Figure 5.6). Twenty-three of the top-performing false stories circulating on Facebook concerned the election. These stories received nearly 9 million shares, while the top 20 real stories were shared by only 7 million.

It took several months for Facebook and Twitter to acknowledge the fake news problem, suggesting that the significant advertising revenues being generated by the strong user interest in fake posts took precedence over concerns about the integrity of the platform and the potential distorting impact on the election. Executives from Facebook were quick to point out that the Russian ad campaign represented a tiny sliver of all the ads that aired on their network. (The Trump and Clinton campaigns together spent some $80 million advertising on Facebook.) Initially, the corporate response was to minimize the extent of the problem. Following the election, Facebook CEO Mark Zuckerberg debunked the possibility of any opinion manipulation: "Personally, I think the idea that fake news on Facebook—of which it's a small amount of content—influenced the election in any way is a pretty crazy idea" (Seetharaman, 2016). Twitter also discounted the importance of fake news. According to a Twitter spokesperson, "Anyone who claims that automated spam accounts that tweeted

FIGURE 5.6

Social Media Interest in Fake News, February–November 2016

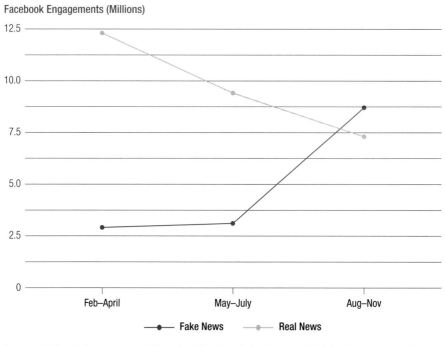

Facebook Engagements (Millions)

- ●— Fake News   ●--- Real News

about the U.S. election had an effect on voters' opinions or influenced the national Twitter conversation clearly underestimates voters and fails to understand how Twitter works" (Markoff, 2016).

Eventually, news coverage of the fake news stories and increasing alarm in policy-making circles that the integrity of the American electoral process had been compromised forced both Facebook and Twitter to admit to the true extent of the problem, acknowledge responsibility, and develop appropriate safeguards. At Facebook, these took the form of three interventions. First, in an attempt to short-circuit the economic incentives, the company prohibited advertisers from linking to stories flagged as false. The identification process itself was delegated to a consortium of major fact-checking organizations (including PolitiFact and FactCheck.org). Once identified, these posts were flagged as suspicious, with clearly visible warnings ("Before you share this story, you might want to know that independent fact-checkers disputed its accuracy"). Users were also directed to "related articles" by the fact-checkers. Initial data released by Facebook in 2018 indicate that these interventions are having some impact. In the first three months of 2018, Facebook identified and shut down 583 million fake accounts on the site (Rosen, 2018). At Twitter, where there is minimal editorial screening of incoming content, the company's response was limited to shutting down hundreds of accounts linked to Russian operatives.

Self-regulation by the social media companies intensified after the 2020 election. In the aftermath of the violence on January 6, both Facebook and Twitter suspended Trump's social media access. Twitter enacted a permanent suspension on the grounds that Trump's tweets had incited the violence. For their part, Facebook banned Trump indefinitely, effective ending his presence on their platform. Facebook's Oversight Board—a group made up of distinguished jurists, journalists, and scholars—upheld management's decision in May 2021 but rejected the notion of an indefinite expulsion. They ruled that Facebook must either make the ban permanent or provide a specific timeline for ending it. They gave Facebook six months to make this decision. Facebook ultimately decided to ban him from the platform until at least 2023, at which point they would decide whether to extend or rescind the ban.

Did the extensive circulation of fake news on social media have an impact on the outcome of the election? Many journalists and commentators suggested that Trump owed his election to the one-sided flow of information on social media (see, for instance, Kreiss & McGregor, 2018; Jamieson, 2020). In the absence of compelling experimental evidence, however, it is difficult to reach any firm conclusions (see Chapter 8 for a discussion of the types of evidence necessary for inferring the causal impact of media messages). What is clear is that any potential impact, given the slant of fake news, would have favored Trump over Clinton. Given the razor-thin margin of Mr. Trump's victory, the fake news campaign might well have made the difference. After all, defections from Trump to Clinton on the part of fewer than 40,000 voters would have flipped the results in Michigan, Wisconsin, and Pennsylvania and resulted in a Clinton Electoral College victory.

What little evidence we do have on voters' reactions to fake news stories in 2016 does not support the inference that these stories were pivotal to the outcome. In the first place, most of the fake news reports were extremely implausible (see Pennycook, Cannon, & Rand, 2017), and few Americans believed in their accuracy. In a study by Hunt Alcott and Matthew Gentzkow (2017), Americans from across the country were shown headlines corresponding to the major fake news stories from the 2016 campaign, and more than 90 percent of the respondents correctly identified the reports as false. On the basis of the percentage of their respondents that accurately recalled having seen a fake news report and the extent to which these reports were shared on Facebook, the authors calculated that the average American voter saw and could remember about one fake news report. Given this level of exposure (and the additional assumption that a fake news story is equally persuasive as a political advertisement), the authors went on to estimate that the persuasive impact of exposure to fake news was too small (around one-hundredth of 1 percentage point) to have altered the outcome of the election, even in the most closely contested states.

While acknowledging that the actual impact of foreign interventions on voter behavior in the 2016 and 2020 elections is unknown and will likely be debated for many years, there is no denying that these interventions occurred— on an unprecedented scale—in both presidential campaigns. Despite the steps taken by the social media giants to crack down on fake accounts, the 2020 election demonstrated continuing efforts by foreign actors to influence American voters. The porousness of social media platforms, the ease with which individuals can fabricate their identities, and the vast quantity of misleading information on offer all served as warning signals to policy makers. At the congressional hearings held after the 2016 election, executives from Facebook, Twitter, and YouTube (Google) were subjected to scathing criticism. With the Democratic takeover of Congress in 2020, it appeared likely that these companies would be subjected to greater regulation targeting foreign-based disinformation campaigns. But, as of August 2022, Congress has failed to act.

IMPACT OF THE INTERNET ON POLITICAL ORGANIZATIONS

In democratic societies, it goes without saying that candidates are attracted to media outlets in direct proportion to the size of their audience. In the early days of the internet, most campaigns felt it unnecessary to establish a Web presence. As the technology spread and innovative new forms of online networking attracted large numbers of users, so too did the incentives for internet-based campaigning. By 2008, the payoffs of internet-based campaigning were sufficient to allow a relatively unknown candidate to capture the Democratic presidential nomination.

In principle, campaigns can harness the immense networking power of the internet to accomplish multiple campaign objectives, including fund-raising; producing and distributing information that increases the candidate's visibility and likability; and most critically, recruiting and mobilizing a cadre of activists.

To date, the impact of technology has been greatest on the goal of mobilization. Although other facets of the campaign remain more oriented toward conventional (especially broadcast) media because there are still more voters to be reached in front of their television sets than at their computers and smartphones, the gap is narrowing. With the growth of video streaming and the speed with which videos circulate around the Web, campaigns are increasingly targeting online audiences. (Exactly what campaigns do to influence public opinion is the subject of Chapter 6.) Nonetheless, it is the ability to organize and communicate with online networks of supporters that has transformed the conduct of campaigns.

Before the internet, candidates recruited volunteers and raised money by making phone calls, sending mass mailings, or going door to door. These low-tech forms of mobilization and fund-raising were both capital- and time-intensive; successful campaigns had an existing organization, professional (paid) staff, and access to phone banks or mailing lists of prospective supporters. Candidates themselves might spend long hours on the phone with prospective donors. The amount of time between the initial contact and receipt of a financial contribution might take weeks or even months. These infrastructure costs made it nearly impossible for lesser-known candidates to develop and manage a hard-core group of activists.

By lowering the cost of communication, the internet has opened up the political arena by enabling any group, no matter how large or small its electoral constituency, to assemble a network of supporters. Any candidate with the ability to mount a basic website can instantly sign up volunteers and send them assignments for upcoming events, thus developing the nucleus of a viable field organization. Once formed, these groups become smart mobs, capable of acting in a coordinated manner despite the absence of any face-to-face contact (for examples of smart mobs in action, see Rheingold, 2002). In effect, the internet has lowered the eligibility requirements for groups to engage in collective action.

In this country, the first instance of a campaign organization using the internet to organize its supporters was Jesse Ventura's 1998 campaign for governor of Minnesota. Running as the Reform Party candidate, Ventura was heavily outspent by his Republican and Democratic opponents. But Ventura's campaign launched a website in early 1998 (at a monthly cost of under $30) and began to develop a statewide e-mail list of volunteers. The list was used to publicize information about local organizational meetings; one such meeting drew a standing-room-only crowd of more than 250 people.

Despite being outspent and outstaffed by his opponents (the campaign had only one paid staff member, the campaign manager), Ventura was elected governor. It is difficult to say precisely how much difference Ventura's use of technology made to the upset victory. After all, his unusual persona and career as a professional wrestler combined to make him a highly visible candidate, and his antigovernment, populist platform resonated well in a state with a long history of supporting progressive reformers. In one respect, however, the payoff of using technology was clear: young people, who are most likely to be reached online, turned out to vote in large numbers. Over half of them voted for Ventura—more than enough to account for the margin of his victory.

The success of the Ventura campaign made it clear to campaign operatives that the internet could and should be exploited for political action. By 2000, all reputable candidates had elaborate, interactive websites and online contacts of prospective supporters. It was during the 2004 campaign that internet campaigning came into its own. Vermont governor Howard Dean tied his presidential candidacy inextricably to the internet. Although Dean was eventually forced to withdraw from the campaign for lack of support, his campaign's innovative use of technology contributed to his meteoric rise from the relatively unknown governor of a small state to the front-running contender for the Democratic nomination. The Dean campaign hired a full-time internet consultant. The next step was to use the networking portal Meetup.com to recruit supporters from across the nation. The Dean campaign used Meetup to schedule events, several of which were attended by the candidate himself. For the campaign, mailing out campaign materials was the only cost of maintaining this network of activists.

The most significant accomplishment of the 2004 Dean campaign was its ability to raise funds online. In one instance, the campaign responded to a Bush–Cheney $2,000-a-plate dinner (which raised $250,000) by hosting an online eat-in challenge featuring a Web page with an image of Dean eating a turkey sandwich and a "Contribute Now" button. In response, 9,700 people visited the page, and the campaign netted over $500,000. In the second quarter of 2003 alone, the campaign took in more than $7 million.

Given the Dean campaign's effective use of the internet to mobilize supporters, why did he fail to win even one primary? In the language of social scientists, the Dean campaign was doomed by a self-selection bias. The American technoliterati, most of whom were eager to drive Bush from the White House and who seized the opportunity to volunteer for Dean, were much too small a group to swing even a small-state primary. In other words, the Deaniacs were not representative of Democratic primary voters. A Pew Research Center survey of Dean activists found that 54 percent had attended graduate school (for all Democratic activists, the comparable figure was 11 percent)

New Media and Regime Change

In nondemocratic countries, the reduced costs of collective action have worked to the disadvantage of authoritarian rulers seeking to suppress dissent. In recent years, several dictatorships have been toppled mainly because anti-regime groups were able to mobilize thousands of their supporters to take to the streets. In what came to be known as the Arab Spring, authoritarian rule was ended in Tunisia, Egypt, and Libya, leading some to speculate that cell phones and text messages have become necessary ingredients of regime change. This is certainly the view taken by dictators, who typically disrupt internet and cell-phone service during periods of mass unrest. However, as a study of the 2011 Egyptian revolution suggests, such shutdowns made Egyptians living in urban areas more likely to take to the streets so that they could acquire information face-to-face, thus creating a cascade of protest activity that eventually forced President Mubarak to resign (Hassanpour, 2014). Of course, in countries without densely populated urban centers, where the population is dispersed across a wide area, the strategy of disrupting cellular communication may prove effective in neutralizing protest.

China provides an especially interesting case study of the technological challenges facing authoritarian governments. With the diffusion of the internet, large numbers of Chinese have become active on popular blog sites where they regularly post messages critical of government officials and voice displeasure with the Communist Party. The Chinese authorities, in response, have implemented a vast censorship operation (Shambaugh, 2007), taking down blog posts they deem objectionable (that is, those identified as potentially destabilizing). A systematic analysis of the content of the blog posts that attract censorship demonstrates that the messages most likely to be censored are not those criticizing the regime but messages referring to any form of collective action (King, Pan, & Roberts, 2013).

and that they were significantly more liberal and anti-Bush than mainstream Democrats (Pew Research Center, 2005). Dean's candidacy itself was clearly faithful to his supporters, but it also made Dean less appealing to most Democratic voters.

Thus, the main lesson of 2004 was that although the internet provided a cost-efficient means of developing a network of campaign workers and donors, it was not yet the best platform for candidates to appeal for votes. It is one thing to develop an electronic network of enthusiastic supporters; it is quite another to attract enough votes to win a primary election. In 2004, the internet was not yet competitive with television as a way of communicating with rank-and-file voters. In 2008, however, the story was quite different; it was now possible for the internet platform to be harnessed not just to mobilize activists and raise money but also to win votes.

INTERNET CAMPAIGNING COMES OF AGE

The 2008 presidential election was, in the words of the *Wall Street Journal,* "the first real Internet election" (Rhoads, 2008). And no one used the power of the Web more effectively than Barack Obama. According to Joe Trippi, the architect of Dean's groundbreaking campaign, "The tools [for elections] changed between 2004 and 2008. Barack Obama won every single caucus state that matters, and he did it because of those tools, because he was able to move thousands of people to organize" (Miller, 2008).

From the day he declared his candidacy in Springfield, Illinois (February 10, 2007), the campaign's sensitivity to online marketing was evident. Blue State Digital, the Democratic consulting firm that had handled the Dean campaign, managed Obama's online campaign. The website barackobama.com was designed for a general audience; it attracted more than 2.6 million unique visitors, while visitors to the McCain website numbered fewer than half that (Rhoads, 2008). Another site, my.barackobama.com, was designed to provide resources (scheduling, call lists, fund-raising scripts) to volunteers and to encourage blogging. Eventually, more than 2 million individuals posted user profiles at my.barackobama.com; 200,000 campaign events were planned; and 35,000 volunteer groups were formed. All the major social networking sites from Facebook and MySpace to BlackPlanet and AsianAve were actively engaged. More than 3 million Facebook users became fans of Obama's Facebook page.

Given the interactive nature of online communication, the Obama campaign was able to compile a massive database of supporters by requesting e-mail addresses and phone numbers whenever a person visited the website. Using cookies, the campaign tracked the Web-browsing behavior of online supporters. Based on the browsing profile of a particular voter, the campaign would have a good idea of that voter's interests and then could e-mail that voter messages or banner ads of likely interest.

In developing a vast network of supporters and volunteers, Obama's use of the internet was no different from other candidates'. But where the campaign broke new ground was in its systematic use of online campaign communication. YouTube played a critical role in the dissemination of campaign messages. Faced with the controversy surrounding his friendship with Reverend Jeremiah Wright, the Obama campaign decided to meet the uproar head-on in a prime-time speech on the subject of race relations (see Video Archive 5.1). Obama used the speech both to distance himself from Wright and to call for racial understanding and reconciliation. On YouTube the speech was immediately viewed by more than a million people. By the end of the campaign, the entire speech had been viewed 7 million times online (Hill, 2009).

Video Archive 5.1
Obama Race Speech
(Introduction)

The most recent development in the gradual encroachment of technology into campaign management, also pioneered by the Obama team, is the incorporation of sophisticated data metrics into day-to-day decision making. The 2012 Obama campaign hired a major data analytics firm to test the persuasion potential of TV ads and develop detailed profiles of voters in swing states based on their likelihood of voting for Obama. These profiles became the basis for targeted voter mobilization efforts on Election Day. The sophisticated use of big data continued in 2016. Hillary Clinton brought in an analytics team that included many veterans from the 2012 Obama campaign. They developed an algorithm—named Ada, after Ada Lovelace, a nineteenth-century mathematician—that provided daily data on the state of the race nationwide and in key battleground states. The campaign then used this information to make decisions concerning the candidate's travel schedule and the targeting of their television advertising. On the Republican side, the Trump campaign did not rely extensively on voter files to develop demographic and marketing profiles of potential supporters. "I've always felt it was overrated," Trump remarked back in May 2016. "Obama got the votes much more so than his data-processing machine. And I think the same is true with me" (Cilizza, 2016). However, the campaign did hire Cambridge Analytica, a consulting firm known for its expertise in reaching voters through social media. After the election, a former employee revealed that the company had harvested the Facebook activity of more than 80 million Americans without their consent to construct psychological profiles that could predict individuals' support for Donald Trump. (The ensuing scandal and loss of clients led Cambridge Analytica to declare bankruptcy in early 2018.) Eventually, the 2016 election set a new record for advertising on social media, with the total amount spent on Facebook ads alone exceeding $60 million.

FIGURE 5.7

Online Campaign Advertising, 2020

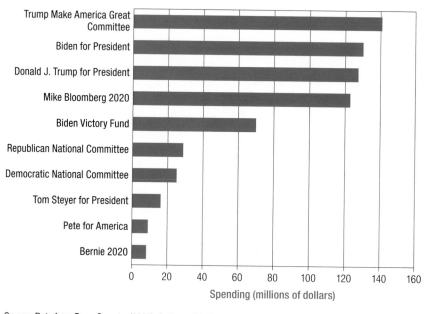

Source: Data from Open Secrets. (2020). Online political ad spending. Retrieved September 3, 2021, from the Open Secrets website: https://www.opensecrets.org/online-ads.

The COVID pandemic in 2020 forced campaigns to double down on their ad strategies, given the unavailability of in-person campaigning. Political advertising on social media and the internet increased exponentially, topping $1 billion. As shown in Figure 5.7, the presidential candidates alone spent more than $500 million on online ads. Billionaire Mike Bloomberg, by himself, accounted for $122 million of this total.

Our brief history of campaigning using the new-media platforms suggests several broad generalizations. First, the internet has made it possible for campaigns to reach and mobilize supporters at relatively low cost. Second, the internet is a rich source of campaign cash. Third, new sources of data and sophisticated data analyses make it possible for campaigns to target potential supporters with a high level of precision. Fourth, social media networks have emerged as important battlegrounds, raising the specter of foreign-based involvement in American campaigns. Finally, and most important, these developments make it possible for candidates to reach a large online audience on their own, thus making them autonomous from the news media.

CONCLUSION

The scholarly evidence concerning the emerging role of the internet in public life suggests that the audience for news is becoming more fragmented. Given the availability of unlimited choice, Americans with limited interest in politics prefer to avoid news coverage entirely. For those who care about politics, the amount of information and increased availability of online news sources forces them to exercise choice. Because many online media outlets deliver partisan messages, consumers can choose based on their partisan affiliation. Social media has emerged as an important platform for news consumption, and the homogeneity inherent in social networks provides further opportunities for partisans to encounter information supportive of their political preferences.

Even though partisans can still encounter objective, nonpartisan news coverage from mainstream news organizations, they are nonetheless apt to ignore or discount highly publicized facts when these facts are at odds with their political preferences. The heightened state of party polarization has led partisans to view mainstream news sources as biased against their side and to cling to inaccurate beliefs despite an abundance of evidence to the contrary. In the aftermath of the 2016 election, for instance, more than 60 percent of Republicans refused to acknowledge that the Russians had attempted to influence the election. This form of "motivated reasoning" in interpreting objective news reports is discussed in Chapter 8.

Quite apart from the ambiguous verdict of the scholarly literature concerning the effects of the internet on civic engagement or exposure to diverse points of view, there is a different reason to feel optimistic about the potential impact of technology on the political process. We have already documented that media-based campaigns fail to deliver substantive information. In place of the candidates' positions and past performance on the issues, news coverage gravitates inevitably toward the more entertaining facets of the campaign: the horse race, the strategy, and, whenever possible, instances of scandalous or unethical behavior. Against this backdrop, technology at least makes it possible for voters to bypass or supplement media treatment of the campaign and access information about the issues that affect them. Rather than waiting (typically in vain) for news organizations to report on the issues they care about, voters can take matters into their own hands and seek out information about the candidates' positions on these issues. This form of motivated exposure is hardly an impediment to deliberation: paying attention to what the candidates have to say on the issues facilitates issue-oriented voting; paying attention to the media circus does not.

Finally, the brief history of the campaigns and social movements that have embraced new forms of voter outreach make it clear that technology, in this respect at least, has leveled the political playing field. Even the poorest candidate has the capacity to publicize his or her candidacy and solicit support online, and grassroots protest movements are able to mount serious challenges to entrenched and ruthless dictators. As technology spreads even further and the next generation of software makes possible even closer contact and cooperation among like-minded individuals, we may expect the internet to become the principal arena for American campaigns.

Summary

1. The development of information technology and the spread of new media have changed the communication landscape. Traditional forms of communication were either point-to-point (between a single sender and recipient) or broadcast (between a single sender and multiple recipients). New media—particularly the internet—have broken down those distinctions. Any internet user can send messages to individual recipients and at the same time communicate with a worldwide audience. Moreover, unlike conventional media, internet-based communication is multichannel, allowing the intermingling of text, voice, still images, and video.

2. The internet has greatly increased both the amount and the variety of material available to the public, as well as consumers' control over the information to which they're exposed. There are three main arguments about how people choose which political communications they will recognize:
   - The *attentive public hypothesis* suggests that the act of seeking out political information is simply a matter of generic political interest. People captivated by politics tune in to all forms of news, while the apolitical majority tune out politics.
   - The *partisan polarization hypothesis* suggests that people prefer to encounter information that they find consistent with their beliefs. Some fear that if partisanship is the dominant basis of selectivity, the spread of new media will lead to increased political polarization, since liberals and conservatives will both have greater ability to select information sources that they agree with and to ignore others.
   - The *issue public hypothesis* suggests that people seek out information about subjects that are particularly important or interesting to them and tune out information about other subjects. Evidence for this type of selectivity has been more consistent than that for partisan polarization.

3. Online social networks such as Facebook have become important carriers of political information. Because online social networks are politically homogeneous, users are usually exposed to news and commentary consistent with their partisan leanings. The unregulated and uncontrolled nature of social media makes it possible for voters to encounter misleading and inaccurate information.

4. The widespread proliferation of the internet has increased its use to mobilize individuals for political action. It has been used to great effect by protest groups seeking to topple authoritarian rulers, by campaign organizations to raise funds and target electioneering activities, and, most recently, by agents of a foreign government to attempt to influence the 2016 and 2020 presidential elections.

FURTHER READINGS

Alcott, H., & Gentzkow, M. (2017). Social media and fake news in the 2016 election. *Journal of Economic Perspectives, 31*, 211–226.

Bessi, A., & Ferrera, E. (2016, November 7). Social bots distort the 2016 presidential election online discussion. *First Monday, 21*(11).

Flaxman, S., Goel, S., & Rao, J. M. (2016). Filter bubbles, echo chambers, and online news consumption. *Public Opinion Quarterly, 80*, 298–320.

Gentzkow, M., & Shapiro, J. (2011). Ideological segregation online and offline. *Quarterly Journal of Economics, 126*, 1799–1839.

Hassanpour, N. (2014). Media disruption and revolutionary unrest: Evidence from Mubarak's quasi-experiment. *Political Communication, 31*, 1–24.

Hindman, M. (2009). *The myth of digital democracy.* Princeton, NJ: Princeton University Press.

Ingram, M. (2015). Facebook has taken over from Google as a traffic source for news. Retrieved from http://fortune.com/2015/08/18/facebook-google/.

Iyengar, S., & Hahn, K. (2009). Red media, blue media: Evidence of ideological polarization in media use. *Journal of Communication, 59*, 19–39.

Mummolo, J. (2017). News from the other side: How topic relevance limits the prevalence of partisan selective exposure. *Journal of Politics, 78*(3), 763–773.

Sears, D. O., & Freedman, J. L. (1967). Selective exposure to information: A critical review. *Public Opinion Quarterly, 31*, 194–213.

Smith, A., Schlozman, K. L., Verba, S., & Brady, H. (2009). *The internet and civic engagement.* Washington, DC: Pew Research Center.

Sunstein, C. (2001). *Republic.com.* Princeton, NJ: Princeton University Press.

Tyler, M., Grimmer, J., and Iyengar, S. (2021). Partisan enclaves and information bazaars: Mapping selective exposure to online news. *Journal of Politics*, forthcoming. Retrieved from https://www.journals.uchicago.edu/doi/10.1086/716950.

NOTES

1. It is well known that interest in politics and other indicators of engagement in civic life are strongly correlated with education and socioeconomic status. In one sense, then, political interest is an indicator of access to and proficiency with information technology.

2. Production of the CD was made possible through the generous support of the Pew Charitable Trusts, the Carnegie Corporation, and the active cooperation of the Bush and Gore campaigns. Produced by the Political Communication Lab at Stanford University, the CD was titled *Vote 2004: Presidential Candidates in Their Own Words* and was distributed broadly to the general public as well as to the study participants.

3. Some of the authors' indicators of issue public membership were, at best, approximations. For example, "reading a great deal of international news in the newspaper" was seen as indicating membership in the issue public for international events.

4. In December 2017, in response to widespread criticism of the social media giant for having spread "fake news" during the 2016 campaign, Facebook announced that they were changing the algorithm that determined the prominence of posts within an individual's news feed to favor posts from individuals and downgrade posts from publishers or businesses.

6

Campaigning through the Media

In the weeks leading up to the 1948 election, President Harry Truman crisscrossed the country on his campaign train, making daily appearances before enthusiastic crowds of voters. Shaking hands, kissing babies, and greeting voters were standard practice in the era of in-person, retail politics.

By 1960, the rapid spread of television had altered the behavior of candidates. In-person appearances were time-consuming for the candidates and attracted only the most faithful of partisans. Most Americans, especially those lacking a strong party affiliation, stayed away from campaign events. These same people, however, watched lots of television. Candidates soon realized that television provided efficient access to a national audience. Unlike personal appearances, with their idiosyncratic hit-or-miss quality (attendance at an event might be cut in half by bad weather), televised news programs attracted a more predictable audience.

As a campaign medium, television provided still further advantages, including the ability to deliver different messages and appeals, depending on the needs and interests of particular television markets. Most notably, the medium of television advertising guaranteed campaigns maximum control over the content and form of their message. These ads ensured there would be no hecklers interrupting the candidate's message and distracting voters from the candidate's appeal; no news editors selecting the particular sound bites actually aired; and no hovering journalists probing for weaknesses or opponents standing ready to pounce on any misstatement of fact. From the perspective of candidates, television seemed to have it all.

Beginning in 1952, presidential campaigns began to experiment with different forms of television-based campaigning. The first political ads appeared in that year. During the 1960 presidential campaign, John F. Kennedy and Richard Nixon debated each other on four occasions before an average audience amounting to 60 percent of the US population. By 1968, campaigns were designed explicitly for television, and no serious campaign was without its cadre of full-time, highly paid media strategists. As the late Roger Ailes, the doyen of Republican campaign consultants (who later rose to be the CEO of Fox News), declared, "This is the beginning of a whole new concept. This is it. This is the way they'll be elected forevermore. The next guys will have to be performers" (Diamond & Bates, 1992, p. 398). Since the turn of the twenty-first century, video remains the dominant form of campaign communication, even though many people are watching not on their television set but on their smartphone. Campaign advertising has followed the same trajectory from television to the internet and, as noted in Chapter 5, to social media in particular.

Campaigns play out on two parallel stages, corresponding to *free media* (news coverage) and *paid media* (advertising). In most statewide and congressional races, advertising tends to dominate news as the principal stage for the simple reason that these campaigns attract only sparse news coverage. In recent contests for governor of California, for instance, less than 1 percent of all local news that was broadcast in October focused on the election to be held the next month. Unable to crack the newsworthiness barrier, gubernatorial candidates are forced to invest heavily in advertising. In the 2010 race for governor of California, between Republican Meg Whitman and Democrat Jerry Brown, the candidates spent more than $280 million, most of it on television ads. The 2018 gubernatorial contest in Illinois—between two billionaires—was almost as expensive, with total expenditures of $244 million. Campaigns for the US Senate also require heavy investments in advertising. In 2020, total spending in the 10 most expensive Senate races amounted to the staggering sum of $1.5 billion.

In contrast to statewide or congressional races, presidential races enjoy virtually unlimited news coverage, making the ad campaign only a small trickle in the cumulative message stream. This does not mean that advertising strategy is unimportant in presidential races—far from it. The continuous and often acrimonious conflict between journalists and candidates over the content of news coverage has only intensified the importance of advertising as the one truly unmediated form of campaign speech.

In 2016 Donald Trump elicited so much coverage his campaign scaled back spending on ads. Data from the 2020 cycle, however, indicate that both campaigns increased their level of advertising dramatically over 2016, primarily because they could not schedule live events due to the coronavirus pandemic, thus reducing the level of news coverage and increasing the need for advertising.

Biden outspent Trump on advertising by $140 million (Wesleyan Media Project, 2021).

In this chapter, we will address three forms of contemporary media campaigning: the candidates' efforts to exploit press coverage, their advertising strategies, and their performance in televised candidate debates.

STRATEGIES FOR MANAGING THE PRESS

In the ideal campaign, each candidate hopes to enjoy a regular stream of favorable news coverage while his or her opponent either suffers from inattention or is portrayed in unflattering terms. In this scenario, the news media would play the role of a credible spokesperson for the campaign. The professional norms governing journalism make it almost certain that reporters will refuse to act as campaign surrogates. As we noted in Chapter 3, the practice of interpretive journalism requires journalists to dismiss the candidates' rhetoric out of hand. The need to make news entertaining and eye-catching is a further drag on the candidates' ability to insert their messages intact into the news stream. The latest position paper on combating international terrorism might contain myriad specific proposals, none of which can be conveyed in a 10-second sound bite.

In the real world, various factors influence the ability of a campaign to spin the press. We begin with the worst-case scenario and then describe a series of specific strategies that provide campaigns at least some leverage over the content of the news.

AVOIDING FEEDING FRENZIES

The ability of a campaign to influence the press is at a low ebb in races in which the media scent evidence of personal misbehavior or character issues. When candidates demonstrate obvious personal flaws, they are completely at the mercy of the media. Given the premium value of the story, the ensuing feeding frenzy can prove fatal. Former vice-presidential candidate John Edwards was forced to suspend his 2008 run for the presidency after the *National Enquirer* published a series of stories alleging an extramarital affair with a campaign worker while his wife was fighting cancer. As mentioned in Chapter 3, Herman Cain's 2012 presidential campaign effectively ended the day *Politico* broke the news that two female employees of the National Restaurant Association had filed complaints of inappropriate behavior against the candidate. One year later, Congressman Anthony Weiner resigned his seat after revelations he had sent a sexually suggestive photograph of himself to a 21-year-old woman.

In 2016, both major party presidential candidates became ensnared in multiple media storms over their behavior, both personal and official. In Trump's case, the inappropriate behavior included his refusal to release his tax returns, insulting remarks directed at Senator John McCain, and his mocking of a disabled reporter at a campaign rally. These incidents, no doubt controversial, were completely overshadowed by the release of the *Access Hollywood* tape in which Trump was heard bragging about his ability to fondle and grope women at will (see Video Archive 6.1). The audio played endlessly on all outlets for several days, prompting many Republicans, who anticipated a tidal wave of voter revulsion, to call on Trump to withdraw from the race. Trump issued a mea culpa on national television ("I said it, I was wrong, and I apologize"), and his wife dismissed the language as "boy talk." The wave of adverse publicity brought on by any of these incidents would normally inflict serious if not fatal damage on most candidacies. But Trump emerged unscathed, setting a modern record for the candidate with the most "Teflon"—attacks couldn't stick to him. His supporters remained steadfast, leading Trump to comment, not entirely in jest, that "I could stand in the middle of Fifth Avenue and shoot somebody and I wouldn't lose voters." For her part, Hillary Clinton faced continuous media scrutiny over her use of a private e-mail server for official State Department business and the ensuing FBI investigation into her handling of classified information. Clinton also appeared to collapse at a ceremony commemorating the fifteenth anniversary of the 9/11 attacks, prompting speculation over her

Video Archive 6.1
Herman Cain and Donald Trump Feeding Frenzies

physical fitness. Later, she condescendingly referred to Trump supporters as a "basket of deplorables." Predictably, each of these developments brought on a media feeding frenzy that the campaign would have preferred to avoid.

DEALING WITH THE OBJECTIVITY IMPERATIVE

On the substantive or performance side of the ledger, candidates rarely eke out an edge in news coverage. Unlike character issues, which tend to be viewed in black-and-white terms (a candidate is either an adulterer or happily married), the candidates' credentials and positions on the issues represent a gray zone: there are no clear winners and losers. Journalists purport to be self-consciously objective in their discussion and take pains to provide point-counterpoint reporting. The rare occasions when the norm does not preclude one-sided coverage arise either when one candidate has a clear-cut advantage over the opponent or, as we will discuss here, when a candidate makes a major misstatement of fact or reverses course on a matter of public policy.

The norm of journalistic objectivity sometimes leads journalists to equate the misdeeds and weaknesses of competing candidates, even when they are not necessarily comparable. This so-called "false equivalence" was on full display in 2016, when both candidates displayed significant liabilities. Critics of the press pointed out that Trump's unstable temperament and bellicose nature were far more significant risks, particularly given the consequences of nuclear war, than Clinton's history of playing fast and loose with the facts. The press refused to make such qualitative distinctions between the candidates' flaws; virtually every story on Trump's divisiveness and racist rhetoric was matched by an equally critical story on Clinton's role in the Benghazi attacks or the shady financing of the Clinton Foundation. In those instances when the race features two relatively flawed candidates, the press is meticulously objective in subjecting both to critical coverage.

As in the case of character-related disclosures, the candidate's pronouncements on policy issues may provide journalists with a convenient excuse to attack. A candidate whose words and deeds are inconsistent or who revises a previously stated position is a ripe target for critical scrutiny. Senator George McGovern, the Democratic presidential candidate in 1972, was widely criticized for dropping Senator Tom Eagleton as his running mate after the press revealed that Eagleton had once been treated for clinical depression, even though he had initially stated that he would support Eagleton anyway. A similar media cloud enveloped Hillary Clinton during the 2008 campaign when she said she had opposed the North American Free Trade Agreement.

Journalists were quick to point out that Clinton had actually worked for its passage while serving as First Lady.

PLAYING THE EXPECTATIONS GAME

Recognizing the difficulty of directly influencing the content and tone of news coverage, the candidates have turned to more subtle media strategies. One approach is to try to influence reporters' treatment of the candidate's electoral prospects. We have seen that the state of the horse race is the foundation of campaign news. In the early stages of the primary campaign, favorable coverage of the candidate's position in the race can prove pivotal; candidates thought to be doing well (thanks to press reports) can use their standing to attract additional financial contributions and, as several scholars have documented, to attract additional voters in upcoming primaries.

Even more important than favorable horse-race coverage is the surprise factor. Candidates who "beat the odds" and surpass journalists' expectations benefit from electoral momentum. Consider the case of Senator John Kerry in the 2004 presidential race. In the months before the Iowa caucuses, Kerry was dismissed as an underachieving contender whose national poll numbers remained steadily in the single digits and whose finances were so shaky that he had to take out yet another mortgage to compete in Iowa. Given this baseline, Kerry's victory in Iowa was equivalent to a home run: he had defied journalists' expectations. The Iowa results elicited a wave of favorable coverage, and Kerry went on to win New Hampshire; eventually, he captured the Democratic nomination quite handily (see Chapter 7).

Setting journalists' expectations, by making sure their expectations aren't too high or too low, is crucial during the early days of the primary season. High expectations for Hillary Clinton's 2008 and 2016 presidential bids hurt her candidacy. As the presumptive nominee, she was the target of attacks by both Democrats and Republicans, and the media subjected her campaign to an extra level of scrutiny. While her rivals—Obama in 2008 and Bernie Sanders in 2016—could get away with the occasional stumble, even a minor slip by Clinton was front-page news. Biden's weak showing in the early contests similarly cast a pall over his prospects in 2020. He came in fourth in Iowa and fifth in New Hampshire. His strong showing in South Carolina, where he outpolled his main rival Bernie Sanders two to one, fundamentally altered the dynamics of the race, allowing Biden to coast to the nomination.

Campaign spokespersons typically downplay poll results that show their candidate comfortably ahead in Iowa or New Hampshire in the hope that the outcome will be more surprising and hence covered more extensively and favorably by the media. Conversely, campaigns sometimes attempt to persuade reporters that the opponent has a substantial lead—when they know that the poll numbers represent a short-term blip that will inevitably wear off. Before the 2008 Democratic National Convention, Sarah Simmons, the director of strategy for the McCain campaign, released a statement to the press claiming that they expected to be trailing in the polls by as much as 15 points after the Democratic convention. Not to be outdone, David Axelrod, Obama's senior strategist, told newspapers that he expected little or no bounce after the convention. Both Simmons and Axelrod knew full well that the increase in a candidate's support after the convention is a short-term bubble and that the two conventions generally neutralize each other, restoring the status quo that existed before the conventions.

The expectations game can also apply to debates between candidates. Fearing that Sarah Palin would be given underdog status in the coverage of the 2008 vice-presidential debate, the Obama campaign hyped Palin's abilities, with one spokesperson stating that Biden was "going in there to debate a leviathan of forensics, who has debated five times and she's undefeated in debates" (CNN, 2008). The 2016 campaign featured perhaps the most one-sided expectations ever over debate performance, providing Donald Trump a significant advantage. The journalistic consensus was that Clinton knew more about the details of policy and had considerably more experience with presidential debates than Trump. Trump's unwillingness to engage in serious debate preparation only lowered the expectations bar further. As *New York Times* correspondent Yamiche Alcindor said in an appearance on MSNBC, "A lot of people are going to look at Donald Trump and think, 'Hey, if he can even get out a good sentence and show off his experience, then he's doing well'" (Graham, 2016). A similar script played out in 2020 with the Trump campaign raising the bar for Joe Biden given his extensive Washington experience. In an interview with ABC News, Lara Trump—a senior adviser to the campaign—quipped, "Biden's been in this game for 47 years. Quite frankly, the bar has been lowered so much for Joe Biden that if he stays awake for the whole thing, it's like maybe he won" (Peoples, Miller, & Barrow, 2020).

MANAGING EVENTS

The nuts and bolts of press management is the strategic scheduling of events. Put simply, events must be designed and scheduled to attract maximal news coverage. In the days of old-fashioned descriptive journalism, the selection of the vice-presidential candidate was delayed until the convention because the presidential nominee was assured adequate coverage in advance of the convention. The increased resistance of the press corps to campaign spin has forced candidates to use the announcement of the vice-presidential selection as a media opportunity.

Rather than wasting the vice-presidential selection by announcing it during a period of ordinarily high media coverage (the party's national convention), the announcement is now typically made in advance of the convention so as to capitalize on the news and analysis that follows. John Kerry announced his selection of John Edwards on Monday, July 5, 2004, three weeks before the Democratic National Convention. The duo immediately left on a multistate bus tour, riding a crest of publicity sparked by the surprise announcement. Mitt Romney's selection of Paul Ryan fit the same timeline, the announcement coming 16 days before the opening of the Republican National Convention. Because Donald Trump was the subject of ample news coverage in 2016, he did not need to stage-manage the selection of his running mate. The announcement that it was to be Mike Pence came two days before the convention. Similarly, Joe Biden announced the selection of Kamala Harris as his running mate one week in advance of the virtual convention.

Nominating conventions were once significant opportunities for the candidates and their allies to posture at length before a nationwide audience. Since the advent of primaries, however, conventions have become ceremonial occasions with no possibility of delegations walking out in protest or the eruption of heated arguments over the platform—either of which might pique the media's attention. In contrast to the 1968 Democratic National Convention in Chicago, which precipitated a full-scale riot in that city's streets, present-day conventions are tame affairs. Speakers are screened to ensure that dissent or strident partisanship (which may throw off independents) is minimized. One reason there was considerable advance media attention given to the 2016 Democratic Convention was that journalists anticipated some "fireworks" in the form of conflict between Clinton and Sanders supporters. As it turned out, the conflict did not materialize; Senator Sanders delivered an impassioned plea for party unity, and the rift between the progressive and centrist wings of the party was, at least temporarily, put aside.

The trade-off for scripted conventions is reduced press coverage. Gavel-to-gavel coverage was last provided in 1976. Since then, television coverage of the conventions has been sporadic. In 2004, the three major networks allocated each convention 3 hours of total coverage on only three of four days (at the least desirable prime-time slot of 10:00 PM).[1] The networks did air an hour of coverage on each of the four days of each convention in both 2008 and 2012, but again chose not to air the coverage during the peak viewing hours (8:00 PM–10:00 PM). The Romney campaign was forced to move Ann Romney's speech from Monday to Tuesday because the three major networks decided to ignore the first day of the convention.

The absence of in-person conventions in 2020 led not only to reduced "live" coverage of the events but also to smaller audiences. Nielsen ratings for the Republican convention fell by 15 percent from 2016 and by 20 percent for the Democrats (Nielsen, 2020).

The reduced newsworthiness of the convention has forced campaign strategists to work harder for news coverage. The appearance of celebrities (such as singer Katy Perry and basketball legend Kareem Abdul-Jabbar at the 2016 Democratic convention) attracts news, but the overall theme of party unity tends to dampen press interest. In an unusual move designed to stimulate media interest, the Republicans decided to hold their 2004 convention in early September rather than the usual July–August timing. Their choice of New York as the host city was not mere coincidence. President Bush's advisers realized that the third anniversary of the 9/11 attacks would provide them with a convenient photo opportunity immediately after a convention dominated by terrorism and national security as the Bush campaign's signature issues.

The decision to delay the convention is a textbook example of the strategy of *riding the wave*—coordinating the campaign with events of consequence so that the campaign will benefit from the additional coverage elicited by the newsworthy event. In 2008, the collapse of Lehman Brothers in September signaled the onset of the banking crisis. This story became the overriding focus of the news media. Both presidential campaigns attempted to ride the wave of economic news. McCain went so far as to suspend his campaign on the grounds that helping to save the American banking industry took precedence over partisan politics (see Video Archive 6.2).

> ▶ **Video Archive 6.2**
> McCain Announces Temporary Suspension of Campaign

REGULATING ACCESS

Providing the press with access to the candidate is an important ingredient of campaign management. On one end of the spectrum, there is the open-door strategy, designed to maximize the candidate's availability. As one might expect, this strategy is favored by candidates who trail in the polls—the ones who typically lack the resources to engage in advertising. When a candidate is more competitive or when they are emerging as the front-runner, the campaign limits access: the press secretary may be made available for questioning, but the candidate does not appear in person. A less than subtle form of restricting press access is the Rose Garden strategy, named for incumbent presidents who enjoy such substantial leads in the polls (for example, in the 1972, 1984, and 1996 elections) that the candidate prefers to ignore the press altogether and stay on the White House grounds. Thus, there is an inverse relationship between press access and electoral standing. Candidates throw themselves at the press (such as Senator McCain's "Straight Talk Express" in 2000) when they anticipate that every additional news report may help them gain on their opponents, but they maintain a closed-door posture and ration information once they attain a more competitive position in the polls. In an exception that proves the rule, the trailing McCain campaign severely restricted media access to Sarah Palin in 2008. This decision hurt the campaign, as it seemed to confirm analysts' sup-

> ▶
> **Video Archive 6.3**
> Palin Interviews

positions that she was unprepared for office. (When Palin finally agreed to do news interviews, her comments—and her inability to name a single newspaper that she read—only raised more doubts about her credentials, illustrated in Video Archive 6.3.)

Exactly the same ritual is played out in the context of debates. Front-runners are loath to participate in debates at all, but trailing candidates seek to have as many debates as is humanly possible. As the 2008 Democratic primary contest reached its final stages, Hillary Clinton's campaign, trailing Obama in the polls, pushed for more and more debates, while Obama's campaign came up with more and more reasons to avoid debating. Clinton even ran advertisements that stated, "Maybe [Obama would] prefer to give speeches than have to answer questions."

In a variant of the restriction of access principle, Donald Trump's 2016 and 2020 campaigns engaged in a running battle with the mainstream media (see Video Archive 6.4). Accusing multiple news organizations of bias, his campaign revoked the credentials of reporters from, among others, the *Washington Post*, Politico, and CNN. This meant that reporters from these outlets could not attend and cover Trump's rallies. Responding to Trump's accusation of "incredibly inaccurate coverage," the *Washington Post*'s editor responded that they would continue to cover Trump "honestly, accurately, energetically, and unflinchingly" (Grynbaum, 2016).

Video Archive 6.4
Trump Attacks
the Media

In regulating access, the principle of risk aversion dominates candidate behavior. Candidates who are ahead in the polls know that they represent appropriate targets and that the press will adopt an even more aggressive and skeptical posture when covering them. For the leading candidates, therefore, less press access is better than more.

PLAYING ONE SOURCE AGAINST ANOTHER

The abundance of reporters covering a major campaign provides candidates with the option of awarding access to sources on the basis of the anticipated quality of their coverage. The Bill Clinton campaign emerged from the 1992 primaries with a number of serious character-related liabilities, any one of which could have erupted into a full-scale press crisis. The Whitewater scandal, the Gennifer Flowers affair, the state of the Clinton marriage, and Clinton's draft deferment were all red meat to the national press corps. No serious news organizations would cover Clinton without making reference to these nagging questions.

Rather than subject the candidate to this line of potentially damaging coverage, the Clinton campaign decided to schedule appearances on programs not typically associated with national political news. Clinton played the saxophone on *The Arsenio Hall Show*. His candidacy was the subject of an hour-long special on MTV (during which he was asked about his use of marijuana and responded, "I didn't inhale"). The Clinton team also arranged for the candidate to provide in-person interviews with local TV anchors at every campaign stop. In short, the campaign was able to shield the candidate from the hostile posture of the national press by cultivating less prominent news outlets.

For a local television correspondent, an exclusive interview with a presidential candidate offers significant professional prestige; for candidate Bill Clinton, the naïveté and inexperience of outer-ring reporters allowed him to dominate the interviews, avoid all reference to his troubled past, and stay on message—that is, hammer away on the state of the national economy. What was the end result? A steady stream of favorable news reports that, according to Clinton insiders, allowed the candidate to transform his image from "Slick Willie" to the candidate with a plan to rejuvenate the economy.

The use of local news to spearhead the campaign message not only offers the candidate greater control over the message but also makes for a better fit between the message and the audience. In presidential campaigns, candidates visit states that are up for grabs, not those that are firmly in the grasp of either party. The issues that concern voters are not the same in all battleground states. Disposal of nuclear waste, for instance, is a major concern for residents of New Mexico (the location of a major federal nuclear waste site). And when campaigning in Wisconsin, where dairy subsidies are a major source of farmers' income, the candidate must demonstrate expertise on matters of agriculture policy. Local news, which is typically an intrastate medium, allows candidates the ability to switch messages depending on the local context.

Today, given the hyperpolarized world of contemporary politics, candidates have a clear preference for "friendly" sources. In the aftermath of any of the innumerable controversies that embroiled his presidency, Donald Trump wasted no time making himself available for interviews with sympathetic Fox News pundits. It was no coincidence that President Biden's first televised town hall on the COVID-19 pandemic was hosted by the liberal-leaning MSNBC.

DUELING PRESS RELEASES

A final element of press relations takes its cue from advertising strategy. Candidates continually react to each other's statements and actions, mainly in the form of competing press releases. Each campaign maintains a war room to research and uncover weaknesses in the opponent's record. As soon as Hillary Clinton took the spotlight during the first presidential debate, she asked of Trump, "Why won't he release his tax returns? Maybe he doesn't want the American people, all of you watching tonight, to know that he's paid nothing in federal taxes." But Trump's campaign wasted no time responding in kind. They issued this press release following the debate: "Hillary Clinton has turned over the only records nobody wants to see from her; the American public wants to see the 33,000 emails she deleted to obstruct an FBI investigation." These rhetorical duels offer the media a coherent story line for the day's coverage. In fact, a significant amount of daily news coverage can be attributed to the candidates' strategists. Both teams maintain a complete roster of so-called analysts to represent them on the talk radio, cable television, and social media circuits. Unlike the earlier era, when reporters had to attend a campaign press briefing to receive the press release, today campaigns reach the targeted audience instantly either through Twitter and other social media channels or e-mail.

As the Trump–Clinton exchange illustrates, a first principle of press management is the immediate rebuttal of unflattering stories in the news. One month before the 2016 special election to fill the US Senate seat vacated by Jeff Sessions, the *Washington Post* published a report, based on four different sources, that Republican candidate Roy Moore had initiated inappropriate relationships with underage girls. Defying calls for him to step down, Moore immediately issued a combative press release accusing the newspaper of deliberately reporting false information. The next day, in his first media appearance, he denied the allegations in an interview with Fox's Sean Hannity.

Campaign press releases are designed not only to show the candidate in the most favorable light but also to help simplify the reporter's task of sorting out the various events, announcements, messages, and retorts that make up the daily news cycle. Campaigns are careful to synchronize their daily activities around a common narrative or theme in the hope that reporters will find it more convenient to organize their coverage around the message of the day. Naturally, campaign staffers are well aware of the special needs of the media and maintain a steady supply of colorful comments from their candidate—often attacking the opponent—suitable for inclusion as sound bites in the national news.

The most extreme press strategy, as developed by candidate Trump in 2016, is to wage open warfare on the media. As we have noted, Trump continually found himself the subject of unflattering coverage. He rejected the reports as "fake news"; held press conferences to disparage reporters as "scum," "slime," and "disgusting human beings"; and regularly used his stump speech at campaign rallies to rail against the "dishonest media." He frequently attacked individual reporters on Twitter for everything from liberal bias to insufficient coverage of the applause at his rallies. As we discussed in Chapter 3, this strategy is effective largely because party polarization has intensified to the point where partisans interpret objective reporting as hostility toward their favored candidate.

In sum, candidates are no longer in a position to manufacture news. Since 1988, the press has become more combative and less willing to recycle the candidates' rhetoric. In response, candidates have taken steps to focus the attention of reporters on subjects that they consider advantageous: from a plan to revive the economy to misstatements by the opponent, candidates offer up their version of the message of the day in the hope of providing reporters with a story line they can't resist. When the national press corps proves insufficiently malleable, candidates turn to less prestigious news outlets where they are ensured gentler treatment.

ADVERTISING STRATEGY

Unlike press management, where success requires campaigns to cater to the needs and values of journalists, advertising provides candidates with a much more direct route to the minds of voters. There is a significant trade-off, however: advertising is unmediated, but it is also a much less credible messenger than news reports are.

Effective advertising is not simply a question of designing a persuasive and memorable campaign jingle. The overall game plan is to strengthen the sponsoring candidate's market share. That goal may be accomplished by adjusting the advertising message to the specific attributes of the candidates in the race and by using messages that reinforce the content of campaign news. In addition to synchronizing the advertising message to the context, campaigns must decide on the precise mix of affirmative messages in favor of the candidate (positive advertising) and messages designed to increase voter aversion to the opposing candidate (negative advertising). The extensive use of negative appeals is the hallmark of political advertising. Commercial advertising stays positive; automobile companies and department stores rarely criticize their competitors. Political advertising is different: candidates are much more likely to attack their opponents than praise themselves. As Figure 6.1 shows, the negativity of campaign advertising has increased steadily over time; by 2012, presidential ads were predominantly negative. However, the level of negativity declined in 2016 and 2020. In a significant departure from prior cycles, in which negative ads targeted questions of policy and performance as well as questions of character, the 2016 ad campaign fixated on the latter. Because both candidates were considered relatively unlikable, their campaigns invested heavily in personal attacks (Fowler, Ridout, & Franz, 2016). In the case of the Clinton ads, almost 90 percent focused on Trump's personality, most notably, his misogyny and divisiveness. Despite the belligerence of his rhetoric, Trump's ads were much more positive than Clinton's, suggesting that the campaign feared that ads attacking a woman aired by a candidate known to have groped women might be too distasteful to many voters.

The 2020 ad campaign, conducted in the midst of a deadly pandemic, proved significantly more positive than that of 2016; while the share of positive ads rose only slightly from 25 percent in 2016 to 27 percent in 2020, the share of attack ads dropped sharply from 56 percent in 2016 to around 25 percent in 2020 (Wesleyan Media Project, 2021).

FIGURE 6.1

The Rise of Negative Advertising in Presidential Campaigns, 1960–2020

Percentage of campaign ads that are negative

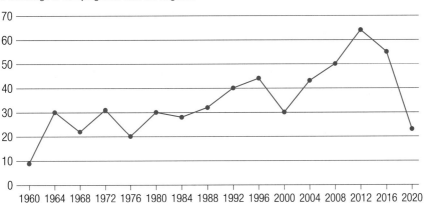

Source: 1960–1996 data from J. G. Geer. (2010). *Fanning the flames: The news media's role in the rise of negativity in presidential campaigns.* Discussion paper, Joan Shorenstein Center on the Press, Politics, and Public Policy, Harvard University, Cambridge, MA. Retrieved September 13, 2021, from the Shorenstein Center website: https://shorensteincenter.org/wp-content/uploads/2012/03/d55_geer.pdf; 2000–2008 data from Wesleyan Media Project. (2012, October 24). 2012 shatters 2004 and 2008 records for total ads aired. Retrieved September 13, 2021, from the Wesleyan Media Project website: https://mediaproject.wesleyan.edu/2012-shatters -2004-and-2008-records-for-total-ads-aired/; 2012–2020 data from Wesleyan Media Project. (2021, March 31). Political ads in 2020: Fast and furious. Retrieved September 13, 2021, from the Wesleyan Media Project website: https://mediaproject.wesleyan.edu/2020-summary-032321/.

TARGETING THE AUDIENCE

Television advertising takes on different roles over the course of a campaign. Before we spell out the temporal contours of advertising strategy, it is important to understand that advertising is a highly targeted form of communication, no matter what the stage of the campaign. Unlike brand-name product appeals, which air on a national basis, political advertising is much narrower in scope. As the use of local news illustrates, candidates are interested primarily in reaching voters whose preferences may be pivotal to the outcome of the race. Senator Obama had little interest in any of the California media markets in 2008 because he fully expected to win the state by a comfortable margin. Conversely, even the most optimistic Democratic strategist will avoid wasting advertising dollars in Texas, where the probability of a Democratic presidential victory is near zero. By this logic, nearly 40 states are off the advertising table. As shown in Figure 6.2, during the 2016 and 2020 presidential races, residents of strongly red (Republican) or blue (Democratic) states saw no

FIGURE 6.2

The Geography of Campaign Advertising, 2016 and 2020

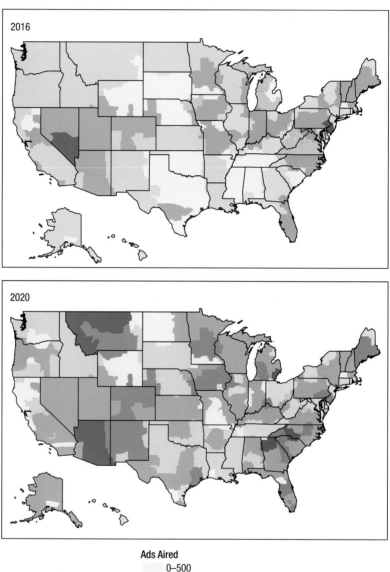

Source: Data from Wesleyan Media Project. (2020, October 29). Presidential general election ad spending tops $1.5 billion. Retrieved September 13, 2021, from the Wesleyan Media Project website: https://mediaproject .wesleyan.edu/releases-102920/.

presidential ads at all. The few battleground states, however, were blanketed with advertising.

The strategy is no different in statewide races. Counties or areas that are heavily Democratic or Republican are bypassed; instead, the candidates invest in markets where a small movement in the numbers can make the difference between winning and losing. In California, for example, voter preferences in the Bay Area are too one-sided to warrant an ad campaign, so candidates for statewide office concentrate on the Central Valley and the densely populated and more competitive Southern California markets.

Given the tiny margin by which Trump defeated Clinton in the key battleground states of Michigan, Wisconsin, and Pennsylvania in 2016, some analysts suggested that the Clinton team took these states for granted and failed to invest sufficiently in advertising. The 2016 advertising numbers support this interpretation, at least in Michigan and Wisconsin. As shown in Figure 6.3, Trump out-advertised Clinton in both Wisconsin and Michigan in the weeks leading up to the election. Suddenly realizing that they were in

FIGURE 6.3

Number of Ads Placed in Wisconsin, Michigan, and Pennsylvania, 2016

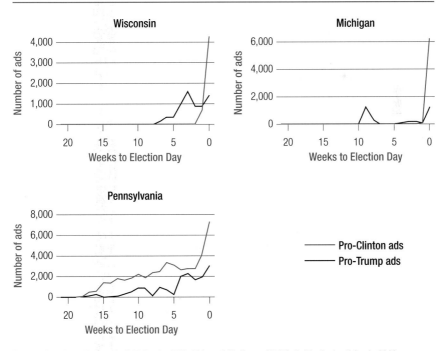

Source: Data from Figure 4 in E. F. Fowler, T. N. Ridout, & M. Franz. (2016). Political advertising in 2016: The presidential election as outlier? *The Forum, 14,* 445–469.

trouble, the Clinton campaign made huge last-minute ad buys in both states but to no avail.

In addition to singling out particular locations, campaigns engage in a different form of targeting designed to maximize the impact of advertising. For advertising to work, the audience must include adults who intend to vote. Clearly, advertising during children's programs would be meaningless, and advertising on MTV would be just as irrational, given the low rate of turnout among youth. Ideally, the ad would air during a program that drew likely voters. Local news, a form of programming that has enjoyed steady increases in viewership, provides just such an audience; people sufficiently motivated to watch the news are also likely to vote. The first half of the local newscast is thus a primetime slot for campaign advertising; the audience is tuning in to the top stories of the day, and their attention has yet to wander. Campaigns also rely heavily on *news adjacencies*—time slots just before or just after a local newscast. In some battleground states, the most desirable advertising slots (during local newscasts in particular) are booked well in advance. Residents of battleground states—at least those who watch television regularly—are sometimes exposed to the same ad so frequently that they claim they can recite the text in their sleep.

One other overarching factor affecting campaign advertising is the budget. Advertising is the single largest expenditure in most major campaigns. A single airing of a 30-second commercial during a 6:00 PM newscast in the two biggest television markets (New York City and Los Angeles) costs approximately $7,000. But a candidate can run the ad 10 different times for that amount in Las Vegas and more than 20 times in South Dakota or Montana.

Thus, allocating resources to ad campaigns depends not only on geography (targeting battleground states) but also on cost considerations. Residents of smaller media markets are likely to receive greater amounts of advertising simply because candidates get more for their advertising dollar.

Given the cost, campaigns attempt to reach as many likely voters as possible with each of their ads. The basic unit of exposure to advertising is the *gross rating point*, or GRP.[2] GRPs are scored to reflect the percentage of the media market exposed to the ad. Buying 100 GRPs for an ad, for instance, would mean one exposure for each viewer; 1,000 GRPs would mean that viewers would see the ad 10 times. In recent years, with the increased proliferation of cable and satellite channels, consultants have been forced to ratchet up their ad buys to fight channel and advertising clutter. In the 1990s, for instance, running a single ad 5 times was considered the norm. Today, an ad is likely to air 10 times.

Given the expanding number of Americans who get their news online, internet and social media advertising is taking up an increasing share of campaign ad budgets. In 2012, the Romney campaign spent about a third of its conventional advertising budget on online ads. For the Obama campaign, the figure was slightly smaller, amounting to 28 percent. In 2016, the Clinton and Trump campaigns spent $80 million on Facebook ads, a figure representing 40 percent of all their online ads, but only one-quarter of their spending on broadcast ads. As noted in Chapter 5, the amount spent on digital ads by the presidential candidates reached an all-time high in 2020, but because the candidates also increased their investment in television ads, the share of digital ads remained at 25 percent.

The attraction to online ads is especially powerful for candidates contesting state and local elections whose financial resources are more modest. The cost of airing social media ads is a bargain by the standards of television advertising. It is not surprising that a recent analysis of the 2018 ad campaign on Facebook found most of the ads were placed by candidates for down-ballot contests (Fowler et al., 2021).

A significant advantage of online ads is that advertisers can target their audiences more precisely because web-browsing behavior has been integrated with a wealth of marketing and political databases revealing individuals' preferences not just about politics but about their recreational interests, charitable giving, and more. Advertisers can therefore more precisely target their messages to designated audiences. In an interview with *60 Minutes,* the head of digital advertising for the Trump campaign explained that they could match messages to narrowly defined groups of voters: "So now Facebook lets you get to . . . 15 people in the Florida Panhandle that I would never buy a TV commercial for. [When it comes to] infrastructure . . . I started making ads that showed the bridge crumbling . . . that's micro targeting. . . . I can find the 1,500 people in one town that care about infrastructure" (CBS News, 2017). Given the ability to match content to the audience's profile and target small subsets of voters with particular interests, social media ads are significantly more likely to position the sponsoring candidate as promoting these interests rather than attacking the opponent. Negativity is much more common in the less targeted form of advertising, that is, television (Fowler et al., 2021).

In the world of old media, ad buying is still more art form than science. Depending on the ad, the stage of the campaign, and the scale of the budget, buyers might opt for the same level of GRPs throughout the campaign or, more likely, vary their buys to synchronize exposure to the ad campaign with the level of news coverage. The expectation is that candidates get more bang for their advertising buck when the campaign is in the news. This logic also influences the content of advertising. When a particular issue or event grabs the headlines, the candidates tend to incorporate that issue into their ads. In the 2001 and 2002 election cycles, for example, it was no surprise—given the aftermath of 9/11—that the most popular spokesperson for Republican candidates across the country was New York City's mayor, Rudy Giuliani.

PLANTING THE SEED: EARLY ADVERTISING

Early in the campaign, advertising introduces the candidate to the electorate. Biographical spots focus on the candidate's personal background and record of public service. Military service is especially noteworthy as an indicator of fitness for office. For candidates who cannot claim to have risked their lives for the nation, alternative qualifications include humble beginnings, the ability to overcome adversity, strong family ties, adherence to a core set of political principles, and a demonstrated commitment to public service. By focusing on personal virtues, campaigns attempt to instill confidence in the candidate's suitability for public office (see Video Archive 6.5). Barack Obama's first ad of the general election, titled "Country I Love," spoke to his professed upbringing in a lower-middle class environment and the "values straight from the Kansas heartland" that were taught to him by his mother and grandparents.

Video Archive 6.5
Introducing the
Candidate

In nonpresidential races, in which candidates might be unknown to voters, the first goal of the ad campaign is more mundane—namely, to deliver a boost to the candidate's name recognition. In some cases, biographical spots focus specifically on the candidate's name. Ed Zschau and Wyche Fowler, both little-known candidates for the US Senate, opened their campaigns with ads that simply explained the correct pronunciation of their names. In politics, familiarity is a necessary condition of electability; voters are disinclined to vote for a name they do not recognize.

IMAGE VERSUS ISSUE SPOTS

Once they have provided voters with a snapshot of their lives, candidates move on to their credentials. *Image ads* maintain thematic continuity with the biographical message by presenting the candidate as a likable human being with a strong sense of public service. *Issue ads* are more substantive and either focus on the candidate's past experience and record in public life or outline the candidate's positions on major policy issues.

The relative importance of image and issue advertising depends on the electoral context. By 1984, the international tensions associated with the Cold War had eased, and voters felt secure on the economic front. This atmosphere of political tranquility was captured by the Reagan campaign in what is generally considered the classic image ad. Labeled "Morning in America," the ad listed President Reagan's accomplishments against a background of idyllic rural landscapes and smiling children (see Video Archive 6.6). Four years later, Vice President George H. W. Bush aired a textbook example of an issue ad, calling into question Governor Dukakis's credentials on the issue of national defense. When voters are concerned about the state of the country, both incumbents and challengers turn to issue ads. As President Bush found out in 1992, voters who are worried about losing their jobs are relatively forgiving of a challenger with questionable personal attributes; they base their choices more on questions of performance. The "Slick Willie" nickname applied to Bill Clinton was not as relevant as "It's the economy, stupid." Similarly, in 2016, Trump's promise to bring back manufacturing jobs took precedence over his personal failings.

> ▶ Video Archive 6.6
> Image and Issue
> Appeals

From the beginning of campaign advertising, image ads have inevitably portrayed the candidate as a man of the people (female candidates were few and far between in the early days of televised campaigns). American voters do not take kindly to millionaire candidates from privileged backgrounds, especially when they make disparaging remarks about ordinary people (as Mitt Romney learned in 2012). Donald Trump, despite his immense wealth, portrayed himself as a down-to-earth candidate who would speak for the "forgotten men and women of our country, people who work hard but no longer have a voice" (Rucker & Fahrenthold, 2016). This focus on the common touch is ironic; like Trump, most presidential candidates are in fact members of a distinctly elite group with appropriate prep school and Ivy League credentials. One of President Bush's greatest liabilities during the 1992 campaign was that he personified the gulf between well-to-do and middle-class America. In a well-circulated story, the president was said to have expressed his delight with the advanced technology of price scanners at a local supermarket, thus revealing his utter unfamiliarity with grocery store shopping.[3] This story line reappeared in the 2008 presidential elections as both McCain and Obama sought to paint the other as out of touch with the average American. In addition to the question of McCain's many homes, Obama's comment about bitter working-class voters gave his opponents (both Hillary Clinton and McCain) ample opportunity to depict Obama as an

Video Archive 6.7
Trump and Clinton
Ads Targeting the
Middle Class

elitist. More recently, the Trump campaign ran ads reminding voters of Hillary Clinton's wealth and the huge speaking fees she received from large corporations and banks (see Video Archive 6.7).

Issue ads fall into two broad classes: performance messages touting the sponsoring candidate's experience and proven accomplishments as a public servant and policy messages summarizing the candidate's preferences on public policy. Campaigns featuring an incumbent invariably gravitate to performance themes, with the challenger habitually framing the choice as a referendum on the performance of the incumbent. Challengers might suggest that the incumbent has weakened the economy or that the administration has done nothing to make the world more secure from terrorism. Conversely, incumbents are quick to take credit for economic growth, balanced budgets, reductions in crime, or other such indicators of effective governance. In 2020, the Biden campaign focused on two key issues to raise questions about Trump's performance: the pandemic and the resulting recession. Biden's ads repeatedly critiqued Trump's response to the health crisis. In one ad that aired immediately after the final debate, the voice-over began with "When coronavirus came, Trump froze like a deer in the headlights."

Even when neither candidate is an incumbent, as in 2016, performance on salient issues is a recurring theme in the ad campaign. Having made immigration the signature motif of his candidacy, Trump ran multiple ads contrasting his posture on illegal immigration and border control ("build the wall") with his

Video Archive 6.8
Illegal Immigration

opponent's "softness" on the issue: "In Hillary Clinton's America, the system stays rigged. . . . Syrian refugees flood in. Illegal immigrants convicted of committing crimes get to stay" (see Video Archive 6.8).

ISSUE OWNERSHIP

Policy advertising follows a simple formula: highlight the candidate's positions but focus only on issues for which your candidate is favored. This directive has two specific implications. First, do not publicize your support for unpopular or controversial positions (that task will be taken up by your opponent); and second, single out issues on which you and, more important, your party are seen as more likely to provide relief. In sum, parties and candidates often *own* certain issues, and these owned issues are featured in campaign advertising.

Issue ownership is a by-product of American political culture. Long before they reach voting age, most Americans are socialized to associate each party

FIGURE 6.4

Perceptions of the Parties on Major Issues, 2020

Which political party do you trust more to handle:

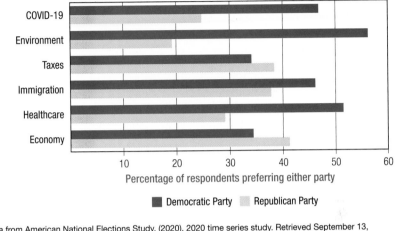

Percentage of respondents preferring either party

■ Democratic Party ▨ Republican Party

Source: Data from American National Elections Study. (2020). 2020 time series study. Retrieved September 13, 2021, from the American National Elections Study website: electionstudies.org/data-center/2020-time -series-study/.

with a set of interests and, by inference, with a set of issues or problems on which they will deliver. In general, Republican-owned issues include national security, government spending, and crime. That is, the public typically assumes that Republicans are better able to deal with these issues than Democrats are. Conversely, voters favor Democrats on most quality-of-life issues, including job and income security, healthcare, and issues affecting women (see Figure 6.4). The public rates the two parties evenly on certain other issues, such as taxes and trade.

How do voters rate the parties on the salient issues today? Polling data from 2020 (provided in Figure 6.4) indicates that Democrats own the environment, COVID-19, and healthcare by wide margins, whereas Republicans are slightly favored on the economy and taxes. Interestingly, immigration—a traditionally Republican issue and one exploited by Trump in the 2016 campaign—now favors the Democrats (by a margin of 8 percent).

Issue ownership was central to George W. Bush's reelection campaign of 2004. The strategy was to make the war on terrorism the centerpiece of the campaign and capitalize on the Republican Party's reputation on the issue. The first round of Republican ads, released on March 5, 2004, made frequent references to 9/11 and terrorist threats. Later in the campaign, the Bush team

Issue Ownership

Issue ownership refers to the fact that the public considers each party to be more capable on different issues: for example, Republicans are thought to perform better in the area of military and defense policy, and Democrats are viewed more favorably on issues such as education and Social Security. Candidates tend to campaign on issues that their party owns because their message is more credible when consistent with the stereotype of the party.

Video Archive 6.9
Advertising on
Owned Issues

produced "Wolves," an ad that attacked Senator Kerry as being weak on defense (see Video Archive 6.9). It is interesting that this ad borrowed heavily from "Bear in the Woods," President Reagan's 1984 ad promoting a strong military posture vis-á-vis the Soviet Union. For its part, the Kerry campaign followed the standard Democratic script and promoted Kerry's positions on job loss and healthcare while attacking Bush as a stooge of the wealthy.

The principle of issue ownership extends to attributes of the candidate other than party affiliation. Gender is an especially visible attribute, and American culture provides ample cues about the traits of men and women (see Video Archive 6.10). Given these widely held gender stereotypes, male and female candidates have reason to project their masculinity and femininity, respectively. Masculine issues, such as defense, terrorism, and crime, resonate well for a male candidate; child care and matters of educational policy confirm voters' beliefs about the credentials of a female candidate. Hillary Clinton, having served as secretary of state, enjoyed high credibility in 2016 on matters of foreign policy and national security; she used this to her advantage by running ads depicting Donald Trump as too inexperienced and temperamentally unstable to be entrusted with the nation's nuclear arsenal. In one ad, a former Defense Department official seated near the launch controls of a nuclear missile says, "The thought of Donald Trump with nuclear weapons scares me to death. It should scare everyone."

Video Archive 6.10
Running as a Woman

In addition to owned issues are policy areas in which neither party enjoys a decisive advantage. These can be seen as leased issues on which parties can claim short-term occupancy, depending on the nature of the times or the track record of a particular candidate. The wars in Iraq and Afghanistan that were largely seen as failures under the Bush administration provided Obama and the

Democrats the opportunity to challenge Senator McCain and the Republicans on issues of national security and foreign policy. A poll taken shortly before the 2008 presidential election asked respondents which candidate would do a better job dealing with the situation in Iraq. Even though McCain had significant military experience and had served on the Armed Services Committee in the Senate, more people thought that Obama would handle Iraq better.

Beliefs about party performance also fluctuate in the short term, driven by events and incumbents' performance. The huge death toll from the coronavirus provided Biden with the opportunity to challenge Trump's handling of the pandemic. In surveys taken before the 2020 election, clear majorities expressed more confidence in Biden's ability to deal with the problem (American National Election Studies, 2020). On the other side, the less than smooth rollout of the Affordable Care Act together with the Obama administration's misrepresentations of the impact of the law on consumer choice allowed Republicans to narrow the gap on the issue of healthcare in several 2013 and 2014 polls.

Although leased issues generate ads from both candidates, the principle of playing to one's strengths creates few opportunities for candidates to engage in an exchange on issues. Advertising campaigns generally do not resemble a dialogue between the competing candidates. Instead, they typically offer two essentially unrelated streams of messages. Candidates prefer to talk past each other in the hope of promoting their comparative advantages.

There is one notable exception to this pattern. The frequent use of negative advertising means that the attack-counterattack spiral is a typical outcome of ad campaigns. Before we discuss negative advertising, however, let's look at another strategy of agenda control.

WEDGE APPEALS: US VERSUS THEM

Consider the following. It is 2024. The US economy continues to recover from the abyss of 2020. Unemployment is at a historic low. Most Americans are fully vaccinated and the pandemic is finally under control. The American public supports the Biden administration's firm response to the Russian invasion of Ukraine, and strongly favors the imposition of massive economic sanctions on Russia despite the steep rise in gas prices. Economic growth and international tensions both tend to favor the incumbent Democratic party (as we discuss in detail in Chapter 7). The Republican National Committee concludes—correctly, in the minds of political scientists and election forecasters—that campaigning on the economy, COVID-19, or international affairs would be a losing strategy for their candidates. Instead, Republicans focus the

2024 campaign on the continuing stream of illegal immigrants coming across the Mexican border, their proposed legislation to prohibit transgender women from participating in high school and collegiate women's sports, and their continued opposition to the teaching of courses in public schools that highlight the persistence of systemic racism in the United States. This hypothetical Republican platform in 2024 is a textbook case of the use of *wedge issues,* those designed to pit one group against another and to appeal to voters' sense of racial or gender identity. When candidates turn to wedge appeals, it is generally a tacit acknowledgment that they are unable to win the debate on other issues.

President Obama handed the Republicans a wedge issue in 2010 when he waded into the controversy surrounding the proposed construction of a mosque in Lower Manhattan, two blocks from Ground Zero. At a White House dinner, the president stated that in keeping with the Constitution, Muslims had a right to build a place of worship. Obama's comments ignited a series of partisan retorts from Republicans, who scented an opportunity to score points with the voting public, many of whom have strong anti-Muslim sentiments. Former speaker of the House Newt Gingrich compared the construction of the mosque to placing Nazi swastikas near the Holocaust memorial, while to Senator John Cornyn, Obama's comments suggested that "the White House, the administration, the president himself seems to be disconnected from the mainstream of America" (CBS News, 2010).

The mosque controversy addressed questions of religious tolerance. Most wedge issues, however, represent issues of race and ethnicity. From the Civil War through the passage of landmark civil rights legislation in the 1960s to debates over affirmative action and reparations, Americans have been consistently divided by race. One set of wedge appeals seeks to capitalize on this racial division. Typically, the strategy is used by Republican candidates, who hope to attract white Democrats and independents on the basis of their opposition to race-based policies such as affirmative action in employment and diversity credits in college admissions.[4]

The success of the Trump campaign in 2016 attests to Republicans' ability to exploit the issue of immigration as a wedge appeal. But Trump was hardly the first Republican to run on an anti-immigrant platform. Immigration became the wedge issue of choice in the 1994 statewide campaign in California. When California governor Pete Wilson ran an ad in 1994 that began with the line "They keep coming," most Californians immediately understood what he meant. (We will say more about that 1994 campaign shortly.) As immigration became an issue in other states, Republican candidates nationwide took up the anti-immigration call, and "they keep coming" became a fixture of their ad campaigns. In short, wedge appeals based on race or ethnicity are aimed at capturing white votes by depicting the candidate as taking a stand against the threatening demands of ethnic minorities. The appeal is either explicit—as in the case of immigration or affirmative action—or implicit, as in the case of references to crime or law and order.

Cultural identity (or "family values") provides an alternative basis for dividing voters. Initially tied to Republican opposition to school busing in the 1960s and 1970s, the family values slogan has since broadened into a code word for cultural conservatism, religiosity, and opposition to nonmainstream lifestyles. A call for family values is generally interpreted as opposition to abortion, feminism, and the rights of gay and transgender Americans.

A prominent episode of the family values divide occurred in 2016. North Carolina passed a law requiring individuals to use restrooms that correspond to their gender at birth. LGBTQIA+ groups filed suit to overturn the law, and the controversy quickly spread to the presidential campaign. Hillary Clinton and Bernie Sanders both attacked the law as discriminatory. Republicans with moderate views on cultural issues, including Donald Trump, came out against the law. Conservatives, including Ted Cruz and Marco Rubio, were quick to attack Trump for his "liberal" views. In the words of Cruz, "Donald Trump is no different from politically correct leftist elites. Today, he joined them in calling for grown men to be allowed to use little girls' public restrooms."

One of the most infamous instances of exploiting wedge appeals occurred in 1988. In August, a Republican group began airing what came to be known as the "Willie Horton" ad. The ad attacked Democratic Massachusetts governor Michael Dukakis for his support of prison furlough programs and was thought to have played a major role in the ability of George H. W. Bush's campaign to overcome what was then a double-digit deficit in the polls. Surprisingly, given the historic nomination of the first Black candidate for president 20 years later, wedge issues were of little consequence during the 2008 campaign. Although there were indirect references to race during the Democratic primaries (for example, Hillary Clinton's claim that she championed the interests of "White working-class voters" and her harsh criticism of Obama's pastor, the Reverend Jeremiah Wright), after the conventions, issues of race and ethnicity disappeared from the campaign radar entirely because of the overwhelming magnitude of the economic crisis.

Wedge appeals are not limited to presidential contests. In 1990, conservative Republican senator Jesse Helms was locked in a close race with Black Democrat Harvey Gantt (the mayor of Charlotte, North Carolina). During the closing days of the race, Helms released an ad opposing

Video Archive 6.11
Dividing by Race
and Ethnicity

the use of affirmative action in employment decisions. This "White Hands" ad is credited with producing a significant surge in White support for Helms (see Video Archive 6.11). Eight years later the tables were turned. Opponents of Proposition 209, a measure to end affirmative action in California, aired an ad featuring David Duke, a well-known member of the Ku Klux Klan, in the hope that the negative imagery of hooded Klansmen and cross burnings would weaken moderate White support for the measure. The strategy failed, however, and Proposition 209 passed easily.

Today, immigration is the most salient wedge issue in national and state politics. Trump made it his signature issue during the 2016 election; he famously referred to Mexican immigrants as drug dealers and rapists. He maintained this nativist stance throughout his presidency, at one point demanding that a group of four progressive Democratic congresswomen (three of whom were born in the United States) "go back and help fix the totally broken and crime-infested places from which they came" (*Washington Post*, 2019).

Well before the emergence of Donald Trump, some candidates contesting House seats in 2008 supported construction of a wall along the US–Mexico border. In 2009, Representative Lamar Smith (Republican–Texas) introduced the Birthright Citizenship Act, which would deny citizenship to children of illegal immigrants. In 2010, the Arizona legislature enacted a law granting law enforcement officers broad discretion to detain individuals on the grounds that they were undocumented immigrants. The next year Alabama passed an even tougher bill; police officers were required to arrest individuals without valid documentation. In the first implementation of the law, a German national was pulled over for driving a rental car with expired registration tags. The individual turned out to be an important executive with Mercedes Benz, a major employer in Alabama. After a similar episode involving a Honda executive—and an outcry from the business community—the state legislature backtracked; police were no longer required to arrest people without appropriate identification papers.

Given that California has a Hispanic population amounting to nearly 40 percent of its population and considering the state's proximity to Mexico, it is not surprising that California has been on the front line of the battle to limit immigration. To illustrate how immigration has shaped California political campaigns, see the Case Study on p. 184, where we will compare the 1994 race for governor between incumbent Republican Pete Wilson and Democratic challenger Kathleen Brown with the 2010 campaign between Republican Meg Whitman and Democrat Jerry Brown.

NEGATIVE ADVERTISING

In recent years, research on the subject of negative campaign advertising has become a growth industry. As we have noted, a striking attribute of political advertising campaigns is the heavy reliance (at least in comparison with product advertising campaigns) on so-called negative or attack advertising. Although the number and ratio of positive to negative ads vary across campaigns, there can be no denying that political advertising is a relatively hostile and impolite form of discourse. In contrast to normal discourse, which is characterized by a positivity bias (we normally greet others with a smile and a cheery hello), candidates tend to dwell on the flaws—either personal or ideological—of their opponents. In the case of so-called issue ads—advertisements aired by groups not directly affiliated with a candidate—almost the entire advertising budget is devoted to attack advertising. In the 2012 election, for example, 90 percent of the airtime purchased by Republican-leaning groups went to messages questioning President Obama's fitness for office. It has reached the point where candidates routinely air ads attacking their opponents for running negative campaigns.

Certainly criticism, counterargument, and rebuttal are legitimate and essential ingredients of fair political debate. In the context of political advertising, however, it is possible for candidates to focus exclusively on defining their opponents while remaining silent about their own suitability for office. Gray Davis was reelected governor of California in 2002 using just this strategy. Davis spent millions attacking his Republican opponent (Bill Simon) as a wealthy and corrupt businessman with no political experience. But even before Simon won the Republican nomination, Davis spent millions on ads attacking Simon's Republican rival, Richard Riordan. As the mayor of Los Angeles, Riordan had accumulated an impressive record in office, was well known, and could appeal to moderate voters. Realizing that Riordan would be the stronger direct opponent, Davis broadcast ads attacking Riordan for his frequent policy reversals on abortion (a charge likely to resonate with conservative Republican voters). Subject to attacks from both Davis and Simon, Riordan's poll numbers dropped, and Simon won the primary.

In the end, though, did the Davis strategy really work? It can't be disputed that Simon defeated Riordan in the primary and Davis easily defeated Simon in November. However, having campaigned against both Riordan and Simon without giving voters a single affirmative reason to reelect him, Davis was vulnerable to a rising tide of political discontent that was orchestrated by Republican activists into a full-scale recall campaign. Lacking public support, Davis was ousted from office less than a year after his reelection.

Immigration Campaigns in California, 1994 and 2010

As governor of California, Pete Wilson faced a challenging reelection campaign in 1994. The state was in the throes of a severe recession, with an accompanying exodus of companies and jobs. Wilson, a Republican, faced a popular and well-known Democrat, State Treasurer Kathleen Brown. Naturally, Brown's ads emphasized the recession, Wilson's inability to bring relief to the state, and her own economic expertise (see Video Archive 6.12). With this theme, she established a substantial lead over Wilson.

Video Archive 6.12
1994 Immigration Ads

Recognizing that a debate over the state of the economy was a hopeless cause, Wilson campaigned as a crime fighter and an opponent of illegal immigration. He linked his candidacy to two well-known statewide propositions: 184 and 187. Proposition 184, known as the "three-strikes measure" for its tough stance on lawbreakers, won approval by an impressive 72-to-28 percent margin. Proposition 187, which proposed limiting or eliminating illegal immigrants' eligibility for a variety of government services, also passed with majority support.

Wilson's efforts to shift the agenda were aided by the Brown campaign, which engaged Wilson on the issue of crime despite Brown's opposition to the death penalty. As a result, the California electorate was exposed to a genuine dialogue on the issue of crime and punishment. Voters' impressions of the candidates became increasingly linked to their positions on crime. On this issue, most voters (including many Democrats) favored Wilson over Brown. Brown's support eroded, and Wilson was reelected by a comfortable margin.

In 2010, in the race to succeed Arnold Schwarzenegger as governor, Meg Whitman faced Steve Poizner in the Republican primary. (The Democratic candidate, Jerry Brown, who had previously served as governor and was attorney general at the time, had no primary challenger.) Whitman, a multimillion-aire, outspent Poizner by more than 10 to 1 and opened up a large lead in the polls. The Poizner campaign decided to attack Whitman on the grounds that she was soft

NEGATIVE THEMES

Negative campaigns run the gamut from direct attacks on the personal attributes of a candidate to ads linking the candidate with unsavory groups or causes. Typically, consultants differentiate between character assassination, in which the opponent is depicted as an immoral or nasty human being and on undocumented immigrants and favored a "path to citizenship." As Poizner began to cut into Whitman's lead, she backed off her earlier statements on legalization, ran ads in which she claimed to be "tough as nails" in cracking down on illegals, and enlisted former governor Pete Wilson, the iconic anti-immigration candidate, as one of her major supporters.

Whitman won the primary quite easily but then did an abrupt about-face on immigration for the general election. She ran ads on Spanish-language television asserting that she opposed Proposition 187 and the Arizona immigration law. She described her views on immigration as no different from the views of her Democratic opponent. In the middle of the campaign, Whitman had to deal with the revelation that she had unknowingly employed an illegal immigrant as her housekeeper. Of course, conservative groups and commentators were enraged by Whitman's new centrist rhetoric and threatened to withhold their support. Latino voters were unpersuaded by Whitman, voting Democratic by a 3-to-1 margin and contributing to Jerry Brown's comfortable victory.

The differing trajectories of the Wilson and Whitman strategies on immigration indicate that while ethnicity is still a potent divider in California politics, the sheer size of the Latino electorate has changed the candidates' political calculus. Republicans' efforts to attract White voters by representing themselves as being opposed to immigration now run the risk of alienating a sizable Latino electorate. In 1994, Wilson could do so with impunity because Whites outnumbered Latinos by a wide margin. In 2010, however, Whitman had to reverse course on immigration once the primary campaign was over for fear of losing Latino votes. More generally, as Latinos are mobilized and their turnout increases, Republican candidates in California will be forced to take more nuanced positions on the issue.

As American society becomes more diverse, the costs of taking an overtly hostile position on immigration will increasingly affect campaigns on a nationwide basis, not just those occurring in states adjoining the Mexican border. The 2016 presidential election provides a case in point. While Trump's divisive rhetoric proved appealing to many White voters, he alienated most Black and Latino voters. On Election Day, 11 percent of the electorate was made up of Latinos, and according to the polling firm Latino Decisions, less than one in five Latinos cast votes for Trump. As the share of the electorate tilts more heavily in the direction of minorities, the use of wedge appeals is likely to decline.

performance critiques that focus on the candidate's record. Personal attacks are standard fare in lower-level races. As one moves up the political ladder, attack ads become more of a mix of personality and performance. In 2016, for instance, interspersed with the steady stream of Clinton ads depicting Trump as a misogynist were ads questioning his positions on trade and climate change.

The most common genre of political attack is the flip-flop ad. In 2004, for example, the Bush campaign repeatedly juxtaposed Kerry's criticisms of the Iraq War with his Senate vote authorizing the war (using the punch line "John Kerry: whichever way the wind blows"). And given Mitt Romney's moderate record as governor of Massachusetts (where he supported abortion rights), he has consistently attracted the flip-flopper label. A 2008 primary ad by John McCain—"A Tale of Two Mitts"—became the template for a series of attack ads by Romney's more conservative Republican primary rivals. In the 2010 California gubernatorial race, meanwhile, Jerry Brown was quick to attack Meg Whitman for her dramatic change of heart on immigration. This line of attack is thought to be especially effective because it resonates with voters' stereotypes of politicians as insincere and willing to say anything to get elected.

An especially effective attack on a candidate's record is the guilt by association spot (see Video Archive 6.13). Criticizing a candidate for having voted to weaken the USA PATRIOT Act is unlikely to have much impact because most voters are not very familiar with that act. Linking the candidate with Osama bin Laden, however, would make it crystal clear that the candidate is soft on terrorism. Given President Trump's weak popularity (less than 40 percent of voters approved of his job performance in August 2018, according to Gallup) and the broad scope of the ongoing Mueller investigation, many Democrats running for Congress in 2018 depicted their opponents as supporters of the president.

Video Archive 6.13
Guilt by Association

REACTIVITY: ATTACKS PROVOKE COUNTERATTACKS

The prominence of negative appeals in campaign advertising can be attributed to several factors. Politics is seen as a dirty business, and the public is cynical about the motives and behaviors of candidates for office. In this context, an attack is more credible than a message promoting a candidate's virtues. Equally important, bad news and conflict are far more newsworthy than good news and civility. The ripple effect of negative advertising can be considerable. That is, attacks are especially effective in attracting press coverage; in fact, campaigns often schedule a press conference to announce their latest attack ad.

Sometimes the ad is merely a ruse designed to titillate the press, and no airtime is purchased. The Republican National Committee announced the hard-hitting anti-Clinton "Soldiers and Sailors" ad to the press in 1996, and the attack was summarized and critiqued in all the leading outlets, but the ad was never actually aired (see Video Archive 6.14). From the perspective of the Republicans, putting

Video Archive 6.14
Newsworthy Attacks

Bill Clinton's penchant for sex scandals on the front pages was well worth the criticism of releasing "misleading" information. During the 2004 campaign, a group funded by Republican donors (Swift Vets and POWs for Truth, a group of veterans who served in Vietnam on US Navy swift boats) aired an ad accusing Senator John Kerry of lying about his military record in Vietnam. Although the amount of money invested in both of these ads was trivial, the sponsors attracted a torrent of news reports across the country simply because their message was so controversial. The "Swift Boat" ad not only generated an avalanche of newspaper reports within the United States but also attracted considerable attention in the international press. For the media, personal attacks are big stories. According to one study, the press devoted more attention to the "Swift Boat" ad than to the Iraq War in the 2004 campaigns. As Figure 6.5 shows, the press has increasingly devoted more attention to political ads. Oftentimes, more people hear about the controversial ads from the news than see the actual ads. The added newsworthiness of negative ads gives campaigns a clear incentive to produce ads that will spark controversy.

The most compelling explanation of negative campaigning is that one attack invites a counterattack, thus setting in motion a spiral of negativity. Among campaign professionals, a fundamental principle is that the attacked

FIGURE 6.5

News Media Attention to Advertising, 1960–2008

Source: Data from J. G. Geer. (2010). *Fanning the flames: The news media's role in the rise of negativity in presidential campaigns*. Discussion paper, Joan Shorenstein Center on the Press, Politics, and Public Policy, Harvard University, Cambridge, MA. Retrieved September 13, 2021, from the Shorenstein Center website: https://shorensteincenter.org/wp-content/uploads/2012/03/d55_geer.pdf.

candidate must punch back, and the sooner the better. In this sense, at least, negative campaigns amount to a debate.

There is limited scientific evidence available that supports the efficacy of counterattacks, but the anecdotal evidence is consistent with the view that these ads work. In the 1988 presidential election, Governor Dukakis enjoyed a substantial lead over Vice President Bush after the Democratic convention. The Bush campaign then released a series of negative ads attacking Dukakis on crime (including a version of the "Willie Horton" ad) and the polluted state of Boston's harbor. Inexplicably, the Dukakis campaign ignored these attacks, even though the ads were highly controversial and the subject of interminable news coverage across the country. Eventually, Bush was able to catch up with Dukakis in the polls, and he went on to win the election.

Since 1988, campaign strategists have become convinced of the need to mount counterattacks. Mindful of the Dukakis experience, Clinton's advisers saw to it that every attack in 1992 was rebutted, in some cases even before the Republican ad hit the airwaves. Rapid response became the hallmark of advertising strategy, thus accelerating the pace at which campaign ads accentuated the negative. One of the major themes in postmortems of the 2004 campaign concerned the Kerry campaign's unwillingness to rebut the "Swift Boat" allegations. According to Kerry pollster Mark Mellman, the campaign was hesitant to counter the attacks for fear of adding credibility to the charges.[5]

The maxim of rapid counterattacks has now spread to the candidates' responses to unflattering news coverage. The very next day after the publication of the "sex tape" story in 2016, the Trump campaign arranged for four women who had accused Bill Clinton of inappropriate behavior to participate in a press conference designed to compare Clinton's actions with Trump's words. Roy Moore, the Republican candidate for US Senate from Alabama, labeled the *Washington Post*'s account of his dating young women a smear campaign from "the Obama-Clinton machine's liberal media lap-dogs." In a later tweet, he went further: "The forces of evil will lie, cheat, steal—even inflict physical harm—if they believe it will silence and shut up Christian conservatives."

In one of the few controlled studies to examine the value of counterattacks, Stephen Ansolabehere and Shanto Iyengar (1995) compared the vote shares of candidates who responded to an opponent's attack either by running a positive ad or by attacking the attacker. Respondents in these studies watched the initial attack and the attacked candidate's response. Applying this method to two statewide campaigns, the authors showed that the attacked candidate was significantly better off to counterattack. Moreover, they also demonstrated that support for the attacked candidate who responded with a positive ad dropped substantially among voters who shared the attacked candidate's party. That is, Democrats were less enthusiastic about voting Democratic when the Republican attacked and the Democrat countered with a positive message. Overall, Ansolabehere and Iyengar's results show clearly that rational candidates should counterattack.

The extensive use of negative campaigning raises serious questions about accountability in campaign discourse. Journalists can be sued for knowingly printing inaccurate information about public figures with intent to harm. The victims of negative advertising campaigns, on the other hand, have recourse only to the dictum of more speech—in this context, counterattacks. The lack of accountability for the use of misleading or inaccurate attacks is compounded by the frequent use of surrogates rather than the candidate as the messenger. In general, the more personal or controversial the attack, the less likely it is that the sponsoring candidate will appear in person. In the 2016 campaign, the most hard-hitting attacks on Donald Trump were delivered not by Hillary Clinton but by liberal interest groups such as Priorities USA (which spent $44 million on ads). Conversely, the most vicious attacks on Clinton came from groups backing Trump, including Rebuilding America Now and the National Rifle Association (see Video Archive 6.15). One such ad juxtaposed Bill Clinton's false claims about his relationship with Monica Lewinsky with his wife's statements on the Benghazi attack on the US consulate.

Video Archive 6.15
Third-Party Attacks

As a means of making candidates more responsible for their advertisements, reform-minded groups have been urging the passage of legislation that makes the connection between specific ads and the sponsoring candidate more transparent. Their efforts succeeded in 2003 when Congress adopted a provision requiring presidential candidates to appear on-screen in their ads while stating, "I'm Candidate X, and I approved this message." Because candidates can no longer rely on surrogates to do their dirty work for them, we may anticipate that the negativity quotient in campaign advertising will fall. At the very least, the in-person rule is likely to deter campaigns from engaging in character-related attacks. Of course, these provisions do little to dissuade the political party committees or other groups involved in campaigns to refrain from attacking. In fact, data from recent presidential campaigns show that the share of negative ads in the ad campaigns aired by affiliated groups is double the share for ads sponsored by the presidential candidates (Fowler, Ridout, & Franz, 2017).

DIRECT MAIL AS AN ALTERNATIVE TO TELEVISED ADVERTISING

For nonpresidential candidates, especially those running in geographically compact districts, televised advertising is an inefficient medium. The Los Angeles media market includes all or part of 17 congressional districts. New York City provides even less overlap between the media market and political district boundaries; the audience for New York City television includes voters in three different states (New York, New Jersey, and Connecticut). Congressional candidates who advertise on Los Angeles TV or candidates for governor of New York who buy time on New York City stations are paying top dollar (New York and Los Angeles are the two most expensive markets in the country) to reach people who cannot vote for them.

In congested markets, such as Los Angeles and New York, candidates rely on a more precise method of reaching voters: direct mail. Mail is the most extensive form of advertising in congressional and other localized campaigns. Direct mail is big business; total expenditures on mail during the 2008 campaign amounted to over $1 billion, and in California alone, there are some 75 registered mail consultants. As in the case of television advertising, mail consultants are affiliated by party; they work exclusively for Republicans or Democrats.

Los Angeles provides an ideal test case for comparing the role of mail to other communication channels. The city requires all candidates contesting citywide elections to submit all communications that reach at least 200 voters. These materials are available for public review. In a recent analysis, a Stanford researcher examined a database of 14,000 campaign appeals used in elections between 2008 and 2020. Direct mail and print flyers accounted for 43 percent of all messages, while television and radio ads made up less than 1 percent (Ayson, 2021).

Direct mail is used by all candidates, from the top of the ticket to the bottom. The top six presidential contenders in 2016—Democrats Hillary Clinton and Bernie Sanders and Republicans Donald Trump, Ted Cruz, Jeb Bush, and Marco Rubio—together spent nearly $70 million on direct mail. For Clinton and Trump, mail accounted for 5 percent of their total expenditures. In most cases, mailers focus on an individual candidate, but frequently they urge the voter to support an entire slate. So-called slate mailers are typically financed by state party organizations, but they are also published by private campaign consultants, some of whom mail millions of pieces per election.

Slate mail is the most economical form of political advertising. Not only does it maximize the ability of the candidate to target the message to voters (as opposed to nonvoters), but it also allows several candidates to share in the cost of advertising. For candidates whose budgets do not run into several millions of dollars (which includes virtually every candidate for county or local office), slate mail is the only advertising medium.

Because slate mailers usually feature candidates for several offices, lesser-known candidates benefit from their association with more visible candidates and causes. For instance, in the midst of the impeachment proceedings against President Clinton, a 1998 mailer sent to California Democrats featured the slogan "End the Washington witch hunt."

One final advantage of direct mail, at least from the candidate's perspective, is that the message is generally ignored by the news media. Candidates often resort to using misleading, unsubstantiated, and personal attacks against opponents. Sometimes, however, candidates can go too far. Ted Cruz was widely condemned for sending a mailer just before the Iowa caucuses emblazoned with the header "VOTING VIOLATION." The postcard informed the recipient, "You are receiving this election notice because of low expected voter turnout in your area. Your individual voting history as well as your neighbors' are public record. Their scores are published below, and many of them will see your score as well. Caucus on Monday to improve your score and please encourage your neighbors to caucus as well. A follow-up notice may be issued following

Monday's caucuses." In general, however, direct mail gets a PG rating when compared with negative television advertising.

In the final analysis, despite widespread concern that political ads trivialize democracy and transform campaigns into shouting matches, they remain an essential form of campaign communication. In the era of interpretive journalism, ads represent the only unmediated form of communicating with voters. It is not surprising that candidates use the opportunity to extol their own virtues and denigrate their opponents. If voters seem more responsive to a particular form of advertising, rational candidates converge on that form.

Attempts to regulate the content and form of campaign advertising are exercises in futility. As an ingredient of political speech, advertising is fully protected by the First Amendment. In races with evenly matched candidates, voters come across countervailing and retaliatory messages—that is, the campaign creates a free flow of information. As for the notion that voters need protection from ad campaigns, it suffices to note that voters are not fools. Recognizing the nature of the medium, they discount ads appropriately. The evidence on the effects of exposure to advertising (presented in Chapter 7) demonstrates that the principal effect is to make fellow partisans more enthusiastic about the sponsoring candidate. Seen in this light (preaching to the choir), efforts to police campaign advertising and monitor the accuracy of the charges and countercharges seem both elitist and excessive. Not only do ad watchers have the potential to recycle the message in the guise of a news report, but they are just as lacking in accountability as the ads themselves. And who watches the ad watchers?

Campaign advertising is expensive. Although presidential candidates are eligible for public financing of their campaigns, not one of the major party candidates has accepted public funds since 2008 because they would then be subject to the Federal Election Campaign Act, which limits the total amount they could spend. By opting out, they can raise and spend unlimited amounts. Since 1972, the total amount of money expended on campaigns has increased exponentially, reaching $14 billion in 2020. The huge sums of money involved and the resulting preoccupation with fund-raising have provoked considerable discussion about the role of money in politics. Should candidates who accept money from contributors return the favor by voting for legislation supported by the donors? Does the high cost of campaigning create the appearance that candidates are bought by powerful interests, thus compromising the political process? These and other questions have propelled campaign finance reform to the forefront of the policy agenda.

CAMPAIGN FINANCE REFORM: A BRIEF OVERVIEW

The present era of campaign finance reform began in 1971 with the passage of the Federal Election Campaign Act (FECA), whose stricter requirements concerning the disclosure of sources of campaign funding played a role in the Watergate scandal. The remaining provisions of the 1971 FECA never took effect because Watergate prompted their replacement by the 1974 FECA amendments. Those amendments remain the backbone of federal campaign finance regulation.

Aside from disclosure, the 1974 amendments contained three broad categories of regulation: limits on the size of contributions, limits on the amount of spending, and limits on public financing. The limits on how much a campaign could spend were supplemented by limits on how much candidates could spend of their own money on their campaigns and on how much outsiders could spend independently to help the candidate. The contribution and spending limits applied to all federal candidates, but the public financing was available only for presidential elections. Public funds matched private contributions in presidential primaries, and the public funds were supposed to pay all the costs of the national nominating conventions and of the presidential general election campaigns. The Federal Election Commission (FEC), with members appointed by the president and by party leaders in the House and Senate, was created to administer the new law.

BUCKLEY V. VALEO

The first challenge to campaign finance regulations was considered by the US Supreme Court in 1976 in *Buckley v. Valeo*. The court ruled that all three forms of spending limits were violations of the First Amendment guarantee of freedom of speech. In an oft-quoted passage, the court said, "The concept that government may restrict the speech of some elements of our society in order to enhance the relative voice of others is wholly foreign to the First Amendment" (*Buckley v. Valeo*, 1976, pp. 48–49). Although the court thus rejected promotion of equality as a justification for speech restrictions, it gave more credence to the goal of preventing corruption (such as the buying of influence) and the appearance of corruption. That goal justified the limits on the size of contributions by individuals, political action committees (PACs), and other entities.

The court rejected challenges to most other parts of the law, including the disclosure and public financing provisions. Furthermore, even spending limits could be constitutional if they were conditions attached to the voluntary acceptance of benefits received from the state, such as public financing. However, the court found that the ability of congressional leaders to appoint members of the FEC violated the separation of powers required by the Constitution. Congress quickly amended the law in 1976 to allow the president to appoint all the members. By custom ever since, the president has deferred to the leadership of the other party on half the FEC appointments.

An additional set of FECA amendments was enacted in 1979. In an attempt to strengthen the role of party organizations, Congress excluded party-building activities, such as get-out-the-vote efforts and administrative upkeep, from regulation. This provision became significant in later years as parties took advantage of the party-building exclusion to raise unlimited amounts of contributions known as *soft money*.

Federal campaign law then remained stable for nearly a quarter of a century. Campaign practices evolved, however, usually to the discomfort of reform activists, who tended to be Democrats. The first major development was the rise of business-oriented PACs during the 1970s. As is often the case with political reform, this development contained some irony in that it had been labor unions, not corporations, that had pressed Congress to make clear the legality of PACs in the 1974 amendments. But business took the most advantage. Four major types of organizations sponsored PACs in the 1970s: unions, corporations, trade groups, and ideological groups. All were significant, but it was the corporate PACs that grew the fastest and raised the most money.

Nevertheless, the PAC situation eventually stabilized, and in the meantime, activists became preoccupied with a new development: independent spending. Because the Supreme Court had upheld limits on the size of contributions but protected the right to independently spend unlimited amounts for a candidate, some organizations found that to have a noticeable effect on elections they had to turn to independent spending. In particular, certain conservative PACs had considerable success in 1978 and 1980 using independent spending to defeat incumbent Democratic senators. Reformers who were Democrats clamored for control of independent spending for both partisan and ideological reasons. But by 1982, Democratic senators had learned how to defend themselves against attacks driven by independent spending. Reformers' attention turned to the issue of soft money and, later, to the related matter of issue advocacy.

SOFT MONEY AND ISSUE ADVOCACY

Soft money has been defined in various ways. Its original meaning was money that political parties could raise and spend that was exempt from the disclosure requirements and, especially, the contribution limits imposed by FECA.

Now the term often denotes campaign money that is exempt from limitation, whether or not it is spent by a party. Concern over soft money began to be expressed in the 1980s and grew steadily through the mid-1990s. Despite the reformers' concern, however, soft money does not appear to have played a major role until the 1996 election.

To understand *issue advocacy,* which also emerged as a major issue in 1996, we must go back to the Supreme Court's decision in *Buckley v. Valeo.* The FECA definition of campaign expenditures turned on whether money was spent for a *political purpose,* a term that the court regarded as unduly vague. To avoid that vagueness, the court in *Buckley* interpreted FECA to cover only expenditures for speech that expressly urged the election or defeat of a clearly identified candidate. Phrases such as "Vote for Smith," "Defeat Lopez," or "Reelect the President" would qualify. Ads referring to candidates but not containing express advocacy were referred to as *issue ads* or *issue advocacy,* and they were not covered by FECA.

The court itself admitted in *Buckley* that the narrow definition of what was included as a campaign expenditure would allow evasion of the campaign law. Nevertheless, and perhaps surprising, for about two decades very little advertising took advantage of this loophole. But the new possibilities of both soft money and issue advocacy exploded in 1996.

In that year, parties began raising soft money in much larger amounts than in the past, much of it in contributions of six or seven figures. Furthermore, much of the soft money was more directly related to particular federal campaigns than it had been before. The clearest and most important example was issue advertising that targeted particular candidates but that evaded regulation because it did not use words such as *vote for* or *defeat.*

In addition to the explosion of soft money raised by parties, the 1996 election saw a new large-scale use of issue advertising by nonparty groups. Unions paid for ads attacking Republican candidates, and business funded ads attacking Democrats. Unlike the use of soft money by the parties, nonparty issue advertising evaded not only the contribution limitations and prohibitions but also the disclosure requirements.

Soft money and issue advocacy expanded dramatically in 1996 and grew even more in subsequent elections. Reformers, who in the early and mid-1990s had been proposing broad new campaign regulations that were going nowhere in Congress, began focusing on soft money and issue advocacy. They enjoyed widespread support from the press, but the passage of legislation might not have been possible without a political boost from scandals that erupted early in 2002 regarding fraudulent accounting practices of Enron and other large corporations.

BIPARTISAN CAMPAIGN REFORM ACT

The legislation, passed by Congress in 2002 and signed by President George W. Bush, was known as the McCain–Feingold bill in the Senate and the Shays–Meehan bill in the House. Its official name is the Bipartisan Campaign Reform Act (BCRA), which is a misnomer because despite support from a few prominent Republicans, such as Senator John McCain, it relied primarily on Democratic support.

Although BCRA doubled the limit on contributions from individuals to federal candidates from $1,000 to $2,000, virtually all the remaining provisions consisted of new or tightened regulations. These regulations cover a wide variety of subjects, but the most important provisions are aimed at parties (and therefore at soft money) and at issue advocacy.

The BCRA method of dealing with soft money is rather severe. All money raised by parties at the national level has to be *hard money*—specifically, money raised within the federal contribution limits and subject to federal prohibitions, such as those relating to corporate and union contributions. This restriction applies even to money raised for purposes far removed from campaigns, such as building party headquarters. Furthermore, restrictions on state and local parties are greatly tightened. Suppose, for example, that a state party spends $100,000 on get-out-the-vote activities. Before BCRA, a formula would be applied to determine the portion of the expenditure attributable to federal races. If that portion were 40 percent, then $40,000 of the state party's expenditure would have to be paid for out of contributions raised within the federal limits and prohibitions, but the remaining $60,000 would be subject only to whatever limits were imposed by state law. Under BCRA, all the funds must come from hard money if the ballot contains any federal candidate at all.

BCRA's approach to issue advocacy is equally broad but surprisingly incomplete. To deal with the vagueness that caused problems in *Buckley*, BCRA created a new category called *electioneering communications*, consisting of any broadcast advertising that identifies a federal candidate and is run within 30 days before a primary or 60 days before a general election. Electioneering communications must be disclosed and must be paid for out of hard money. The concept sweeps broadly because it includes not only ads clearly targeted at the campaign but other ads that mention, say, the president or a senator while debating a particular legislative or policy controversy having no direct relation to the campaign. On the other hand, all nonbroadcast advertising and all advertising airing more than a month or two before the election are excluded.

Despite BCRA's early success in court, it had little impact on the money chase in the 2004–2008 election cycle. To the surprise of some, parties were able to make up for the loss of large contributions by raising increased amounts of hard money, partly with the aid of relatively small donations raised through the internet. But the large donors, blocked from giving to the parties, found a new vehicle in the so-called 527 groups (named after the section of the Internal Revenue Code under which they are organized). George Soros and other wealthy Democrats announced that they would be contributing millions to 527s in their efforts to defeat President Bush, and the Republicans were quick to follow suit, claiming they would raise an equivalent sum to support the president's campaign. Most analysts agree that the 527 groups are evidence of the perverse consequences of campaign finance regulation. By eliminating soft money raised by political parties—whose role in the electoral process is essential and legitimate—reformers have encouraged the development of a class of groups with no electoral accountability whatsoever.

In addition to the rise of the 527s, tighter campaign finance restrictions may be a cause of increased incumbency advantage in congressional elections. Incumbents are reelected more than 90 percent of the time, primarily because they are better known to voters than their challengers are. Incumbents receive regular media exposure and various other perks (free use of television studios to produce videos, multiple trips to their district, all costs of mailings to their constituents being covered by taxpayers, and so on) that contribute to their greater visibility. Placing equal limits on challengers' and incumbents' fund-raising inevitably has unequal consequences because challengers need to spend more money to overcome the incumbent's considerable recognizability advantage.

Another drawback of BCRA is its incredible complexity. It used to be said that if you wanted to run for office, the first thing you had to do was hire a lawyer. In this post-BCRA era, it is likely that your lawyer will have to hire a lawyer because only a few specialists have a firm grasp on the ins and outs of the law. Although the effects are hard to quantify, campaign finance regulations of this order of magnitude may tend to discourage some people from becoming active in politics as candidates, party officials, or activists.

CITIZENS UNITED AND McCUTCHEON

In recent developments, the Supreme Court ruled, in *Citizens United v. Federal Election Commission* (2010), that corporations and labor unions have the same First Amendment right to make unlimited independent expenditures in election campaigns that individual citizens and other kinds of organizations have. In the aftermath of the decision, public attention has focused on the possible unleashing of corporate political power, although whatever increases there may be in corporate and union expenditures are likely to offset each other. Four years later, in *McCutcheon v. Federal Election Commission* (2014), the court decided that the cap on the total amount individuals could donate to multiple campaigns (which was $123,000) was an unconstitutional impediment to freedom of speech. The court did leave intact the cap on donations to individual candidates ($2,600 across primary and general election races). The practical impact of the decision, therefore, is that wealthy individuals can make contributions to as many candidates and causes as they like. As expected, the removal of the cap on individual spending has resulted in significantly higher levels of campaign fund-raising since 2014 (Lioz, Navarro-Rivera, and McElwee, 2017).

CANDIDATE DEBATES

The final element of campaign strategy in the post-television era concerns debates. On September 26, 1960, an audience of 70 million gathered around their television sets to watch the first of four debates between John F. Kennedy and Richard Nixon. Nixon was in poor health and appeared without make-up (thus revealing that he had not shaved). Kennedy, in contrast, appeared tanned, fit, and youthful. Audience reaction to the historic debate was remarkably one-sided; a significant majority gave the nod to Kennedy (see Video Archive 6.16). In future debates, candidates would be more attentive to matters of appearance and imagery.

Video Archive 6.16
Nixon–JFK Debate

Oddly enough, debates occur more frequently in primary than in general election campaigns. In the 2007–2008 Democratic primary and preprimary seasons, there were so many debates (26 in all) and joint appearances on the schedule that the candidates found it difficult to carry on with their normal activities (such as fund-raising). Even more important is that the opportunity to participate in multiple debates gives candidates who do not have the backing of the party establishment an incentive to prolong their campaign by attacking the front-runner. The Republicans held more than 20 primary debates in 2012, allowing the candidates to "slice and dice" each other for months on end. Following the election, the Republican National Committee decided that there would be fewer debates in 2016 (only 13). The Democratic National Committee followed suit, reducing the number of primary debates to

10 in 2016 and 12 in 2020. By cutting down on the number of opportunities for the candidates to attack each other on national television, the party leaders hope to make the primary process less divisive and thus boost the general election prospects of the nominee.

Typically, primary debates attract tiny audiences, consisting for the most part of party activists. However, the presence of Donald Trump and the circus-like atmosphere of the 2016 debates provided a significant boost to the size of the debate audience. In 2012, on average, the 20 Republican primary debates attracted an audience of 5.1 million viewers. The same average in 2016 shot up to 15.4 million, an increase of 300 percent! At a campaign rally, Trump floated the idea that he would demand $5 million from CNN to participate in their debate (the money would go to charity) because he had driven up the ratings. In fact, Trump's presence did correlate with higher ratings. We can assess the "Trump effect" by comparing viewership for the 12 primary debates in which he participated with the one debate he skipped (on January 26, 2016). Without Trump, the audience fell by nearly 3 million viewers. Not surprisingly, the percentage of the public saying that the presidential campaign was "interesting" reached an all-time high of 67 percent in 2016 (Pew Research Center, 2016).

In fact, the term *debate* is something of a misnomer when applied to campaigns. It is true that the audience observes the candidates answering questions and offering summary introductory and closing statements, but these resemblances to conventional debates are superficial. In fact, debates—at least those occurring in the fall of election years—are closely managed by the candidates so as to maximize their ability to score points with the relevant judges, namely, the viewing audience. From the subject matter of the questions, to the identity of the questioners, to scheduling preferences and even the details of the shape of the stage and the podiums, campaigns control the protocol. The Bill Clinton campaign, for instance, pushed hard for adoption of a town hall format in the 1992 campaign; the George H. W. Bush campaign, knowing that its candidate was more reserved and less apt to connect with ordinary people, argued in favor of the more conventional panel of questioners. In the end, the town hall format was used for one debate, and the other two debates relied on a panel.

A recurring issue with televised candidate debates concerns eligibility. Major party candidates may participate, but all minor party candidates are excluded. In fact, the reason for the suspension of debates between 1964 and 1976 was that the television networks (who were then the principal sponsors) were legally bound to include minor party candidates under the provisions of the FCC's Fairness Doctrine. If one candidate was offered 90 minutes of prime-time exposure, then all other candidates for the same position were entitled to similar treatment. In 1976, the rule was evaded, and the debates resumed by use of a third-party sponsor—the League of Women Voters. The league invited only the major party candidates, giving the networks the freedom to televise the debates as a newsworthy event. Today, organization of the debates is in the hands of a nonpartisan commission on presidential debates. The commission has formulated a set of criteria for eligibility, the most notable of which is that a candidate must demonstrate a level of public support (in reputable polls) of at least 15 percent. By this standard, virtually all third-party candidates are excluded. In 2016, there were so many Republicans in the presidential field— too many to fit on a single debate stage—that the networks adopted a two-tier system, with candidates falling below a minimum polling threshold relegated to a debate that aired in the afternoon and the prime-time platform reserved for the "first string." The overcrowding problem got even worse in 2020, when the Democratic field included no less than 29 candidates.

With the advent of cable television and the greater freedom afforded the viewing audience, fewer people are tuning in, even to the general election presidential debates. As Figure 6.6 shows, the size of the debate audience has

FIGURE 6.6

The Shrinking Audience for Presidential Debates, 1960–2020

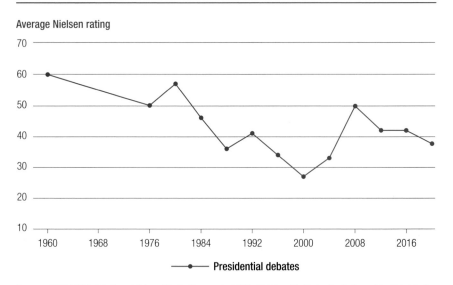

Source: 1960–2008 data from Nielsen Media Research. (2008, October 6). Highest rated presidential debates 1960 to present. Retrieved from the Nielsen Media Research website: https://www.nielsen.com/us/en /insights/article/2008/top-ten-presidential-debates-1960-to-present/; 2012–2020 data compiled by the author from Nielsen press releases.

declined substantially from its peak in 1960. If we translate the Nielsen ratings into the percentage of households watching, the decline amounts to nearly 20 percentage points between 1960 and 2016. The debates held in 1960, 1976, and 1980 attracted well over half the total viewing audience. Since 1984, however, only once has the debate audience amounted to one-half of the total audience and that was in 2008 with the historic candidacy of Barack Obama.

The declining trend in audience size also applies to entertainment programming, including such high-profile events as Major League Baseball's World Series and the Academy Awards, suggesting a generalized fragmentation of the national television audience. Even with their diminished share of the audience, debates reach a much larger number of voters than any single advertisement or news report can. For the candidates, the benefits (and risks) of performing before 70 million viewers mere weeks in advance of the election are huge. Campaigns understandably go to great lengths to prepare their candidates. They suspend the travel schedule, hold no other events, and devote several days to preparation, even to the extent of holding full-scale dress rehearsals.

The fact that the debates are far from spontaneous exchanges does not seem to have reduced their credibility with the public. In comparison with television ads and news reports, debates are easily the most favorably evaluated form of campaigning. Two-thirds of the electorate reported that they took debates into account in 2016. Surveys also indicate that, unlike opinions about advertising and news coverage, both of which the public dismisses as unhelpful to the task of voting, large majorities generally rate the debates as either "very helpful" or "somewhat helpful." This was not the case, however, in 2020. The first debate between Biden and Trump degenerated into utter chaos (see Video Archive 6.17) with Trump constantly interrupting both Biden and the moderator (Chris Wallace from Fox News). Immediately after the debate, the polling company YouGov asked a sample of likely voters for their reactions; only 17 percent said they found the debate informative. Instead, most voters said the debate left them feeling annoyed.

Video Archive 6.17
Debate Gaffes

From the candidates' perspective, the benefits of debates include an opportunity to demonstrate their fitness for office: their command over the issues, their demeanor under duress, their sense of humor, and their ability to deal with conflict. The principal risk is that they will say or do something that makes them look less than presidential. Their first priority, accordingly, is to avoid committing a *gaffe*—a major misstatement of fact. The best example of such a misstatement occurred in the 1976 foreign policy debate between incumbent Republican Gerald Ford and Democrat Jimmy Carter. President

Ford incorrectly asserted that the countries of Eastern Europe were generally free of Soviet domination—a statement that he made not once but twice. Remarkably, as we will discuss in the next chapter, this blunder had no immediate impact on viewers' evaluations of Ford and Carter.

Scoring points with undecided voters sometimes calls for more than verbal fluency or command over the subject matter. Candidates must also convey cues concerning their personality, emotions, and people skills. When Michael Dukakis was asked in 1988 if his position on the death penalty (he was opposed) would change if his wife, Kitty, were raped and then murdered, his relatively calm response led many commentators to suggest that he was a cold fish, incapable of expressing emotion. Newt Gingrich adopted precisely the opposite approach in 2012 when asked by John King of CNN about his alleged extramarital affairs. Gingrich turned the tables on King by condemning the question as an attempt by the "liberal media" to sabotage any discussion of political issues.

Sometimes candidates send the wrong signal not by what they say but rather by their demeanor. In the first debate of the 2000 campaign, Vice President Al Gore repeatedly cut off Governor George W. Bush's answers, generally coming across as an arrogant know-it-all. President George H. W. Bush committed a nonverbal gaffe in the town hall debate of 1992; obviously uncomfortable with the format and the proceedings, the president was seen studying his watch, thus conveying the impression that he found the discussion, which concerned mostly middle-class worries, of little interest. Donald Trump, in the second debate of 2016—which followed a town hall format—chose to walk around the stage rather than sit still in his seat. He often appeared behind Clinton while she was speaking, leading the Clinton campaign to accuse him of "stalking" behavior. In the following debate, Trump was guilty of a verbal gaffe when, in effect, he became the first presidential candidate to deny the legitimacy of the election by refusing to answer "yes" to the question of whether he would accept the result should he lose.

The gold medal for debate gaffes clearly goes to Texas governor Rick Perry who, in an early 2012 campaign debate, repeated his campaign pledge to eliminate three major federal agencies (see Video Archive 6.17). He identified two—the Departments of Commerce and Education—but was unable to remember the third (the Department of Energy). Perry responded to questions about his debate performance by noting that "everybody makes mistakes," but his poll numbers stayed low and a few weeks later he withdrew from the race.

In nonpresidential campaigns, debates contribute little. It's not that candidates for statewide office do not debate. They do, and frequently. But voters have little opportunity to view these debates because they are rarely televised in prime time. In a study of statewide campaigns in 10 states, the Committee for the Study of the American Electorate found that two-thirds of the debates were televised, but only half were shown on network affiliates with large shares of the audience. Debates between candidates for the US House were even less newsworthy: only 30 percent were televised.

CONCLUSION

The basic objective of any campaign strategy is simple: maximize the number of positive messages about yourself and the number of negative messages about your opponent. Given the role of the press, candidates can no longer expect reporters to do their bidding. As a result, the campaigns have taken to more subtle forms of spin, from staging events to uncovering newsworthy information concerning opponents. On the advertising front, candidates attempt to promote their candidacies with personal and performance-based appeals. More often than not, advertising campaigns do not address the same issues; instead, candidates talk past one another, each emphasizing their respective strengths. In the case of negative campaigns, the candidates engage in a debate of sorts, not about the strengths of their policy proposals but about the veracity and fairness of the charges and countercharges they hurl at each other. Finally, debates provide candidates with opportunities to close the deal—to demonstrate to voters that what they see in the ad campaign is what they get for real.

Summary

1. Media-based campaigns take place on two *stages: free media* (news coverage) and *paid media* (candidate advertisements). Presidential races enjoy virtually unlimited news coverage, making the ad campaign only a small trickle in the cumulative message stream; advertising strategy is still extremely important to presidential candidates, however, because it represents their only opportunity to present their case unfiltered by journalists. In the case of nonpresidential races (congressional, gubernatorial, and so on), paid media dominate because news coverage is sparse.
2. Although advertising provides candidates with much greater control over their message than news coverage does, there is a significant trade-off; advertising is a much less credible messenger than news reports.

3. Candidates take numerous steps to focus news coverage on subjects that they consider advantageous:
   - Candidates try to avoid the media feeding frenzies that arise whenever they demonstrate a personal or character flaw.
   - Candidates can gain an advantage in coverage if the opponent makes a major misstatement of fact or reverses course on a matter of public policy.
   - Campaigns often attempt to set low expectations about their candidates' prospects or standing—especially during the primary season—so that any level of achievement above this low baseline will be more surprising to journalists and hence be covered more extensively and favorably.
   - The nuts and bolts of press management is the strategic handling of events, which are scheduled in such a way as to maximize press coverage.
   - Campaigns regulate media access to candidates on the basis of the candidates' standing in the polls: candidates who are trailing may follow an open-door strategy with the press, while candidates who are ahead tend to severely limit media access.
   - Candidates can limit the access of journalists who are more likely to be critical, while devoting time to outlets more likely to provide favorable coverage. Campaigns dogged by critical coverage may try to shield the candidate from the national press by cultivating less prominent outlets, such as local news and talk show formats.
   - Candidates react to each other's statements and actions on a continuous basis, mainly in the form of competing press releases. Campaigns research the opponent's record and monitor the opponent's actions and words, with the aim of pouncing on any particularly newsworthy item.
4. Candidates follow several strategies in designing their advertising campaigns:
   - Campaigns aim their advertisements at voters whose preferences may be pivotal to the outcome of the race—that is, voters in states or areas considered competitive.
   - Candidates change the content and tone of their advertisements over the course of the campaign, from biographical spots early in the campaign to image and issue ads later.
   - In their advertising campaigns, candidates emphasize issues on which they enjoy an advantage over their opponent. A particularly important aspect of this strategy is issue ownership.
   - Candidates may also use wedge appeals in their advertising, particularly if they are losing the debate on generic issues. Wedge issues are designed to pit groups against each other, to appeal to voters' sense of group identity.

- A striking attribute of political advertising campaigns is the heavy reliance on negative (attack) advertising.
- Negative messages dominate campaign advertising both because they tend to be more newsworthy than civil discourse and because the public's low opinion of politicians makes attacks on opposing candidates more credible than promoting one's own virtues. Furthermore, among campaign professionals, a fundamental principle is that a candidate must punch back when attacked.
- Candidates often use direct mail to target voters more effectively. Direct mail is especially important in lower-level races, where TV advertising is inefficient.

5. Advertising is expensive and necessitates the raising of huge sums of money for political campaigns. In recent decades, concern about the role of money in politics has led to several attempts at campaign finance reform. In most cases, however, these attempts have merely encouraged campaigns to find loopholes and new, creative financing techniques.

6. Another important element of campaigns is the candidate debates. Campaigns closely manage debates to maximize their candidates' ability to score points with the viewing audience.

FURTHER READINGS

Ansolabehere, S., & Iyengar, S. (1995). *Going negative: How attack ads shrink and polarize the electorate.* New York: Free Press.

Bartels, L. M. (1988). *Presidential primaries and the dynamics of public choice.* Princeton, NJ: Princeton University Press.

Fowler, E. F., Franz, M. M., Martin, G. J., Peskowitz, Z., & Ridout, T. N. (2021). Political advertising online and offline. *American Political Science Review, 115,* 130–149.

Geer, J. (2010). *Fanning the flames: The news media's role in the rise of negativity in presidential campaigns.* Discussion paper, Joan Shorenstein Center on the Press, Politics, and Public Policy, Harvard University, Cambridge, MA.

Jacobson, G. C. (1997). *The politics of congressional elections* (4th ed.). New York: Longman.

Petrocik, J. R. (1996). Issue ownership in presidential elections, with a 1980 case study. *American Journal of Political Science, 40,* 825–850.

Popkin, S. L. (1994). *The reasoning voter: Communication and persuasion in presidential campaigns* (2nd ed.). Chicago: University of Chicago Press.

Vavreck, L. (2008). *The message matters: The economy and presidential campaigns.* Princeton, NJ: Princeton University Press.

NOTES

1. The networks were quick to point out that this limited coverage did not amount to an abdication of their civic responsibility, stating that they intended to provide gavel-to-gavel coverage on their online subsidiaries.

2. A GRP is defined as the sum of all Nielsen rating points for the programs in which the ad was placed. (One Nielsen point is approximately 1 percent of the media market in which the ad airs.)

3. After the campaign, the story was exposed as Democratic spin; no such event occurred.

4. Because there are more Democrats than Republicans in the national electorate and the Democrats have traditionally enjoyed near-unanimous backing from the African American community, the incentive to use wedge appeals based on race is especially enticing for Republican candidates.

5. Mark Mellman, conference remarks, "The 2004 American Presidential Election: Voter Decision-Making in a Complex World," Institute for Research in the Social Sciences, Stanford University, November 9, 2004.

7

Campaigns That Matter

Candidates spend millions of dollars on political campaigns and deploy small armies of professional consultants in hopes of gaining a competitive edge. But in the end, would they be any worse off without this investment? Do campaigns really make a difference?

This chapter begins by providing an overview of two competing perspectives on this question and suggesting how these disparate perspectives may be reconciled. We then turn to the dynamics influencing voter behavior, the role of campaigns in providing civic education, and factors influencing voter turnout.

POLITICAL CONTEXT VERSUS CAMPAIGN EFFECTS

There are two competing perspectives on the question of how much campaigns matter. In the minimalist view typically advanced by academics, political campaigns represent "sound and fury signifying nothing." The evidence shows that, at least in the case of presidential elections, the results can be predicted with a high degree of accuracy from indicators of economic growth and public approval of the incumbent administration. In this account, changes in gross national product (GNP) during the preceding 12 months and the level of public approval of the incumbent president 4 months before the election are relevant to election outcomes; day-to-day tactics of the candidates in October, seemingly, are not. At the very least, this evidence suggests that the general political and economic context in which elections occur is just as important as anything the candidates themselves might do or say over the course of the campaign.

The view from the trenches is quite different. Campaign consultants claim considerable prowess in improving their clients' electoral prospects.

By the consultants' account, well-executed campaign maneuvers can produce a significant increase in the candidate's level of support. They claim that political advertising, news coverage of campaign events, and the candidate's verbal dexterity and demeanor in the debates make all the difference to voters. The theory is that image matters; therefore, image is what campaigns seek to project, using creative and intensive interventions.

Mounting evidence supports the existence of short-term campaign effects. Typically, a presidential candidate's visit to a state generates considerable media publicity and increases that candidate's support statewide. But an opposing candidate who arrives the very next day creates an equally powerful ripple in the opposite direction. It seems that day-to-day tactics can significantly move public opinion; however, if campaigns have similar levels of resources (in terms of both funding and professional expertise), then campaign-induced shifts in voter support will cancel each other out over the course of the campaign.

Between the strictly context-driven and engineered explanations of electoral outcomes is a more realistic middle ground. Every election occurs within a distinct political context to which the candidates adapt their messages. During the recession of 1992, Americans' general sense of economic insecurity led the Clinton campaign to adopt "It's the economy, stupid" as its core message and mantra. In 2004, in the aftermath of the 9/11 attacks and the first stages of the war in Iraq, President Bush ran for reelection on the grounds that he had made the country more secure from terrorist attacks. In 2020, Joe Biden ran as the candidate with the competence to get the COVID-19 pandemic under control, suggesting that President Trump had failed to do so. Four years earlier, Trump used his "Build the wall" slogan to capitalize on anti-immigration sentiment. Each campaign was seeking to position itself advantageously within the current political context to which the candidates had to respond. Economic messages were paramount in 1992 and 2012 but less important in 2004 and 2016, when concerns over national security and illegal immigration were more salient.

No matter the nature of the current political context, a perennial element of campaigns is the track record of the candidate or party in power. Voters tend to rely on their assessments of the incumbent's performance as a guide for choosing between the candidates. In their eyes, the state of the country reflects either favorably or unfavorably on the incumbent. Ronald Reagan understood the intuitive appeal of this psychological barometer when he asked voters, "Are you better off today than you were four years ago?"

However, well-entrenched perceptions of the state of the nation and the qualities of the incumbent administration do not make campaign strategies irrelevant. To the contrary, campaign professionals know full well that voters care about the current political context, and they design their messages accordingly. They position their clients to capitalize on what voters deem important. Thus, in any given campaign, exposure to the candidates' messages makes voters even more reliant on the underlying fundamental or contextual forces.

VOTER DYNAMICS: FORECASTING PRESIDENTIAL ELECTIONS

Political scientists have devised a variety of statistical models for forecasting the results of presidential elections. In most cases, the forecasts combine the incumbent's popularity with the state of the economy. The dynamic underlying the forecasting models is exactly as implied by Reagan's rhetorical ploy—namely, the logic of reward or punishment based on the incumbent's stewardship of the country. Voters are expected to reelect the incumbent during times of economic growth but opt for change during times of distress.

Forecasters capture this logic by incorporating some measure of public support for the incumbent (typically the incumbent's standing in trial-heat polls that predict the two-party vote on Labor Day or the percentage of the public who approve of the president's job performance) with standard indicators of economic performance. The economic indicators are generally recorded considerably in advance of the campaign; examples include annual change in disposable personal income, consumer satisfaction with personal finances in the second quarter of the election year, or the percentage change in GNP between the fourth quarter of the preceding year and the second quarter of the election year.

Basing their predictions on a combination of public opinion and the past state of the economy, the forecasting models have proven generally accurate: with the exception of the 2000 and 2016 elections (elections in which the candidate with the most votes actually lost), most models have predicted the winner in elections from 1948 to 2020 with only a small spread between the predicted and actual results. For the 2008 and 2012 elections, the average forecast proved accurate to within a half of a percentage point of the actual outcome.

Figure 7.1 shows the overall correspondence between the 2019–2020 percentage change in real disposable income per capita and the fate of the incumbent party's presidential candidate. Clearly, more money in voters' pocketbooks tends to benefit incumbents. On the basis of this particular model—devised by

FIGURE 7.1

The Economy and the Vote for President, 1948–2020

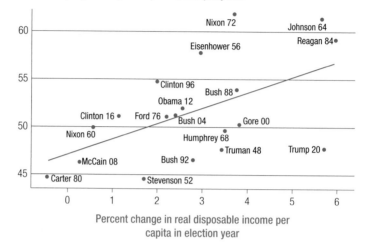

Incumbent party share (percent) of the two-party vote

Percent change in real disposable income per
capita in election year

Note: Blue line indicates predicted share of the popular vote.
Source: Data from Bureau of Economic Analysis. (2020). GDP and personal income. Retrieved September 14, 2021, from the Bureau of Economic Analysis website: https://www.bea.gov/iTable/index_nipa.cfm.

political scientists Larry Bartels and John Zaller (2001)—President Bush won reelection in 2004 by almost exactly the expected margin, given the state of the economy. Hillary Clinton's victory in the popular vote over Donald Trump exceeded the model's prediction; given the lackadaisical state of the economy, the model predicted a victory for the nonincumbent party. In 2020, given the significant boost to disposable income from the pandemic-related stimulus checks issued by the federal government, this model predicted a comfortable victory for Trump. The fact that Trump fell well short of the forecast suggests that other factors—most notably, the state of the COVID-19 pandemic—took precedence over economic concerns.

The data in Figure 7.1 show that in addition to Trump, Harry Truman (1948), Adlai Stevenson (1952), George H. W. Bush (1992), Hubert Humphrey (1968), and Al Gore (2000) fared worse than they should have given the state of the economy. On the positive side, "overachievers" (who exceeded their expected vote) included Presidents Dwight Eisenhower (1956), Richard Nixon (1972), Bill Clinton (1996), and Joe Biden (2020). Overall, Figure 7.1 suggests that, at the margin, presidential campaigns infrequently produce significant deviations from the outcome one would see if voters cared only about the state of the economy.

TABLE 7.1

Forecasting the 2020 Presidential Election

Model	Predicted Trump Share of Two-Party Vote	Predicted Share Minus Actual Share
Erickson and Wlezien—leading economic indicators model	45.0	−2.7
DeSart and Holbrook—state-level candidate preference model	45.6	−2.1
Jerome, Jerome-Speziari, Mongrain, and Nadeau—state by state model	48.3	0.6
Lewis-Beck and Tien—popularity plus growth model	43.3	−4.4
Graefe—issues and competence model	47.2	−0.5
Enns and Lagodny—state presidential approval model	45.4	−2.2
Gruca and Reitz—Iowa electronic markets model	49.9	2.2

Source: Data from R. Dassonneville & C. Tien. (2021). Introduction to forecasting the 2020 U.S. elections. *PS: Political Science and Politics*, 54, 47–51.

As shown in Figure 7.1, the forecasting model based on changes in per capita disposable income incorrectly forecast a Trump victory. However, notwithstanding the unprecedented political context of the 2020 election (a raging pandemic and extensive voting by mail), most published forecasts proved accurate. Table 7.1 shows the predicted share of the Trump two-party vote versus the actual share for seven different models. With the exception of one model, the forecasters fared well, typically underestimating Trump's share of the vote, with an average forecast error of around 2 percent.

THE INFLUENCE OF CAMPAIGNS

The fact that presidential elections generally follow the reward-or-punish rule is not in and of itself an argument against the influence of campaigns. First, when the contest is competitive and the candidates are separated by only a few points in the polls, the efforts of campaign strategists may make all the difference between winning and losing. In the case of the 2016 election, a difference of less than 40,000 votes in the key battleground states of Michigan, Wisconsin, and Pennsylvania would have made Hillary Clinton the winner. In 2020, a total of 44,000 vote switches in Arizona, Georgia, and Wisconsin would have produced a tie between Trump and Biden in the Electoral College. Second, as we will discuss, considerable evidence suggests that exposure to campaign messages encourages voters, especially those with lower levels of political interest and motivation, to behave in ways that are exactly as anticipated by the forecasting models.

Contrary to conventional wisdom, the evidence suggests that campaigns do not manipulate voters into supporting the candidate with the most attractive appearance or compelling advertisements. Instead, one of the principal effects of campaigns is to bring candidate preferences into line with the voter's sense of party identification. By the end of the campaign, very few partisans contemplate voting for the out-party candidate.

In the rest of this chapter, we will look at the ways in which campaigns influence voters. After presenting the evidence concerning the reinforcing effects of campaigns, we will turn to the ways in which campaigns attract so-called swing, or undecided, voters. Typically lacking an attachment to a party, these voters are susceptible to image- and issue-oriented appeals. They might vote for the candidate deemed more trustworthy or the candidate who stands for policies that more closely approximate their own preferences.

Next we will take up the educational or informative impact of campaigns. Presumably, the onslaught of advertising, news coverage, and partisan rhetoric adds something to voters' store of knowledge about the candidates and the issues. The evidence suggests that voters do indeed learn from campaigns, but they find it easier to learn about image than about issues. In the case of primary elections, voters are especially likely to gain information about the question of *viability*—a candidate's ability to win. The proliferation of early primaries and the fact that primary voters cannot fall back on their party affiliation create the possibility of significant bandwagon effects whereby voters flock to candidates who demonstrate vote-getting prowess in the early primaries.

Finally, we will address the role of campaigns in influencing the level of voter turnout. In recent cycles, both parties have invested significant resources in the ground game—contacting their potential supporters and getting them to the polls (for a review of recent research on getting out the vote, see Kalla & Broockman, 2017). For voters who may be less than enthusiastic about politics, get-out-the-vote efforts can be especially effective. While striving to increase turnout among their supporters, campaigns may simultaneously take steps to discourage would-be opponents from voting. One of the objectives of negative campaigning is to make undecided voters cynical about both candidates, thus weakening their incentive to vote.

VOTING AS AN EXPRESSION OF PARTISANSHIP

Decades of research into why individuals vote the way they do has made it abundantly clear that party affiliation is the single most important determinant of vote choice. Most Americans are socialized into identifying with one of the two major political parties even before they enter kindergarten. This basic sense of loyalty to the party sticks with individuals throughout their entire lives. In the jargon of voting research, party identification is the *long-term* influence on elections; year in and year out, Americans vote according to their standing commitment.[1] Contrary to popular accounts, party identification is alive and well within the electorate; if anything, in this era of polarized politics, party-line voting is on the increase with defection rates in the single digits.

Of course, not all Americans claim to identify with a political party. As Figure 7.2 shows, more than a third of the electorate rejected partisan labels in 2020, preferring to call themselves *independents*.[2] In fact, many independents are partisan "leaners," who are just as partisan as strong Democrats or strong Republicans. For the less than 15 percent of the electorate who have no

FIGURE 7.2
Party Identification in the Electorate, 2020

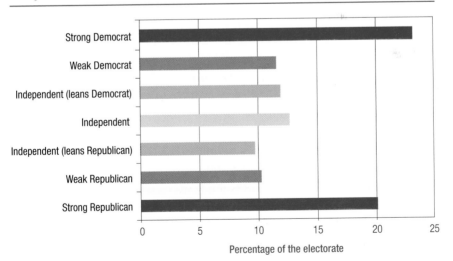

Source: Data from American National Elections Study. (2020). 2020 time series study. Retrieved August 16, 2021, from the American National Elections Study website: electionstudies.org/data-center/2020-time-series -study/.

partisan leanings whatsoever ("pure" independents), their voting decision varies from election to election—hence their designation as *swing voters*. Swing voters might choose candidates on the basis of the candidates' positions on the issues or according to their assessments of incumbent performance. More likely, swing voters are attracted to a candidate on personality grounds; they are willing to vote for someone they believe is a strong leader with the necessary experience or, alternatively, a person of impeccable character. In short, swing voters choose on the basis of candidate and not party considerations. We will consider the evidence concerning candidate-based voting shortly.

Going into the campaign, Democrats and Republicans have a strong predisposition to support their nominee. Except when the party nominates a candidate who is largely unrepresentative of rank-and-file voters (such as Barry Goldwater in 1964 and George McGovern in 1972), the great majority of partisans can be counted on to vote accordingly. Rather than responding objectively or "on the merits," partisans interpret campaign events and messages in ways that confirm rather than contradict their sense of political identity, a phenomenon known as motivated reasoning. For Democrats, candidate Hillary Clinton was seen as a supporter of workers' rights despite the fact that she received millions in speaking fees from banks and hedge funds. For Republicans, a twice-divorced candidate who bragged about his ability to fondle women was seen as a supporter of evangelical Christian values. Despite the 2016 candidates' many liabilities and involvement in multiple controversies over the course of the campaign, more than 90 percent of partisans stuck with their candidate on Election Day. In 2020, despite the Trump administration's dismal performance in dealing with the COVID-19 pandemic, some 90 percent of Republicans voted for Trump. Over the course of the campaign, the pressure to maintain consistency between party affiliation and beliefs about the candidates representing their party makes partisans increasingly likely to "distort" their perceptions and vote for their party's nominee. Exposure to the campaign thus reinforces party loyalty.

Unlike partisans, independents enter the campaign with an open mind. As the campaign progresses, they encounter information and form impressions of the candidates. When the information flow is relatively balanced (an equal number of favorable and unfavorable encounters with both candidates), non-partisans may remain undecided until the very last moment. In other cases, when one candidate generates more favorable messages than the opponent, independents are persuaded accordingly.

Thus, campaigns have multiple objectives. The first is to ensure that their partisans remain steadfast (holding the base). In the context of polarized politics, this is an easy task. The second is to attract a sufficient number of independents to win a plurality. Implicit to both of these goals is the task of informing voters about the personal characteristics, political credentials, and policy visions of the candidates. Finally, campaigns seek to optimize turnout by encouraging supporters and discouraging opponents and would-be opponents from voting.

HOLDING THE BASE

Beginning in the 1940s, large-scale sample surveys noted that campaigns induced very few voters to cross party lines. Instead of converting partisans, campaigns made Republicans even more enthusiastic about voting Republican and Democrats all the more inclined to vote Democratic. The reinforcement effect means that campaigns typically polarize the electorate along partisan lines. As the campaign progresses and more voters encounter the candidates' messages, voters increasingly come to align with their party affiliation, their evaluations of the incumbent administration, or their assessments of the state of the country.

In the 1988 presidential campaign, for instance, Republican candidate George H. W. Bush trailed Michael Dukakis by double digits in June and July. Once the campaign began in earnest, more and more Americans reacted in a partisan manner; those whose standing connections were predominantly Republican became more likely to declare their intention to vote for Bush. As a result, the gap between Bush's expected support (based on voters' partisan predispositions) and his actual support narrowed. Of course, Bush went on to win the election. In the 2008 campaign, there was the opposite trend. Early in the campaign (July–August), John McCain and Barack Obama were locked in a close contest even though the forecasts indicated a comfortable victory for Obama. While McCain's early numbers were close to his forecast, Obama was underachieving among Democrats, in part due to some voters' concerns over his race and lack of political experience. The onset of the economic crisis on September 18, however, fundamentally altered the trajectory of voter preference. McCain's support dropped from a high of 48 percent in early September to 43 percent in mid-October. Over the same period, Obama's support increased from 45 percent to 52 percent. Over the final weeks of the campaign, both candidates' levels of support converged with the forecast models.

A simpler barometer of partisan reinforcement in campaigns is to track the number of voters who say they intend to vote for their party candidate. Using national surveys conducted over the entire period of the 1988, 1992, and

1996 presidential campaigns, researchers found that the level of party voting increased steadily with time, generally peaking by October (see Figure 7.3). A few weeks before the election, strong partisans (those who claim they are strongly affiliated with their party) were almost unanimously behind their candidate (with levels of party voting typically in excess of 90 percent). Note that the reinforcing effect of the campaign proved much stronger among voters whose sense of party loyalty was ambivalent (people who said that they were only weak Republicans or Democrats). Weak partisans registered larger increases in support for their nominee; over time they tended to catch up with their more intense copartisans. By October, the gap between strong and weak partisans was significantly narrowed. As the election approached, more than 70 percent of the weak partisans were prepared to vote for their party's candidate.

The pattern shown in Figure 7.3 suggests that voters' sense of partisanship is activated or strengthened through exposure to specific partisan messages or events. Campaign advertisements and televised debates both contribute to reinforcement. In the case of the former, exposure to a single advertisement is sufficient. During the 1990 and 1992 campaigns, Stephen Ansolabehere and Shanto Iyengar (1995) conducted several experiments in which they inserted a campaign ad into a 15-minute local newscast. Residents of Southern

FIGURE 7.3

Party Allegiance in Voting Patterns

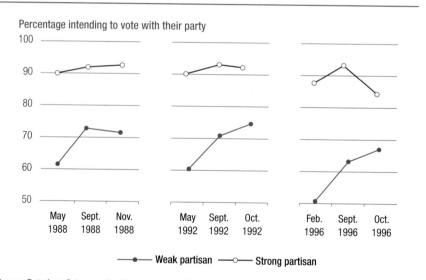

Source: Data from S. Iyengar & J. R. Petrocik. (2000). Basic rule voting: The impact of campaigns on party- and approval-based voting. In J. A. Thurber, C. J. Nelson, & D. A. Dulio (Eds.), *Crowded airwaves: Campaign advertising in elections* (pp. 113–148). Washington, DC: Brookings Institution Press.

California watched the newscast and then completed a survey of their political attitudes. Overall, exposure to the political ad proved persuasive; as shown in Figure 7.4, the percentage of the sample reporting that they would vote for the candidate featured in the ad increased by 7 percent. However, almost all of the effect occurred among viewers who shared the party affiliation of the sponsoring candidate. When the ad was from a Democratic candidate, the Democrats in the study responded favorably, but independents and Republicans were unmoved. Similarly, when the sponsor was Republican, the ad produced significant gains primarily among Republican voters. Averaged across studies, the effect of watching an ad among in-party viewers was a 14 percent increase in support for the sponsoring candidate. Thus, the benefits of advertising were concentrated among partisans. Over time, as more and more voters encounter ads, members of the electorate are increasingly pushed into their respective partisan camps.

What is especially revealing about the experimental studies is the relationship between the reinforcing effects of advertising and voters' level of political interest (see Figure 7.5). Consider strong Republicans who follow the campaign religiously. They are so enthusiastic that their preferences need no

FIGURE 7.4
Reinforcing Effects of Campaign Advertising on Voter Choice

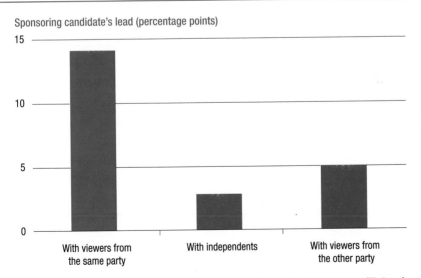

Note: Effects of exposure to a political ad are concentrated among viewers who share the party affiliation of the sponsoring candidate.
Source: Data from S. Ansolabehere & S. Iyengar. (1999). *Going negative: How attack ads shrink and polarize the electorate.* New York: Free Press.

FIGURE 7.5

Reinforcing Effects of Campaign Advertising by Level of Political Interest

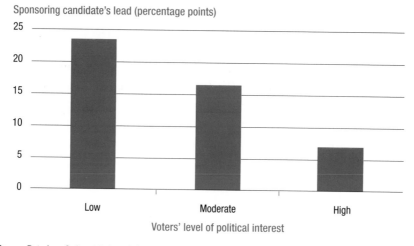

Source: Data from S. Ansolabehere & S. Iyengar. *Going negative: How attack ads shrink and polarize the electorate.* New York: Free Press.

reinforcing. On the other hand, more lukewarm partisans may not be particularly familiar with the candidates or the issues. For these voters, a television advertisement may provide the necessary spark to fire up partisan sentiments. The reinforcing effects of campaigns, accordingly, should be especially pronounced among the less motivated and attentive partisans.

This graded pattern of reinforcement effects by level of interest is precisely what occurred in the advertising experiments. As Figure 7.5 shows, the persuasive effects of exposure to a television commercial were concentrated among the less interested partisans. For Democrats with a relatively high level of political interest, encountering an ad from a Democratic candidate represents overkill: they are already committed to the Democratic candidate. For the less motivated partisan, however, advertising provides a necessary wake-up call; among this group, candidates can increase their level of support by up to 20 percent.[3]

Over the years, the reinforcing effects of campaigns have steadily increased as the level of party polarization has intensified and party identifiers have sorted themselves into liberal and conservative camps. As we note in the next chapter, the party label has become more important to an individual's sense of group identity, making it even less likely that a partisan will defect and support a candidate representing the opposing party. In fact, partisans have become so committed to their party that they are willing to ignore major flaws in their party's nominees. In the 2017 senatorial election in Alabama, Roy Moore (Republican)—a candidate accused of molesting underage women—received 48 percent of the statewide vote and more than 90 percent of the Republican vote. By a similar overwhelming margin, Republicans in her Georgia district supported Congresswoman Marjorie Taylor Greene, who openly voiced bizarre conspiracy theories about school shootings and California wildfires. The evidence indicates that as campaigns enter the closing stages, it is almost impossible to get partisans to desert their party (Kalla & Broockman, 2017). Data from the 2020 American National Election Study show that 84 percent of Democrats who disagreed with Biden's stance on climate change and healthcare—both pressing issues in the campaign—nonetheless voted Democratic. For his part, Trump retained the support of 90 percent of Republicans who disagreed with him on these issues (Parker, Brady, & Iyengar, 2021). Voters may be persuadable early on, before they have begun to pay attention to the election, but these effects are ephemeral. Understandably, the difficulty of swaying entrenched partisans has made both parties allocate more resources to mobilization (getting out the vote) than to persuasion.

As in the case of advertising, the evidence suggests that voters react to televised debates not as objective judges but rather as partisan fans. No matter how poorly their candidate might perform, that candidate is deemed to have outdebated the opponent. Perceptions of who won the debate (in a general election), for all practical purposes, are proxies for voters' party affiliation.

The most extreme case of selective perception occurred in 1976 in a debate between Gerald Ford and Jimmy Carter (see Video Archive 7.1). During the debate, as noted in Chapter 6, Ford was asked a question about American policy concerning the Soviet-controlled nations of Eastern Europe. He replied that the United States did not tolerate Soviet interference in the affairs of sovereign states and that the countries of Eastern Europe were free of Soviet control.[4]

Video Archive 7.1
Ford–Carter Debate, 1976

By any standard, Ford's statement represented a major gaffe. The Soviets exercised tight control over Eastern European governments at the time and, as the Czechs learned in 1968 (and the Hungarians before them in 1956), any attempts at autonomy would be crushed by Soviet military might. President Ford seemed blissfully unaware of recent history. But despite this blunder, polls conducted immediately after the debate showed that voters' support for the candidates remained unchanged. Democrats felt that Carter had won the debate, and by equally wide margins, Republicans gave the nod to Ford. It was not until several days later, in the aftermath of extensive press coverage of Ford's debate misstatement, that Carter eked out a small lead over Ford in the polls.

Although neither Mitt Romney nor Barack Obama committed a major gaffe in their first debate in 2012, it was generally interpreted as a significant victory for Romney. He repeatedly highlighted the weakness of the national economy, while Obama was listless and unwilling to challenge Romney's critical characterization of his economic record. Following the debate, Republicans' support for their candidate surged, especially their views of Romney as bold, strong, inspiring, and effective. However, despite Obama's lackluster performance in the debate, Democrats continued to rate him highly. Eighty-six percent of Democrats viewed Obama as strong before the debate, and this number slipped by only 2 points in the aftermath of the debate. Thus, the main effect of the debate was to solidify Republicans' support for Romney.

The pattern of partisans sticking with their candidate even in the aftermath of weak debate performances was clear both in 2016 and 2020. Most analysts agreed that Hillary Clinton easily bested Trump in their first encounter on September 26. A Public Policy post-debate poll showed that nearly 60 percent of viewers felt that Clinton won the debate, among the most lopsided verdicts in the history of debate polls. Yet 69 percent of Republicans felt that the victor was Trump. In 2020, despite Trump's blatant violation of debate norms during the first debate with Biden, more than 80 percent of Republicans believed he won, according to a poll by CBS News (2020).

In short, viewers evaluate the candidates' performance in debates depending on their party. Even when candidates commit a major faux pas or demonstrate

◎ IN FOCUS

The Reinforcement Effect

- One of the primary effects of campaigns is reinforcement, bringing voters' candidate preferences in line with their party identification. As a campaign progresses and voters increasingly encounter the candidates' messages, voters are increasingly inclined to vote for their party's candidate. By the end of the campaign, very few partisans contemplate voting for another party's candidate. Thus, campaigns typically polarize the electorate along partisan lines.
- Overall, the evidence on reinforcement indicates that contrary to conventional wisdom, media-based campaigns do not manipulate voters. Instead, campaigns steer voters in the direction of their respective parties, encouraging them to vote in accordance with their core political loyalties. Reinforcement of partisanship is a far cry from manipulation.

considerable ignorance about the state of the world, their supporters remain unwavering.

ATTRACTING SWING VOTERS

We have seen that in the eyes of partisans, their candidate can do little wrong. Independents, however, are more open-minded and, depending on the course of a campaign, can be moved in either direction. Once candidates have secured their base, they direct their overtures to this group.

The most important clue to the behavior of independent voters concerns their impressions of the candidates' personalities, especially the traits of competence and integrity. To be seen as intelligent, decisive, and knowledgeable is a prerequisite for attracting voter support. The candidate's moral bearings are also relevant; Senator Edward Kennedy was unable to mount a successful run for the presidency in 1980 because large numbers of the public questioned his integrity in the wake of the notorious Chappaquiddick incident.[5] Herman Cain was forced to drop out of the 2012 campaign after revelations that he had settled complaints of sexual harassment.

As we noted in Chapter 6, advertising early in a campaign tends to portray the candidate as a pleasant, upstanding, experienced problem solver. A favorable personal image can go a long way among independent voters. Independents were drawn to John F. Kennedy's youthful charisma, Jimmy Carter's image as a hardworking and honest public servant, Ronald Reagan's charm and strong values, Barack Obama's change-agent persona, and Donald Trump's reputation as a straight-talking, successful businessman. Sometimes, the effect is reversed. Independents were turned off by Michael Dukakis's lack of personal warmth, by President George H. W. Bush's apparent lack of concern for the welfare of

◎ IN FOCUS

Swing Voters

Swing voters are voters who lack strong partisan ties and who are therefore considered up for grabs in elections. Because voters with partisan affiliations reliably support their party's candidate, swing voters often are the target of most campaign activity. Swing voters are most likely to base their choices on their impressions of the candidates' personalities, especially the traits of competence and integrity.

working people, and by Hillary Clinton's willingness to bend the rules on the treatment of classified information while she served as secretary of state. In the case of the 2012 debate between Romney and Obama, which was dominated by Romney, independents reacted as dispassionate judges. Their rating of Obama as intelligent and effective fell by more than 10 percentage points, while their view of Romney became more favorable by the same margin. In all these instances, images of the candidates' personal traits were one-sided.

In general, voters do not care equally about all facets of a candidate's character. Depending on the circumstances, they seize on particular traits. In 1992, President George H. W. Bush was a decorated war hero with an unblemished personal life. His opponent, Bill Clinton, had not only managed to avoid military service but was also dogged by allegations of womanizing and marital infidelity. During the debates, President Bush repeatedly reminded voters of Clinton's history but to no effect. For most voters, even though Bush was apparently the more trustworthy candidate, Clinton was perceived as the more able manager who would turn the economy around. Because voters assigned higher priority to competence over integrity, Clinton won despite his unfavorable image on the latter.

The 2016 campaign featured two candidates with less than impeccable backgrounds. Donald Trump had led the birther movement against former president Obama, had been caught on tape bragging about his sexual exploits, and refused to release his tax forms. Hillary Clinton was under investigation for mishandling confidential information while serving as secretary of state, the Clinton Foundation had accepted millions in contributions from officials of authoritarian regimes, and she refused to provide transcripts of her speeches to business groups for which she was paid millions of dollars. Independent voters found it difficult to choose between the two. Nearly 50 percent of independents surveyed in the 2016 American National Election Study thought that the term *honest* did not apply to either candidate.

In 2020, voters distinguished clearly between Joe Biden and Donald Trump on questions of personal attributes to the advantage of the former. Biden's ratings exceeded Trump's by an average margin of 15 percentage points, for honesty, likability, and caring about ordinary people. Trump had the advantage on only one attribute; more people viewed him as a strong and decisive leader (Gallup Poll, 2020).

In addition to responding to their impressions of the candidates' personalities, swing voters may base their choices on a more substantive evaluation that focuses on the candidates' policy platforms. In the idealized case, an *issue voter* is one who holds preferences on policy issues and who is aware of both of the major candidates' positions on these issues. Assume that voter Mary Smith is pro-choice and supports affirmative action and government-subsidized healthcare. In the 2020 election, Smith would have concluded that Biden was the closer candidate on all three issues and cast her vote accordingly.

Voting on the issues requires relatively well-informed and opinionated voters. As we will note in the next section, however, relatively few Americans are capable of casting strictly issue-based votes. Many voters do not have a clear preference on any given issue, and even more are unaware of the candidates' positions. The media's penchant for covering the horse race does not make the task any easier. And when voters have the opportunity to watch the candidates debate the issues, they are drawn to evidence of personality rather than ideology. The 1960 debates between Kennedy and Nixon were thought to have given Kennedy an advantage because viewers were drawn to the visual contrast between the youthful-looking, tanned Kennedy and the pale, sickly looking Nixon (see Video Archive 7.2). Among people who listened to the debate on the radio, however, it was Nixon's debating skills that made an impression.[6]

Video Archive 7.2
Kennedy–Nixon
Debate, 1960

In an experimental re-creation of the first Kennedy–Nixon debate (Druckman, 2003), one group watched the debate on television, while another group was given only the audio track. As expected, the television group was more likely to rely on image factors (such as integrity) when considering the candidates' performance in the debate. The radio group, on the other hand, took into account both image and the candidates' positions on the issues. This study confirms that the visual imagery provided by candidate debates encourages voters to focus on personality-related rather than issue-related considerations when evaluating the candidates.

An additional set of candidate attributes can come into play, especially during nonpresidential campaigns, when news coverage and other forms of campaign communication tend to be less prevalent. In state and local races, clearly visible physical attributes, such as gender, ethnicity, or physical attractiveness, may influence the candidate's level of support. Female candidates, for instance, run well among women, as do black candidates in districts with large numbers of African American voters. Because the decibel level of the campaign is lower, voters lack information about the candidates' personal attributes or policy positions. They make do by inferring these attributes from the candidate's gender or ethnicity. Extrapolating from cultural stereotypes, for instance, they may view a female candidate as caring and compassionate and more willing to support government funding for childcare and nutrition programs. Conversely, male candidates tend to be seen as strong leaders who are more likely to support a tough stance on issues of national security.

EDUCATING VOTERS

Partisan voters have a convenient basis for voting, even without the benefit of specific information concerning the candidates and the issues. Independents, however, are not similarly equipped. For independents to express a vote prefer-ence, they must first acquire a basic impression of the candidates. Campaigns facilitate this task by delivering information about their candidate's personal background and positions on major issues. Gradually, voters develop differen-tiated, though not necessarily accurate, images of the candidates.

There are three levels of relevant candidate information. At the most basic level, voters must recognize the candidates' names. Voters are unlikely to select a candidate whose name they encounter for the first time on the ballot. In presidential campaigns, the candidates typically achieve universal name recognition (either through news coverage of their candidacies or by using biographical advertisements) by the time they are officially nominated in late summer. In lower-level races, however, candidates tend to be less visible and must expend more effort to achieve public familiarity. The fact that incum-bents have much higher levels of name recognition than their challengers, as we noted in Chapter 6, makes for an inherently unequal contest. Incumbents attempt to preserve their tactical advantage by limiting their participation in debates, thus denying their lesser-known opponents much-needed opportuni-ties to catch up.

Although it helps to be recognized, candidates cannot count on mere familiarity as a basis for voter support. They must flesh out their candidacies by telling voters about their experience and qualifications (competence), moral values, and concern for the needs of ordinary people (trustworthiness). As demonstrated in Chapter 6, early advertising is designed to provide voters with an image of the candidate as a likable person capable of political leadership.

The final layer of campaign information concerns the candidates' positions on the issues. Given the penchant of the news media to downplay issues at the expense of the horse race and character-related stories, it is not surprising that acquiring information about the candidates' stances on major issues is the most difficult task confronting voters. Not only do they infrequently encounter issue information; they also lack the sophistication and motivation to know where to find this information (such as at the candidates' websites). Compounding the problem, the candidates are often deliberately ambiguous in their messages, hoping to attract votes from both sides of a contested issue.

Unlike the case with issues, voters have little difficulty forming impressions of the candidates' personal qualities. The percentage of voters who can offer an opinion about presidential candidates' intelligence, sincerity, honesty, or other related attributes generally rises dramatically during the initial stages of the campaign. Of course, the learning trajectory varies, depending on the visibility of the candidate and the attentiveness of the voter. Household names such as Ronald Reagan, George H. W. Bush, Donald Trump, and Hillary Clinton all entered the race with universal name recognition. Others, such as Jimmy Carter (initially referred to as "Jimmy Who?"), Bill Clinton, and Barack Obama had to build up voter familiarity through early primary successes. Once again, incumbents enjoy a substantial advantage. At the outset of the 2004 campaign, for instance, almost all Americans could rate President George W. Bush's personal attributes, but only a bare majority could do the same for Senator John Kerry and the rest of the Democratic field. Unlike Senator Kerry, who had to invest substantially in biographical ads, President Bush could proceed directly to discussing the issues.

The 2016 and 2020 elections featured candidates with historically high levels of name recognition. Ninety-four percent of respondents interviewed by the Gallup poll in early December 2015 were familiar with Hillary Clinton, while Trump was almost as visible, with 91 percent familiarity. In 2020, Biden and Trump had name-recognition levels exceeding 95 percent. For Biden, this level of familiarity gave him a significant edge over most of his primary challengers.

Figure 7.6 shows the percentage of voters who could recognize some of the 2016 presidential candidates between March and December 2015. Clearly, for household names such as Trump and Clinton, the benefits of being in the spotlight were minimal, since there were few who hadn't already heard of them. But in the case of the candidates who started out as relative unknowns, such as Vermont senator Bernie Sanders and Republican Ben Carson, media attention produced very large gains in their visibility; the percentage of voters recognizing them more than doubled between March and December. For the candidates with intermediate levels of public familiarity, such as Marco Rubio and Jeb Bush, the gains in visibility were more modest, averaging around 10 percent.

One reason that voters find it easier to acquire personality impressions than policy impressions of the candidates is that the former task is equivalent to the everyday process of forming impressions of friends, neighbors, or colleagues. Small and colorful snippets of information, telltale incidents or events, and the candidate's demeanor at an interview or debate all fuel inferences about personality (a phenomenon psychologists call the *fundamental attribution error*). In 1976, President Ford's unfamiliarity with Mexican cuisine (Ford neglected to remove the husk from a tamale before biting into it at a televised rally in San Antonio) was interpreted by Hispanic voters as revealing insensitivity

FIGURE 7.6

Increases in Familiarity with Presidential Candidates, 2016

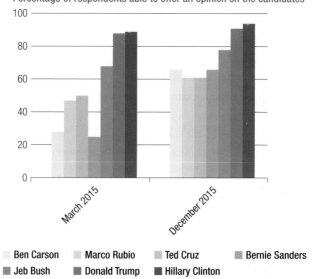

Percentage of respondents able to offer an opinion on the candidates

Legend:
- Ben Carson
- Marco Rubio
- Ted Cruz
- Bernie Sanders
- Jeb Bush
- Donald Trump
- Hillary Clinton

Source: Data from A. Dugan. (2015, December 10). Donald Trump well-known, but not well-liked. Gallup News. Retrieved December 13, 2017, from the Gallup website: news.gallup.com/poll/187607/Donald-trump-known -not-liked.aspx.

to their needs. In a different context, Donald Trump attempted to repair his image as an anti-Hispanic candidate by tweeting an image of him eating a taco bowl with the caption "I love Hispanics." In 1980, Ronald Reagan insisted that a New Hampshire Republican primary debate be open to all the candidates (breaking his earlier pledge to debate only George H. W. Bush). Bush, who had agreed only to a one-on-one debate with Reagan, refused to participate. When the moderator of the debate asked the uninvited candidates to leave, Reagan strode over to the podium, grabbed the microphone, and proclaimed, "I am paying for this microphone, Mr. Green." To voters, his actions conveyed an image of decisiveness and conviction. In 2016, when Hillary Clinton stumbled and fell after attending a 9/11 commemoration event, the incident immediately raised alarm about Clinton's fitness. Trump was quick to weigh in, calling her weak and lacking in stamina.

In contrast with matters of personality, voters generally take much longer to become aware of the candidates' positions on policy issues. By normal standards, issues are considered the most appropriate criteria for evaluating candidates. Against this standard, American campaigns are inadequate; voters tend to be poorly informed at the start of the campaign, and their ignorance generally persists.

Many voters remain unfamiliar with the candidates' positions even when the issues receive extensive attention from the candidates and the media. In the 2016 campaign, Donald Trump and Hillary Clinton made clear their opposing positions on the future of the Affordable Care Act (Obamacare). The two candidates also offered contrasting positions on civil rights and protecting the environment (Trump promised to take the United States out of the Paris Agreement on climate change). Yet, as shown in Figure 7.7, early in the campaign (March 2016), many voters had no idea where the candidates stood on these questions, and some offered opinions that were the direct opposite of the candidates' stated positions. If we combine the percentage of no opinion and incorrect responses, unfamiliarity with the candidates' issue positions averaged nearly 40 percent. Six months later, a few weeks before the election, although the level of unfamiliarity was substantially lower, between 15 and 20 percent of the electorate still failed to recognize the candidates' positions on these hot issues.

The data from the 2016 election suggest that voter familiarity with the issues did increase over the course of the campaign. The results from most previous presidential campaigns paint a more disappointing picture. A study of the 1988 presidential campaign (Buchanan, 1991) compared the number of voters who became reasonably informed about issues that received either extensive press coverage (such as taxes and capital punishment) or minimal coverage (such as the line-item veto and federal tax credits for day care). Between September and October, voters became more informed (on average) about where Vice President Bush and Governor Dukakis stood on the high-visibility issues by a margin of 10 percent. For low-visibility issues, the comparable level of learning was only 3 percent. A mere two weeks before the election, only 29 percent of the public had heard of Bush's pledge to be the "education president." Similar levels of ignorance applied to the Dukakis position on defense: only 30 percent were familiar with his proposals to strengthen US conventional forces.

Despite everything we've said up to this point, the public's ignorance about the candidates' policy positions should not be overstated. Although voters may be unfamiliar with the details of the party platforms, they can compensate through their familiarity with the groups and interests that stand to gain from Democratic or Republican policies—for example, Black Americans and senior citizens in the case of Democrats, business interests and fundamentalist Christians in the case of Republicans. They are also aware of the broad policy emphases of the political parties. A majority, for instance, correctly recognize that Democrats are more sensitive to unemployment than Republicans are,

FIGURE 7.7

Percentage of Voters with Uncertain or Incorrect Perceptions of Candidates' Positions on Issues, 2016

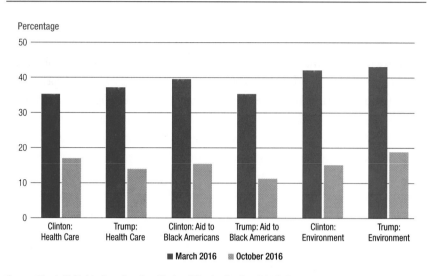

Source: March 2016 data from American National Election Studies. (2016). Recruitment pretest study. Retrieved September 14, 2021, from the American National Election Studies website: https://electionstudies.org/data -center/anes-2016-pilot-study/; September–October 2016 data from American National Election Studies. (2016). 2016 Time Series Study (pre-election survey responses). Retrieved September 14, 2021, from the American National Election Studies website: https://electionstudies.org/data-center/2016-time-series-study/.

and Republicans are seen as more likely to adopt policies that restrict immigration. Thus, although information about specific pledges may be missing, voters do have a gut sense of the candidates' ideology and general policy orientation.

In summary, campaigns seek to flesh out voters' impressions of the candidates. The task is generally easier in the case of personality because voters infer or form impressions from casual incidents and isolated pieces of information. In the case of issue positions, voters tend to be aware of the candidates' overall vision of government, but many people remain uninformed about candidates' specific policy positions.

LEARNING AND MOMENTUM IN PRIMARY CAMPAIGNS

Primary elections represent a special category of campaign effects. The principal determinant of vote choice—party identification—is no longer applicable. With a relatively large field of sometimes unfamiliar candidates, the task of voting is made more difficult. Moreover, candidates in primaries often deliberately state their positions ambiguously, not wishing to alienate voters with opposing views or to unnecessarily constrain their messages later in the campaign. Instead of highlighting issues, they often campaign on the basis of background and personality, seeking to present themselves as likable, competent leaders and the best bet to win in November.

As we noted in Chapter 6, press coverage of the early primaries can play a key role in determining candidate trajectories. Candidates who win the expectations game (who do better than expected in Iowa and New Hampshire) are labeled serious contenders, while the rest of the field is left to gradually wither away. In recent years, the importance of early primary successes has been amplified because the Iowa and New Hampshire contests are no longer isolated events.

Instead, a host of states have moved up their primary dates to follow closely on the heels of New Hampshire. Thus, the primary process has become front-loaded. In 2004, a candidate could accumulate the number of delegates required to win the Democratic nomination as early as "Super Tuesday," which fell on March 2. The process was further compressed in 2008. Iowa and New Hampshire moved up their contests to January 3 and 8, respectively, and "Super Tuesday" (when 21 states held primaries) occurred on February 5. The parties stretched out the nomination process more evenly in the 2012 and 2016 campaigns, prohibiting many states from moving up their primary calendar and thus ensuring that the nomination would not be secured before mid-April or May at the earliest.

The news media plays an important role in whittling down the field of primary candidates, a phenomenon known as winnowing the field. When there are many candidates seeking the nomination, the task of covering the race becomes more complex, and there is no clear story line for journalists. Candidates who fare poorly in the early races are dismissed as also-rans, with the media anticipating their withdrawal from the race. (Consultants refer to this type of coverage as the "death watch.") This was the case in 2016, when a huge field of 17 candidates entered the Republican race. In the span of six weeks—between the Iowa caucuses and March 15—the field had been narrowed to three: Donald Trump, Ted Cruz, and John Kasich.

The major consequence of front-loading—scheduling multiple primaries early in the campaign—is a serious reduction in the flow of information between candidates and voters. In a context of rapid-fire primary elections occurring in far-flung locations, it is virtually impossible for the candidates— no matter how well financed they might be—to reach a majority of primary voters. There is simply not enough time to mount an adequate advertising campaign or to schedule multiple visits to primary states. Time and resource constraints make it inevitable that voters in early primaries will lack information when they go to the polls.

When they don't have much information, voters must fall back on available cues. Given the media's penchant for horse-race coverage of primaries, voters are likely to know which candidates are doing well and which ones are faring poorly. As primaries occur and the media seize on the latest results to handicap the race further, voters encounter an abundance of information that they can use to assess the relative viability of the candidates. As Henry Brady and Richard Johnston (1987) put it, "Citizens . . . learn too slowly about every aspect of the candidates except their viability. And, one of the major reasons that citizens learn quickly about viability is the enormous emphasis placed on the horse race by the media, especially right after the Iowa caucuses and the New Hampshire primary" (p. 184).

Because viability is all that most voters have to go on, a candidate who comes to dominate the early races benefits from momentum, standing to reap a whirlwind of public support in the upcoming primaries. Thus, early results and media coverage of these results reward candidates who perform especially well.

In primaries, voting on the basis of viability is far from irrational. After all, it is in the voters' interest to select a candidate who can unify the party and defeat the opposition in November. In fact, some primary voters consciously vote for the candidate who may be only their second or third choice in terms of personal attributes and the issues but whom they view as the candidate with the best prospects of winning the White House. In 2004, nearly 30 percent of those who voted in the 2004 Iowa Democratic caucuses rated "Can beat Bush" as the most important attribute they were looking for in the candidates.

The 2004 Democratic primary campaign provides a textbook example of electoral momentum, both positive and negative. Over the space of a few weeks, beginning with the Iowa Democratic caucuses, Senator John Kerry rose from being a self-financed, underachieving candidate to the presumptive nominee, while Howard Dean fell from front-runner to underdog to certain loser.

Figure 7.8 traces the emergence of the Kerry candidacy in nationwide opinion polls between December 2003 and February 2004. For comparative purposes, we also show the level of support for candidates Howard Dean, John Edwards, and Wesley Clark.

In mid-December, Kerry was at the bottom of the group, with less than 5 percent backing from Democrats and independents. Fearing elimination, the Kerry campaign decided to go all out in Iowa. They closed their field offices in

FIGURE 7.8

Trends in Democratic Candidate Support Nationwide during
the 2004 Campaign

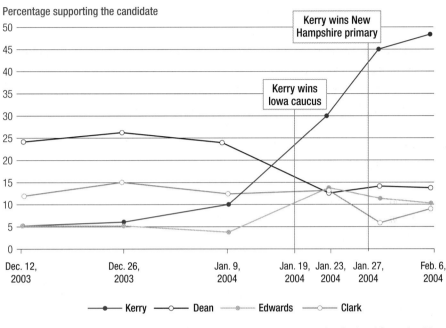

Source: Data from Polling Report, Inc. (2004). White House 2004: Democratic nomination. Retrieved September 14, 2021, from the Polling Report website: www.pollingreport.com/wh04dem.htm.

other states and devoted all their resources to Iowa. Senator Kerry campaigned continuously in the state during the 10 days before the caucuses.

The Kerry campaign's investment in Iowa clearly paid rich dividends. On January 9, only 10 days before the caucuses, Kerry's support nationwide was at 10 percent. Two weeks later, after his unexpected victory in Iowa, his poll numbers had climbed to 30 percent. Between the Iowa victory and his win in New Hampshire, Kerry's national support climbed to 45 percent. Following his victories in Missouri, South Carolina, and four other states on February 6, he climbed still further, to 48 percent. Thus, in a matter of just four weeks (January 9 to February 6), Kerry had registered a meteoric rise in the national polls.

While Kerry's candidacy was booming, Howard Dean's support was collapsing. Dean went into Iowa with a double-digit lead over his closest competitor (at that time, General Wesley Clark). Two weeks later, after his loss in Iowa and the "scream heard around the country," his support was cut in half (from 25 percent to 12 percent). Dean was unable to halt this reverse momentum; for all practical purposes, the loss in Iowa was the death knell of his campaign.

Momentum also played an important role in the 2020 Democratic primaries. Joe Biden began the campaign as the front-runner, but he underperformed in the Iowa caucuses (coming in fourth). His performance went from bad to worse in New Hampshire, where he received fewer than 10,000 votes, ending in a fifth-place finish. The *Politico* headline "Blood in the Water: Biden Campaign Reels after New Hampshire Trouncing"—and many others equally negative—sent shock waves through the Democratic establishment. Fortunately for Biden, the next major contest on the schedule was the South Carolina primary, dominated by African American voters whose support for Biden was rock solid. Biden decisively defeated his chief rival, Vermont senator Bernie Sanders, effectively ending the "death watch" media narrative. Buoyed by the South Carolina results, Biden went on to win 40 of the remaining 46 contests, coasting to the nomination.

Such dramatic fluctuations in candidate support are unusual. Since the large-scale adoption of primaries, initial front-runners have typically maintained their advantage and locked up the nomination at a relatively early stage. Vice President Gore, for example, had relatively little difficulty overtaking Senator Bill Bradley (Democrat–New Jersey) in 2000. On the Republican side that year, even though Senator McCain scored a major upset win over the front-running George W. Bush in New Hampshire, McCain's momentum was short-lived. He was defeated in the next primary (South Carolina) and was out of the race soon after. In other cases, two evenly matched candidates may be unable to deliver a knockout punch, and the primary contest is prolonged. Hillary Clinton entered the 2008 Democratic primaries as the clear front-runner, but Obama's win in Iowa and his strong showing in New Hampshire (where he lost to Clinton by only 2 points) allowed him to catch Clinton in the national polls. For the next two months, the candidates remained tied until Obama pulled ahead for good in April. Clinton eventually conceded the race and endorsed Obama in June. Clinton entered 2016 once again as the front-runner, but she barely won Iowa and then lost New Hampshire to the insurgent candidate Bernie Sanders. Sanders's surprising strength in these early contests led to a significant infusion of campaign contributions, and he competed with Clinton on nearly level terms, winning more than 20 primaries and capturing 43 percent of the votes cast before eventually conceding in June.

Apart from 2004, the only other cases of dark-horse candidates emerging from early primary successes include Jimmy Carter, who was catapulted from relative obscurity to win the 1976 Iowa caucuses and New Hampshire primary and, eventually, the presidency. Eight years later, in a particularly dramatic case of momentum, the little-known Democratic senator Gary Hart of Colorado finished third in the Iowa caucuses behind the odds-on favorite and former vice president Walter Mondale and 1972 Democratic nominee George McGovern of South Dakota. Hart's third-place showing was surprise enough to provide a surge in media attention. Hart went on to score a remarkable upset in New Hampshire, where he defeated Mondale by nearly 10,000 votes. At that moment, national polls showed Mondale with only a slight lead over Hart. The Mondale campaign was forced to invest in a major advertising campaign questioning Senator Hart's credentials (including a famous commercial modeled on the Wendy's "Where's the beef?" query). Mondale eventually hung on to win the nomination, but as Senator Hart himself acknowledged, "You can get awful famous in this country in seven days." (Four years later, when he was forced to withdraw from the 1984 race following revelations of marital infidelity, he might have added that you can become equally infamous just as quickly.)

CAMPAIGNS AND TURNOUT

Campaigns have a clear interest in getting out the vote, but only among voters who support them. Among partisans of the other side or swing voters who are leaning toward voting against them, campaigns would prefer that as few of them vote as possible. The ideal outcome is maximum turnout among supporters, minimum turnout among opponents.

Unlike most other nations, the United States makes voting a relatively difficult task. Despite a series of reforms aimed at increasing the number of eligible voters (such as eliminating literacy requirements and the poll tax and lowering the voting age to 18), Americans still must register before they can cast votes. In most states, voters must register at least a month in advance of the election. Only 10 states and the District of Columbia have adopted same-day registration. The two-step process, coupled with high rates of mobility (each time you move, you need to reregister), is a significant impediment to voting.

In comparison with most other affluent, industrialized societies, American voter turnout is low. Figure 7.9 shows two different indicators of turnout in national elections between 1976 and 2020: the percentages of the population that were eligible to vote and the percentages of the population that were registered to vote.[7] Clearly, most registered voters show up to vote; turnout in this group approximates turnout in the European democracies. Among the

FIGURE 7.9

Trends in Voter Turnout, 1976–2020

Percentage

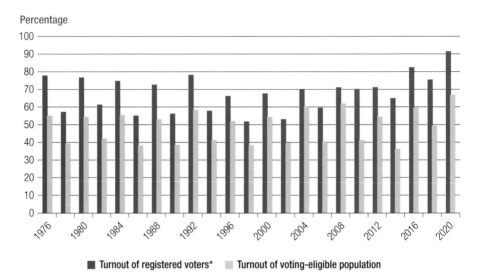

■ Turnout of registered voters* ▨ Turnout of voting-eligible population

*Because the registered-voter turnout figures are based on self-reports, they are likely to be inflated. Source: Data for registered voters calculated by author from the US Census Bureau. (1976–2020). Voting and Registration Tables. Retrieved September 14, 2021, from the US Census Bureau website: https://www.census.gov/topics/public-sector /voting/data/tables.All.List_1863097513.html; data for voting-eligible population from the United States Elections Project. (1976–2020). Voter turnout. Retrieved September 14, 2021, from the United States Elections Project website: http://www.electproject.org/home/voter-turnout.

eligible population, however, turnout is much lower—in most off-year elections, less than a majority.

Since the election of Donald Trump in 2016 and the intensified conflict between Democrats and Republicans, more Americans have become motivated to participate. Nearly 50 percent of the eligible electorate voted in 2018, the highest off-year turnout since 1914. This increased level of engagement carried over to the 2020 election, which set a record for the number of voters (nearly 160 million). The 2020 turnout rate of 67 percent of eligible voters (and 91 percent of registered voters) was the highest since the election of 1900. In addition to polarization having increased the perceived significance of elections, some analysts attribute the increased turnout in 2020 to the use of mail-in ballots which make the act of voting more convenient. However, a careful analysis of the differences in turnout registered by states with more and less extensive absentee voting revealed only minimal effects of mail-in voting (Yoder et al., 2021).

While the increase in 2020 turnout occurred among all demographic groupings, it was especially significant for the young. Voters under the age of 24, many of whom had been galvanized to take part in the protests over racial justice and police violence, voted at the highest rate ever (nearly 50 percent). Since the young tilt heavily Democratic, the youth vote may have proved pivotal to Biden's victory in several battleground states (Frey, 2021).

The sawtooth pattern of voter turnout suggests that the decibel level of the campaign stimulates people to vote. When the candidates and their activities are more visible, more people vote. In presidential elections, the media buzz and the level of advertising (at least in the battleground states) generate a sufficient level of interest and information; turnout increases to two-thirds of registered voters and a slight majority of all adults eligible to vote. In off-year elections, as media coverage drops off, the campaigns generate less excitement, voters find it too burdensome to acquire information, and turnout drops considerably. Thus, turnout depends on the level of voter *stimulation*.

The most effective form of stimulation is personal contact. Campaigns often send volunteers door-to-door, make reminder telephone calls (often with recorded voice messages from VIPs about the importance of voting), provide absentee ballots for those unable to make it to the polls, and generally urge their supporters to vote. These get-out-the-vote efforts are likely to be concentrated in areas where the election is hotly contested. In the case of the 2000 presidential election in Florida, an increased turnout of only 500 voters on the Democratic side would have swung the election to Al Gore.

Voter mobilization efforts are effective. As we have already noted, partisan polarization has increased voters' resistance to persuasive messages, making it a better investment for parties to increase the turnout among their supporters. Both parties have spent millions on developing databases of registered voters so that they may more precisely target their efforts at mobilization. In fact, a systematic examination of voters contacted by either campaign in 2012 (Enos & Fowler, 2016) demonstrates that both campaigns mobilized their supporters effectively and raised the turnout level among their targeted voters by more than 10 percent.

Yale researchers Alan Gerber and Donald Green (2008) have conducted numerous experiments designed to assess the conditions under which voter mobilization efforts succeed or fail. Their work demonstrates that the method of contacting voters makes a big difference. Telephone calls have no effect at all (since most people screen incoming calls), but in-person contacts are highly effective. Contacting voters by direct mail also stimulates higher turnout but only by a slight margin. Gerber and Green also assessed the effects of different get-out-the-vote appeals. Messages that conveyed implicit social pressure to vote (by suggesting that the turnout rate in the targeted household would be publicized to neighboring households) had the strongest impact on actual turnout.

Traditionally, two groups that are the most likely to require campaign outreach if they are to vote at all are young people and members of ethnic minorities. Eighteen-year-olds are busy with their personal affairs—transitioning to college or getting a job—and are less likely to be connected to a network of politically attentive friends or acquaintances. For these reasons and more, the turnout rate of 18- to 21-year-olds, prior to 2020, hovered around 30 percent. The consequences of age-related imbalances in political participation are obvious. Elected officials respond to the preferences of voters, not to the preferences of nonvoters. As rational actors, candidates and parties tend to ignore the young, thereby contributing to the disillusionment of young voters and perpetuating a vicious circle that discourages young voters from participating in the electoral process.

The second group of voters who suffer from electoral underrepresentation are racial and ethnic minorities. In the case of Black Americans, the gap can be attributed to lower socioeconomic status. In the case of Hispanics, language and unfamiliarity with voting procedures may be key barriers. Whatever the explanation, the underrepresentation of minorities in the electorate has significant consequences for the conduct of campaigns. The wedge appeals discussed in Chapter 6 are successful only because White Americans remain the dominant voting bloc. When an influx of Latino immigrants, for example, alters the ethnic composition of the state population quite dramatically (as has occurred in California), the incentives to engage in appeals based on ethnicity are weakened. Whereas White Americans accounted for 60 percent of the adult population of the state in 1992, they numbered only 38 percent in 2016. The Latino share of the population, on the other hand, increased from 24 percent to 39 percent. Among registered voters in the state, the share of Latinos increased from less than 10 percent to 28 percent. The candidate who attempts to use immigration as a wedge issue in California today, therefore, risks alienating a significant number of voters.

What holds true in California today is increasingly applicable to the nation at large. In the 2016 election, the White share of the national electorate dropped to 73 percent (from 80 percent in 2004). On average, Democratic presidential candidates receive only 41 percent of the White vote, meaning that the party's electoral success is based on high levels of support among Black and Latino voters. Among Obama voters in 2012, 62 percent were White and 38 percent were non-White. Romney voters, in contrast, were 91 percent White.

Voter mobilization drives can be especially effective if they reach groups that lack the motivation to vote. The Yale studies demonstrate that canvassing young people significantly increases the probability that they will turn out to vote (Gerber, Green, & Nickerson, 2002). Unfortunately, the reality is that get-out-the-vote efforts typically reach only the relatively motivated strata of the electorate. A recent *meta-analysis* assessing the results of several voter turnout experiments conducted in the United States suggests that the effects of campaign mobilization are significantly stronger among groups that are more inclined to vote (Enos, Fowler, & Vavreck, 2014).

Campaigns are not only interested in boosting turnout but at times may also attempt to achieve the opposite result by discouraging would-be opponents from voting. The incentives to demobilize are considerable. In the first place, as virtually every study of campaign effects demonstrates, very few partisans can be converted. Running ads that attempt to persuade Democrats to vote Republican is not a good use of scarce resources. Persuading Democrats that the Democratic candidate may have undesirable attributes, however, may be easier to accomplish. If some Democrats become sufficiently unenthusiastic about their candidate, they may decide not to bother with the election. Rather than casting a vote for the other party, these Democrats may prefer not to vote.

Thus, negative campaigning can have a negative impact on turnout. In the experiments conducted by Ansolabehere and Iyengar (1995), exposure to negative rather than positive campaign ads reduced participants' interest in voting by nearly 5 percent. Among viewers who considered themselves independents (who tend to find political campaigns far from interesting to begin with), the demobilizing effects of negative advertising were doubled: independents who watched negative rather than positive ads were nearly 10 percent less likely to say that they intended to vote. For nonpartisans, negative campaigning not only diminishes their opinion of the candidates but also engenders cynicism about the process.[8]

Campaign managers and candidates are well aware of the effects of negative campaigning on turnout. Why else would negative campaigning prove so popular? They are more diplomatic, however, in their public accounts of the strategy. Fearing the controversy that accompanies discussion of intentional vote suppression, practitioners are not inclined to acknowledge their efforts publicly. In the immediate aftermath of the New Jersey gubernatorial election of 1993 between incumbent Democrat Jim Florio and Republican candidate Christine Todd Whitman, Republican consultant Ed Rollins openly admitted (in a C-SPAN broadcast) that the winning Republican strategy included systematic efforts to reduce Black voter turnout. Once Rollins's comments had made the news, civic groups threatened litigation to overturn the election result on the grounds that minority voters had been disenfranchised. Rollins immediately recanted, claiming that he had exaggerated the role of campaign tactics. In an op-ed piece for the *Washington Post,* Rollins explained, "I spun myself out of control" (Merry, 1996).

A number of states, particularly those with Republican-controlled legislatures, have recently passed strict voter identification requirements in the name of enhancing election security and reducing fraudulent votes. These requirements, typically involving presentation of an official photo ID or birth certificate, have come in for criticism on the grounds they may have the effect of vote suppression when applied to the poor or to racial minorities. Historically, such identification requirements had frequently been overturned by federal courts as violating the 1965 Voting Rights Act (which mandated federal oversight of voter eligibility requirements in states with a history of racial discrimination). In 2013, however, the US Supreme Court ruled, in a case involving an Alabama statute, that these provisions of the Voting Rights Act were unconstitutional. Accordingly, Southern states, and indeed all states, are now empowered to enforce strict voter identification requirements (Liptak, 2013).

Following the 2020 election, Republican-controlled state legislatures passed laws making it more difficult to vote. The laws reduced the number of polling places in urban areas, made it a felony to distribute food or water to people waiting in line to vote, and shortened the time window for casting absentee votes. By July 2021, 18 states had passed laws to this effect, with similar legislation pending in another 30 states. Democrats have attempted to fight back by proposing legislation that would protect the right to vote in federal elections. The For the People Act, passed by the House of Representatives in March 2021, would require states to register voters automatically anytime voters provide information to state agencies (for example, the Department of Motor Vehicles), mandate same-day registration for federal elections, and require states to offer at least two weeks of early voting. The bill is unlikely to pass the Senate, since a key Democratic senator—Joe Manchin from West Virginia—announced he would side with the Republicans against the bill.

Whether laws that impose identification and other burdensome requirements in fact reduce voter turnout, and whether any such effect is concentrated among groups less inclined to vote, is as yet unclear. Most studies report minimal effects (Ansolabehere, 2009; Mycoff, Wagner, & Wilson, 2009; Pastor, Santos, Prevost, & Stoilov, 2010; Cantoni and Pons, 2021); these authors attribute their results to the possibility that the groups targeted by these laws, such as individuals without the necessary IDs, are less likely to vote in any event— without regard to the specific eligibility requirements applied at the polling place. Alternatively, the effects of laws that restrict ballot access may be counteracted by significant voter mobilization drives that target low turnout groups (Neiheisel & Horner, 2019). Finally, some scholars suggest that restrictive laws may induce a boomerang effect by angering Democrats and liberal-leaning groups, thus making them more determined to vote (Valentino & Neuner, 2017). Notably, the literature also demonstrates that these laws, enacted in the name of enhancing election integrity, have minimal impact on the level of voter fraud (see, for instance, Cantoni & Pons, 2021).

CONCLUSION

Campaigns do not occur in a vacuum. Candidates design their messages to fit the political environment. During times of international tension, candidates run as advocates of a strong military; during times of recession, they propose policies to stimulate economic expansion. Individually and cumulatively, the effect of campaign messages is either to activate or to reinforce viewers' long-term political predispositions (their party identification) as well as their assessments of the performance of the incumbent administration. The most frequent instance of the reinforcement effect is the shepherding of wayward partisans back into the fold. Thus, the contradiction between the ability to forecast elections on the basis of structural indicators that have little to do with day-to-day campaign activities and the candidates' substantial investments in media campaigning is more apparent than real.

A common criticism of modern campaigns is that they are light on substance (issues). Sound bites, ads, and social media pronouncements, the critics suggest, are inherently superficial forms of political discourse. The news media are equally responsible, given their unwillingness to elevate issues to the same level of newsworthiness as campaign strategy and the horse race. Voters have to look harder to become informed about the issues, and in most cases they don't. At the level of the candidates' personal qualities, however, campaigns do prove informative. By Election Day, most voters can compare the candidates on questions of competence, experience, and integrity.

A second criticism of media-based campaigns is that they intend to deceive and manipulate. Campaigns that deal in symbols and slogans rather than careful and well-documented analysis are thought to deflect voters from the real issues of the day. While the evidence presented in this chapter suggests that few votes are changed, there is growing concern about the increasing use of campaigns to spread misinformation. We take up the rise of "alternative facts"—a consequence of extreme party polarization—in the next chapter.

Summary

1. There are two competing perspectives on the question of how much campaigns influence voter behavior:

   - In the minimalist view, the general political and economic context in which elections occur is just as important as anything the candidates themselves might do or say during the campaign. Evidence shows that, at least in the case of presidential elections, the results can be predicted with a high degree of accuracy from indicators of economic growth and public approval of the incumbent administration.

   - The booming campaign industry suggests a different conclusion. Campaign consultants claim that well-executed campaigns can produce a significant increase in the candidate's level of support. Growing evidence supports the existence of campaign effects.

2. Between these two positions is a more realistic middle ground: Every election occurs within a distinct political context to which the candidates adapt their messages. Campaign professionals are aware of the political context and design their messages accordingly, positioning their clients to capitalize on what voters deem important.

3. Political scientists have devised a variety of statistical models—most of which combine the incumbent's popularity with the state of the economy—for forecasting the results of presidential elections. Voters are expected to reelect the incumbent during times of economic growth but to opt for change during times of economic distress.

4. One of the primary effects of campaigns is reinforcement, bringing voters' candidate preferences in line with their party identification. As a campaign progresses and more voters encounter the candidates' messages, they are increasingly inclined to vote for their party's candidate.

5. Another task of campaigns is to attract swing (undecided) voters, who lack strong attachment to a party and thus are susceptible to image- and issue-oriented appeals. The behavior of independent voters is most clearly linked to their impressions of the candidates' personalities. Swing voters may also base their choice on candidates' policy platforms, siding with the candidate whose positions most closely match their own.

6. Campaigns also have an educational impact. This is especially important for independent, or swing, voters, who must figure out how to decide between candidates during the campaign. Campaigns deliver information about their candidate's personal background and positions on major issues.

7. Primaries represent a special case because the principal determinant of vote choice—party identification—is no longer applicable. With a relatively large

field of sometimes unfamiliar candidates, voters must fall back on cues such as the relative viability of the candidates.

8. Campaigns can also significantly affect the level of voter turnout. While striving to increase turnout among their supporters, campaigns may simultaneously take steps to discourage would-be opponents from voting.

FURTHER READINGS

Ansolabehere, S., & Iyengar, S. (1995). *Going negative: How attack ads shrink and polarize the electorate.* New York: Free Press.

Campbell, A. (1960). Surge and decline: A study of electoral change. *Public Opinion Quarterly, 24,* 397–418.

Cantoni, E., & V. Pons (2021). Strict ID laws don't stop voters: Evidence from a U.S. nationwide panel, 2008–2018. *Quarterly Journal of Economics, 136,* 2615–2660.

CBS News. (2020, September 30). Debate-watchers say Biden won first debate, but most felt "annoyed." CBS News poll. Retrieved from the CBS News website: https://www.cbsnews.com/news/who-won-debate-first-presidential-biden-trump/.

Fiorina, M. P. (1981). *Retrospective voting in American national elections.* New Haven, CT: Yale University Press.

Frey, W. H. (2021, May 5). Turnout in 2020 election spiked among both Democratic and Republican voting groups, new census data shows. Brookings Institution report, Washington, DC. Retrieved from the Brookings Institution website: https://www.brookings.edu/research/turnout-in-2020-spiked-among-both-democratic-and-republican-voting-groups-new-census-data-shows/.

Gallup Poll. (2020, October 9). Americans view Biden as likable, honest; Trump, as strong. Retrieved from the Gallup website: https://news.gallup.com/poll/321695/americans-view-biden-likable-honest-trump-strong.aspx.

Gelman, A., & King, G. (1993). Why are American presidential election polls so variable when votes are so predictable? *British Journal of Political Science, 23,* 409–451.

Gerber, A. S., & Green, D. P. (2008). *Get out the vote.* Washington, DC: Brookings Institution Press.

Green, D., Palmquist, B., & Schickler, E. (2002). *Partisan hearts and minds: Political parties and the social identities of voters.* New Haven, CT: Yale University Press.

Iyengar, S., & Petrocik, J. R. (2000). Basic rule voting: The impact of campaigns on party- and approval-based voting. In J. Thurber, C. J. Nelson, & D. A. Dulio (Eds.), *Crowded airwaves: Campaign advertising in elections* (pp. 113–148). Washington, DC: Brookings Institution Press.

Kalla, J. R., & Broockman, D. E. (2017). The minimal persuasive effects of campaign contact in general elections: Evidence from 47 experiments. *American Political Science Review, 112,* 148–166.

Lazarsfeld, P. F., Berelson, B. R., & Gaudet, H. (1948). *The people's choice.* New York: Columbia University Press.

McDonald, M. P., & Popkin, S. L. (2001). The myth of the vanishing voter. *American Political Science Review, 95,* 963–974.

NOTES

1. Although partisan attachments are considered stable dispositions, there is evidence that some voters change their identification to make it consistent with their opinions on the issues and the candidates.

2. Because the label independent speaks well of the respondent's civic virtue, the designation is likely to include many closet partisans. Note that most tabulations of the number of independents include respondents who indicate they lean toward one of the parties.

3. It is important to note that the effects of exposure to particular ads are momentary rather than persistent. The successive "waves" of ads from opposing candidates serve to neutralize or counteract any lingering effects of ads encountered earlier.

4. Much later, after he had retired from public life, former president Ford joked that he had merely been 15 years ahead of his time!

5. Senator Kennedy drove his car off a bridge into a pond. The accident killed his passenger, Mary Jo Kopechne.

6. It is difficult to make strong causal claims about these media differences because television viewers and radio listeners at the time differed in several ways, including their pre-debate feelings about Kennedy and Nixon.

7. The voting-eligible population is a more appropriate definition of the electorate than the voting-age population because it excludes two groups that are deprived of voting rights: noncitizens and, in some states, convicted felons.

8. It is important to note that evidence of demobilization is limited to a handful of experimental studies in which the tone of the ad campaign was manipulated while all other factors were held constant. Survey-based studies, which lack any semblance of control over the content of the advertising message, have found no connection between advertising tone and turnout. Some survey-based studies even suggest that negative campaigning boosts turnout. A compilation of all published studies on the subject (both experimental and survey based) thus concluded that there is no relationship between negative campaigning and turnout (Lau, Sigelman, Heldman, & Babbitt, 1999). It should further be noted that these studies were all conducted prior to the onset of partisan polarization. In the current polarized era, it is possible that negative messages mobilize rather than demobilize partisans.

8

News and Public Opinion

Despite politicians' fixation on their public image as presented by the media, surprisingly, the conventional wisdom in academic circles until quite recently was that the media's influence on public opinion is somewhere between weak and nonexistent. Communication scholars have long bought into the doctrine of *minimal consequences*.

What can explain the astounding divergence between the observed behavior of practitioners and the judgment of scholars? The paradox of so much media campaigning with so little apparent effect is, in part, a question of definition. Communication scholars initially conceptualized media effects simply as changes in voter preference; no other outcomes were recognized as evidence of media influence. Against this standard, evidence that campaigns reinforced rather than altered voters' preexisting partisan sentiments was taken as a symptom of minimal effects.

Over time, researchers began to incorporate other measures of influence instead of relying simply on evidence of change in voter preference. When additional indicators were included in research studies—for example, changes in the prominence of particular political issues and in the weight ascribed to particular issues in evaluations of candidates—the effects of media campaigns quickly became more apparent.

The earlier verdict that mass media exerted minimal consequences on public opinion was a result not only of a limited definition of *effects* but also of a methodological artifact. As in all fields of social science, there is more than one possible approach to studying a phenomenon of interest (in this case the political effects of media on citizens). The doctrine of minimal consequences was predicated on decades of survey research. Unfortunately, survey research simply lacks the power to detect evidence of influence because it cannot assess causation. More recent scholarship has increasingly turned to experimental methods, which, unlike survey research, provide unequivocal evidence of causal impact.

To illustrate the difference between the power of survey methods and the power of experimental methods, consider, for example, a scholar who wants to find out whether use of Facebook has any influence on voter turnout. In this case, intention to vote is the *dependent variable*, the variable that the researcher believes might hinge on or be influenced by some other, *independent variable*, such as time spent on Facebook. The researcher can conduct either surveys or experiments to investigate whether the independent variable (Facebook use) has any effect on the dependent variable (intention to vote). For a survey, the researcher might select a representative sample of citizens and ask them how often they use Facebook and whether they intended to vote. For an experiment, the researcher might select a group of Facebook users and get half of them—selected at random—to stop using Facebook for one month.[1] At the end of the study, the researcher asks participants in both groups whether they intended to vote.

Both research methods (surveys and experiments) have strengths and weaknesses, which we will discuss in detail. In short, though, experiments are especially powerful for detecting causation. By contrast, surveys lack the ability to detect causation, but their results can be generalized more easily to larger populations.

Unlike other areas of mass communication, such as marketing, the field of political communication (particularly in its earlier years) relied predominantly on survey research. For reasons that we will discuss, surveys are notoriously imprecise instruments for detecting media or campaign effects. As soon as scholars increased the power of their methodology by turning to experimentation and more elaborate survey designs, the balance of evidence turned in the direction of maximal rather than minimal consequences. Thus, any account of the development of research on media effects must cover both changing conceptualizations of media influence and advances in the methodologies employed in mass communication research.

CONCEPTUALIZATIONS OF MEDIA INFLUENCE

Serious research into the effects of mass communication can be dated to about the 1930s, following the large-scale spread of radio. Political events in Europe, most notably the rapid development of extremist political parties in Germany and Italy, prompted widespread speculation that public opinion could easily be swayed by demagoguery or xenophobic appeals. To horrified observers in the United States, Hitler and Mussolini appeared to have capitalized on effective propaganda. If the Nazis and fascists could move public opinion so successfully, might the American public be equally susceptible to extremist appeals? Answers to these questions were of considerable interest to senior administrators in the US Department of Defense (DOD), who in the late 1940s commissioned a series of studies to understand the dynamics of propaganda campaigns.

The DOD-sponsored research was carried out by a group of social psychologists at Yale University. The leader of the group, Carl Hovland, was one of the founding fathers of the field of media effects. Hovland's team designed a series of experiments to identify the conditions under which people might be persuaded to change their positions on social and personal issues (Hovland, Janis, & Kelley, 1953; Hovland, Lumsdaine, & Sheffield, 1949). Their research program, which remains a backbone of the literature on media effects, was guided by an overarching analytic framework known as *message learning theory*. Attitude change, according to this theory, depends on the source (who), the message (what), and the receiver (whom)—factors we will discuss later in this chapter.

While developing the essential ingredients of message learning theory, Hovland's team was especially interested in DOD movies that were meant either to encourage young men to enlist or to boost civilian morale. Through experimental research, they found that although the films were informative, they generally failed to shift attitudes toward the war or willingness to volunteer for military service. Thus, the team concluded that concerns over the power of propaganda seemed unfounded.

After World War II, scholars turned their attention to the persuasive effects of political campaigns. Social scientists at Columbia University and the University of Michigan undertook large-scale survey studies of attitude change over the course of several presidential campaigns, expecting to find widespread political conversion (Republicans deciding to vote Democratic or vice versa) resulting from campaign messages (Lazarsfeld, Berelson, & Gaudet, 1948; Campbell, Converse, Miller, & Stokes, 1960). The survey evidence, however, showed no traces of last-minute shifts in opinion. In fact, voters who followed campaigns the most closely were the least likely to be influenced.

The results from the 1948 election proved to be no fluke. A series of election studies carried out between 1948 and 1960 all reached the conclusion that political campaigns persuaded almost no one (for a summary of the evidence, see Klapper, 1960). People who intended to vote Democratic or Republican at the start of the campaign generally became all the more convinced of their preference. Only a handful of voters switched from one candidate to the other. Thus, any concept of an all-powerful media gave way to the idea of minimal media effects.

Naturally, these results eventually caused scholars to question whether persuasion was, or should be regarded as, the only indicator or criterion of media influence. Researchers began to change their approach. Rather than asking, "What do people think?" researchers focused on asking, "What do people think *about*?" Changes in the political agenda became the operative definition of media influence. The media were thought to act as gatekeepers—selecting some issues for presentation and ignoring others—rather than as marketers of specific points of view.

As scholars began to test and refine the idea of agenda setting by the media, they discovered that the process of defining the political agenda did, in fact, contribute to attitude change or persuasion. Consider the case of the 2020 election. COVID-19 first arrived in the United States in January. In early March, the Trump administration declared a national emergency, and most states enacted mandatory stay-at-home orders. By April, the virus was killing 2,000 Americans every day, with cataclysmic consequences for the economy. Between March and April, the unemployment rate jumped from 4.3 to 14.7 percent, the largest monthly increase since the federal government began compiling the data. Given these developments, it is no wonder that the media subjected their audience to nonstop news coverage of the pandemic and rising unemployment. In response, Americans deemed the state of the economy and the virus as the most important problems facing the nation. Because COVID and the economy became paramount concerns, during the presidential campaign, voters focused on Biden's and Trump's ability to deal with these problems. In other words, the doctrine of agenda control holds that the more news coverage is assigned to an issue, the more weight voters will accord that issue when evaluating the candidates. This extension of the agenda-setting logic (which we will take up later in this chapter) is called the *priming effect* of news coverage.

The gradual extension of the agenda-setting argument to the determination of voter choice in effect delineated a process of indirect persuasion. If, by increasing the visibility of a particular issue, campaigns also attract voters to that issue as a basis for voting, for all practical purposes the effect is equivalent to persuasion. Substitution of the criteria on which candidates are evaluated produces a different bottom-line choice. Thus, the theoretical orientation of research on media effects turned full circle. In the early days of mass media, researchers set out with a notion of powerful media capable of altering all manner of social and political attitudes. In the aftermath of repeated failures to document widespread persuasion during campaigns, scholars assigned media a more limited agenda-setting function. Eventually, studies showed that agenda setting and priming could generate effects that were similar to persuasion.

THE CHOICE OF METHODS

Just as the concept of media influence has waxed and waned, so, too, has the debate over the appropriate tool kit for measuring the effects of the media. Within the field of mass communication are two distinct methodological traditions: experimentation and survey research. Each tradition is associated with a set of distinctive results. The discovery of agenda-setting and priming effects resulted predominantly from the extensive use of experimental methods; the earlier period of minimal consequences, on the other hand, was marked by exclusive reliance on surveys. This pattern suggests a general effect caused by the methodology itself—namely, that experimental and survey studies lead to diametrically opposing conclusions about the effects of mass communication.

The impact of methodological choices on research findings was first identified by Hovland (1959). After enumerating the complementary strengths and weaknesses of experiments and surveys, Hovland warned that exclusive use of one or the other would inevitably lead to biased results. Accordingly, the optimal research strategy was a combination of survey and experimental methods. Here we retrace and update Hovland's classic analysis.

Identifying Causes: The Advantage of Experiments

The major advantage of the experiment over the survey—and the focus of the discussion that follows—is the experiment's ability to isolate the effects of specific components of political messages. Consider the case of political campaigns. At the aggregate level, campaigns encompass a set of messages, channels, and sources, all of which may influence the audience, often in inconsistent ways. The researcher's task is to identify specific causal factors and specify the range of their relevant attributes.

What was it about the infamous "Willie Horton" ad (discussed in Chapter 6) that is thought to have moved so many American voters in 1988? Was it, as widely alleged, the race (African American) of Willie Horton, whose crimes the ad highlighted? Alternatively, was it the violent and brutal nature of his behavior, the fact that he was a convict, the dramatic voice-over used in the ad, or another factor? By manipulating the possible causal attributes, experiments make it possible to isolate the explanation. Surveys, on the other hand, can provide evidence only on self-reported exposure to the causal variable in question; respondents are unlikely to remember whether they saw a particular campaign commercial, let alone its unique features. (In fact, as we will discuss, many people do not even accurately report whether they have seen an ad, watched the news, or voted.)

Experimentation is the method of choice in every scientific discipline, therefore, because the researchers can tightly control the phenomenon under investigation. Potential causal factors can be switched on and off. Consider the key phenomenon of media exposure. The experimenters can measure exposure with almost total precision because they create it. Using random assignment, they can ensure that the treatment group (those exposed to the message) and the control group (those not exposed to the message) will be similar on average; for example, the two groups will have approximately the same proportion of Democrats and Republicans.[2] Thus, any observed difference between the treatment and control groups after the experiment will have been caused by the manipulation of the message.

For example, using the context of the 1990 gubernatorial campaign in California between Republican Pete Wilson and Democrat Dianne Feinstein, Stephen Ansolabehere and Shanto Iyengar (1995) manipulated the negativity of the candidates' advertising on the environment and examined the effect of this manipulation on intention to vote. In the positive-ad condition, the sponsoring candidate was depicted as being opposed to offshore oil drilling; in the negative-ad condition, the sponsor's opponent was said to be in favor of offshore drilling. This difference in the candidates' positions was accomplished by the substitution of two words into the soundtrack of a 30-second commercial—"no" for "yes" and "will preserve" for "will destroy" (see Video Archive 8.1). Because this was the sole difference between the positive-ad and negative-ad conditions and because study participants were randomly assigned to either condition, the researchers could attribute any observed difference in the participants' response to negativity. The experiment showed that participants who watched the negative version of the ad were less likely to report that they intended to vote in the election.

Video Archive 8.1
Experimental
Manipulation of
Advertising Tone

Experimental studies, of course, do have their own limitations. Long considered the Achilles' heel of experiments, the lack of generalizability—being able to generalize the results observed in an experiment to the population as a whole—manifests itself on three levels: mundane realism, sampling bias, and the nonrandom nature of selection in the real world.

Mundane Realism Because of the need for tightly controlled stimuli, the setting in which the typical laboratory experiment is conducted is often quite different from the setting in which individuals ordinarily experience the target phenomenon. Although asking participants to report to a location on a university campus may be convenient for the researcher, it is also a highly unnatural environment for media use or for other types of activities that are of interest to political communication researchers. The artificial properties of laboratory experiments are likely to influence the behavior of participants. To avoid the reactivity of the laboratory setting, researchers have increasingly turned to so-called field experiments, in which the procedures and settings more closely reflect ordinary life (providing participants with a milieu that better matches the setting of their living room or den, for example).

In general, building realism into experimental designs necessitates some loss of experimental control. Watching treatments in a mock living room means that some respondents may not pay attention to the stimulus, for example, just as many people zone out when watching TV at home.

Sampling Bias The most widely cited limitation of experiments concerns the composition of the participant pool. Typically, laboratory experiments are conducted on "captive" populations—for example, college students who often serve as guinea pigs to gain course credit. College sophomores may be a convenient subject population, but they are hardly representative of the general population; they have been found, for example, to have less resolute attitudes and a stronger tendency to comply with authority than do older adults. College sophomores might be persuaded by a stimulus, but what about likely voters?

In the pre-internet era, one solution to the sampling problem was to transport the experiment to public locations and recruit participants from nonstudent populations. Ansolabehere and Iyengar, for instance, administered their experiments on campaign advertising at three different shopping malls in and around Los Angeles, and they offered a financial incentive to attract participants.

Fortunately, technology has both enlarged the pool of potential experimental participants and reduced the per capita cost of administering subjects. Today, most researchers run their experiments online. Advantages of using the internet as the experimental site include the ability to reach diverse populations without geographical limitations, since respondents can easily self-administer experimental manipulations in their own homes. The rapid diffusion of the internet has made it possible for market research companies to assemble large online panels consisting of individuals willing to participate in research studies for a token incentive (such as the chance to win an iPod). YouGov, a firm founded in Silicon Valley, maintains an online research panel of 1.5 million adult Americans and millions more in 35 other nations. Because of the size of their panel, YouGov is able to deliver samples that match the population on key attributes, including party affiliation, gender, and education. In the 2016 and 2020 US elections, the accuracy of YouGov preelection online polls equaled or exceeded that of conventional telephone-based polls.

Self-Selection An especially important difference between experimental and real-world contexts concerns the nature of exposure to media messages. The defining advantage of the experiment is that exposure is made equivalent to a lottery, thus guaranteeing equivalence between the experimental and control groups. In the real world, however, exposure to political messages is far from a lottery. Some people receive the message while others do not, and the distinction is based on self-selection. The audience for news consists disproportionately of relatively attentive voters, and the increased level of consumer choice only makes it easier for less interested voters to tune out. Thus, the challenge facing experimental researchers is to design communication-related manipulations that more closely reflect processes of self-selection by the audience.

One approach is to give participants some control or choice over their exposure to the experimental treatment (Knox, Yamamoto, Baum, & Berinsky, 2019). In one study, for example, researchers had participants watch video clips of talking heads on cable shows arguing with each other to test the proposition that watching uncivil and rude behavior decreases political trust (Arceneaux & Johnson, 2013). Previous research had detected this effect but had used a design that forced participants to watch some version of the political program (Mutz & Reeves, 2005). When participants were given the choice to watch some other program entirely, however, the effect of argumentative talk shows on those who chose to watch them disappeared.

In summary, the experiment is unsurpassed in its ability to isolate cause from effect. By physically manipulating the causal factor and holding all other factors constant, the researcher provides unequivocal evidence of causation. At the same time, by maximizing control, the researcher necessarily sacrifices realism, often casting doubts on the generalizability of experimental results to the real world.

Generalizability: The Advantage of Surveys

Surveys are almost the exact complement of experiments: they yield evidence that is ambiguous with respect to causation but that may be confidently generalized. For communication scholars, the most fundamental weakness of the survey is that it provides little control over the key phenomenon of media exposure. In the experimental context, exposure is turned on or off; in the survey context, it is approximated by the request that participants reconstruct their past behavior. In the closing days of a campaign, for instance, respondents might be asked to recall which political commercials they watched on television. Survey researchers treat respondents' self-reported exposure to campaign communication as a substitute for actual exposure. Accordingly, the standard test for campaign or media effects is to compare voting choice or candidate preference across respondents who self-report high or low levels of exposure to the campaign. If those with higher levels of self-reported exposure are more likely to prefer one candidate over another (all other factors being equal), the researcher concludes that this preference was due to exposure to the campaign.

The assumption that self-reported exposure is an accurate approximation of actual exposure is problematic on several grounds. People have notoriously weak memories for past events, especially when the event in question concerns an encounter with a political campaign or media message. In the experiments conducted by Ansolabehere and Iyengar (1998), over 50 percent of the participants who were actually exposed to an advertisement were unable—a mere 30 minutes later—to recall having seen the advertisement. On the other side of the coin, survey respondents tend to err in the opposite direction, often overreporting exposure, possibly because they feel that these affirmative responses speak well of their civic virtue. For example, although ratings data showed that only 6 percent of adults listened to NPR at least once per week, fully 35 percent of respondents in a 1989 American National Election Studies pilot study reported that they did so (Price & Zaller, 1993). In a comparison of self-reported network news exposure with actual exposure, one study found that the former provided estimates of audience size that were, on average, three times higher than the actual size. Overreporting also differs between subgroups, with younger people overreporting their exposure to TV news by a factor of nine (Prior, 2009; see also Vavreck, 2007). The gross inaccuracy in self-reports necessarily weakens the ability of survey researchers to detect media effects.

Fortunately, technology provides researchers with the tools to monitor actual rather than self-reported exposure to news. As people increasingly turn to their cell phones and tablets for news reports, it is possible to track what they read quite precisely. In a recent study, scholars tracked browsing behavior over the period of the 2016 presidential campaign to assess which news sources partisans accessed most frequently. Not surprisingly, the results showed clear differences between Democrats and Republicans, with each group gravitating to "friendly" providers (Peterson, Goel, & Iyengar, 2017).

Even more problematic for the survey researcher is the fact that self-reported media use is typically a by-product of the very same political attitudes that are considered effects of media consumption. Those who remember encountering political messages (candidate ads, for example)—and therefore are likely to report having seen them when asked about it in a survey—are likely to be those who are already highly politically engaged. People who are not already interested in politics are less likely to pay attention to campaign ads that appear when they are watching television and therefore are unlikely to remember—and report—having seen them.

The fact that those who are highly politically engaged are more likely to report exposure to political messages has predictable consequences for research on media effects. In experiments that manipulated the tone of campaign advertising, researchers found that exposure to negative messages discouraged turnout (Ansolabehere & Iyengar, 1995). On the basis of self-reports, however, survey researchers concluded the opposite—that exposure to negative campaign advertising stimulated turnout (Wattenberg & Brians, 1999). But was it recalled exposure to negative advertising that prompted turnout or the greater interest in campaigns among likely voters that prompted higher recall? When statistical techniques were used to control this problem, the sign of the coefficient for recall was reversed, indicating that those who recalled negative advertisements were less likely to intend to vote (see Ansolabehere, Iyengar, & Simon, 1999). Unfortunately, most survey-based analyses fail to disentangle the reciprocal effects of self-reported exposure to the campaign and partisan attitudes or behaviors.

Over the years, survey design has improved, survey measures of media exposure have become more finely calibrated, and scholars have become more adept at data analysis. Panels (before and after surveys) and aggregate time-series designs make causal inferences from the results much more reliable. During the 2004 election, for instance, the National Annenberg Election Study interviewed a large number of respondents on a daily basis to yield evidence that spanned the entire life of the campaign (Johnston, Hagen, & Jamieson, 2004). Because respondents were interviewed more or less continuously from the earliest stages of the campaign, the researchers could aggregate respondents into precise temporal groupings corresponding to before and after major events. It is not surprising that work based on longitudinal surveys replicates several experimental findings of significant campaign effects. All told, these significant methodological advances have strengthened survey researchers' ability to detect media effects.

Surveys do have their advantages. A relatively small sample yields evidence that reflects a much larger population because the respondents can be a microcosm

Methodological Trade-Offs

Surveys and experiments each have strengths and weaknesses as methods of establishing the nature of relationships between independent and dependent variables. By giving the researcher greater control, *experiments* provide the most unambiguous evidence of causation. Because of issues of mundane realism, sampling bias, and self-selection, however, the results from experimental studies often cannot be generalized to the real world.

Surveys do not have such generalizability problems. But because they rely on self-reported data (which are often inaccurate because of errors of memory and self-presentation biases), they often fail to reveal the true relationships between cause and effect.

of the entire population rather than a sample limited to college students. Estimates based on probability samples come very close to approximating the true value of a particular population parameter. In addition to providing generalizable evidence, surveys are less intrusive than experiments. Answering the phone is a routine task for most people as compared with visiting the local college campus, which participants still must do in the case of many experiments.[3] Survey responses on the phone are less likely to be contaminated by the novelty of the situation.

Combining Experimental and Survey Approaches

Given the complementary strengths and weaknesses of experiments and surveys, the least biased methodology for the study of communication effects is to combine the two. Using experiments in tandem with surveys, as Hovland (1959) put it, amounts to "the royal road to wisdom" (p. 17). Over the years, researchers have come to heed Hovland's advice. Their tool kit now includes experiments, quasi-experiments, telephone surveys, in-person surveys, survey experiments, and, as noted, Web-based surveys and experiments.

Methodological advances and the adoption of multimethod research strategies have gradually eroded the minimal consequences verdict in the scholarly literature. Today, it is generally acknowledged that media presentations leave their mark on the audience and that media campaigns can affect the outcome of an election. We explored the effects of media campaigns in Chapter 7. We will now summarize the evidence regarding the effects of news presentations on public opinion.

VARIETIES OF NEWS MEDIA EFFECTS

Ordinary people encounter the political world only through what they see and read about in the media. This dependence has motivated political elites to invest heavily in efforts to shape the content of the news. As we'll describe in this section, this strategy is not irrational; what appears in the news does indeed influence public opinion.

BECOMING INFORMED

The dissemination of public affairs information is considered a basic responsibility of the news media in democratic societies. By tuning in to the news, Americans can acquire factual information about the course of events—for example, that the number of Americans who have died from COVID-19 has almost hit the 1 million mark or that President Biden has nominated a new Supreme Court justice. However, as we will note shortly, the media do not write on a blank slate. Voters' partisan beliefs affect their willingness to learn.

One of the most striking characteristics of American public opinion is that it does not appear to rest on a command of political facts. Americans offer opinions about candidates or issues even when they possess minimal amounts of information. Examples abound: despite Donald Trump's repeated pledges to pull the United States out of the Paris Agreement on climate change, more than 40 percent of American voters could not identify Trump's position on the environment. Another 2016 survey found that one-third of the public could not name any of the three branches of the federal government (Annenberg Public Policy Center, 2016). Especially striking, as noted in Chapter 2, is the extent to which Americans lag behind citizens of other industrialized nations. While 75 percent of the British and Finnish respondents in a cross-national study correctly identified the Taliban as a fundamentalist Islamic group based in Afghanistan, less than 60 percent of Americans could do so, despite the substantial involvement of the United States—both militarily and economically—in the affairs of that nation. When asked to identify the Tamil Tigers—the separatist group representing Tamil speakers in Sri Lanka—the answer chosen most frequently by Americans referenced an endangered species of the Bengal tiger!

There are several explanations for the unusually high level of political ignorance in the most media-rich society on earth. Americans' relative affluence is thought to contribute to their inattentiveness to politics. For most citizens, decisions made in Congress or the state legislature are seen to have little impact on their daily lives. The benefits of knowing who does what in government are minimal. Hence, voters may consider it unnecessary—even irrational—to accumulate large amounts of political information.

A variation on this theme is that people do not need facts to express informed opinions. The public is able to arrive at reasonable approximations of informed political decisions using shortcuts, or *heuristics,* such as voting on the basis of their liking or disliking the groups that support a particular candidate or cause or supporting a candidate because of that candidate's party affiliation. Although not all scholars agree that the public's use of heuristics produces opinions equivalent to opinions that are based on hard factual information,[4] opinions and voting behavior are undeniably much less affected by information per se than by relevant cues.

It is one thing to be uninformed about current events, but it is quite another to stake a claim to knowledge based on demonstrably false information. Over the past three decades, as American politics has become intensely polarized across party lines, a more insidious form of ignorance has emerged in the form of partisans' willingness to believe in rumors, innuendo, and "alternative facts." Perhaps the first instance of large-scale partisan bias in factual beliefs occurred in the aftermath of the 2003 invasion of Iraq. The Bush administration had justified the invasion on the grounds the regime of Saddam Hussein possessed weapons of mass destruction. Once the Hussein regime fell, it became clear— and was widely reported in the media—that the invading forces had failed to find traces of chemical or biological weapons. However, large numbers of Republicans continued to believe that the United States had in fact found the weapons in question (Kull, Ramsay, & Lewis, 2003).

Republicans' misinformation over Iraq stemmed not only from their unwillingness to accept that the Bush administration had waged a war based on faulty intelligence, but also from the availability of news and commentary that propagated news coverage with a partisan slant. Viewers of Fox News, for instance, were especially likely to express false beliefs (Kull, Ramsay, & Lewis, 2003).

The election of Barack Obama as the first African American president created further ripples of misinformation. Many opposed to Obama doubted his citizenship. The lingering controversy engendered by the "birther" movement (organized by Donald Trump) made it necessary for the president to release his official "long form" birth certificate. Despite overwhelming evidence to the contrary, large numbers of Republicans continued to believe that Obama was Muslim and a noncitizen. In a 2016 national poll, while more than 80 percent of the Democrats in the sample agreed with the statement "Barack Obama was born in the United States," among Republicans the level of agreement fell to 25 percent. Strikingly, Republicans who were relatively knowledgeable on other factual questions were just as likely to provide the misinformed response as their less aware counterparts (Clinton & Roush, 2016). Misperceptions of Obama's religion were no less prevalent, with 54 percent of Republicans as recently as 2015 identifying him as Muslim (Benen, 2015).

Especially worrisome is the increasing willingness of partisans to dispute facts concerning elections. In 2016, the consensus within the intelligence community was that the Russian government interfered with the presidential election. Nonetheless, large majorities of Republicans surveyed in 2017 and 2018 claimed that allegations of Russian interference were false. And contrary to all evidence, clear majorities of Republicans continue to believe the false assertions of former President Trump that he and not Joe Biden was the legitimate victor of the 2020 election.

Biased beliefs also apply to politicized policy domains. In the case of health care, opponents of the Affordable Care Act rallied around false claims that the legislation would create so-called death panels with the power to deny treatment to critically ill elderly patients (see Berinsky, 2017). (In fact, the law included a provision that Medicaid would cover patients' consultations with their physicians on living will and related end-of-life concerns.) In experimental settings, erroneous beliefs about policy provisions persist despite exposure to information rebutting the claims in question (Hart & Nisbet, 2012; Swire, Berinsky, Lewandowsky, & Ecker, 2017).

Since misperceptions typically reinforce partisans' sense of identity, it is tempting to attribute the misinformation phenomenon to motivated reasoning. Indeed, several scholars have pointed out that survey respondents may use the information questions as opportunities to "cheerlead" for their party, in many cases knowing full well that their responses are inaccurate (Bullock, Gerber, Hill, & Huber, 2015; Prior, Sood, & Khanna, 2015). While it is difficult to distinguish between genuinely misinformed partisans and those who behave strategically as cheerleaders, in practice the distinction may be less than significant. By knowingly responding in a biased manner, partisans are waving the party flag, a signal that is certainly received by elected officials.

In the era of the internet and social media, there is a plausible alternative explanation (to partisan motivated reasoning) for the rise of misinformation. In the context of a media market with biased news providers, misperceptions may spread through repeated exposure to biased information rather than motivated processing of unbiased information. The increased supply of news and commentary with a partisan slant, much of which is not subject to editorial gatekeeping, makes it possible for relatively "unmotivated" individuals—that is, those not subject to strong consistency pressures including independents and weak partisans—to become misinformed. As noted in Chapter 5, millions of Americans encountered false reports about the 2016 election on Facebook and Twitter; given the political naïveté of the electorate, many may have believed in the reports' accuracy, although the available evidence indicates that the level of exposure was insufficient to have had an impact on the election (Alcott & Gentzkow, 2017).

In summary, the literature suggests two explanations for the acquisition of misinformed beliefs. The first is dispositional; partisans, especially those with a strong sense of identity, distort the information they encounter in order to maintain in-party favoritism. By this account, partisans who are sufficiently aware of the affective implications of correct and incorrect responses to knowledge questions (for example, the more educated) should exhibit more misinformation. Alternatively, misinformation may be a product of the information environment. Exposure to information providers and platforms that propagate rumors and unverified information inculcates misinformation among unmotivated and motivated members of the audience alike. The former are unable to distinguish fact from fiction; the latter are capable of doing so but choose to accept false reports that cast their party in a favorable light.

Finally, there is the opinion leadership explanation for misinformation. In the current era of polarization, politicians have become willing to spread false or misleading information. Americans' misinformation on controversial issues may simply reflect the rhetoric they hear from their elected leaders. (We will elaborate on this thesis shortly, in the upcoming discussion of persuasion research.) When President Trump asserted, without a shred of evidence, that the Obama administration had ordered the wiretapping of his offices in Trump Tower, his words had considerable impact on fellow Republicans; in the 2017 survey cited earlier, nearly two-thirds of the Republicans responded that Trump had been wiretapped (compared with less than 5 percent of Democrats). We will address the implications of this troubling trend in Chapter 10; disagreement over the facts of political life is not conducive to the practice of democratic citizenship and can threaten fundamental democratic norms and institutions.

AGENDA CONTROL

As casual observers of the political scene, most Americans notice only those issues that are in the news; events, issues, and personalities not covered by the media might as well not exist. What the public notices becomes the principal

🎯 IN FOCUS

Agenda Setting and Priming

The central idea of *agenda setting* is that, by giving differential attention to certain issues, the media set the agenda of public discourse. That is to say, by covering some issues and ignoring others, the media influence which issues people view as important and which they view as unimportant.

Priming, an extension of agenda setting, refers to the way in which the media affect the criteria by which political leaders are judged. The more prominent an issue becomes in the public consciousness, the more it will influence people's assessments of politicians.

basis for their beliefs about the state of the country. Thus, the relative prominence of issues in the news is the major determinant of the public's perceptions of the problems facing the nation (see, for example, Dearing & Rogers, 1996; McCombs & Shaw, 1972). The media's issue agenda becomes the public's agenda. This is particularly true in the case of national and international issues, about which the public has almost no opportunity to learn from firsthand experience.

The sudden surge in the number of high-profile companies and institutions that fired employees accused of sexual harassment in the immediate aftermath of the Harvey Weinstein scandal is a classic case of responsiveness to the media agenda. In October 2017, the *New York Times* and the *New Yorker* published detailed reports documenting that Harvey Weinstein, a major Hollywood producer, had sexually abused a number of women going back decades. Weinstein was quickly fired by the movie studio he cofounded. In the weeks that followed, prominent men in the world of journalism (including Matt Lauer and Charlie Rose), entertainment (Dustin Hoffman and Kevin Spacey), and politics (Senator Al Franken and Congressman John Conyers) also faced sexual harassment or assault allegations. NBC and CBS immediately fired Lauer and Rose. Senator Franken and Congressman Conyers were forced to resign their offices. This "zero tolerance" policy toward sexual harassment stands in stark contrast to the situation a year earlier, when 13 women accused candidate Donald Trump of inappropriate sexual overtures. He denied the accusations and dismissed his accusers as liars. A few weeks later, he was elected president.

The increased sensitivity to issues of sexual harassment in 2017 reflects changes in both the media agenda and the public agenda. Once the media spotlight focused on the issue, Americans began to think of sexual harassment as an important national problem, even though high-profile instances of harassment date back decades to the 1990s, including an episode we discuss in Chapter 9 featuring a nationally televised confrontation between a nominee to the US Supreme Court and his accuser. We can use the Gallup poll to document the seismic shift in the public agenda brought about by the feeding frenzy surrounding the Weinstein scandal. In October 2017, after the Weinstein revelations, Gallup respondents were asked whether they considered sexual harassment in the workplace to be a major problem, a minor problem, or no problem at all. The identical question had been asked 20 years earlier, in March 1998. We plot the differences over time in responses to this question in Figure 8.1. In 1998, the public was evenly split; 50 percent of respondents considered harassment a major problem, and an equal number thought it was not significant. By 2017, the number of Americans who considered the issue a major problem was more than double those who did not.

The relationship between news coverage and public concern has come to be known as the *agenda-setting effect*. An early statement of the hypothesis was formulated by B. E. Cohen (1963): the media, Cohen said, "may not be

FIGURE 8.1

Public Concern about Sexual Harassment, 1998 versus 2017

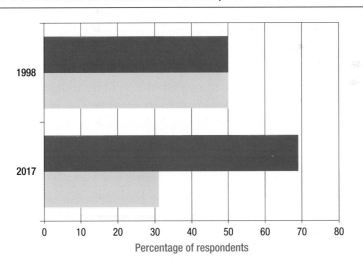

■ Harassment a significant concern   ▨ Harassment not a significant concern

Source: Data from L. Saad. (2017, November 3). Concerns about sexual harassment higher than in 1998. Gallup poll. Retrieved September 16, 2021, from the Gallup News website: http://news.gallup.com/poll/221216 /concerns-sexual-harassment-higher-1998.aspx.

successful most of the time in telling people what to think, but it is stunningly successful in telling its readers what to think *about*" (p. 13). The first study to test for the effect was conducted by Maxwell McCombs and Donald Shaw (1972) in the context of the 1968 presidential campaign. They surveyed a random sample of Chapel Hill, North Carolina, voters, asking them to identify the key campaign issues. Simultaneously, they monitored the news media used by residents of the Chapel Hill area to track the level of news coverage given to different issues. They found almost a one-to-one correspondence between the rankings of issues based on amount of news coverage and the number of survey respondents who mentioned the issue as important.

Although evidence of agenda-setting effects of media coverage is plentiful, some scholars have suggested that the convergence of the public and the news media on the same issue agenda may result simply because both respond to the same real-world events and *not* because the media are influencing the public. This explanation is unlikely to be correct, however, because most political issues can be experienced only through exposure to the news. How would ordinary voters know about global warming, for example, without encountering any discussion of the problem in the news?

The case of crime provides a striking example of public concern and real-world indicators moving in opposite directions. As Figure 8.2 shows, the FBI nationwide violent crime index has declined significantly since the early 1990s. Despite the substantial reduction in crime, the percentage of the public that viewed crime as among the three most important national problems remained at a high level, averaging 25 percent in the 1990s and peaking in 1999. Not coincidentally, the decade of the 1990s witnessed a dramatic increase in the availability of local television news, which is likely to feature stories on crime. Figure 8.2 suggests, at least in the case of crime, that public opinion is more responsive to what appears in news reports than to the state of the real world. It was not until the September 11 terrorist attacks that public concern for crime fell as terrorism and national security became the focal points of media coverage.

Survey-based studies of agenda setting have difficulty establishing the direction of causality. That is, some scholars suggest that the correlation between the media's agenda and the public agenda reflects editors' decisions to run stories on issues deemed important by the public rather than the other way around. Researchers have attempted to tease out the direction of causality by tracking changes in public opinion and news coverage over time, thus establishing whether it is the media that lead public concern or vice versa. In one such study—the first to test for feedback from the level of public concern to

FIGURE 8.2

Violent Crime Rate and Public Concern about Crime, 1994–2015

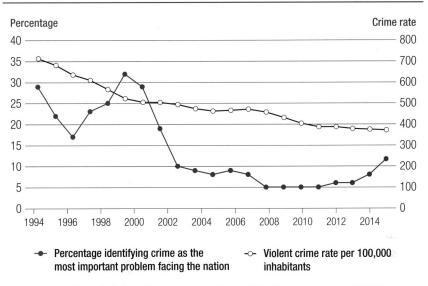

Source: Data from Gallup Poll, "Most important problem" series; https://news.gallup.com/poll/1675/most
-important-problem.aspx; Federal Bureau of Investigation. (2013). Crime in the United States, 2013. Retrieved
September 16, 2021, from the FBI website: http://www.fbi.gov/about-us/cjis/ucr/crime-in-the-u.s/2013/crime
-in-the-u.s.-2013/tables/1tabledatadecoverviewpdf/.

news coverage—the authors found no traces of shifts in the amount of news
devoted to the economy induced by changes in public concern for economic
issues (Behr & Iyengar, 1985). The authors thus effectively dismissed the possibility that news panders to the concerns of the audience. The same study, however, also showed that television news coverage of economic issues predicted
the level of public concern for these issues independent of real-world economic
conditions. The researchers concluded that correspondence between the media
agenda and the public agenda was not a result of both responding to the same
real-world conditions.

Experiments provide the most compelling evidence concerning the direction of causality in agenda setting. By manipulating the issue content of news
programs, researchers have shown that even small amounts of coverage are
enough to significantly shift people's perceptions of the importance of various
issues. In the early 1980s, for example, Shanto Iyengar and Donald Kinder
(1987) administered a series of experiments that varied the level of news coverage accorded to several target issues. They found that participants who watched
one story every day for a week on a particular issue came to see that issue as
one of the three most important problems facing the country (see Table 8.1).

TABLE 8.1

Agenda Setting by Network News: Changes in the Public's Perception
of the Importance of a Problem

	Percentage of Viewers Naming the Problem as One of the Country's Most Serious		
Problem	Before the Experiment	After the Experiment	Change
Defense	33	53	+20[a]
Inflation	100	100	0
Pollution	0	14	+14[a]
Arms control	35	65	+30[a]
Civil rights	0	10	+10[a]
Unemployment (experiment 8)	43	71	+28[a]
Unemployment (experiment 9)	50	86	+36[a]

[a]The reported change is statistically significant.
Source: Data from S. Iyengar & D. R. Kinder. (1987). *News that matters: Television and American opinion.* Chicago:
University of Chicago Press.

In the most convincing test of media agenda setting to date, Gary King and
his collaborators enlisted 48 small news outlets to participate in a controlled
experiment (King, Schneer, & White, 2017). The authors then coordinated
within a set of 2 to 5 outlets to create a "pack" and let the pack select a specific
policy to cover. The news outlets published their "treatment" content over the
period of a week. The results showed that Twitter posts on the same policy
area as the news reports increased by 20 percent on the first day after the news
report appeared, with smaller increases on days 2 to 5. Over the course of the
week, the news coverage produced a 10 percent increase in Twitter posts on
the target policy. At least in terms of the audience's social media behavior, this
study provides convincing evidence of an agenda-setting effect.

Overall, the evidence in support of the agenda-setting effect is overwhelming. One-shot surveys, time-series analyses of public opinion, and laboratory
experiments all agree on the finding that issues in the news *are* the issues that
people care about.

Setting the Elite Agenda

The effects of news coverage on the perception of which issues are important
extend beyond public opinion. The fact that ordinary citizens care about an
issue is of considerable interest to policy makers, who view public opinion

as a strategic resource. Policy makers know that when the media spotlight is aimed at a particular issue, they are likely to have greater success in proposing or moving along legislation on that issue, because it is more difficult for those who might normally try to block such efforts to do so when the public is clamoring for action. Legislators interested in regulating the tobacco industry, for instance, are more likely to propose policy initiatives designed to curb smoking when health issues are moving up the public agenda. In fact, as Frank Baumgartner and Bryan Jones (1993) have demonstrated, congressional hearings on the public health consequences of smoking were preceded by periods of relatively heavy media coverage of the issue. Across a variety of policy issues, Baumgartner and Jones found that the frequency of congressional committee hearings on particular issues over time corresponded to the level of news coverage. As Figure 8.3 shows, hearings on environmental issues were scheduled more frequently when the state of the environment attracted more attention in the pages of the *New York Times*.

Several researchers (for example, Edwards & Wood, 1999; Eshbaugh-Soha & Peake, 2005, 2008) have found that the relationship between media attention

FIGURE 8.3

Attention Trends in Congress and the Media on Environmental Issues, 1946–2010

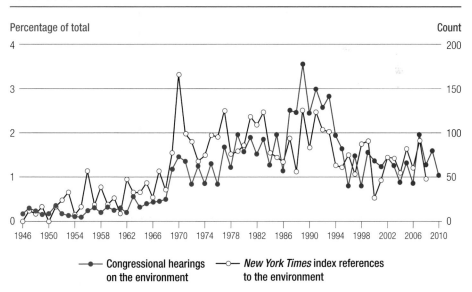

Note: Nonreferred hearings may be of an investigative or oversight nature and signify general committee interest in the issue.
Source: Data compiled by the author from Policy Agendas Project. https://www.comparativeagendas.net/us.

and elite attention to issues differs across policy areas. On foreign policy issues, as well as some domestic issues (such as crime and education), presidential attention follows the level of media attention. In other domestic policy areas, however, the relationship is reciprocal, with the level of media attention also responding to the level of presidential attention. On issues that are already high on the public agenda, presidents are especially responsive to news coverage. For other less visible issues, however, it is the media that responds to presidential actions (Eshbaugh-Soha & Peake, 2011).

Thus, media coverage not only moves public concern but also motivates policy makers to take action. And because political elites (most notably the president) are the primary generators of news stories, they are in an especially advantageous position to simultaneously influence the media agenda and the public agenda.

Psychological Accounts of Agenda Setting

Scholars have identified at least two psychological mechanisms that influence agenda setting. First, people may respond to news coverage because the issues receiving attention in the news are more likely to be top-of-the-head—that is, coming to mind more quickly and easily—and are therefore more likely to be cited when respondents are asked to name important national issues. If every newspaper headline and every TV news report you saw prominently featured a story on school shootings, it would not be surprising if that were the first thing that sprang to mind if somebody asked you to name the important problems facing the country today.

An alternative perspective treats agenda setting as a more thoughtful process. In this view, people treat journalists as credible sources for judging the importance of issues. When a particular issue receives regular and high-profile coverage, citizens surmise that it must be an important issue for the nation.

Researchers studying agenda setting have also looked at the conditions that underlie the media's ability to shape the public's priorities. Such factors include the personal relevance of the issue and the visibility of the coverage. In general, the more prominent the coverage of an issue, the more likely it is that issue will move up the public agenda. Front-page news, newspaper stories accompanied by photographs, and lead stories in television newscasts tend to be particularly influential. This could be taken as evidence in favor of the thoughtful account of agenda setting. On the other hand, the greater impact of front-page and lead-story coverage might indicate that the public's attention to news is so limited that they notice only glaring headlines or lead-story coverage.

Some individuals are more responsive to the media agenda than are others. In general, the further removed an issue or event is from direct personal experience, the weaker the agenda-setting effects of news coverage are. In other words, when an issue is in the news, people personally affected by it are the first to have their agendas set by that issue. Iyengar and Kinder (1987) found, for example, that after being exposed to broadcast news reports detailing the financial difficulties of the Social Security fund, older viewers were much more likely than their younger counterparts to name Social Security as one of the most important problems facing the country. In the Gallup poll question on sexual harassment, women were more likely than men to see it as a major problem—73 percent of women, 55 percent of men (Saad, 2017).

Finally, given the state of party polarization, there is growing evidence of significant differences between the issue agendas of Democrats and Republicans. In a 2021 survey, Pew researchers presented a national sample with a list of issues and asked whether each "should be a top priority for the president and Congress to address this year." While there was a consensus on Social Security, terrorism, and strengthening the economy as top priorities, when it came to climate change, issues around race relations, and dealing with COVID, significantly more Democrats than Republicans expressed concern. Conversely, compared to Democrats, Republicans were more apt to nominate reducing crime and strengthening the military as national priorities (Pew Research Center, 2021).

PRIMING EFFECTS

Beyond merely affecting the perceived importance of issues, news coverage influences the criteria that the public uses to evaluate political candidates and institutions—a phenomenon known as *priming*. An extension of agenda setting, priming is a process by which news coverage influences the weights that individuals assign to their opinions on particular issues when they make summary political evaluations, such as which candidate deserves their vote. As Stephen Ansolabehere, Roy Behr, and Shanto Iyengar (1993) put it, "Priming refers to the capacity of the media to isolate particular issues, events, or themes in the news as criteria for evaluating politicians" (p. 148).

In general, the evidence indicates that when asked to appraise politicians and public figures, voters weight their opinions on particular policy issues in proportion to the perceived importance of those issues: the more prominent the issue, the greater the impact of opinions about that issue on the appraisal (for reviews of priming research, see Krosnick & Kinder, 1990;

Miller & Krosnick, 2000). If crime is the issue receiving the most attention in the news, for example, people will be more likely to support the candidate or public official they think is best able to deal with crime.

Priming effects can be especially important during election campaigns. The closing days of the 1980 presidential campaign provide an especially dramatic example of priming. With less than a week to go before the election, the polls showed Jimmy Carter and Ronald Reagan to be dead even. Suddenly, the Iranian government offered President Carter a last-minute proposal for releasing the Americans whom they had held hostage for over a year. Carter suspended his campaign to devote full attention to these negotiations. The hostage issue and the progress of the negotiations became the major news story of the day. The media's preoccupation with the hostage story caused voters to seize on the candidates' ability to control terrorism as a basis for their vote choice. Given his record in office, this logic proved disadvantageous to President Carter.

Similar volatility in the public agenda bedeviled President George H. W. Bush in the 1992 election. In the previous year, as he presided over the successful liberation of Kuwait from Iraqi occupation, his popularity ratings had soared to 90 percent. Following the end of the Gulf War, news coverage of the economy drowned out news about military and international issues; on economic issues, voters preferred Clinton over Bush by a wide margin. Had the media played up military or security issues, of course, it's likely that the tables would have been turned.

Yet another instance of priming comes from the post-9/11 era. Prior to the terrorist attacks, President George W. Bush's overall popularity was closely tied to perceptions of his performance on economic issues (see Figure 8.4). After September 11, 2001, and extending through 2003, Bush's popularity moved more closely in tandem with public assessments of his performance on terrorism. Terrorism and national security had replaced the economy as the yardstick for judging Bush's performance. Only in 2004, after the onset of the presidential campaign, were economic performance and overall performance again linked. Our analysis of presidential popularity in Chapter 9 reinforces this finding. There we note that following the 9/11 attacks, news coverage of terrorism became the single most important determinant of President Bush's public approval.

As already noted in Chapter 6, voters' tendency to focus on highly visible issues creates strong incentives for candidates to introduce issues on which they enjoy an advantage. September 11 gave George Bush a significant advantage over John Kerry on national security. Among the exit-poll respondents who cited terrorism as the most important issue facing the country, 86 percent said

FIGURE 8.4

Terrorism versus the Economy as Criteria for Evaluating President George W. Bush

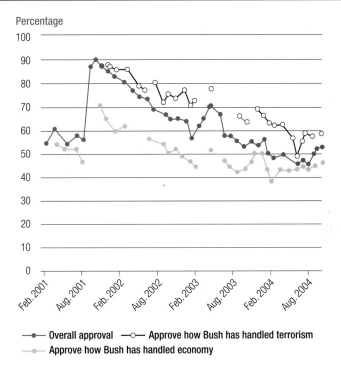

Percentage

—•— Overall approval   —○— Approve how Bush has handled terrorism
—•— Approve how Bush has handled economy

Source: Data compiled by the author from CBS News polls & Gallup polls. (2001–2004). Retrieved from multiple CBS News polls and https://news.gallup.com/interactives/185273/presidential-job-approval-center.aspx.

they voted for Bush. Among voters concerned about the economy, however, 80 percent said they voted for John Kerry. As these data suggest, elections often turn on the issue that voters find most important. Had the state of the economy been more prominent, Kerry would likely have been elected. Conversely, if even more voters had been preoccupied with terrorism, Bush would have won by a landslide.

The economic crisis of 2008 provides another classic case of priming. Before the onset of the crisis, Americans were concerned about a variety of issues, including the war on terror, illegal immigration, education, and the economy. In June 2007, for instance, 15 percent of the public named immigration as one of the most important problems facing the nation, while another 15 percent named corruption and dishonesty in government as important. In the aftermath of the economic crisis, however, the economy became the overriding concern, and previously hot issues such as immigration disappeared entirely from the public's agenda. In early 2009, the portion of those surveyed who named immigration as an important problem was barely 1 percent. The emergence of the economy as the national concern is shown when we compare the public's overall evaluation of President Obama with ratings of his performance on the economy and immigration (as shown in Figure 8.5). Clearly, for this period, ratings of Obama's performance on the economy show closer correspondence with ratings of his overall performance, suggesting that it is the economy rather than immigration that explains the downward trend in his overall popularity. Had people evaluated Obama more in terms of immigration, his popularity would have been considerably lower. (We will provide more evidence on the relationship between economic conditions and presidential popularity in Chapter 9.)

It is important to distinguish the concept of priming from other psychological mechanisms that might induce the same observed outcome, such as a greater impact of salient issues on evaluations of elected officials or the

FIGURE 8.5

The Economy versus Illegal Immigration as Criteria for Evaluating President Obama

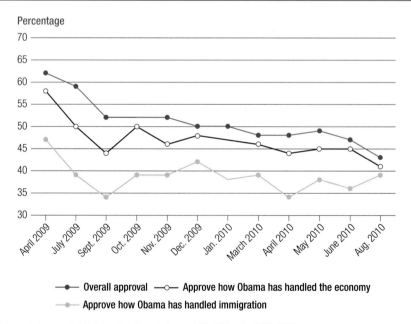

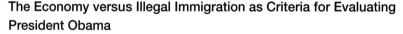

Source: Data compiled by the author from Gallup and AP-GFK polls (2009–2010).

tendency of voters to attribute favorable qualities to leaders they like—called projection. For example, a voter who had a generally favorable impression of President Trump may have evaluated his performance on immigration favorably, even though the voter lacked meaningful information about the president's actual performance regarding the issue. Projection and priming support opposite inferences concerning the direction of causality; in the case of the former, the general evaluation drives the performance evaluation with the opposite holding for priming. To date, most studies of priming fail to consider projection.[5] However, a 2014 study investigated both possibilities with respect to President Obama's performance on education and the environment. The researchers found that the effects of priming surpassed the effects of projection (Hart & Middleton, 2014).

Media priming effects have been documented in a series of experiments and surveys targeting the evaluation of presidents and lesser officials and covering a variety of attitudes, including assessments of incumbents' performance in office and ratings of their personal attributes. Overall, news coverage of issues elicits stronger priming effects in the area of performance assessments than in the area of personality assessments.

A special case of priming concerns the phenomenon of momentum in primary elections. News coverage during the early primaries tends to focus exclusively on the state of the horse race. Because horse-race coverage is so pervasive (as explained in Chapter 3), primary voters are likely to rely heavily on information about the candidates' electoral viability when making their choices. In a study of the 2004 primary campaign, researchers found that the single most important determinant of Democrats' primary-vote preference between Senators John Kerry and John Edwards was perception of the two candidates' personalities (Luskin, Iyengar, & Fishkin, 2005). The second most powerful predictor of vote choice was the candidates' electoral viability. Viability was more important to voters than the candidates' positions on major issues, including the war in Iraq and outsourcing of American jobs. But among voters who were given ample information about the candidates' positions on the issues, policy agreement (defined as the extent to which a voter's own opinion on major issues matched the voter's perception of where the candidates stood on these issues) proved more important than viability as a determinant of candidate preference.

Priming can also lead citizens to give greater weight to other evaluative criteria, such as character traits. James Druckman and Justin Holmes (2004) found that President Bush successfully used his 2002 State of the Union address for image priming, increasing the influence of trait evaluations (strong leadership, integrity) on his approval rating. Similarly, Matthew Mendelsohn (1996) found that voters in the 1988 Canadian election who were heavily exposed to media reports were more likely to base their vote choice on candidate character evaluations and less likely to base them on issues.

Just as the influence of news coverage on the state of the public agenda is conditioned both by properties of news stories and by characteristics of individual members of the audience, the ability of the news to prime political evaluations is similarly tempered. It is not surprising that priming effects peak when news reports explicitly suggest that politicians are responsible for the state of national affairs or when they clearly link politicians' actions with national problems. Thus, evaluations of President Reagan's performance were more strongly influenced by news stories when the coverage suggested that Reaganomics was responsible for rising American unemployment than when the coverage directed attention to alternative causes of unemployment.

In another parallel with research on agenda setting, individuals differ in their susceptibility to media priming effects. Joanne Miller and Jon Krosnick (2000) found that priming effects occurred only among people who were both highly knowledgeable about political affairs and highly trusting of the media. Iyengar and Kinder (1987) found that partisanship affected the issues on which people could be primed: Democrats tended to be most susceptible to priming when the news focused on issues that favor Democrats, such as unemployment and civil rights; and Republicans were influenced most when the news focused on traditional Republican issues, such as national defense.

In sum, people use patterns of news coverage as an indicator of the state of the nation. Issues and events in the news are deemed important and weigh heavily in evaluations of incumbent officials and political candidates. As is clear from the way in which President George H. W. Bush benefited from media coverage of the 1991 Gulf War and then suffered from coverage of the economy, priming results equally from news of political successes and news of political failures. Priming is a double-edged sword.

FRAMING EFFECTS

The term *framing* refers to the way opinions about an issue can be altered by emphasizing or de-emphasizing particular facets of that issue. Framing theory was developed by psychologists Amos Tversky and Daniel Kahneman, who showed that choices could be reversed if outcomes were simply defined as potential gains or losses. A program that would certainly save 200 out of 600 people from an outbreak of a rare disease, for example, was chosen by a majority of subjects over an alternative with the identical outcome that was couched in terms that made it seem riskier ("a one-third probability of 600 people saved"). But when the choice was presented in terms of loss (400 deaths for sure, or a two-thirds probability of 600 deaths), the majority now preferred the riskier-seeming alternative (see Tversky & Kahneman, 1981). Similar presentation effects occur in surveys. Trivial changes in the wording of survey questions can bring about large shifts in public opinion; for example, people respond far less charitably when asked about the desirable level of government aid for "people on welfare" than when asked about aid for "poor people."

Media researchers have identified two distinct types of framing effects: equivalency framing effects and emphasis framing effects. *Equivalency framing effects* involve "the use of different, but logically equivalent, words or phrases" to describe the same possible event or issue; *emphasis framing effects* involve highlighting different "subset(s) of potentially relevant considerations" of an issue (Druckman, 2001, pp. 228, 230).

The previous example—"people on welfare" versus "poor people"—belongs more in the category of *emphasis* framing because the two phrases emphasize different aspects of poverty: referring to poor people puts the focus on the plight of the less fortunate, whereas referring to welfare brings up the question of whether the government has the responsibility to take care of them, as well as the negative stereotype that Americans have of people "on the dole." Other examples of emphasis framing effects include presenting a Ku Klux Klan rally as either a free speech issue or a public safety issue (respondents reported higher levels of support for allowing such a rally when it was framed as a free speech issue) and presenting gun control as either an individual rights issue or a public safety issue. Because equivalency framing rarely occurs in real-world political contexts, emphasis framing effects are most relevant to our discussion here—especially as it concerns the issue of who is responsible for national problems.

News coverage of political issues comes in two distinct genres of presentation: thematic and episodic news frames. A *thematic* news frame places a public issue in a general context and usually takes the form of an in-depth background report. An example of thematic framing would be a story about a war that addressed the historical context of the relations between the two sides, the factors that contributed to the current conflict, and so on. *Episodic* framing, on the other hand, depicts issues in terms of individual instances or specific events—the carnage resulting from a particular terrorist bombing, for example. Episodic coverage typically features dramatic visual footage and pictures; thematic reports tend to be more sedate, consisting primarily of talking heads.

In the United States, episodic framing is by far the predominant mode of presentation in news stories, largely as a result of market pressures. The preponderance of episodically framed news has serious political repercussions, for it affects viewers' attributions of responsibility for political issues. Most political issues are capable of being viewed either as the creations of societal and/or governmental forces or as the result of private actions of individuals. Rising unemployment, for instance, might be attributed to the changing nature of the job market or to government economic policies (societal responsibility). Alternatively, unemployment might be attributed to the unwillingness of the unemployed to work for low wages (individual responsibility). The tendency of people to attribute responsibility to societal or individual factors depends, in part, on how television frames political issues.

In a series of experimental studies (see Iyengar, 1991), viewers exposed to thematic framing attributed responsibility for issues to government and society. Following exposure to news reports about increases in malnutrition among the US poor, participants in the study discussed poverty in terms of inadequate social welfare programs; confronted with news accounts of the shrinking demand for unskilled labor, participants described unemployment as a result of inadequate economic policies or insensitive public officials; and provided with news reports on increasing rates of crime in the inner cities, participants cited improved economic opportunities for the underprivileged as the appropriate remedy for crime. Thus, when television news coverage presented an analytic frame of reference, attributions of responsibility—both for causing and curing national problems—were societal in focus.

When provided with episodic news, however, viewers attributed responsibility not to societal or political forces but to the actions of particular individuals or groups. For example, when poverty, crime, and terrorism were depicted in episodic terms, viewers attributed causal and treatment responsibility primarily to poor people, criminals, and terrorists. In response to news stories

◎ IN FOCUS

Framing

Framing refers to the way the media, by highlighting some aspects of an event or issue and ignoring others, can influence how people think about that event or issue. Changing the manner of presentation of a news story can result in a very different audience perception of that story.

describing particular illustrations of national issues, viewers focused on individual and group characteristics rather than on historical, social, political, or other general forces.

The importance of episodic and thematic news frames extends beyond viewers' attributions of responsibility. In each of the framing experiments (and in replications with national survey data), individuals who attributed responsibility for national issues to general societal factors were found to be significantly more critical of the performance of elected officials than were individuals who attributed responsibility to nonsocietal factors. Thus, television news is generally a significant asset for incumbent officials; the predominance of event-oriented and case study news coverage tends to insulate them from any rising tide of disenchantment over unemployment, poverty, corporate corruption, or other such problems. In contrast, when television casts its coverage in thematic terms, issues are more likely to become campaign ammunition with which to attack incumbents.

Framing scholars have extended analysis of the episodic frame to local news coverage of crime (see Video Archive 8.2). Typically, local crime reports provide a physical description—and perhaps a police sketch or even security camera footage or an old mug shot—of the suspect. The visual emphasis of television, together with the focus of crime reports on particular offenders, means

> ▶ **Video Archive 8.2**
> Episodic versus Thematic Framing of Crime

that, as depicted in the news, the principal determining factor of criminal behavior appears to be race (since race is something that is clearly evident in a news report, whereas poverty and other social factors obviously are not). Episodic framing thus necessarily introduces racial stereotypes into the public's understanding of crime. Viewers are compelled to evaluate their racial beliefs in light of what seem to be empirical realities. Thematic framing, by contrast, lacking the focus on an individual suspect or perpetrator, directs the viewers' attention to alternative and more contextual accounts of crime.

Experiments by Franklin Gilliam and Shanto Iyengar (2000) further demonstrated that the race of the suspect in episodic crime reports is a meaningful cue. The researchers presented the suspect as either a White or an African American male suspect (see Video Archive 8.3). Their results showed that when the suspect depicted in the news was African

> ▶ **Video Archive 8.3**
> Race Manipulation in Crime News Study

American, the number of viewers who endorsed punitive criminal justice policies increased significantly. In addition, exposure to the Black suspect strengthened viewers' racial stereotypes (ratings of Black Americans as lazy and unintelligent) and their hostility to Black leaders such as Jesse Jackson.

Interestingly, in the case of crime, episodic and thematic framing have the same effects. In a recent study, participants who were given statistical information about racial disparities in the US prison population (a significant overrepresentation of African Americans) expressed greater fear of crime and more support for punitive crime policies (Hetey & Eberhardt, 2014).

Racial stereotypes, particularly those associating crime and race, are also exploited by politicians (hence the rise of wedge appeals, as discussed in Chapter 6). Not only does exposure to information about crime influence viewers' attitudes toward crime and race; it can also prime racial stereotypes as a basis for judging the performance of elected officials or for choosing between candidates for elective office. A study by Tali Mendelberg (1997) found that among voters who watched the infamous 1988 "Willie Horton" ad, racial prejudice was more closely linked to their attitudes about civil rights and social welfare policies than among voters who did not view the ad. Similarly, Thomas Nelson and Donald Kinder (1996) found that frames that focused attention on the perceived beneficiaries of a policy (such as homosexuals in the case of AIDS spending) increased the importance of attitudes toward that group in determining attitudes toward the policy.

Some news frames originate with the media themselves (as by-products of news production processes). Episodic coverage is one such media-generated frame, since in most cases it results from the organizational and commercial pressures on news organizations. Other frames are inserted into the news by politicians and candidates in pursuit of political advantage (as in the case of the "Willie Horton" ad used by the George H. W. Bush campaign). If politicians can increase their support by using appeals—either explicit or coded—to racial prejudice, it is only to be expected that such appeals will become even more frequent during political campaigns.

Frames can occur on a number of levels as well. Political elites generate frames both on the level of specific issues (for example, is spending on social welfare an equality issue or an economic issue?) and on the level of specific events (did the events on January 6, 2021, amount to a violent insurrection or, as argued by many Republicans, mere acts of vandalism?). Campaigns often amount to framing battles between parties, each fighting to define voters' choices in terms of the issues or concerns on which they enjoy a strategic advantage.

Framing can also be used to evoke a sense of group identity. A candidate might be framed as an in-group (or out-group member, in the case of negative messages) on the basis of race, gender, age, or other physical attributes. In the 2008 contest between Obama and McCain, for instance, the negative ads aired by the McCain campaign featured darkened images of Obama (Messing, Jabon, & Plaut, 2016). Evolutionary psychologists argue that physical similarity is a powerful kinship cue and that humans are motivated to treat their kin preferentially. Experimental studies support the idea that voters are more likely to vote for the candidate whose face more closely resembles their own. In one study, participants were asked to provide their photographs in advance of the 2004 presidential election. One week before the election, these same participants took part in an online survey of political attitudes that included a variety of questions about the presidential candidates (President George W. Bush and Senator John Kerry). In some cases, the photograph of Bush had been morphed with the face of the participant; in other cases, it was the photograph of Kerry that had been morphed. Figure 8.6 shows two of the morphs used in this study. The researchers found that weak partisans and independents moved in the direction of the more similar candidate (see Bailenson, Iyengar, Yee, & Collins, 2009). Thus, this study demonstrates that nonverbal frames can influence voting, even in the most visible and contested of political campaigns.

FIGURE 8.6
Facial Morphing

Source: Data from J. N. Bailenson, S. Iyengar, N. Yee, & N. A. Collins. (2008, December). Facial similarity between voters and candidates causes influence. *Public Opinion Quarterly, 72,* 935–961.

More generally, candidates whose looks convey group membership (as in the case of skin complexion or feminine facial features) are likely to be evaluated through the lens of the voter's own sense of group identity. Candidates with typical Afrocentric features will lose support among Whites and gain support among African Americans (Messing, Jabon, & Plaut, 2016).

Frames that originate with the media also occur on a number of different levels. On one level, what the media tend to cover and not cover over the long term amounts to a frame; as documented in Chapter 3, the heavy emphasis on campaign strategy and poll standings overwhelms coverage of the candidates' issue positions, thus framing elections—and politics more generally—in terms of superficial rather than substantive matters (Patterson, 2016). Indeed, in some ways a specific medium can itself be considered a frame; for example, television—as a visual medium—tends to focus attention on superficial aspects of political presentations, such as candidate appearance or demeanor. And as we have already discussed, the media generate frames by deciding between thematic and episodic coverage.

Like agenda setting and priming, framing effects are conditioned by individual and contextual factors. Source credibility (believing a source to be knowledgeable and/or trustworthy) has been shown to be necessary for framing effects to occur. Researchers have also demonstrated that when given an opportunity to deliberate on issues, people are less susceptible to framing. Moreover, people are more likely to accept frames that are congruent with their political predispositions. This conclusion is consistent with the finding, mentioned earlier, that Republicans and Democrats are each more easily primed by issues traditionally associated with their own parties. Findings concerning the role of political knowledge are more ambiguous, with some studies showing the less informed to be more open to framing effects and other studies finding them to be less so.

The abundance of research on framing and the often shifting definitions of the concept have led some researchers to call for more precise terminology. In the case of emphasis framing, since there are multiple differences in content between the frames in question, it is difficult to pinpoint what exactly caused the framing effect. One advantage of nonverbal frames, as described in the face-morphing study, is that they provide very strong control; the different frames differ in one and only one respect, allowing the researcher to make a "clean" causal inference.

In summary, despite mediating factors on both contextual and individual levels, the manner in which the news media frame issues and events affects the public in a number of important ways. Politicians fight to frame issues and elections in terms that are advantageous to themselves. The news media assist them in their task, focusing on nonsubstantive facets of elections and presenting individualistic rather than contextualized accounts of political issues that discourage citizens from holding politicians accountable for national problems.

PERSUASION EFFECTS

Persuasion is typically defined as attitude change. As discussed at the outset of this chapter, early political communication researchers, looking for evidence of reversals in voter preference, found little evidence of persuasion effects. However, attitude change does not necessarily mean converting from one candidate or one side of an issue to the other. For example, persuasion can involve switching from having no opinion at all to having an opinion, from having a weak opinion to having a strong opinion, or from not intending to act on an opinion to intending to act. Television news coverage of the abortion issue might encourage viewers to alter their position from uncommitted or slightly pro-choice to strongly pro-choice. A political advertisement might induce some undecided citizens to vote for a particular candidate. News reports on business activity might increase consumer confidence in the economy. And under certain circumstances, people may reverse their preferences or opinions.

Communication theorists typically analyze persuasion situations from the perspective of "who says what to whom." Thus, the major determinants of attitude change are source, message, and receiver characteristics. Applied to politics, the sources are either the news media in general, particular news organizations, or candidates and political parties. Message-related factors might include the particular subject matter of a news report (crime versus the economy), the content of news reports (such as accounts suggesting that Russia interfered in the 2016 election versus reports suggesting that it did not), or the tone of a candidate advertisement (positive versus negative appeals). Receiver factors include a wide variety of political predispositions (is the voter Republican or Democrat?) and general background characteristics (is the voter young or old, more educated or less?). As we will describe, the evidence suggests that political persuasion, like persuasion in other contexts, requires a set of joint contingencies among message, source, and receiver factors.

Receiver-Related Contingencies

In his classic paper on persuasion effects in campaigns, Philip Converse (1962) demonstrated that the most and the least attentive strata of the electorate remained equally stable (unpersuaded) over the course of political campaigns. The most attentive encounter a host of campaign messages in the form of either news reports or candidate advertisements but reject most of them. This is because attentiveness is associated with partisanship: those most likely to tune in to campaigns are strongly Republican or Democratic in affiliation. The less attentive, on the other hand, are drawn disproportionately from the ranks of nonpartisans. Although willing to consider any campaign message, they encounter none.

Political campaigns thus typify the golden-mean maxim of attitude change theorists: voters at the upper end of the attentiveness curve cannot be persuaded because they already have strong preferences; those at the bottom cannot be persuaded because they are never exposed to political messages. Therefore, the middle strata of political engagement—citizens who are moderately interested or informed—are the most influenced by campaigns. Those who paid no attention to news during the 2020 presidential campaign, for instance, would have had no exposure to the uniformly unfavorable coverage of Trump's behavior in the first televised debate and could not possibly have been persuaded by it. Strong Democrats and Republicans, two groups that were especially likely to have tuned in to the news following the debate would have been equally unpersuaded— the former because they were already staunchly anti-Trump, the latter because they rejected the coverage as coming from pro-Biden news sources. However, weak Democrats and Republicans who were only mildly interested in the campaign could have been swayed by the post-debate coverage to vote against Trump on the grounds that his behavior was erratic and unpresidential.

The opposing effects of exposure and acceptance on susceptibility to persuasion help explain why reinforcement rather than persuasion is the typical outcome of political campaigns (as described in Chapter 7). Voters' partisan loyalties provide a filter for interpreting campaign messages: messages that oppose viewers' attitudes are actively resisted; those that agree with viewers' attitudes are accepted. Of course, nonpartisans are far less attentive to campaigns than partisans are; nonpartisans' attitudes remain unaffected because they are unaware of what the candidates are saying. Thus, the principal effect of campaigns is to push Republicans and Democrats further into their respective camps.

Source- and Message-Related Contingencies

While exposure to and acceptance of persuasive messages are both conditioned by the political predispositions of receivers, some scholars have uncovered a different family of interactions—this time between message and source factors. Their argument is that persuasion effects also depend on the degree of fit between the *what* and *who* factors. Readers should recognize this argument as none other than the strategy of issue ownership. That is, Republican candidates are more persuasive when they (the source) discuss issues on which Republicans are generally preferred (the message), and the same is true for Democrats and their preferred issues.

Ansolabehere and Iyengar (1995) experimentally tested for the interaction of source and message factors. The identical advertisements (one on unemployment and one on crime) were attributed to either the Democratic candidate or the Republican candidate running for US Senate in California. Whereas exposure to the unemployment ad elicited greater gains for the Democratic candidate, exposure to the crime ad did the same for the Republican candidate. In a related study, voters rated campaign ads aired by presidential candidates Bob Dole and Bill Clinton during the 1996 presidential campaign. Republicans were more likely to rate Dole's ads as informative (and less likely to rate them as misleading) when the ads addressed Republican issues (Iyengar & Valentino, 2000). Conversely, Democrats were more impressed by Clinton's ads dealing with Democratic issues. Thus, the parties' policy reputations are tantamount to assessments of source credibility.

The logic of differential source credibility extends easily to attributes of the candidates beyond their party affiliation. Gender is an especially visible attribute, and the popular culture provides several cues about the traits of men and women—cues that are amply reinforced by the media's depiction of female candidates (Kahn, 1994). Given the availability of gender stereotypes, certain issue messages might be expected to have differential effects across male and female candidates. In fact, the evidence reveals that "masculine" issues, such as defense or crime, are especially persuasive as campaign material for male candidates, whereas preschool funding and other matters of educational policy work well for female candidates. Not surprisingly, given their ownership of issues of social welfare, Democratic politicians are deemed more compassionate than Republicans (Hayes, 2005).

In short, persuasive messages are not encountered in a vacuum and must blend in with voters' partisan motives and attitudes. As we discuss in the next section, partisan motives have become especially important in recent years as party polarization has intensified. Party identification increasingly affects not only voting choices and candidate evaluations but a variety of nonpolitical preferences and behaviors.

Polarized Politics: Implications for Media Effects

The conventional definition of polarization concerns the increasing divergence in the policy platforms of the two major parties. Over the past several decades, Democratic and Republican leaders have moved to the liberal and conservative extremes, respectively, leaving very few elected officials in the political center (McCarty, Poole, & Rosenthal, 2006). As the elites have gravitated to the ideological extremes, rank-and-file partisans have aligned their positions on the liberal-conservative continuum with their party affiliation, which means that there are very few liberal Republicans or conservative Democrats. This phenomenon is known as "sorting": the opposing political camps are now based on both party and ideological affiliation (Levendusky, 2009; Mason, 2014).

One effect of the more extreme policy positions taken by party leaders is the growing discrepancy in the preferences of politically attentive Democrats and Republicans. The more attentive the partisans, the more likely they recognize and adopt the position taken by their party. In this "polarization" model of attitude change, attentiveness (or any proxy for attentiveness such as education) has the *opposite* effect on policy preferences, depending on the individual's party affiliation. For instance, more attentive Republicans will be more opposed to government-run healthcare than less attentive Republicans, with precisely the opposite pattern holding for Democrats. More attentive Republicans and more attentive Democrats are both more likely to toe the party line.

As the electorate has become more sorted, a different form of division—referred to as affective polarization—has emerged among Americans with a party identity. Since the early 1970s, the American National Election Studies (ANES) has included a "feeling thermometer" question measuring positive or negative feelings about several groups, including the two parties. Thermometer scores of 0 indicate an extreme negative evaluation, while a score of 100 represents the opposite. As shown in Figure 8.7, since the late 1970s the thermometer score given by partisans to the "out" party—the party they do not affiliate with—has declined significantly from a high point of around 60 to the mid-30s, whereas the rating of the "in" party has remained steadily enthusiastic (thermometer scores in the mid-70s). In the 2008 ANES survey, the average thermometer rating of the "out" party was around 30, making the out party the most disliked of all the groups included in the survey, even more so than Muslims and atheists, two groups that traditionally receive unfavorable evaluations in ANES surveys (for details on the thermometer data, see Iyengar, Sood, & Lelkes, 2012). In the 2016 ANES survey, for the first time on record, the most frequent thermometer score given the opposing party was 0! In 2020, the trend continued with nearly 45 percent of partisan respondents rating the opposing party at 0.

The ANES thermometer data represent but the tip of an iceberg of survey evidence showing animus and ill will across party lines. A 2014 Pew poll found that 27 percent of Democrats and 36 percent of Republicans believed that the policies of the opposing party actually threatened the well-being of the country (Pew Research Center, 2014). Around 40 percent of the partisans in this survey (those who said they identified as Democrat or Republican) viewed the out party in

FIGURE 8.7

A Rising Tide of Partisan Animus

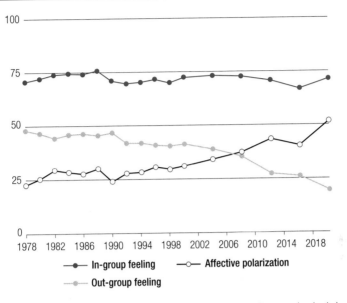

Note: Republicans include Republican-leaning independents; Democrats include Democrat-leaning independents.
Source: Data compiled by the author from American National Election Studies. Retrieved from the American National Election Studies website: https://electionstudies.org/.

very unfavorable terms, a level of animosity more than double that expressed in 1994. Politics may not be a contact sport, but Democrats and Republicans harbor generally hard feelings toward their opponents. The sense of partisan identity is increasingly associated with an "us against them" view of the political world.

The harshly critical image of the opposition party suggests that political divisions run deep for Americans, so much so that party affiliation has become an important cue for the initiation and conduct of interpersonal relationships. We increasingly socialize with and develop close personal ties with people whose political views we find congenial. Almost 60 years ago, in their classic study of political culture, Gabriel Almond and Sidney Verba asked a national sample of Americans how they would feel if their son or daughter were to marry someone from the party they did not favor. Barely 5 percent of the partisans in the sample expressed any concern at the prospect of their progeny entering into an interparty marriage (Almond & Verba, 1963). But when a similar version of the question was asked in 2010, nearly half the Republicans and a third of the Democrats responded that they would feel somewhat or very unhappy at the prospect of their son or daughter marrying across party lines (Iyengar, Sood, & Lelkes, 2012).

The startling increase in partisans' unease over a family member crossing party lines cannot be dismissed as survey respondents simply conforming to what they believe is expected of them. Examination of the actual party registration of male and female adults residing at the same address (using national voter registration files) reveals a level of spousal agreement that exceeds 80 percent, suggesting the tendency of people to select a mate on the basis of political similarity (see Iyengar, Konitzer, & Tedin, 2019). The evidence from online dating sites is no less compelling. In one recent study (Huber & Malhotra, 2017), partisan agreement increased the likelihood of recipro- cal messaging on a major dating site by 10 percent. To put this difference in context, the comparable attraction based on individuals' level of education was 11 percent. Thus, partisanship appears to be just as important as socioeconomic status in the process of selecting a romantic partner.

Perhaps the most startling evidence of affective polarization comes from research that documents the applicability of party cues to entirely non- political settings. In one such study, participants were asked to indicate which of two high school students was more deserving of an academic scholar- ship. The résumés of the two students were manipulated so that in all cases, one student's grade average was higher than the other's. The résumés also revealed a difference in the students' extracurricular interests: one was active in the student wing of the Republican Party, while the other was described as similarly active for the Democratic Party. Rather than nominating the student with the better grades, partisans on both sides overwhelmingly preferred the student whose political affiliation matched their own (Iyengar & Westwood, 2015). Thus, it appears that the party cue is now all-encompassing and just as likely to influence nonpolitical as political choices (for a review of the evidence, see Iyengar, Lelkes, Levendusky, Malhotra, & Westwood, 2019).

EXPLAINING AFFECTIVE POLARIZATION

The period over which partisan animus has intensified (1980 to today) coin- cides with several major changes in American society and politics, most nota- bly changes in the media environment, increased ideological polarization and partisan sorting, and elevated levels of negative campaigning (as documented in Chapter 6). Each of these factors is a likely contributor.

First, as described in Chapter 5, the revolution in information technology has empowered consumers to self-select into segregated audiences that regularly encounter news and analysis reinforcing their point of view. Many partisan outlets depict the opposing party in harsh terms and focus disproportionately on out-party scandals (real or imagined). The creation of vast online social networks has permitted extensive recirculation of news reports, even to those not particularly motivated to seek out news. Several scholars have thus singled out partisans' ability to encounter "friendly" information providers as an especially influential agent of affective polarization.

Second, over the last 50 years the percentage of "sorted" partisans, that is, partisans who identify with the party most closely reflecting their ideology, has steadily increased (Levendusky, 2009). When most Democrats are also liberals or most Republicans are also conservatives, they are less likely to encounter conflicting political ideas and identities and are more likely to see their opponents as socially distant (Levendusky & Malhotra, 2016).

As partisan and ideological identities have come into alignment, other salient social identities, including race and religion, have also converged with partisanship. Democrats are increasingly the party of women, non-Whites, professionals, and residents of urban areas, while Republican voters are disproportionately older White men, evangelical Christians, and residents of rural areas. This decline of crosscutting identities has contributed to affective polarization (Mason, 2018).

A third explanation focuses on shifts in partisans' policy preferences. In effect, the claim is that ideological polarization has caused affective polarization and that as the ideological distance between parties grows, so too does out-party animus (Orr & Huber, 2020; Rogowski & Sutherland, 2016). At present, the jury is still out on the question of ideological disagreement as the driver of partisan affect. A handful of studies demonstrate the causal connection (for instance, Orr & Huber, 2020), while a similar number find no relationship, or even the opposite effect, that is, that partisan identity determines policy preferences and perceptions of ideological extremity (for instance, Dias & Lelkes, 2021). Given the mixed state of the evidence, we must await additional studies.

Finally, there is the "opinion leadership," or persuasion, explanation we have just covered for why partisans have become sworn enemies. It is abundantly clear that elite rhetoric and campaign messaging in America have become more shrill and hostile over time (see Berry & Sobieraj, 2014; Geer, 2012). Even in nonelection contexts, political elites engage in name calling and taunting of their opponents (Grimmer & King, 2011). Given the extreme negativity of elite discourse, we can expect that relatively attentive partisans will be both exposed to and accepting of the sentiment expressed by their party leaders. There is only one direct test of this explanation; Gaurav Sood and Shanto Iyengar (2018) documented that out-party animus increased over the course of recent presidential campaigns and that this change is attributable specifically to exposure to negative campaign advertising.

Overall, at present we do not know enough about the psychological underpinnings of affective polarization to offer any firm generalizations. Given the power of the party cue and its widespread applicability in any number of nonpolitical domains, one suspects that partisan social identity is implicated as a causal force. Possibly, the sense of identity is sufficient to engender out-party animus. Alternatively, their sense of identity may lead partisans to perceive their opponents as holding extreme preferences, and this "illusory" state of ideological polarization may fan the flames of partisan animus. Finally, there is the possibility that elites bear the responsibility for the widespread partisan rancor; their hostile rhetoric and behavior instill animus in the minds of their supporters.

The heightened state of affective polarization has clear implications for research on persuasion and attitude change. Given their strong views, partisans can be persuaded by party cues but little else. They will resist information and arguments damaging to their cause and even go so far as to deny established facts. W. Lance Bennett and Shanto Iyengar (2008) have argued that the entrenched views of partisans, coupled with their exposure to one-sided news coverage supporting their point of view, make it increasingly unlikely that we will witness persuasion effects at all during campaigns. In fact, the literature on media effects may have practically come full circle, with a return to the theory of minimal consequences.

The implications of polarization extend well beyond the reduced persuadability of partisans. As we document in Chapter 9, polarization also alters the dynamics of incumbent approval. No matter how ineffective a president might be in managing the problems at hand, in the era of polarization the president will always be evaluated favorably by supporters of his party. Conversely, evidence of effective leadership and policy accomplishments does little to moderate unfavorable evaluations of the incumbent's performance among opposing partisans. In essence, polarization weakens mechanisms of electoral accountability.

CONCLUSION

Writing 100 years ago with remarkable foresight, Walter Lippmann (1922, 1925) offered a series of concerns about the health of American democracy. First, he warned that the great majority of American citizens were too apathetic and uninformed to govern themselves. Lacking firsthand knowledge, the public had no recourse but to rely on the "pictures in their heads" when attempting to make sense of political issues and events. Second, he warned that opportunistic political elites could take advantage of citizens' apathy and dependence on the media to manipulate public opinion to their advantage.

The evidence summarized in this chapter matches the first part of Lippmann's argument quite closely. Ordinary citizens are preoccupied with their personal lives and pay little attention to public affairs. Unable to weigh the pros and cons of policy debates, citizens make do with what they have: the images and sound bites transmitted by the media. They follow the lead of news programming when asked to identify the important issues of the day. Those who influence the media agenda also hold a great deal of power to mold public opinion because issues in the news become the principal yardsticks for evaluating public officials. The impact of media messages on political attitudes, however, is significantly curtailed by the audience's partisan predispositions.

Lippmann's second conjecture—that political leaders could manipulate public opinion—has also come true, but not because of voter indifference and ignorance. Instead, Americans who support their political "team" have become mere robots, content to accept the proclamations and posturing of their leaders, even when the rhetoric clashes with the facts and their leader has a well-known propensity to stray from the truth. This willingness to accept messages based entirely on the logic of "us against them," as we discuss in Chapter 10, has grave implications for the practice of democratic politics.

Another lingering question in media effects research concerns the duration or persistence of media effects on public opinion. Most experiments expose subjects to a single message and then measure the effects of the message immediately afterward. There is very little evidence concerning the long-term implications of agenda-setting, priming, or framing effects.

Taken cumulatively, the evidence indicates that media presentations achieve considerable influence over public opinion. When most news providers parrot the views of political elites—as is the case during periods of military conflict—the journalistic consensus allows elites to bolster their popularity and gain an important strategic advantage in the policy arena. In Chapter 9, we will demonstrate that fluctuations in presidential popularity have become less dependent on the state of the country and the accomplishments (or failures) of the incumbent administration. Instead, presidents receive unconditional support from adherents of the governing party—a finding we take as suggestive of Lippmann's concern over the ability of ordinary citizens to hold political leaders accountable for their actions in office.

Summary

1. As a result of a limited conceptualization of media effects (defining them only in terms of persuasion) and a reliance on survey methodology (which tends to underestimate media effects), political communication researchers have long held that media effects were minimal. Methodological advances (including wider use of experiments), along with a broadened definition of media effects, have since led scholars to acknowledge that media presentations can make a difference in politics.

2. Surveys and experiments, the two methods used to study media effects, each have strengths and weaknesses. Experiments give researchers control over the stimuli to which study participants are exposed, allowing them to isolate causality, but the results from experiments cannot be easily generalized. Surveys, on the other hand, are highly generalizable, but inaccuracy in participants' self-reports weakens the ability of survey researchers to detect media effects.

3. A variety of media effects on citizens have been examined by researchers:
    *   *Becoming informed.* By tuning in to the news, Americans can acquire factual information about events. However, in recent years, many Americans also acquire factual beliefs that are false (misinformation).
    *   *Agenda setting.* The term *agenda setting* describes the way in which the media set the agenda for public opinion by highlighting certain issues and ignoring others.
    *   *Priming.* An extension of agenda setting, priming is the way the media affect the criteria by which political leaders are judged. The more prominent an issue becomes in the public consciousness, the more that issue will influence people's assessments of politicians, candidates, and other public figures.
    *   *Framing.* By highlighting some aspects of an event or issue and ignoring others, the media can influence how people think about that event or issue.
    *   *Persuasion.* Although most early studies on media effects failed to find evidence of persuasion, the media do have some persuasive influence—especially when the definition of persuasion is not limited to conversion from one candidate or one side of an issue to the other.

4. Party polarization has elevated the importance of the party cue for voters. As hostility across the party divide has spread, partisans become more motivated to acquire information that reinforces their point of view, making it less likely that they can be persuaded by media messages.

FURTHER READINGS

Alcott, H., Braghieri, L., Eichmeyer, S., & Gentzkow, M. (2020). The welfare effects of social media. *American Economic Review*, 110, 629–676.

Bennett, W. L., & Iyengar, S. (2008). A new era of minimal effects? The changing foundations of political communication. *Journal of Communication*, 58, 707–731.

Berelson, B., Lazarsfeld, P. F., & McPhee, W. (1954). *Voting.* Chicago: University of Chicago Press.

Cohen, B. E. (1963). *The press and foreign policy.* Princeton, NJ: Princeton University Press.

Gilliam, F. D., Jr., & Iyengar, S. (2000). Prime suspects: The influence of local television news on the viewing public. *American Journal of Political Science*, 44, 560–573.

Hovland, C. I. (1959). Reconciling conflicting results derived from experimental and survey studies of attitude change. *The American Psychologist*, 14, 8–17.

Iyengar, S. (1991). *Is anyone responsible?* Chicago: University of Chicago Press.

Iyengar, S., & Kinder, D. R. (1987). *News that matters: Television and American opinion.* Chicago: University of Chicago Press.

Iyengar, S., Levendusky, M., Lelkes, Y., Malhotra, N., & Westwood. S. (2019). Affective polarization: A review of the evidence. *Annual Review of Political Science*, 22, 129–146.

King, G., Schneer, B., & White, A. (2017). How the news media activate public expression and influence national agendas. *Science*, 358, 776–780.

Lenz, G. S. (2012). *Follow the leader: How voters respond to politicians' performance and policies.* Chicago: University of Chicago Press.

Popkin, S. L. (1994). *The reasoning voter: Communication and persuasion in presidential campaigns* (2nd ed.). Chicago: University of Chicago Press.

Price, V., & Zaller, J. (1993). Who gets the news? Alternative measures of news reception and their implications for research. *Public Opinion Quarterly*, 57, 133–164.

Zaller, J. R. (1992). *The nature and origins of mass opinion.* New York: Cambridge University Press.

NOTES

1. This procedure, known as a "deprivation" design, is implemented by offering social media users a financial incentive to temporarily suspend their use of their preferred social media platform (for a recent application of this design, see Alcott, Braghieri, Eichmeyer, & Gentzkow, 2020).

2. Of course, as in any probabilistic outcome, there is some chance (typically small) that the two groups might not be equivalent.

3. Perhaps the imposition of answering the phone is not so trivial. The response rate in most major surveys has dropped in recent years and now approaches 30 percent.

4. Critics of the "heuristics as equivalent to information" argument cite evidence showing that when voters are made to acquire factual information, they express opinions that are often significantly different from the opinions they held previously.
5. An exception is the work by Gabriel Lenz (2012), which documents significant projection effects.

9

Going Public

Governing through the Media

It used to be that when an election was over, the winning candidates took office, put away their campaign paraphernalia and rhetoric, and got down to the serious business of governing. For a US president, this meant cultivating majority support in Congress for the key provisions of the presidential platform. The White House became the center of serious, behind-the-scenes negotiations. The end result was the passage of legislation that reflected and accommodated competing interests. In the premedia era, an essential element of presidential leadership was the ability to create winning coalitions from across the party or ideological divides.

Amassing support for the president's proposals typically required both patience and a horse trader's knack for compromise. Presidents with extensive personal networks on Capitol Hill (Lyndon Johnson, for example) were in the best position to readily elicit bipartisan support. In the Johnson era, conservative Southern Democrats supported civil rights legislation in return for increased defense spending directed to Southern states. This bargaining model of policy making rested on face-to-face communications among a relatively small group of elites who felt a common sense of obligation to place the interests of the nation ahead of the narrow confines of party or ideology.

Of course, bargaining among the elites did not guarantee sound policy. "Pork barrel" considerations typically trumped cost-benefit analysis of political problems as the basis for compromise. Powerful committee or subcommittee chairs could see to it that a significant share of federal spending was deposited into the pockets of their constituents. Despite these flaws, however, the bargaining model did, for the most part, result in smoothly functioning governance. The federal budget, for instance, was routinely enacted into law in advance of the fiscal-year deadline.

As elections became more media-centric, the president's increasingly important role as direct spokesman to the public began to alter the policy-making process. Rather than dealing directly with congressional leaders, presidents preferred to influence them indirectly by making them respond to "the people." As political scientist Samuel Kernell (1986) defined the new approach, "It is a strategy whereby a president promotes himself and his policies in Washington by appealing to the American public for support" (p. 2).

The increased reliance on the modern bully pulpit of television intensified partisan conflict and ill will, making it more difficult for rival elites to engage in good-faith bargaining. The more confrontational atmosphere in Washington led to the shutdown of the federal government on 20 occasions between 1977 and 2018 because of irreconcilable policy differences between the president and Congress over the federal budget. In most cases, federal offices were closed for only a day or two. In 2018, however, in the longest shutdown in history, involving 800,000 federal employees, essential government services were unavailable for 35 days because President Trump and the Democrats in Congress could not reach agreement on funding for the border wall. Several airports shut down because of insufficient Transportation Security Administration staff to conduct security checks. Gridlock rather than compromise had become the order of the day. An earlier impasse occurred in 2013 when Republicans in Congress refused to support an increase in the debt ceiling without extracting concessions from Democrats in the form of changes to the Affordable Care Act (Obamacare). When the Democrats refused, the government shut down for 16 days before the Republicans—in response to poll results showing that the public held them responsible—capitulated and voted to raise the borrowing limit.

The deterioration in the relationship between the president and Congress and between competing party elites can be attributed in significant part to media-based electoral campaigns. When hard-edged rhetoric and personal attacks are directed at opponents during a campaign, it becomes difficult for elected leaders to extend the olive branch once the election is over. Donald Trump insisted that the FBI investigate the Clinton Foundation during the 2016 campaign and promised to send Hillary Clinton to jail if he won. After taking office, as his own legal issues mounted, he continued to demand prosecution of Clinton for corruption.

Winning candidates must look over their shoulders constantly, for fear of offending potential donors and campaign activists or of casting a vote that might become the focus of the next round of attack ads. A vote on raising the debt ceiling is no longer a routine legislative duty but rather an opportunity to go on the record as opposing "big government." During the Trump presidency, almost all Republicans in Congress refused to criticize the president (and voted to acquit him in two separate impeachments) to avoid provoking the wrath of Trump supporters in their district. More generally, the very same tools and strategies that are used to win the election are now applied for purposes of policy making. Going public has gradually superseded give-and-take bargaining as the preferred approach to governance.

The movement away from bargaining has only accelerated in the current era of online news, social media, and instant leader-to-follower communication. President Trump would immediately take to Twitter to condemn legislators and other officials who refused to go along with his proposals or who dared criticize his behavior in office. After a federal judge ordered a halt to Trump's travel ban targeting individuals from Muslim nations, Trump tweeted that the decision by a "so-called" judge was politically motivated. In 2017, after the failed attempts to repeal Obamacare, Trump lashed out at Republicans who voted against the bill to repeal (most notably, Senator McCain). Do opponents back down in the face of presidential criticism? It depends on the president's popularity with the public and, for officials from the president's party, his standing among the activist base. The Republican base's complete devotion to Trump meant that any Republican who offended him would almost certainly face a primary challenge in the next election. After Congresswoman Liz Cheney broke with Trump over his role in inciting the violence of January 6, her Republican colleagues in the House voted to strip her of her leadership position. She faces no fewer than six challengers in the 2022 Wyoming Republican primary.

The central ingredient of going public as a strategy of leadership is the cultivation of public approval. A president's popularity creates an important bargaining advantage; a president who enjoys a high level of public approval is more able to persuade Congress to go along. When the public backs the president, the president's credibility is enhanced; members of Congress become more likely to defer to the president's legislative proposals because they fear that the potential costs of opposition are too high. As Richard Brody (1991) puts it, popularity enables the president to "achieve his program, keep challengers at bay, and guide his and other political leaders' expectations about the president's party's prospects in presidential and congressional elections" (p. 4).

The effects of a president's popularity on the ability to garner legislative support are most evident when the president's proposals address issues that are salient to the public but concern subject matters about which the public possesses little information. For example, the public is unanimously in favor of policies that reduce terrorism but has little ability to discriminate between

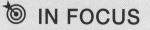

IN FOCUS

Going Public

Going public is a strategy used by presidents and other politicians to promote their policies by appealing to the American public for support. If a president enjoys strong public support, that popularity creates an important bargaining advantage. A president with a high level of public approval can often count on being able to persuade a few members of the opposition who may fear that they will not be reelected if they take a stand against a well-liked president.

the pros and cons of military intervention versus economic development as possible solutions. In such circumstances, presidential rhetoric has a double-barreled effect: it makes the targeted issues more prominent for the public, and it makes Congress more responsive to the president's proposals.

Conversely, a president buffeted by allegations of illegal or immoral behavior will be much less effective at pushing through a legislative program. Nixon's credibility with Congress was minimal once the Watergate allegations began to hold the public's attention. Forty-five years later, the investigation led by Special Counsel Robert Mueller into collusion between the Trump campaign and the Russian government and the resulting impeachment inquiry weakened an already less-than-credible president (given his consistently low levels of popularity). Despite Republican control of both houses of Congress, Trump's legislative accomplishments consisted of one major tax cut and a handful of minor bills.

In stark contrast to the Trump presidency, Ronald Reagan's presidency provides a textbook case of a popular president using his power to persuade to get things done. Reagan had defeated incumbent president Jimmy Carter on a platform of smaller government and tax cuts. Reagan's first budget proposal (in 1981) called for unprecedented cuts in social welfare programs coupled with significant increases in defense spending. On both counts, the budget was an abomination to congressional Democrats, who still controlled the House. Undeterred, Reagan embarked on a systematic media campaign to promote the budget. The president gave several speeches across the country urging citizens to convey their support for his budget to their congressional representatives. The speeches were carefully designed (with catchy sound bites) to attract coverage from local and network newscasts. Reagan also made it plain that he would personally campaign against any Democrats who voted against his budget. Here's how David Gergen (Reagan's director of communications) described the closing stages of the campaign:

> We learned about it [the impending congressional vote on the budget resolution] the next day. . . . Reagan was flying off to Texas. I was back at the White House, and we worked it out by sending statements to the plane for Reagan to make a planeside statement in time to get it on the evening news. We wanted to give it hype, to elevate the issue on the evening news so that the nation was getting a message. We were calling the press and doing whatever we could to build the issue. At the same time, the political office went to work, notifying all their allies around the country, bringing the calls and pressure onto Congress as quickly as possible. (Hertsgaard, 1988, p. 120)

Reagan's strategy paid off. Despite the radical nature of his proposals and the deep hostility of congressional Democrats to the Reagan agenda, the budget was passed. Recognizing President Reagan's considerable popularity, a sufficient number of Democrats voted against their party. Fear of angering voters rather than some form of political inducement had become the basis for creating policy coalitions in government. Using a president's public standing as leverage had replaced negotiations among elites as the basis for governance.

As we have already noted, President Trump elevated the strategy of going public to new heights. There was no policy debate or ongoing controversy on which he did not stake out his position—often in black-and-white terms—via Twitter. He also regularly scheduled campaign-style rallies (nearly one per week after taking office, and also throughout the COVID-19 pandemic leading up to the 2020 election) in which he fiercely attacked his critics and extolled his accomplishments. In contrast to their reaction to Reagan, however, Democrats in Congress ignored Trump's outbursts knowing that the president was extremely unpopular among their party's supporters.

Overall, the evidence suggests that going public has become the principal strategy underlying presidential leadership in the current era. According to Brandice Canes-Wrone (2001), "Modern presidents systematically achieve policy goals by promoting issues to the public" (p. 326).

The transition from a style of governance based on negotiations among elites to one based on media rhetoric and imagery has occurred in part because of the growing prominence of media professionals in the policy process. Increasingly, political appointments in the White House have come to be distributed among the members of the winning campaign team rather than among party officials. Key campaign professionals have taken up positions in the executive branch with the principal agenda of ensuring the president's

A Tale of Two Disasters

The contrasting ways in which George W. Bush dealt with Hurricane Katrina in 2005 and Barack Obama dealt with the Gulf of Mexico *Deepwater Horizon* oil spill in 2010 illustrate the overriding importance of news media coverage to the president's ability to govern effectively. In the case of Katrina, the Bush administration failed to recognize the urgency of the situation and allowed the continuous stream of vivid images depicting "an environmental disaster of biblical proportions" to dominate the news. When the president finally traveled to New Orleans to deliver a televised speech to the American people, he was forced to admit that "the system at every level of government was not well-coordinated, and was overwhelmed" (*Washington Post*, 2005). In the weeks after Katrina, Bush's public approval plummeted.

In the case of the Gulf oil spill, the Obama administration immediately orchestrated a series of events suggesting that the president was in control of the situation. Secretary of the Interior Ken Salazar was dispatched to BP's command center to review their procedures. Admiral Thad Allen, of the Coast Guard, was appointed to head the Unified Command Center, the group overseeing BP's efforts to cap the well. In a nationally televised address President Obama announced that BP would establish a victim compensation fund. The president made multiple trips to Louisiana to express his solidarity with the residents of the affected region. As the oil spill dragged on, Obama's public approval remained stable.

reelection. At the other end of Pennsylvania Avenue, members of Congress have behaved in similar fashion, recruiting political operatives for their office staff whose major responsibility is to prepare for the next campaign.

The revolving door between the campaign and the White House staff means that the president's closest advisers, while experts in dealing with the media, have limited experience with congressional outreach. George W. Bush's closest confidant was Karl Rove, his campaign manager. David Axelrod, President Obama's senior political adviser, was a little-known political consultant in Illinois before working on Obama's 2008 campaign. President Trump continued this tradition of staffing the White House with campaign operatives. Steve Bannon, his chief strategist, previously ran the conservative website Breitbart. com. Once in the White House, Bannon's advice to Trump came straight out of the going-public textbook: force the Washington establishment to go along by appealing to the Republican base. Joe Biden has continued this revolving-door tradition; Anita Dunn, who masterminded the 2020 Biden campaign, joined the White House staff as "senior advisor to the president."

The remainder of this chapter will discuss the role of public communication by the president today. Why is communication with the public so essential? What are the key forms of presidential communication and why? And what are the payoffs, if any? Does the preoccupation with media imagery strengthen the president's power to persuade?

PRESIDENTIAL COMMUNICATION

The conventional wisdom in Washington is that the president's media messaging is indeed essential to political success. As explained by President Bush's political guru Karl Rove,

> I think in the post-1980 era we all owe it to [Michael] Deaver who said turn off the sound of the television and that's how people are going to decide whether you won the day or lost the day, the quality of the picture. That's what they're going to get the message by, with the sound entirely off. I think that's simplistic, but I think it's an important insight. There's a reason why the old saw, a picture is worth a thousand words, how we look, how we sound and how we project is important. So winning the picture is important. (Kumar, 2003, p. 385)

Validating Rove's analysis, recent presidents have all adapted their behavior to harness the power of mass media. Exercising control over the media narrative rather than cultivating good relations with Congress has become an absolutely essential element of presidential leadership. Herbert Hoover's media staff consisted of a single assistant for press relations. In the 1950s, the White House media operation expanded to include the press secretary, the press secretary's deputy, and five secretarial employees. Today, the vast White House media complex (see Figure 9.1) has more than 70 full-time employees and five distinct organizational units. Clearly, the strategy of going public has magnified the function of press management in the contemporary presidency.

THE PRESIDENT'S MEDIA MANAGERS

The nerve center of the executive branch's communication efforts is the Office of the Press Secretary, commonly referred to as the Press Office. Alongside the Press Office is the Office of Communications, headed by the communications

FIGURE 9.1

Media Operations in the White House

Source: Data from M. J. Kumar. (2003). The White House and the press: News organizations as a presidential resource and as a source of pressure. *Presidential Studies Quarterly*, 33, 669–683.

director. The Press Office issues all press releases and responds to inquiries from the national media. The Office of Communications is responsible for planning the president's media appearances, including press conferences and other public events. The communications director is also responsible for coordinating the message of the various spokespersons throughout the administration. The Office of Media Affairs provides the same services as the Office of Communications but for the benefit of local and regional news outlets. The Office of Global Communications provides "strategic direction and themes" to government agencies (such as the Voice of America) that produce information and media content for overseas audiences. The Office of Speechwriting is entrusted with drafting the president's speeches and public remarks. Finally, the newly created Office of Digital Strategy ensures that the president's message is made widely available through live video streaming and text posts on the White House website, its YouTube channel, its Facebook page, its Twitter account, and other online sources.

The communications director is responsible for overseeing the production and release of information throughout the administration. Given the number of agencies and offices that deal with the media, message coordination is often impossible. Getting the federal government to speak with one voice is the goal, but more often than not, there are inconsistencies and misstatements that must be explained. After triumphantly announcing a bipartisan deal over infrastructure legislation in 2021, President Biden went on to state that he would not sign the bill unless Congress also passed additional legislation that included paid leave, free childcare, and other priorities championed by liberal Democrats. Republicans immediately responded that Biden's stance was a deal killer. The next day the White House walked back Biden's comments.

On other occasions, conflict and disagreements between advisers within the White House led to information about internal debates being leaked to the press. In the first few months of the Trump administration, leaks from the White House occurred on such a regular basis that the president had to reshuffle his inner circle. Reflecting the turmoil in White House communications, Stephanie Grisham became the sixth person to hold the post of communications director under Trump. One of her predecessors—Anthony Scaramucci—held the position for less than 10 days!

Unlike the press secretary, who acts mainly as a conduit between the press and the White House, the communications director is more of an ideas person, a strategist who seeks to define and market the president's image. Fearing Ronald Reagan's penchant for off-the-cuff remarks, his communications director, Michael Deaver, prohibited the press from asking questions during photo opportunities.

The press secretary, the president's point person for dealing with the national media, is much more likely to occupy the spotlight. The press secretary (or the secretary's deputy) typically conducts two daily press briefings for the White House press corps. During the Trump administration, the briefings often featured hostile confrontations between the press secretary and reporters, attracting continuous coverage on cable news and elevating the public profile of the press secretary. Sarah Huckabee Sanders, Trump's press secretary for two years, announced her candidacy for governor of Arkansas soon after leaving Washington.

On occasion, the press office also arranges special background briefings for reporters (usually by a policy specialist). In addition, there are more informal off-the-record sessions between reporters and administration officials. Behind the scenes, the press office regulates journalists' access to the White House (by issuing credentials) and maintains the elaborate on-site facilities necessary for journalists to transmit their news reports.

The press secretary must walk a fine line between meeting the political objectives of the White House staff ("spin and more spin") and maintaining journalistic credibility. As a member of the president's inner circle, the press secretary is expected to do as much as possible to score points for the administration.

Some press secretaries engage in so much spinning, however, that they find themselves facing an increasingly disbelieving press corps. The credibility of the Trump press office came into question early, when Sean Spicer, the press secretary at the time, claimed that the media had deliberately understated the number of people in attendance at Trump's inauguration ceremony "to minimize the enormous support that had gathered on the Mall" (White House Press Office, 2017). Spicer went on to claim (falsely) that the crowd was the largest ever to witness an inauguration. His claims were widely debunked, and he was regularly spoofed on *Saturday Night Live* as a character who made outrageously inaccurate statements.

As media management has increasingly become a critical aspect of the presidency, reporters have adapted by more aggressively challenging the press secretary at the daily briefings and other appearances. The press secretary may not even know whether the information being channeled from the White House is true or false. According to Ari Fleischer (President George W. Bush's first press secretary), the resulting pressures are so intense that no press secretary can hope to serve out a full four-year term (Auletta, 2004). Spicer lasted only seven months before being replaced by Sanders. As Spicer's case illustrates, the press secretary's reputation is damaged irreparably when he or she repeatedly delivers disinformation.

The Trump administration's generally hostile posture toward the mainstream media has cast the press secretary in the new role of media watchdog. When reporters asked Sanders about inaccuracies in Chief of Staff John Kelly's characterization of a Florida congresswoman who had criticized the president, she responded that it was "entirely inappropriate" for journalists to question the word of a four-star general. Facing intense questioning following the controversial firing of FBI director James Comey, Sanders claimed that she had "heard from countless members of the FBI that are grateful and thankful for the President's decision." Later, when questioned by Special Counsel Mueller, she admitted the claim was false but attributed it to a "slip of the tongue."

The more effective press secretaries, while enjoying the trust and confidence of the White House political operatives and the president, have maintained an "objective" posture with the press. Mike McCurry, press secretary to President Clinton, was able to draw on his reputation as a straight shooter to weather the storms of the Monica Lewinsky scandal, when all too often he was forced to claim ignorance in response to reporters' questioning. In the case study "A Day in the Life of a Presidential Press Secretary," McCurry describes his daily routine as press secretary.[1]

As the complexity of the White House media apparatus suggests, managing the press has become a key function within the administration. Going public requires that the administration orchestrate the news media to present a consistently positive image of the president. At the same time, as discussed next, the president must be protected against being put on the defensive by aggressive or unexpected questioning of actions the administration has taken.

GETTING THE MESSAGE OUT

There are three distinct media opportunities that presidents may pursue. In each case, the amount of resources invested varies with the payoffs; namely, the number of people who can be reached and the degree of control over the message. In the ideal scenario (from the president's perspective), the president would command a nationwide news audience and be granted free rein to influence public opinion, unimpeded by skeptical reporters or critical commentary from opposing elites. This was the goal of President Trump's political team when they decided that Trump would hold daily press briefings to update the administration's efforts to deal with the COVID-19 pandemic. Trump used the briefings to consistently downplay the threat posed by the virus and did not permit the public health experts on the virus taskforce (for example, Dr. Anthony Fauci) to provide their assessment of the situation. A systematic analysis of Trump's remarks at these briefings by reporters from the *New York Times* (Peters, Plott, & Haberman, 2020) found that Trump devoted most of his speaking time to self-congratulation rather than displaying empathy for the hundreds of thousands of Americans impacted by the virus.

Over the years, as media audiences have shrunk and the national press corps has adopted a more critical perspective, presidents have taken to speechmaking before a supportive audience as their principal communication strategies. The presidential press conference, once prized as an opportunity to demonstrate the president's leadership before a captive audience, has all but fallen into disuse. During the Trump administration, rallies outnumbered solo presidential press conferences by more than 2 to 1.

News Coverage

As Mike McCurry points out in the speech excerpted in the "Day in the Life" case study, the president is the focal point of the national government. Given reporters' reliance on official sources, the president can count on regular and sustained news coverage from all forms of news media. Studies of national news repeatedly demonstrate the visibility of the White House. In the

FIGURE 9.2

Coverage of Congress and the President, 1948–2014

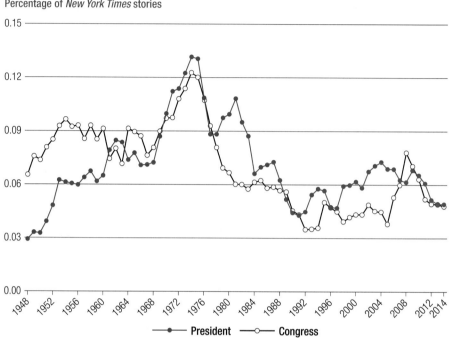

Percentage of *New York Times* stories

President ———●——— President ———○——— Congress

Note: These observations represent a moving average of three consecutive observations. A moving average has the effect of smoothing a data series.
Source: Data from Policy Agendas Project. (2010). University of Texas at Austin Department of Government. Retrieved December 2017 from the University of Texas Policy Agendas Project website: https://www.comparativeagendas.net/us.

case of *New York Times* coverage between 1948 and 2014 (see Figure 9.2), the proportion of news reports accorded to the president was initially below the level of coverage accorded to Congress. Beginning just before the election of John Kennedy, however, presidential coverage increased and reached the level of congressional news reporting. By the 1980s, the president was the principal source of news; averaging across the presidencies from Carter to Obama, presidential coverage exceeded congressional coverage, but by the relatively small margin of around 5 percent.[2]

Executive power is especially pronounced in the arena of foreign policy. By virtue of the president's constitutional prerogatives as commander in chief, the president is unquestionably the principal source of news on American foreign policy. When we examine news reports about foreign policy (see Figure 9.3), the dominance of the president is apparent: since Reagan, the president's

FIGURE 9.3

Coverage of Congress and the President, Foreign Affairs, 1948–2014

Percentage of *New York Times* stories

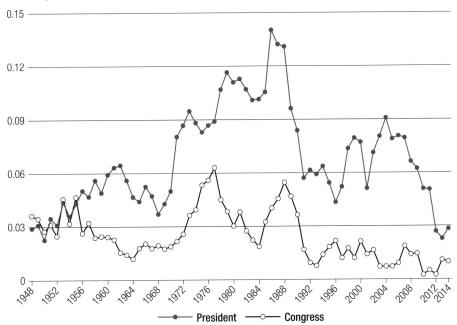

Note: These observations represent a moving average of five consecutive observations. A moving average has the effect of smoothing a data series.
Source: Data from Policy Agendas Project. (2010). University of Texas at Austin Department of Government. Retrieved December 2017 from the University of Texas Policy Agendas Project website: https://www.comparativeagendas.net/us.

share of foreign affairs news coverage has been nearly four times the level of congressional coverage. Foreign policy news, for all practical purposes, is presidential news.

Unfortunately, there is no comparable database for broadcast news coverage of the president (archived videotape recordings of network news began only in 1968). In tracking CBS News coverage between 1968 and 1978, Michael Grossman and Martha Kumar (1981) found that the network devoted substantial attention to the executive branch, even more so than print news did. On average, CBS aired four news reports each day on the president, amounting to approximately 20 percent of the newscast.

Clearly, the president can command the attention of the national media at will. But does the president also influence the story line? Studies of news content suggest that news coverage of incumbent presidents follows the same pattern as coverage of presidential candidates—evolving from generally positive coverage in the 1960s and 1970s to more interpretive and critical coverage in the 1990s. In Grossman and Kumar's 1968–1978 comparative study of coverage in *Time,* the *New York Times,* and CBS News, favorable coverage of the president exceeded unfavorable coverage by a wide margin in both print outlets. Only in the case of CBS was the assessment mixed: the network aired an equal number of positive and negative reports (Grossman & Kumar, 1981, p. 256). Although the content of the CBS News reports was mixed, the accompanying visual imagery was invariably flattering: 40 percent of the pictures used in the newscasts were positive, and only 8 percent were negative (p. 258). Thus, the evidence suggests that during this period at least, the efforts of the White House media apparatus paid rich dividends.

Over time, as journalists learned to resist the persuasiveness of media consultants and press secretaries alike, news reports began to take on a sharper tone. Presidents Bill Clinton and George W. Bush both elicited news coverage that proved more critical than complimentary. Even though it is acknowledged that the press and the political opposition generally defer to the president's proposals during the first few months of an incoming administration (the so-called honeymoon period), Clinton and Bush were not treated kindly by the press during their first hundred days in office. According to a study by the Pew Project for Excellence in Journalism (2009), network news coverage of Bush was more negative than positive by a margin of 6 percent (28 percent negative, 22 percent positive, 50 percent neutral); and for Clinton, positive and negative reports aired with equal frequency (28 percent negative, 27 percent positive, 45 percent neutral). However, President Obama's news coverage over this same period was more positive than negative by a ratio of 2 to 1 (42 percent positive, 20 percent negative, 38 percent neutral).

The advent of cable outlets with a tendency to slant the news has made it more difficult for partisan leaders with opposing views to get their message out. In 2009, President Obama described Fox News as biased in a CNBC interview with reporter John Harwood, stating, "I've got one television station that is entirely devoted to attacking my administration. . . . That's a pretty big megaphone. You'd be hard-pressed if you watched the entire day to find a positive story about me on that front" (CNBC, 2009). The president's comments were only slightly exaggerated; during his first year in office—a time when most news organizations provided favorable coverage—the ratio of negative-to-positive reporting on Fox News was 3 to 1. As Obama's communications director Anita Dunn pointed out in an interview with the

New York Times, "As they are undertaking a war against Barack Obama and the White House, we don't need to pretend that this is the way that legitimate news organizations behave" (Stelter, 2009).

In the case of President Trump, a study by researchers at Harvard's Kennedy School of Government found that the level of coverage over Trump's first 100 days in office was three times higher than the level accorded previous presidents (Patterson, 2017). However, the coverage was overwhelmingly more negative than positive by a 4-to-1 margin. In comparison with Obama, Bush, and Clinton (his three predecessors), Trump's coverage was by far the most negative. However, a related Pew study showed that the tone of White House coverage during the first year of the Trump administration varied significantly across news organizations. Conservative-leaning outlets (for example, Fox News) provided the least critical coverage, while those on the left (for instance, MSNBC) offered the harshest criticism (Pew Research Center, 2017). We will return to the unusually adversarial relationship between Trump and the media when we discuss trends in presidential popularity.

While media are clearly willing to run hypercritical coverage of the president, overt conflict with the White House can be a risky strategy for news organizations because presidents have considerable means at their disposal to retaliate. The Obama administration punished Fox News, for instance, by excluding *Fox News Sunday* with Chris Wallace from a round of Sunday presidential appearances in September 2009. Hours after he asked Trump tough questions on immigration at a press conference, the White House suspended CNN correspondent Jim Acosta's press credentials "until further notice." CNN took the matter to court, arguing that authorities had abridged Acosta's First Amendment rights. A federal judge ruled in favor of CNN and ordered the Trump administration to reinstate Acosta's credentials.

The increasingly negative tone of press reports is symptomatic of decreased presidential control over the national press corps. In response, presidents and their media advisers have pursued alternative media strategies. President Obama, facing a more hostile press corps during his second term, turned to off-the-record interviews in Washington and frequent speaking trips, where he attracted more sympathetic coverage from local and regional news outlets. For his part, President Trump used his Twitter account to regularly lash out at critical news reports.

Speechmaking

Speechmaking is a relatively recent form of presidential leadership. The framers of the Constitution did not expect the president to interact with the public.

A Day in the Life of The Presidential Press Secretary

The hardest part of the job is to just get on top of the flow of information that is crushing, all-consuming, surrounding you every waking moment of the day with some new plotline that you have to think about. Because part of the problem is that the White House has become, for most of the US press corps, the prism through which every story anywhere can sometimes be seen. I don't know if, when Princess Diana died, what was that, a Saturday night? It was like a Saturday night that she died in Paris. And it was awful and tragic but I was watching a ball game or something. And I suddenly got this flood of calls at home from angry network executives saying "Your people said they won't open up the White House press office so we can go live from the White House." And I said, "Well, what does the White House have to do with Princess Diana dying in this car accident?" But the immediate thought was that this big, significant, huge moment had to be reflected through this stage that most Americans associate with big events. If it's a big event, clearly the White House has something to do with it. . . . But anyhow, the reality is that every single day everything happening in the world is going to at least be a possible source of questions in the White House.

I'd get to work about 7, 7:30 and then start a process by which the White House would decide, well, what's the news we want to make today versus what's the news that's coming at us because that's going to be the agenda of the press corps that day and how do you reconcile the two and how do you make some guess over which is going to top the other? Because a successful day for the White House was a day in which the story that we put out there and wanted to drive made the network news that night and was the dominant focus of the press corps that day versus some other story line that presented us with more risk and less advantageous coverage of our own point of view. . . .

They preferred that the president spend the time in office deliberating with Congress and other leaders. During the early days of the republic, presidential speechmaking was limited to formal presentations to Congress.[3]

With the rapid development of radio in the twentieth century and the gradual enfranchisement of adult voters, presidents took to communicating

But the press corps would then come into my office in the West Wing and we would sit and go through our schedule, and they would want me to try to react to any breaking news or anything that had happened overnight or if some big news organization had a big story on the front page that day they would want an initial reaction to that story. This was the working briefing. It was off-camera and we did not make a transcript of it. At that first briefing of the day, it was perfectly legitimate for me to say, "I'll do that question at 1 o'clock," because that would then give me time to research what the right answer was.

At some point every morning I would either see Clinton or swing by the Oval Office and kind of walk through my briefing book and say, "Here's what we are going to say about this, that or the other," and he would kind of like dial me one way or the other. If he wanted me to be sharper or more provocative on one point, or usually he would dial me in the other direction and want me to tone it down and not be as pithy or as partisan as probably my own instinct would have had me be. But he kind of got me where he wanted me to be as I articulated an answer. And then when

Mike McCurry

I would give the briefing for the press at 1 o'clock, I would then spend the next hour cleaning up whatever messes I had created or get more information or trying to deal with the immediate aftermath of the briefing, and then just a lot of one-on-one work with reporters to get additional information for them. . . .

And then everybody would kind of watch the news collectively at 6:30 and 7, and that was your report card at the end of the day because either your story made it and you got that out there, or something else came in to dominate the story line about the White House that day.

Source: From a speech by Mike McCurry at Stanford University on May 8, 2001. Photo courtesy of Cynthia Johnson/Time Life Pictures/Getty Images.

with the public on a regular basis. The use of presidential rhetoric to rally public opinion was pioneered by Teddy Roosevelt, whose frequent appeals for public support proved instrumental in his efforts to persuade Congress to enact significant trust-busting legislation. A few years later, Franklin Roosevelt introduced his *fireside chats*, held before a nationwide radio audience. These were occasions for Roosevelt to explain what his administration intended to do to combat the Depression. He used these addresses to mobilize support for key provisions of his New Deal.[4]

With the advent of television, the audience at the president's command climbed still further. A prime-time speech carried by all three of the networks might reach as many as 60 percent of the adult population (see Figure 9.4). The period of the 1970s—when network television was the dominant media source—is referred to as the "golden age of presidential television" because presidents could count on a massive captive audience for their speeches. Of course, presidents were quick to exploit this opportunity; in 1970 alone, Nixon delivered nine major policy speeches in prime time.

The ability to reach a majority of the American public through prime-time appearances proves especially useful when presidents become embroiled

FIGURE 9.4

TV Audience for Presidential Addresses, 1971–2021

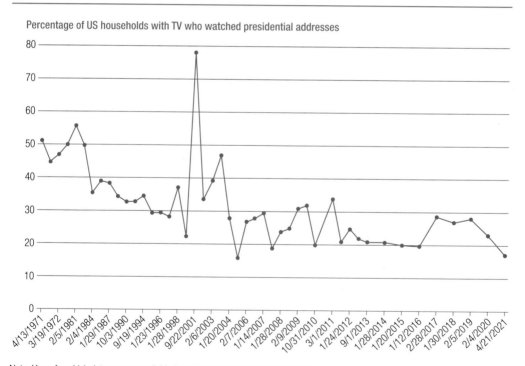

Percentage of US households with TV who watched presidential addresses

Note: Years for which data were unavailable have been excluded from this graph.
Source: 1971–2010 data from S. Kernell & L. R. Rice (2011). Cable and the partisan polarization of the president's audience. *Presidential Studies Quarterly, 41*, 696–711; 2011–2021 data from nielsen.com.

in controversy (see Video Archive 9.1). In the aftermath of revelations that members of his staff had arranged for arms to be sold to Iran and had then diverted the proceeds of the sales to the right-wing Contra rebels in Nicaragua, Ronald Reagan delivered a prime-time address assuring the public that he was indeed awake at the steering wheel. Earlier in his term of office, on the day the *Challenger* exploded, causing the death of all seven crew members, Reagan both consoled and inspired the nation:

▶
Video Archive 9.1
Presidential
Speechmaking as a
Form of Damage Control

> For the families of the seven, we cannot bear, as you do, the full impact of this tragedy. But we feel the loss, and we're thinking about you so very much. Your loved ones were daring and brave, and they had that special grace, that special spirit that says, "Give me a challenge and I'll meet it with joy." They had a hunger to explore the universe and discover its truths. They wished to serve, and they did. They served all of us. . . . We don't hide our space program. We don't keep secrets and cover things up. We do it all up front and in public. That's the way freedom is, and we wouldn't change it for a minute. (NASA, 1986)

Of course, the golden age of television proved short-lived. With the growth of cable networks, not only did people have the ability to tune out the president, but the commercial pressures on the major networks were sufficient to deter the regular provision of free airtime. Since the advent of cable television, the president's prime-time opportunities are limited to the annual State of the Union address and, on occasion, prepared remarks on a topic of unusual importance. For example, President Clinton's apology to the nation for his sexual involvement with Monica Lewinsky occurred during prime time, as did the most-watched speech given by President Obama, concerning the killing of Osama bin Laden in 2011. It is not surprising that the audience for these prime-time addresses is considerably smaller in the post-cable era, averaging around 25 percent of the total television audience. Research by Samuel Kernell and Laurie Rice (2011) shows that the only people who tune in to televised presidential speeches in the post-cable era are those who support the president. Thus, presidential speechmaking today is equivalent to preaching to the choir. There is very little possibility of the president reaching out to his opponents.

The declining audience for presidential addresses has obvious implications for the television networks. Giving the president free time means they have less opportunity to air profitable entertainment programs. In 2013, facing widespread public criticism over the incompetent rollout of Obamacare and the inability of Americans to sign up at the official website, the president sought to deliver a prime-time address announcing that the problems had been fixed and that 7 million people had signed up for health insurance. The networks declined, claiming that the announcement was insufficiently newsworthy.

Deprived of the captive nationwide audience, presidents have turned to other media venues. Local and regional audiences, particularly those living in critical battleground states, are the new targets of presidential rhetoric. This "narrowcasting" approach to going public is designed to attract favorable coverage in areas that could prove pivotal in the next election.

The behavior of recent presidents reveals the new look of going public, with incumbents increasingly synchronizing their official travel with the reelection campaign. Presidents Bush and Obama both visited competitive or battleground states more frequently than noncompetitive states during their first terms in office. Not coincidentally, during Trump's four years in office, his travel schedule targeted either battleground or solidly red states; he held rallies in states carried by Hillary Clinton on only six (out of 97) occasions.

In sum, speechmaking remains the major form of presidential communication, but presidents have substituted regional for national audiences. In the golden age of network television, presidents could count on unmediated access to the whole country, thanks to the programming monopoly enjoyed by the three television networks. Today, with the proliferation of television channels and programming choices, the president is no longer a major draw on national television. In response, presidents have taken to scheduling local and regional events where they are assured of sympathetic audiences.

The Press Conference

Like speechmaking, presidents' use of the press conference has evolved in response to the risks and rewards of the medium. When the prime-time audience was there for the taking, the benefits of reaching the entire nation outweighed the risks of appearing before a group of seasoned reporters who were all bent on asking the toughest question. With the loss of the national audience, however, the risks of committing a gaffe or appearing uninformed have deterred modern presidents from holding frequent press conferences.

Before the development of the press conference, presidents generally granted interviews to reporters and editors on an ad hoc basis. Teddy Roosevelt attempted to systematize the process by increasing reporters' access to the White House while maintaining tight control over their stories. Calvin Coolidge flatly refused to take questions from reporters. Warren G. Harding was willing to take questions but only if they were submitted in advance.

A more open posture toward the press was the hallmark of the first Franklin Delano Roosevelt (FDR) administration. Under FDR, the press conference became the principal source of news; in fact, FDR still holds the record for the number of scheduled press conferences—almost triple the total held by any his successors!

Holding press conferences during prime time was the brainchild of the Kennedy administration. Kennedy's advisers were well aware that his telegenic characteristics would impress the audience. When Pierre Salinger (Kennedy's press secretary) first announced the plan, it was met with uniform derision from the press establishment (which was dominated at the time by newspaper reporters). Still, the first-ever televised press conference attracted more than 400 reporters, and the president's remarks were watched by an audience in excess of 60 million.

Despite the 1960s transformation of the press conference into a television spectacle, the institution has since fallen out of favor. Reporters' interests in catching the president in a moment of spontaneity clash with White House objectives of scripting the president in the best light possible. At press conferences, the risks are high that the president might misspeak or be put on the defensive by a tough line of questioning. Even as accomplished a public speaker as President Reagan stumbled on several occasions, demonstrating that he did not know the answers to important questions and that his command of the facts was, at best, limited.[5] To be revealed as ignorant on national television, of course, is not likely to impress voters.

To reduce the risks of appearing inept, presidential staff personnel have attempted to choreograph presidents' appearances. Presidents Ford, Carter, and Reagan all staged elaborate dress rehearsals, attempting to fine-tune their answers to anticipated questions. The press office is intimately familiar with most White House reporters and on the basis of the daily press briefings can reliably predict what individual reporters might ask. Larry Speakes, press secretary to Reagan, claimed that "out of 30 questions and follow-ups the press would ask, we might fail to anticipate one. And often, we could even predict which reporters were going to ask which questions" (Ansolabehere, Behr, & Iyengar, 1993, p. 114).

The press office often takes advantage of journalistic competition by planting questions. The term *planting* refers to the practice of getting a pliable reporter to ask a softball question provided by the White House. In exchange, the reporter might be awarded a significant journalistic coup (such as an exclusive interview with the First Lady). Although it is difficult to demonstrate the frequency of planted questions, it is generally accepted that all administrations engage in the practice. Planting questions was fairly common during the Eisenhower and Johnson administrations. Eisenhower's press secretary often received questions in advance from reporters, allowing the president to call on a specific reporter and deliver a prepared answer. President Johnson is said to have instructed his staff to arrange a press conference in which all the questions were planted.

A clearer case of planted questions, though not in a national press conference, occurred in December 1990 during a telephone question-and-answer session between President George H. W. Bush and newspaper reporters in Southern California. Not realizing that his microphone was live, the president complained aloud that one of the questions was not "in the right order." In another instance illustrating White House influence over press conferences, President George W. Bush recognized a relatively unknown Web journalist (Jeff Gannon) in the first national press conference after his reelection in 2004. The question Gannon put to the president was not exactly objective:

> Senate Democratic leaders have painted a very bleak picture of the U.S. economy. Harry Reid was talking about soup lines and Hillary Clinton was talking about the economy being on the verge of collapse. Yet, in the same breath, they say that Social Security is rock solid and there's no crisis there. You've said you're going to reach out to these people. How are you going to work with people who seem to have divorced themselves from reality? (CNN, 2005)

Even with all the preparation, however, press conferences can prove damaging to the president's image. Perhaps the most extreme case of presidential blundering occurred during a Reagan press conference held in early 1987 after disclosure of the Iran–Contra scandal. The president's answers to the questions were so frequently confused and inaccurate (for example, he incorrectly stated that Israel had not been involved in the transaction) that the press office took the unprecedented step of issuing a news release immediately after the conference—even before the networks had concluded their coverage—clarifying the president's remarks.

A similar unscripted press conference occurred in New York City in 2017 as President Trump sought to focus attention on his "rebuilding infrastructure" initiative. Flanked by his treasury secretary and Office of Management and Budget director, Trump began by announcing a new executive order that streamlined the permit process for federal construction projects. He then asked for questions. All the questions addressed the president's comments the previous day about the rally by white nationalists in Charlottesville, Virginia.

Rather than denouncing the white supremacists, Trump instead condemned "hatred, bigotry, and violence on many sides." Asked repeatedly to clarify his position, Trump chose to double down on his initial statement: "And you had a group on one side that was bad and you had a group on the other side that was also very violent. And nobody wants to say that. But I'll say it right now." Trump's comments elicited a chorus of criticism from both Democrats and Republicans. House Speaker Paul Ryan saw fit to tweet, "We must be clear. White supremacy is repulsive. There can be no moral ambiguity."

Presidents have adopted several routines to help bolster their performance at press conferences. They typically make an opening statement in the hope of setting the agenda for reporters' questions. They may also schedule the event on short notice. The most extreme case of this tactic was one occasion in which President Johnson held a press conference without notice to reporters, addressing only those who happened to be present in the White House press room at the time. Presidents have also taken to sharing the spotlight by holding joint press conferences (usually with a visiting foreign leader). This approach not only shifts the burden of performance from the president, but it also permits the administration to present the image of a unified front.

Despite their considerable ability to stage-manage the event that is afforded them by their position, presidents have concluded that the risks of frequent press conferences outweigh the benefits. As noted in Chapter 3, reporters have become savvier about officials' efforts to spin the news and have reacted by adopting a more adversarial approach. This applies to press conferences as well; the number of hostile questions asked during televised press conferences has increased significantly over time (Clayman, Elliot, Heritage, & Beckett, 2010; Clayman, Elliot, Heritage, & McDonald, 2007). The overall trend is one of fewer press conferences per month. Although George H. W. Bush held more conferences than any of his predecessors while in office, most of the occasions were reserved for discussion of foreign affairs, a subject on which Bush was especially authoritative. Naturally, the press office sought to minimize Bush's exposure to tough questions on domestic issues; between 1989 and 1991, Bush answered a total of four questions on AIDS and two questions on the widespread bankruptcy of savings-and-loan institutions.

When we compare the frequency of solo press conferences with joint appearances (usually with a visiting head of state), the aversion of recent presidents to the media spotlight is quite clear (see Figure 9.5). Since the first President Bush, all presidents have taken to sharing the stage. The average

FIGURE 9.5

Solo and Joint Presidential Press Conferences

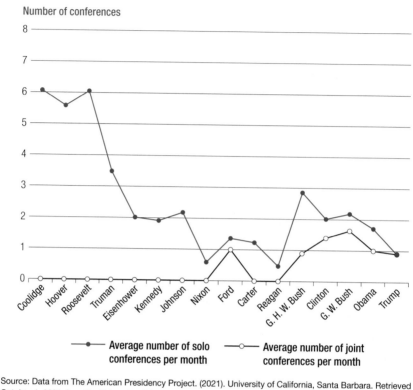

Number of conferences

Average number of solo conferences per month

Average number of joint conferences per month

Source: Data from The American Presidency Project. (2021). University of California, Santa Barbara. Retrieved October 4, 2021, from the University of California, Santa Barbara, website: https://www.presidency.ucsb.edu /statistics/data/presidential-news-conferences.

number of solo press conferences has declined precipitously. President Obama, in his first term, went seven months without holding a press conference, the longest interval in 10 years. In President Trump's tenure, he averaged less than one press conference every month.

In short, the recent history of the presidential press conference illustrates the fundamental tension in the relationship between the national press and the president. Reporters crave information, particularly information that is objective and free of political spin or distortion. Presidents demand control over the story. With today's interpretive reporting, the risks of critical news coverage have come to outweigh the benefits of television exposure, especially in the era of consumer choice when presidents no longer command vast audiences. As a result, the frequency of the presidential press conference has decreased dramatically.

Alternatives to the Press Conference

Instead of subjecting themselves to the entire White House press corps, presidents often negotiate appearances on individual television programs or grant interviews to small groups of reporters. President Reagan granted more than 200 private interviews to reporters during his first term. Question-and-answer sessions with local reporters (sometimes referred to as end runs) are particularly rewarding from the administration's perspective because local reporters are more easily impressed than their Washington counterparts are.

As in the case of the press conference, presidents have increasingly reduced their availability for questioning by the press. One occasion on which presidents are expected to take questions is when a pool of journalists is brought to the White House to cover some official event, such as the president meeting with a foreign leader. These *pool sprays* provide reporters with a rare opportunity to catch the president off-script, but in recent years, their questions have been increasingly ignored. During his first year in office, President Obama answered only 47 questions during these sessions. His predecessor, George W. Bush, responded to 147 questions during his first year. Both Bush and Obama were less accessible than President Clinton, who answered 252 impromptu questions in his first year.[6] In the latest wrinkle on question-and-answer sessions, President Trump would take questions from reporters just before he departed Washington on Marine One (the presidential helicopter). The noise from the helicopter proved to be a convenient distraction, allowing the president to selectively ignore questions on the grounds he could not hear the reporter.

When the White House loses control over the message, as is the case during major scandals (such as the affair between Clinton and Monica Lewinsky) or policy debacles (such as the failed rollout of Obamacare or the furor over President Trump's telephone call with the president of Ukraine), the president may be forced to engage in a variety of fire-extinguishing maneuvers. Such measures might include scheduling newsworthy events on diversionary issues (for example, inviting injured servicemen to the White House for an awards ceremony), providing previously classified material that is thought to show the president in a favorable light (as when Trump ordered the release of the full transcript of his call with the Ukrainian president), or enlisting popular celebrities to promote a controversial program. In the aftermath of widespread press ridicule over the inability of the Department of Health and Human Services to host a website capable of enrolling Americans seeking health insurance, the White House asked NBA superstar LeBron

James to appear in a YouTube public service announcement encouraging people to enroll.

As epitomized by the Trump press strategy, the White House often responds to press criticism combatively by attempting to repudiate particular reports or by denying opportunities for one-on-one interviews with the president to news organizations that provide critical coverage while providing access to others. During his time in the White House, Trump gave more than 115 interviews to programs aired by Fox News and not a single interview to CNN. Trump chose to ignore CNN (and other practitioners of mainstream journalism) on the grounds that their coverage was too critical.

Another strategy designed to boost favorable news coverage is for the president to enlist members of the press to deliver a message on his behalf. The George W. Bush administration paid Armstrong Williams, a syndicated columnist and cable television pundit, $240,000 to write columns and make speeches extolling the virtues of No Child Left Behind, the administration's signature education policy. And while Sean Hannity of Fox News had no formal role in the Trump administration, he could be counted on to be the staunchest defender of the president, no matter how controversial Trump's words and actions. In the immediate aftermath of any number of controversies, Trump's first media appearance was with Hannity.

Overall, there can be no denying the inherent newsworthiness of the presidency. Presidents are not so much subjects of news coverage as they are sources of news about the actions of the federal government. Presidential media management is essentially a process of spoon-feeding: the president holds a rally, gives a speech, or schedules a press conference, and reporters write stories about what the president had to say. The president stages a photo opportunity with a visiting foreign dignitary, and images of the two leaders appear in every media outlet. Of course, as we demonstrate later in this chapter, the power to set the media agenda can have significant downstream effects on the public's perceptions of the president.

◉ IN FOCUS

Three Principal Forms of Presidential Communication

- Attracting news coverage.
- Making speeches.
- Holding press conferences.

THE PUBLIC CONGRESSPERSON

The president is not alone in seeking to use the media for political gain. Everyone else in Washington plays the same game. However, members of Congress find it more difficult to achieve media leverage because there are so many of them, each promoting a different story or angle. Reporters are much more likely to gravitate to a story that can be personalized and that offers a clean story line. Reports on parliamentary procedures or legislative protocol typically do not meet the requirements of appropriateness or simplicity, making it difficult for journalists to put the legislative branch in the spotlight.

COMMITTEE HEARINGS

Committee hearings provide the best opportunity for congressional media coverage. The subject matter is timely, the number of congressional participants is relatively small, and in many cases the witnesses who appear have considerable star power. As early as the 1950s, congressional hearings attracted national television coverage. The first televised hearings were organized by Senator Estes Kefauver's special Senate committee investigating the influence of organized crime. Shortly thereafter, Senator Joseph McCarthy's hearings on security lapses at military installations (the Army–McCarthy hearings) became big news and led eventually to the end of McCarthy's crusade to root out American communists. In the 1970s, the spotlight was directed at the House Judiciary Committee proceedings to consider the impeachment of President Nixon. By the late 1970s, elected representatives understood that regular television coverage of Congress would facilitate the policy and electoral interests of members and also enable the public to monitor the actions of their representatives. C-SPAN coverage of the House began in 1977, followed by Senate coverage in 1986.

Following the 2016 election, multiple committees held hearings to investigate the extent of Russian interference during the political campaign. High-ranking executives from Facebook, Twitter, and Google were grilled over their inability to identify and prevent foreign operatives from disseminating inaccurate reports about the election. These same committees were also tasked with investigating the extent of the interactions between representatives of the Russian government and members of the Trump presidential campaign.

The Trump presidency provided Congress with especially high-profile media opportunities in the form of two different presidential impeachments.

In the first instance, the House Judiciary Committee scheduled four days of hearings about Trump's dealings with Ukraine in November 2019. On average, these hearings attracted between 11 million and 12 million viewers. The second impeachment occurred after the storming of the Capitol on January 6. There were no televised committee hearings, but 12 million Americans watched the vote to impeach Trump in the House of Representatives on January 13, 2021.

Even though hearings and high-stakes confrontations with the president provide legislators much-needed media exposure, the fact that Congress is divided along party lines makes it difficult to produce a unified, coherent media message. Whereas the White House provides a solo speaker, congressional media opportunities feature a chorus of disparate voices. The famous Hill–Thomas hearings provide a striking case of the more divided nature of the congressional message.

In 1991, President George H. W. Bush nominated Clarence Thomas for the US Supreme Court. Senate Democrats had challenged the nomination on a number of grounds, including Thomas's weak judicial credentials, his stance on abortion, and his record as head of the Equal Employment Opportunity Commission (EEOC). When a young Black college professor (Anita Hill) publicly accused Thomas of sexual harassment, the possibility of lukewarm support from within the Black community appeared to doom the nomination. The confrontation, featuring sexually explicit material, made for dramatic television (see Video Archive 9.2). On the first day (a Friday), the television audience numbered 30 million viewers. Over the following weekend, the networks cut away to their regularly scheduled sports programming, leaving PBS to cover the hearings. The interest in the controversy was so intense that PBS achieved its largest audience ever; more people watched the hearings than watched college football, the baseball playoffs, or the NFL.

▶ **Video Archive 9.2**
The 1991 Hill–Thomas Hearings

Despite the intense and potentially damaging media coverage, Thomas was confirmed. Opponents of the nomination had no common argument. Some Democrats took issue with his pro-life stance; others singled out the ambiguity of his testimony or his lack of judicial experience. On the other hand, the president offered a succinct defense of his nominee as a deserving minority candidate who had acquired his credentials through effort and hard work. Against this simple and understandable theme of mainstream American individualism, the Democratic message—"Some of us think he's not qualified. Some of us don't like him because he may not be pro-choice.

Some of us think he lied to us. And some of us think he's just fine"—was no match (Ansolabehere, Behr, & Iyengar, 1991, p. 119).

Despite the media opportunities provided by hearings, the fact remains that Congress is much less newsworthy than the presidency. In fact, the vast majority of congressional hearings are treated as routine events and ignored by the media. It requires unusual circumstances and high-profile witnesses for these events to warrant media attention.

POLICY VERSUS ELECTORAL GOALS

Political scientists generally assume that the overriding aspiration of all legislators is political survival or reelection. A secondary aspiration is moving up the legislative hierarchy and becoming known as an effective legislator with high-profile committee memberships and policy clout. In the premedia days, congressional representatives worked their way up the career ladder by acquiring seniority and by currying favor with party and committee leaders (which meant obediently voting the party line). Today the road to legislative success is much more likely to include maintaining a media profile. Congressional press secretaries are now ubiquitous; their principal role is to flood all media outlets, both new and old, with daily press releases claiming credit for Congressperson X's legislative accomplishments. Not surprisingly, congressional use of Twitter follows this pattern; studies that track the content of congressional tweets have found that more often than not the tweet provides a link to a press release (Golbeck, Grimes, & Rogers, 2009; Straus, Glassman, Shogan, & Smelcer, 2013).

The principal goal of congressional press strategy is to advertise legislators' accomplishments: sponsoring important legislation, shepherding bills through the intricacies of the legislative process, eventually getting bills enacted into law, and—most important—obtaining federal funds for local projects (typically referred to as "pork"). Research demonstrates that the ability to deliver federal funds is an important electoral asset for legislators and that voters are especially likely to approve of incumbents who deliver multiple projects (Grimmer, Messing, & Westwood, 2012).

Policy or performance coverage is more likely to come from the national press or from regional outlets with full-time Washington correspondents. Congress is able to compete with the presidency on more level terms in the pages of the *New York Times* when the subject is domestic rather than international and most of the coverage focuses on matters of policy. National media coverage is likely to boost a congressperson's reputation and lead to increased influence with party leaders.

Policy-oriented reports in national news outlets are unlikely to reach a congressperson's home district or state, however. To serve the goal of reelection, incumbents turn to local news sources. As we noted in Chapter 3, local television news attracts large audiences. Most television stations do not have full-time Washington correspondents. Instead, they subscribe to a video wire service that feeds cookie-cutter reports to multiple stations across the country. Wire services have a strong economic incentive to provide congressional news with a local angle because they are paid by the report. Members of Congress take advantage of this system by creating an appropriate local angle—by inviting local VIPs to testify at committee hearings or by holding a press conference to announce the funding of local programs.

Which of the two branches of Congress is better able to generate news? The smaller size of the Senate, coupled with the greater prestige of the office, grants senators a distinct advantage. In a comparative study by Tim Cook (1998), almost all senators (90 percent) were interviewed on network news at least once; for House members, only one-third were given similar treatment.

One form of notoriety that members of Congress would do well to avoid is involvement in scandal or being the target of ethics-related investigations. To be the subject of an investigation is to be featured in the news. In 2017, it was revealed that Hollywood mogul Harvey Weinstein had subjected multiple women—including several famous actresses—to sexual harassment. It wasn't long before the scandal spread to Congress. Senator Al Franken was forced to resign after several women complained about his inappropriate behavior. Democratic congressman John Conyers took early retirement after BuzzFeed reported that he paid a former staffer $27,000 to settle a harassment complaint. Republican congressman Blake Farenthold paid out a larger sum of taxpayer money ($84,000) to settle a similar complaint and eventually resigned. Congressman Matt Gaetz, known as a vocal supporter of former president Trump, is currently the target of a criminal investigation for allegations of sex trafficking.

The ability to attract news depends not only on the degree to which members of Congress "make news" but also on the nature of the media market in the areas that they represent. In Los Angeles or New York, an individual representative rarely makes the news, simply because the competition for coverage is too intense; to give one of the 17 Los Angeles–area House members a story in the *Los Angeles Times* is bound to generate complaints of favoritism from the remaining 16. When the *Times* has provided such coverage, it has generally been buried in the metro section rather than appearing in the national section (Arnold, 2004, p. 67).

The problem is especially acute in broadcast news. Local newscasts in the Los Angeles area rarely mention a congressperson by name, because then they would be obliged to provide coverage of all the others in their viewing area. In Danielle Vinson's 2003 study of Los Angeles local news, not a single congressional representative or senator appeared in the news over a four-week period. Thus, *incongruent media markets*—areas where a media outlet is shared by multiple elected officials (the classic case is New York City, where media serve residents of three different states: New York, New Jersey, and Connecticut)—generate fewer local reports on incumbent legislators.

In sum, in this era of going public, elected officials' ability to lead depends increasingly on their public image. Presidents and members of Congress invest heavily in efforts to attract media coverage and to shape the media message. Favorable coverage is seen as contributing to public approval, and public approval is thought to strengthen the official's hand in Washington. In comparison with Congress, the president enjoys significant media advantages: the presidential office is the classic authoritative source, and the president is one person rather than an impersonal institution. Legislators can also generate news, but their multiple messages often amount to a confusing jumble, making it difficult for them to compete with the executive branch's message of the day.

PRESIDENTIAL POPULARITY

In October 1983, a suicide bomber rammed a truck filled with explosives into the barracks used by American marines on peacekeeping duty in Beirut, Lebanon. Nearly 300 marines died. By any measure, the event represented a military disaster. That evening, President Reagan addressed the nation on prime-time television. Surprisingly, his popularity actually increased in the immediate aftermath, leading some to label Reagan the "Teflon president."

Do the media strategies outlined earlier in this chapter in fact bolster the public image of incumbent presidents? Can rhetoric and imagery overcome economic downturns and foreign policy failures? Certainly, the Beirut tragedy suggests that presidents can use staged rhetoric to maintain high approval ratings even in the face of events that signify obvious policy or performance failures. Does the popularity imperative create incentives for leaders to pander to public opinion rather than doing what's best for the nation?

In the rest of this chapter, we focus on theories of presidential popularity and the implications of going public for the exercise of leadership. We begin by assessing the degree to which the public responds to real-world events or to news media coverage of these events. For some issues that voters can directly experience (such as rising prices or unemployment), there is evidence that voters are prepared to reward or penalize presidents running for reelection depending on real-world conditions (for example, the state of the economy). However, in the case of foreign policy and national security issues, which rarely impact voters directly, the president's popularity responds more to news coverage than events. Since the president exercises significant control over media coverage of foreign policy and national security matters (as discussed in Chapter 4), in this case media management would seem to matter.

Research suggests that three principal factors influence presidential popularity: length of time in office, the course of events, and public relations. To these, we add a fourth, more recent explanation—the extent of party polarization.

INEVITABLE DECLINE?

Some theorists have suggested that given sufficient time, even the most popular president will eventually decline in popularity. This systematic erosion in public approval is attributed to presidential decision making: over the course of the term, as presidents make decisions and take positions, they accumulate opponents. The downward trend in popularity has led some scholars to propose the idea of the *throwaway presidency*, which suggests that "the probability of failure is always tending toward 100 percent" (Lowi, 1981, p. 11).

However, several presidencies have not conformed to the general theory of inevitable decline. President Reagan experienced two major drops in popularity, and on both occasions he recovered. During the prolonged 1981–1982 recession, his approval dropped 20 points, but by the summer of 1984, his approval rating had rebounded, and he was reelected in a landslide. During his second term, Reagan's standing fell in early 1985 after allegations of corruption in the Department of Labor. A more serious scandal erupted in November 1986, when it was revealed that the administration had secretly sold arms to Iran and illegally channeled the proceeds to the Nicaraguan Contras. The Iran–Contra scandal caused Reagan's approval rating to fall from 63 percent to 47 percent. Once again, however, Reagan proved buoyant. By the end of his second term, his popularity stood at 63 percent, higher than when he first entered office.

The case of Bill Clinton provides an even more convincing rebuttal of the theory of inevitable decline. The Monica Lewinsky scandal erupted early in President Clinton's second term, creating a firestorm of controversy that eventually developed into a full-scale effort to remove him from office. Yet in the immediate aftermath of the allegations, Clinton's job approval actually increased! The rebound in his popularity continued during the period leading up to the House vote on impeachment. Ultimately, Clinton's approval ratings stabilized in the 60 to 65 percent range.

The case of President Obama (shown in Figure 9.6) bears the closest resemblance to Lowi's notion of the throwaway presidency. Taking office with more than two-thirds of the country behind him, his popularity declined steadily and by mid-2014, more people disapproved than approved of his performance. On only a handful of occasions did his standing benefit from events: it improved in 2009 after he signed the massive stimulus bill committing $787 billion toward the economic recovery, in 2011 following his announcement of the end of US military involvement in Iraq, and in the immediate aftermath of the 2012 attacks on the American consulate in Benghazi. Obama's popularity moved up slightly in the closing months of his term, to around 55 percent.

One reason Obama's approval was generally unaffected by events is the heightened state of partisan polarization. As discussed in Chapter 8, the president's performance is increasingly viewed through a partisan lens (for evidence, see Jacobson, 2008). The partisans from the president's party serve as cheerleaders,

FIGURE 9.6
Obama Approval Ratings, 2009–2016

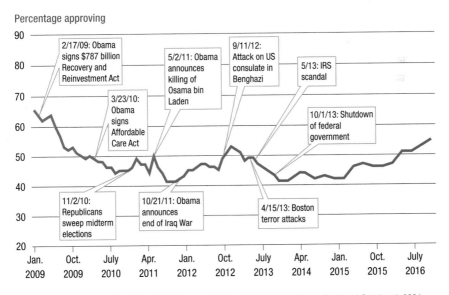

Source: Data from Gallup. Presidential Job Approval Center. (2021). Gallup News. Retrieved October 4, 2021, from the Gallup website: http://www.gallup.com/poll/124922/Presidential-Job-Approval-Center.aspx.

while those from the other side remain critics from beginning to end, no matter the course of events. The case of Donald Trump illustrates the massive partisan divide in evaluations of the incumbent president. Trump came into office with the lowest recorded level of popularity (44 percent), and over his first year in office, his numbers gradually got worse. In December 2017, his approval was at 35 percent, a historic low for presidents in their first year of office. When we disaggregate the approval data by party affiliation (see Figure 9.7), the gap between Democrats and Republicans is huge. Trump's support from Democrats seldom reached double digits, but his approval from Republicans never fell below 80 percent. Independents' views resembled Democrats, a clear indication of Trump's damaged electoral prospects for 2020.

REAL-WORLD CUES

Ebbs and flows in presidential popularity can reflect the unfolding of events and issues. Peace and prosperity generally produce high approval ratings and assured reelection; recessions, military defeats, policy debacles,

FIGURE 9.7
Polarized Evaluations of President Trump

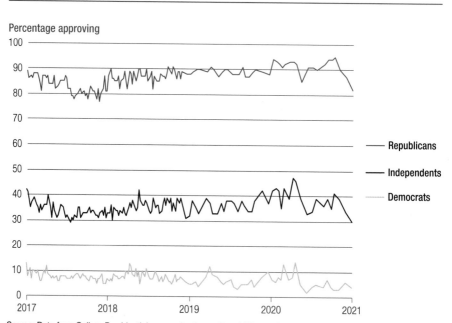

Source: Data from Gallup. Presidential approval ratings—Donald Trump. (2021). Gallup News. Retrieved October 4, 2021, from the Gallup website: http://news.gallup.com/poll/203198/presidential-approval-ratings-donald-trump.aspx.

and allegations of official misconduct do the opposite. According to this *environmental connection* account, the American public holds the president responsible for the state of the nation. When the country is doing well (for example, the unemployment rate drops or the Saddam Hussein regime is toppled with minimal loss of American life), the president is rewarded with an approval bonus. Conversely, when events imply less satisfactory outcomes for the country (for example, the number of American troop casualties overseas continues to increase, with no end in sight, or when the federal government fails to mount a response to a pandemic that kills hundreds of thousands), the president is punished.

In the pre-polarization period of American politics, the frequency and duration of such approval-enhancing and approval-diminishing events were the major determinants of presidential popularity. During the Monica Lewinsky scandal—which, other things being equal, should have been an approval-diminishing event for President Clinton—the American economy expanded significantly; personal income grew by more than 2 percent, a rate of growth higher than at any other time during Clinton's term in office. In the immediate aftermath of the allegations of an inappropriate relationship with the White House intern, Clinton's job approval actually increased! When the president appeared on television to deny the affair with Lewinsky, with the

◉ IN FOCUS

Theories of Presidential Popularity

Research suggests that four principal factors influence presidential popularity:

- **Length of time in office.** Over the course of the term, as presidents make decisions and take positions, they accumulate opponents and thus lose popularity.
- **The course of real-world events.** The American public holds the president responsible for the state of the nation. When events suggest that the United States is doing well, the president's popularity increases, but it drops when events imply less satisfactory outcomes for the country.
- **Public relations efforts.** By influencing the way events are defined and framed in news accounts, the president is able to exert substantial influence over his standing with the public.
- **Polarization.** Supporters of the president's party approve of his performance and opponents disapprove, no matter the state of the country and news media coverage of the president.

First Lady at his side, one poll showed an 8-point increase in popularity from the previous day. The rebound in his popularity continued during the period leading up to the House vote on impeachment. The net change in Clinton's popularity during this period was therefore positive: the booming state of the economy more than neutralized the Lewinsky revelations.

The impact of events raises important questions about the real significance of rhetorical leadership and going public for presidential popularity. Is it simply that popular presidents are those who happen to be lucky enough to hold office during prolonged periods of peace and prosperity? Or does prowess as a communicator and the ability to reach millions of supporters through daily social media pronouncements protect the president from the course of events? Or alternatively, in the words of Richard Neustadt (1960), is "merchandising no match for history?" (p. 73).

The Role of Presidential Rhetoric

Scholars have tried to trace the connection between presidential rhetoric and shifts in popularity but have had inconsistent results. Some studies show that major presidential speeches boost public approval and that the effects of speechmaking on popularity are stronger than the corresponding effects of events. Other studies show precisely the opposite—namely, that once the effects of events and the state of the economy are taken into account, the frequency of presidential speechmaking and international travel add little to approval ratings. This view implies that President Clinton owed his surprising buoyancy during the Lewinsky scandal not to any media tour de force but to the public's satisfaction with the state of the nation. Collectively, the studies suggest that practitioners' beliefs about the importance of spin and public relations may be exaggerated. Perhaps presidential rhetoric falls on deaf ears. Had Ronald Reagan—the "great communicator"—held office during the energy crisis or prolonged periods of inflation, he, too, probably would have suffered significant declines in popularity.

The early phase of the Trump era provided an unusual opportunity to test the ability of the president to use rhetorical posturing to shore up his standing with the public. Trump, of course, tweeted on a daily basis from @realDonaldTrump. His tweets often became front-page news, but even without the coverage, his messages had the potential to influence the millions who followed him on social media. If Trump's outbursts on Twitter were helpful to his image, we should have been able to observe some association between his Twitter activity and increases (or absence of declines) over time in his level of public approval. As shown in Figure 9.8, however, Trump's

FIGURE 9.8

President Trump's Twitter Activity and Presidential Approval

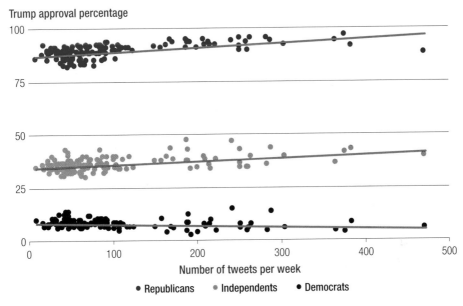

Trump approval percentage

Number of tweets per week

● Republicans   ● Independents   ● Democrats

Source: Data from Trump Twitter Archive. (2017). (Twitter activity [2,123 tweets] between January 20, 2017, and November 14, 2017). Retrieved October 4, 2021, from Trump Twitter Archive website: http://www.thetrumparchive.com/; approval data from Gallup. Presidential Job Approval Center. (2021). Gallup News. Retrieved October 4, 2021, from the Gallup website: http://www.gallup.com/poll/124922/Presidential-Job-Approval-Center.aspx.

Twitter output mainly helped strengthen his image among Republicans, who already approved of his performance. Among Democrats, Trump's Twitter activity seemed to increase disapproval of his performance. Among independents, Trump's Twitter activity only modestly increased his standing. Overall, the Twitter data corroborate the evidence from studies of the effects of political campaigns: the principal effect is to reinforce partisan evaluations of the president.

WHY MEDIA MANAGEMENT MATTERS

Despite President Trump's inability to move his numbers upward through social media activity, there are good reasons to believe that media management nonetheless has an impact on presidential popularity, especially in the arena of international affairs. Media coverage of the economy might not have much impact because voters experience economic conditions themselves. During periods of rising unemployment, for instance, people hear about layoffs either through word of mouth or by observing activity in the workplace. For economic issues, accordingly, news coverage may be redundant; people hold the president responsible based on their own experiences. However, the real-world events surrounding national security and international affairs are classic mediated events—they can be encountered only through news coverage—and the president exercises especially strong leverage over these events as commander in chief. When terrorists strike on American soil, people look to the president for the implementation of appropriate security measures. For much of the country, the 9/11 attacks were encountered only through news coverage and not through direct experience. Indeed, an analysis of presidential popularity after 9/11 reveals that changes in the level of television news coverage of terrorism proved to be a more powerful predictor of presidential popularity than changes in the actual incidence of terrorism (Hahn & Iyengar, 2007).

In the final analysis, the key difficulty with the argument that history eclipses media management is that events require interpretation and explanation. Thus, the distinction between an event that represents successful leadership and one that represents failed leadership is typically blurred and contingent on media treatment.

The case of the American invasion of Grenada in 1983, which proved to be a significant approval-enhancing event for the Reagan administration, is revealing. As we noted in Chapter 4, the administration prevented the press from directly covering the invasion and then fed reporters a steady stream of stories and images that portrayed the invasion in the most favorable light possible. Thus, the public's understanding of the invasion reflected the administration's framing of the event rather than any independent reading of conditions in Grenada. Had the media treated the invasion of Grenada as a public relations exercise or another case of US domination in the Americas, public reaction might have been less than enthusiastic.

In short, events do not speak for themselves. The public interprets events through the filter of news coverage, especially in the case of events concerning national security or foreign affairs. History may dominate merchandising in the case of the economy, but for issues with no direct "observables," news coverage is pivotal. The amount of news coverage devoted to terrorism was the paramount influence on President George W. Bush's popularity. On September 1, 2001, President Bush's approval stood at 54 percent. The immediate impact of the September 11 terrorist attacks on his popularity was to raise his approval level to 87 percent. Although the legacy of the 9/11 attacks included two major US military interventions and occupations, it was nearly two years later (August 2003) before Bush's popularity returned to the pre-9/11 baseline.

In summary, popularity is not driven entirely by media management or by history, but by a combination of the two. In the case of unemployment, an issue with several visible indicators (such as friends and neighbors who have lost their jobs), increasing joblessness can damage the president's popularity. As we discuss in the next section, however, the effect of economic conditions on presidential approval may be weakened in the era of polarized politics. In the case of national security issues, however, the tables are turned. Events have less significance than media representations of the events. Because the Oval Office exercises considerable influence over the content of national security news, presidents can more easily maintain their popularity independent of the course of events.

THE RALLY EFFECT

The importance of media management to presidential popularity comes into sharp relief in the case of the so-called *rally effect*. In the aftermath of major foreign policy actions undertaken by the US government, people rally behind the president. George H. W. Bush achieved a new high in the history of the Gallup poll when his approval rating soared to 85 percent in the immediate aftermath of Operation Desert Storm. As we have just noted, after the 9/11 attacks, his son's popularity while president increased even further, to 87 percent (see Figure 9.9). In both instances, Americans were nearly unanimous in evaluating their president favorably. Generally, whenever the president acts as the nation's commander in chief, Americans are more inclined to bury their partisan differences and rally to the side of their leader. Note, however, that we have not had a major international crisis involving the use of American troops (other than the recently ended wars in Afghanistan and Iraq) since the election of President Obama, and it remains unclear whether the polarized state of presidential approval will impede the normal rally phenomenon.

What is intriguing about rally effects is that they sometimes occur when the triggering event represents a failure of American policy and leadership. President Kennedy's popularity increased after the attempted invasion of Cuba, even though it proved to be a spectacular failure. President Carter actually benefited when Iranian militants stormed the American embassy in Tehran, taking all the occupants hostage in a brazen violation of international law.

FIGURE 9.9

Operation Desert Storm and 9/11 as Rally Points

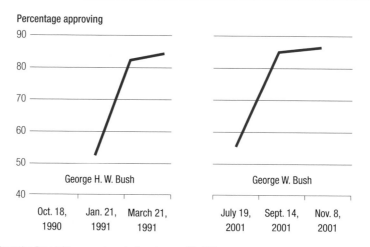

Note: Operation Desert Storm was launched on January 17, 1991.
Source: Data from Gallup. Presidential approval ratings—Gallup historical statistics and trends. (2021). Gallup News. Retrieved October 4, 2021, from the Gallup website: http://news.gallup.com/poll/116677/presidential -approval-ratings-gallup-historical-statistics-trends.aspx.

Reagan's popularity improved in the immediate aftermath of the *Challenger* disaster, and George H. W. Bush gained significantly in the polls when in August 1990 Iraq annexed Kuwait, a major US ally (and oil supplier) in the Middle East.

The most plausible explanation of rally events is the indexing process described in Chapter 4. Foreign policy and national security events are easier to frame in a manner that supports administration policy. During times of international tension, the president's spin is less subject to challenge, and the public responds accordingly. But when opposition leaders openly contest the president's interpretation of events (as is typical during a political scandal), the media messages become one-sided in the opposite direction, and the public turns against the president.

The 1990 Iraqi invasion of Kuwait provides a clear example of the ebb and flow of elite discourse. Initially, the event was a significant rally point because of the silence of congressional Democrats. Congress happened not to be in session during the first month of the Iraqi occupation, and the administration's accounts of its various "successes" (such as the creation of a worldwide coalition in opposition to Saddam Hussein) went unchallenged. After Congress reconvened in September, some prominent Democrats expressed skepticism about

⊚ IN FOCUS

The Rally Effect

The term *rally effect* describes how, in the aftermath of major foreign policy actions undertaken by the US government, people rally behind the president. Generally, whenever the president acts as commander in chief, Americans bury their partisan differences and throw their support behind their leader.

the timetable proposed by President Bush, suggesting that economic sanctions against Iraq should be given more time. On September 20, 1990, the *New York Times* noted, "Congressional criticism of the Bush Administration's position on the Persian Gulf, nonexistent in the first days after Iraq's invasion of Kuwait, then muted, is growing louder on both sides of the aisle as lawmakers openly attack the President on several major points" (Apple, 1990). As Americans began to encounter more critical news reports, President Bush's popularity fell from 71 percent in August to 55 percent in November. In general, then, the public's evaluations of an incumbent president rise and fall in accordance with elite cues provided by the media: the louder the criticism of the president's actions, the lower the probability that the public will rally around the president.

In sum, the sensitivity of presidential popularity to ongoing issues and events depends on the ability of the White House to portray events as either good news or bad news and its ability to silence would-be critics. The president's level of influence over the news is thus the critical mediator between the onset of events and the ensuing changes in the public's evaluations of the president.

In recent years, the increased polarization of the electorate has cast significant new light on the dynamics of presidential popularity; with partisans so entrenched in their views of the president, it will take a much stronger "shock" in the form of events or news coverage to bring about short-term changes in the president's popularity. The Trump presidency provides clear evidence of the weakened influence of both real-world and media cues over evaluations of presidential performance. The onset of the COVID-19 pandemic and the ensuing public health and economic catastrophes represent perhaps the greatest domestic crisis in recent memory. If the theory of electoral accountability for events is accurate, the Trump administration's inability to mount a significant response to the virus should have led to a substantial decline in his approval.

If previous history is a guide, the huge increase in unemployment caused by the pandemic should similarly have worked against Trump's popularity. However, as shown in Figure 9.10, the rising death toll from the pandemic and increased unemployment only exerted modest impacts on Trump's approval. If anything, Republicans and independents became somewhat more likely to approve of Trump's performance as unemployment worsened. Increasing deaths from COVID-19 did make Trump less popular, but once again the effects were conditional on party identification. If we compare the level of approval at the highest and lowest levels of COVID-19 deaths, for Republicans, approval dropped from 93 to 82 percent; for independents, it fell from 42 to 30 percent; and for Democrats, the percentage approving fell from 10 to 4 percent.

FIGURE 9.10

COVID-19 Deaths, Unemployment, and Trump Approval

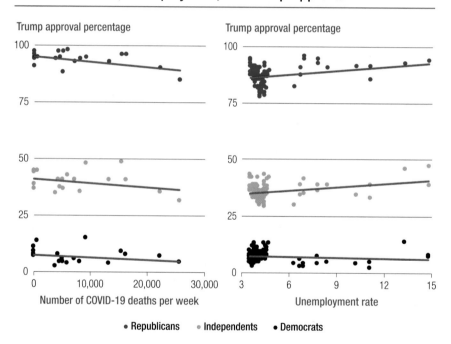

Source: Monthly unemployment data from US Bureau of Labor Statistics. Economy at a glance. (2021). Retrieved October 4, 2021, from the US Bureau of Labor Statistics website: https://www.bls.gov/eag/eag .us.htm; COVID-19 death data from Centers for Disease Control and Prevention (CDC). (2021). Provisional death counts for coronavirus disease 2019 (COVID-19). Retrieved October 4, 2021, from the CDC website: https:// www.cdc.gov/nchs/nvss/vsrr/covid_weekly/index.htm; presidential approval data from Gallup. Presidential Job Approval Center. (2021). Gallup News. Retrieved October 4, 2021, from the Gallup website: http://www.gallup .com/poll/124922/Presidential-Job-Approval-Center.aspx.

The case of Trump thus suggests that polarization has short-circuited the conventional explanations for presidential approval. Partisans have become so motivated to keep their party in office, they are unwilling to withhold support from a president from their party no matter how dismal the president's performance in office. Conversely, we can infer that opposing partisans will be unwilling to credit the president even when there is clear evidence of strong and effective leadership. Today, it appears that independents are the only voters whose views are sensitive to the course of events; for their part, Republicans and Democrats are relatively "blinded" by their strong sense of partisan identity.

CONCLUSION

The power of elected officials to govern depends increasingly on their public image. The number of people who support the president is a key barometer of the president's persuasiveness in Washington, and maintaining a high level of popularity requires close attention to the media. Presidents and their advisers strive to capitalize on the inherent newsworthiness of presidential events, speeches, and press conferences to focus the media spotlight on success stories, while avoiding reference to issues or outcomes that cast aspersions on the president's leadership. In recent years, travel and speeches have replaced press conferences as the president's principal media opportunity because they provide the president with more control over the message and access to a supportive audience while minimizing reporters' ability to ask difficult questions and scrutinize the president's claims. In general, cost-benefit media management has become central to effective governing.

The focus on using media relations to maintain a high level of public approval is not without cost. At the very least, the time and effort devoted to working the press detracts from elected leaders' ability to develop and implement policy initiatives. Moreover, the fear of alienating public opinion may be a disincentive for leaders to tackle difficult problems that may require the prescription of bitter medicine (such as higher taxes). Under media politics, officials face strong incentives to cater to public opinion. Rather than formulating policy on the basis of a coherent theory or systematic cost-benefit analysis and then attempting to bring voters on board, public officials may be guided primarily by their need to maintain high levels of popularity.

A further liability of going public is that it exacerbates conflict between the executive and legislative branches, making compromise and accommodation more difficult. As the president increasingly turns to rhetorical leadership, opponents in Congress and their backers respond in kind. The prolonged battle to repeal Obamacare is typical. President Trump made numerous appearances and public pronouncements to make clear his support for repeal (and his disdain for the Republican senators who voted against it). For their part, Democrats took every opportunity to publicize the widespread public support for Obamacare and the catastrophic consequences of repeal for people with limited means. The conflict finally ended in 2021 when the Supreme Court upheld the Affordable Care Act by a vote of 6 to 3.

Summary

1. Going public is a strategy used by presidents and other political actors to promote their policies by appealing to the American public for support. Given the overriding importance of reelection to the strategic calculations of elected officials, a president's popularity creates an important bargaining advantage; a president who enjoys a high level of public approval can often count on being able to persuade a few members of the opposition.
2. The effects of a president's popularity on the ability to garner legislative support are most evident when the president's proposals address issues that are salient to the public but concern subject matter about which the public possesses little information (such as the best way to combat terrorism).
3. The White House media complex has become a vast bureaucracy with multiple branches. Two of the key players are the communications director and the press secretary:
   - The communications director, who seeks to define and market the president's image, is responsible for overseeing the production and release of information throughout the administration.
   - The press secretary, who conducts daily press briefings for the White House press corps, must walk a fine line between meeting the political objectives of the White House staff (spin and more spin) and maintaining personal credibility with the media.
4. Presidents have three distinct media opportunities: attracting news coverage, making speeches, and holding press conferences. In recent years, they have also taken to using social media as a form of directly reaching the public.
   - Given reporters' reliance on official sources, the president can count on regular and sustained news coverage from all forms of news media.
   - In response to the increased negativity of news coverage and the decrease in the size of the audience for national television appearances, presidential

speeches around the country, often in front of enthusiastic audiences, have become more common as presidents hope to attract more favorable coverage from local and regional news outlets.

- With the decrease in size of the national audience, presidents have lost the incentive to make themselves available for tough questioning by the press; the risks of holding press conferences—committing a gaffe or appearing uninformed—have led presidents to increasingly abandon this form of public communication.

- As the case of President Trump illustrates, the popularity of social media has led presidents to increasingly communicate via this platform.

5. Like the president, members of Congress seek to use the media for political gain, with two particular goals: reelection and moving up within the legislative hierarchy. Members of Congress (particularly in the House of Representatives) find it much more difficult to garner media attention than the president does, however, because there are so many members, each promoting a different story or angle, and because legislative dynamics do not make for clean, easily explicated story lines.

6. Legislators typically seek out two forms of press coverage. First, with the aim of boosting their reputation and increasing influence with party leaders, they hope to attract attention from national and important regional news outlets. Second, with the goal of reelection in mind, they target local news in their home districts.

7. Research suggests that four principal factors influence presidential popularity:
- *Length of time in office.* Some theorists have suggested that over the course of the term, as presidents make decisions and take positions, they accumulate opponents and lose support. But some presidencies have not conformed to this theory.
- *The course of real-world events.* The American public holds the president responsible for the state of the nation. When events signify that the United States is doing well, the president's popularity increases; but it drops when events imply less satisfactory outcomes for the country.
- *Public relation efforts.* By influencing how events are defined and framed in news accounts, presidents can significantly affect their personal standing with the public.
- *Party polarization.* Because partisanship has become so fundamental to evaluations of government officials, today the president's popularity has become less affected by the course of events and media management.

8. In the *rally effect,* the public supports the president in the aftermath of major foreign policy actions—even when those actions may represent a failure of

American policy and leadership. During times of international tension, opponents are afraid to speak out against the president, making the president's spin less subject to challenge, and the public responds accordingly.

FURTHER READINGS

Arnold, R. D. (2004). *Congress, the press, and political accountability.* Princeton, NJ: Princeton University Press.

Auletta, K. (2004, January 19). Fortress Bush: How the White House keeps the press under control. *The New Yorker.* Retrieved March 28, 2006, from the *New Yorker* website: www.newyorker.com/fact/content/?040119fa_fact2.

Baum, M. A., & Kernell, S. (1999). Has cable ended the golden age of presidential television? *American Political Science Review, 93,* 99–114.

Cook, T. E. (1998). *Governing with the news: The news media as a political institution.* Chicago: University of Chicago Press.

Grimmer, J., Messing, S., & Westwood, S. J. (2012). How words and money cultivate a personal vote: The effect of legislator credit claiming on constituent credit allocation. *American Political Science Review, 106,* 703–719.

Kernell, S. (1986). *Going public: New strategies of presidential leadership.* Washington, DC: Congressional Quarterly Press.

Kumar, M. J. (2003). The White House and the press: News organizations as a presidential resource and as a source of pressure. *Presidential Studies Quarterly, 33,* 669–683.

Tulis, J. K. (1987). *The rhetorical presidency.* Princeton NJ: Princeton University Press.

Wildavsky, A. (1991). The two presidencies. In S. Shull (Ed.), *The two presidencies: A quarter century assessment* (pp. 11–25). Chicago: Nelson-Hall.

NOTES

1. Mike McCurry served as President Clinton's press secretary from 1995 to 1998. Before that, he served as spokesperson for the Department of State from 1993 to 1995 and as director of communications for the Democratic National Committee from 1988 to 1990.

2. The *New York Times* data quoted throughout this discussion come from the Policy Agendas Project (2010) at the University of Texas. The data were originally collected by Frank R. Baumgartner and Bryan D. Jones, with the support of National Science Foundation (NSF) grant number SBR 9320922, and were distributed through the Center for American Politics and Public Policy at the University of Washington and/or the Department of Political Science at Pennsylvania State University. Neither NSF nor the original collectors of the data bear any responsibility for the analysis reported here.

3. In fact, one of the articles of impeachment brought against President Andrew Johnson alleged excessive use of rhetoric. Specifically, he was accused of "intemperate, inflammatory and scandalous harangues . . . [and of being] unmindful of the high duties of his office and the dignities and proprieties thereof" (Tulis, 1987, p. 91).

4. Roosevelt broadcast 30 fireside chats between 1933 and 1944.

5. As we noted earlier, President Reagan's fondness for off-the-cuff remarks led the White House to implement the Deaver rule (named for Michael Deaver, the president's communications director), which stipulated that no reporter was permitted to ask Reagan questions during photo opportunities. The networks initially threatened to boycott these sessions if the rule was enforced, but NBC capitulated immediately and within two days the rule was in force.

6. These statistics were compiled by Professor Martha Kumar.

10

Evaluating Media Politics

Media politics in the United States involves interdependencies among three sets of players: politicians, whose overriding objective is to stay in office; journalists, who strive to maintain their professional autonomy while also delivering news that "sells"; and voters, who often lack the time or interest to follow political developments closely and therefore simplify their decision making based on party preferences. In all three cases, the motives driving the behavior include strong elements of self-interest rather than the public good. In this sense, media politics represents a tragedy of the commons; the players optimize their own self-interest, but the body politic suffers. In this closing chapter, we elaborate on just how the behavior of the key players leads to unsatisfactory outcomes, at least from the perspective of democratic theory. We also offer some suggestions for short-circuiting the incentives that detract from the common good.

POLITICIANS AND THE POPULARITY GAME

Popularity is the basic currency of media politics, and this has significant policy consequences. Elected officials have every incentive to pander to public opinion rather than engage in serious efforts to solve problems. If a politician's focus on popularity reflected an appeal for meaningful public input, arguably the process would be inherently democratic, approximating government by referendum. The problem, however, is that public opinion is largely ill informed about the complexities and trade-offs involved in policy decisions. Indeed, members of the public tend to adopt uncritically the positions taken by party leaders. But party leaders frequently promote positions based on ideological thinking or reelection-related posturing that do not reflect factually informed or expert analysis. Because reelection is the overwhelming priority of politicians, and because policy development does involve trade-offs that can be unpalatable to important groups, attention to comprehensive policy approaches is all too frequently neglected. For example, increasing taxes to pay for much-needed infrastructure modernization is considered tantamount to political suicide.

All of this is not to say that public opinion cannot provide meaningful guidance or that experts and the public are always on opposite sides. When the results of theory, cost–benefit analysis, and public opinion polling all point in the same direction, elected officials have an easy choice: they select the optimal and most popular policy. But their task is seldom that simple; most policy areas are sufficiently complex that nuanced positions cannot be taken for fear of electoral repercussions. One such policy area is criminal justice.

PANDERING ON "LAW AND ORDER"

For over 50 years, elected officials representing both political parties at all levels of government have positioned themselves as "tough" on crime. As we have seen, media coverage of violent crime makes the public especially fearful and supportive of measures that crack down on criminals. The popular approach to criminal justice emphasizes strengthened law enforcement (focusing on retribution). An alternative approach, proposed by experts, is to deal with the perceived underlying problems of educational access and employment opportunities (focusing on economic mobility). Which model (or combination of models) will work best in practice? Should voters opt for three-strikes laws or similar policies of punishment, or would they benefit more from supporting rehabilitation and job-training programs?

Meaningful evidence on these questions suggests that "toughness" and deterrence have minimal effects on crime rates. However, the subject is complex, and candidates who argue for nuanced positions risk appearing sympathetic to criminals. Accordingly, most candidates rely on slogans and symbolism in lieu of serious analysis. The news media, preoccupied with the horse race and strategy, do little to encourage informed debate. Under these circumstances, voters have little choice but to align themselves with proposals that they find intuitively plausible or that resonate with their strong feelings about crime—no matter how shortsighted or counterproductive these proposals might be in reality.

Politicians' and voters' support for harsh criminal justice policies has consequences that ripple across American society and politics. Most notably, the United States has the highest rate of incarceration of any industrialized nation. The prison population has exploded over the past five decades, from 300,000 in 1972 to over 2 million today (Gottschalk, 2009). On a per capita basis, the United States imprisons nearly four times the number of citizens as other industrialized nations.

The increased prison population has forced states and counties to invest in the construction of new prisons and hire armies of prison guards. Criminal justice is now a major employment sector, with a variety of firms and businesses providing ancillary support services, from meal suppliers to manufacturers of tasers and stun guns. California has built 25 new state prisons since 1982, and state spending on prisons quadrupled from 2 percent to 8 percent of the overall budget.

The increased prison population is only one consequence of politicians' emphasis on law and order. The United States is one of only two advanced democracies (the other is Japan) to implement capital punishment. More than 20 states have passed some version of a "three-strikes" law under which repeat offenders are jailed for life. California provides a good case study of the rush to adopt punitive criminal justice policies. In 1994, prompted by the abduction and brutal murder of 12-year-old Polly Klaas, California adopted three-strikes legislation. Fanned by sensationalized media coverage of the Klaas murder and public outrage, the California legislature enacted the most stringent of the three-strikes bills that had been introduced. No public hearings were held; no policy experts were called to testify. As Willie Brown, the longtime speaker of the California Assembly advised his Democratic colleagues, "Better get the hell out of the way" (Domanick, 2004, p. 141).

The law that passed made the number of felony convictions (strikes) rather than the severity of the crime the basis for sentencing. Hundreds of people were sentenced to a minimum of 25 years in prison for theft or drug use because the offense represented their third felony conviction. In one of the most glaring cases of strikes-based sentencing, Leandro Andrade was sentenced to two consecutive 25-year terms for stealing $150 worth of videotapes from two stores.[1]

Reform-minded groups attempted—unsuccessfully—to persuade the California legislature to amend the law. In 2004, with the financial support of a wealthy corporate executive, these groups placed Proposition 66—a measure to restrict the definition of the third strikes to violent felonies—on the California ballot. Proposition 66 was endorsed by virtually every major newspaper in California and backed by the Democratic, Green, and Libertarian party organizations. However, the overwhelming majority of the state's elected officials, including Governor Arnold Schwarzenegger, declared their opposition to Proposition 66. Armed with an infusion of funds from billionaire Henry Nicholas III, opponents of Proposition 66 subjected the electorate to a last-minute barrage of television advertising. In one of the ads, Schwarzenegger warned that "child molesters, rapists, and killers" would be roaming the streets if the measure passed.

The impact of the "No on Proposition 66" campaign was pivotal. Nearly three-fourths of the California public had expressed support for the measure during the early stages of the campaign. Then, in response to the advertisements and the campaign appearances of the governor, public sentiment shifted dramatically. On Election Day, the measure was defeated, 53 percent to 47 percent.

The rise of the "carceral state" (Weaver & Lerman, 2010) has significant spillover effects in other policy domains. Most notably, punitive criminal justice policies have clear racial overtones impacting African Americans and Hispanics disproportionately. While the ratio of the imprisoned to free population is 268 per 100,000 for Whites, it rises dramatically to 797 per 100,000 for Hispanics and to 1,501 per 100,000 for Blacks (Gramlich, 2020). Compounding the racial bias in incarceration, most states disenfranchise prison inmates (as well as those released from prison following a felony conviction), thus creating racial disparities in access to the ballot.

Finally, the growing prison population also contributes to a redistribution of resources from urban to rural America. While most crime occurs in urban areas, most prisons are located in rural parts of the country. For census purposes, prison inmates are considered residents of the county in which they are imprisoned, not the county they lived in prior to (and after) imprisonment. As a result federal funds flow increasingly to rural, Republican-leaning areas at the expense of urban, heavily Democratic areas (Gottschalk, 2009).

PANDERING VERSUS LEADERSHIP

Criminal justice policy provides a clear case of politicians pandering to public opinion. When might we expect politicians to do the opposite of pandering—that is, to propose unpopular policies that they know to be effective? Over the years, the issue of taxes has provided a litmus test of true leadership in Washington. The public instinctively opposes higher taxes but insists that government continue to deliver benefits and services. Efforts to persuade voters that it's impossible to have their cake and eat it too are risky. At the outset of the 1984 presidential campaign, Democratic nominee Walter

Mondale announced on national television that the size of the federal budget deficit left him no choice but to raise taxes if elected. In November, Mondale carried only his home state of Minnesota. His resounding defeat is still cited by campaign consultants as a textbook example of how not to campaign.

Six years later, President George H. W. Bush faced a similar dilemma. In 1988, he had run under the slogan "Read my lips: no new taxes" as a means of cementing the Republican conservative base to his generally moderate candidacy. When Bush took office, the budget deficit was less than 3 percent of the gross domestic product (GDP). As the economy slowed, however, the deficit ballooned. By the summer of 1990, the debt-to-GDP ratio had topped 4 percent, and it was clear that unless Congress and the president took action, the trend would continue.

In mid-1990, after lengthy negotiations with the Democratic-controlled Congress, the president announced that he would support "tax revenue increases." His budget package increased the marginal tax rate and phased out exemptions for high-income taxpayers. Bush also reneged on his pledge to reduce the capital gains tax. The budget deal did not go down well with conservatives. They bashed Bush for breaking his promise on taxes, and the conservative commentator Patrick Buchanan ran against Bush in the 1992 primaries. Bush's popularity never fully recovered; in November 1992 he was defeated by the relatively unknown Bill Clinton.

The Mondale and Bush cases suggest that politicians who advocate raising taxes suffer at the polls. In both cases, the actions occurred relatively close to the next election. Some scholars have suggested that politicians can survive unpopular policies if the policy debate occurs a considerable time before the next election, giving voters enough time to observe the beneficial consequences of the unpopular policy and the elected official enough time to persuade voters of the merits of the decision. Even when there is an initial disconnect, alignment may develop over time. Consider, for example, the Affordable Care Act, which was passed in 2010 over considerable popular opposition. More than a decade down the road, as millions of low-income individuals have gained health insurance, the ground has shifted, and now a majority enthusiastically supports the policy.

Personal popularity may also help to insulate politicians from negative reactions to unpopular policies. For one thing, a personally popular incumbent will scare off candidates who might strategically seek to run in opposition. Popularity also conveys credibility; the well-liked candidate may be able to persuade voters of the long-term benefits of the policy in question.

In sum, leadership is more likely when there is a longer time horizon and the incumbent is not subject to a serious reelection threat. Research by Brandice Canes-Wrone and Kenneth Shotts (2004) shows that incumbents with unusually high or low levels of public approval are more likely to lead on the merits—the former because they are secure in their position, the latter because they have nothing to lose and everything to gain. Republican senator Jeff Flake, faced with the prospect of a primary challenge, announced his intention not to seek reelection in 2018. Liberated from the need to cultivate support from the Republican base, he became a vocal critic of President Trump. But when elections are likely to be close, as is typical in presidential races, candidates refuse to lead.

Sometimes elected officials pander not to a partisan base but to the activists and donors who finance their campaigns. In 2017, having gained control of the presidency and both houses of Congress, Republicans made repeal of the Affordable Care Act (also known as Obamacare) their top policy priority. However, millions of Americans had signed up under the law for government-subsidized healthcare, and most states (39 as of April 2022) had chosen to participate in provisions expanding Medicaid eligibility. Thus, as early as 2017, a majority of Americans supported Obamacare and opposed congressional efforts to dismantle the law. Despite this clear signal from the public, Republicans in Congress pressed on, introducing multiple "repeal and replace" bills (all of which were defeated in the Senate). What explains the curious disconnect between legislators and public opinion in this case? The answer lies in the special relationship between politicians and the interest groups and wealthy individuals who donate large sums of money to their campaigns. Many of these donors were steadfastly opposed to "socialized medicine" and made their position clear to Republican incumbents: either repeal Obamacare or they would stop providing campaign contributions. The donor class was so influential that Republican members of Congress chose to defer to their views rather than to the increasingly clear preferences of their constituents.

Similar pressures have made it difficult for lawmakers to address the immigration status of "Dreamers," undocumented children brought to the United States by their parents. Dealing with the status of Dreamers has been one of the key roadblocks to immigration reform since 2001, when the original Development, Relief and Education for Alien Minors Act was proposed in Congress. Over the past 20 years, 11 different bills have been introduced (all of which provided a pathway to citizenship), but none of them passed, mainly because Republicans are held hostage by conservative activists who equate a path to citizenship with "amnesty."

In 2012, in the aftermath of another failed congressional effort to enact immigration reform, President Obama took executive action to protect the Dreamers from deportation: they were allowed to apply for two-year temporary visas and were made eligible for work permits. Five years later, shortly after he took office, President Trump announced that he was rescinding the policy and gave Congress a deadline of March 2018 to come up with a legislative solution. On January 9, 2018, in a meeting with a group of legislators, President Trump surprised everybody by announcing his willingness to support a bipartisan bill legalizing the status of Dreamers: "I will take all the heat. You are not that far away from comprehensive immigration reform" (Davis & Stolberg, 2018). The next day, after conservatives took to social media to condemn the president's intentions, Trump backtracked, repeating his demands for the construction of a border wall in a joint appearance with the Norwegian prime minister. "Any solution has to include the wall. We need the wall for security. We need the wall for safety. Without the wall, it [immigration reform] doesn't work." Two days later, the president declared that the bill drawn up by a group of Republican and Democratic senators was "horrible, the opposite of what I campaigned for." Once again, the pressures of electoral politics had taken precedence over bipartisan problem solving.

The failure to respond to a major national problem is even more glaring in the case of gun control. The United States stands alone among all societies in providing easy access to firearms, including assault rifles capable of firing 1,000 rounds per minute. The United States also stands alone among industrialized democracies in the number of annual gun-related deaths. Following the almost continuous spate of deadly mass shootings, increasingly large majorities of Americans now favor background checks and other limited regulations over gun ownership. However, Republican legislators continue to oppose all such proposals, despite the massive toll in human life, because they are often financially (and politically) indebted to the National Rifle Association and their activist base views the Second Amendment as sacrosanct.

As the examples of criminal justice, immigration, and gun control illustrate, policy makers interested in self-preservation bend to electoral pressures. It is far from clear that society benefits when we impose life sentences on petty criminals, when we deport individuals who entered the United States illegally as children, or when we make it possible for people with a history of mental illness to purchase assault rifles; but these policies are favored because politicians have to signal their "toughness" on crime and illegal immigration, and their hard-line stance on gun control. Although the immediate responsibility for making these policy choices rests with elected officials, citizens who respond more to slogans and party cues than to dispassionate analysis, together with news organizations that deliver sensationalized rather than in-depth coverage of crime and immigration, have also contributed to shortsighted policy making.

UNINFORMED AND POLARIZED VOTERS

Writing nearly a century ago, the great American journalist Walter Lippmann concluded that ordinary citizens are incapable of controlling the actions of their government because the political world is "out of reach, out of sight, out of mind" (1925, p. 18). Lippmann's critique of public opinion seems even more appropriate today—and fundamentally discouraging—given that political ignorance is not inevitable among busy people; citizens of most industrialized democracies manage to stay considerably more informed about current events than Americans.

What has changed relatively recently is that public opinion now is often not merely uninformed but, much more ominously, misinformed, even deliberately misinformed. As noted in Chapter 8, Americans who identify with either of the major parties have become reliable team players whose loyalty provides politicians considerable leeway to guide and lead public opinion. The more attentive the partisans, the more likely they are to follow the positions taken by their leaders. As a result, when candidates make claims that are false, there is the very real possibility of voter manipulation. Well before he became a presidential candidate, Donald Trump was the principal sponsor of the conspiracy-oriented "birther" theory concerning former president Barack Obama's place of birth and citizenship. When confronted during the 2016 campaign with his well-documented role in promoting that claim, he falsely accused Hillary Clinton of originating the rumor. While in office, Trump continued to show little respect for facts and evidence. He claimed that extensive voter fraud was responsible for his loss in the 2016 popular vote, that charges of possible collusion between his campaign and the Russian government amounted to a "hoax," and that senior officials in the FBI and CIA were involved in a "deep state" conspiracy to undermine his presidency. Throughout, he frequently attacked the credibility of the American press by referring to stories critical of his leadership as "fake news."

A divided electorate willing to adopt opinions founded on prejudice or falsehoods rather than evidence is fundamentally more dangerous to democracy than an electorate that is merely ignorant of the facts. Prior to the era of polarization, the uninformed would accept the facts, however inconvenient to their political loyalties, once those facts came to light. The vast majority of Americans who voted for Richard Nixon in 1972 had no idea of the extent to which the Nixon White House engaged in a systematic cover-up of the break-in at the Democratic National Committee headquarters in the Watergate Hotel. But as the media reported on the story and Congress began its own investigation, increasing numbers came to acknowledge that President Nixon had engaged in corrupt and illegal behavior. Eventually, the Judiciary Committee of the House of Representatives adopted a bill of impeachment. Voting for the bill were all the Democrats on the committee as well as 6 of the 17 Republicans. In the aftermath of further revelations, many of the remaining Republicans announced that they, too, would vote on the floor of the House to impeach Nixon. Realizing that he had lost the support of Republican legislators, Nixon decided to resign. In fact, he was forced out because of bipartisan agreement over the facts of the scandal. Republicans did not question the integrity or credibility of Carl Bernstein or Bob Woodward, the two reporters from the *Washington Post* who originated the media investigation into the scandal. There was no Republican-leaning cable news channel that offered up conspiracy theories alleging that the investigation was part of a communist plot to destabilize America. Instead, the process worked as expected: a free and vigorous press unearthed information implicating key White House staffers as part of a conspiracy to cover up a burglary, and the cumulative pattern of news reports was treated as "common knowledge"—accepted at face value by both Democrats and Republicans. It was this bipartisan agreement over the facts that led to Nixon's resignation.

When Americans disagree over the facts and refuse to accept information that is at odds with their preferences, the concept of common knowledge disintegrates; there are liberal facts and conservative facts, each with their hard-core adherents. The men and women who stormed the Capitol on January 6 were convinced that Donald Trump had won the election. In this polarized environment, when news organizations provide information suggesting that politicians have engaged in illegal or unethical behavior, supporters of these politicians either ignore the information or dismiss the allegations as false and the journalists as biased. That was the response of Roy Moore's supporters during the 2017 Senate campaign in Alabama after the *Washington Post* exposed Moore's relationships with underaged women. Moore eventually lost an extremely close race to Democrat Doug Jones but secured more than 90 percent of the Republican vote. Unwillingness to accept damaging information about a fellow partisan runs even deeper among political elites. President Trump's telephone call with Ukrainian president Volodymyr Zelenskyy, in which he suggested an exchange of US military aid for the release of damaging information about Joe Biden, convinced only one Republican senator (Mitt Romney) that Trump had committed an impeachable offense.

In addition to using the White House to spread disinformation, President Trump consistently made statements that detract from the moral stature and prestige associated with the office. He equated the moral standing of White supremacists with that of civil rights protesters. He described African nations as "shithole countries" and asked why the United States could not attract more immigrants from a country like Norway. He refused to reprimand an aide who derisively commented about Senator John McCain, "It doesn't matter, he's dying anyway," when McCain opposed Trump's nominee for head of the CIA. Yet despite the trajectory of the president's comments, approval of his performance among Republicans never fell below 80 percent, confirming the president's assertion that his supporters would stand by him no matter what.

Partisans did not always blindly support the candidates and leaders endorsed by their party. Prior to the onset of polarization, there were frequent instances of large-scale defections. In 1964, the Republicans nominated Senator Barry Goldwater—a conservative firebrand—as their presidential candidate. Goldwater supported the use of tactical nuclear weapons in Vietnam and a more aggressive approach to the Cold War. On domestic issues, he opposed the landmark civil rights laws on the grounds that states had the right to discriminate against racial minorities. Goldwater's extreme views disenchanted many moderate Republican voters; on Election Day, Lyndon Johnson received nearly 30 percent of the Republican vote.

A similar scenario played out in 1972. This time it was the Democrats who nominated a flawed candidate. Like Goldwater, Senator George McGovern was out of the moderate mainstream, in this case representing the extreme liberal wing of his party. In addition to his unrepresentative policy positions, McGovern seriously mismanaged his campaign. He initially selected Missouri senator Tom Eagleton as his running mate. This decision proved controversial after media reports revealed that Eagleton had been treated with electric shock therapy for clinical depression. Despite the ensuing controversy, McGovern pledged "1,000 percent" support for his running mate. But a week later he reversed himself, asked Eagleton to step down, and selected Sargent Shriver, a brother-in-law of John F. Kennedy. McGovern's ideology and erratic behavior turned off large numbers of Democrats; 37 percent of those who voted chose Nixon over McGovern. Thus, prior to the onset of polarization, partisans were willing and able to penalize their party for selecting flawed candidates.

The current state of polarization and misinformation extends well beyond partisans' willingness to ignore the personal liabilities of their preferred candidate. It also extends to partisans' perceptions of politicians' issue positions. We have noted at some length the increased ideological extremity of elected Democrats and Republicans. But similar movement has not occurred among rank-and-file partisans, who remain closer to the center on most issues (Fiorina, 2017). Today, there is a real discrepancy between the preferences of candidates and their constituents—an ideological disconnect that produced devastating losses in the 1964 and 1972 elections (and in several more recent off-year elections). However, while the ideological gap between the party elites and rank and file has gradually increased, elected officials taking extreme positions have no difficulty gaining reelection because partisans' *perceptions* of their leaders' positions have become distorted. Partisans perceive their own party's candidate as closer to the center and, conversely, perceive the opposition-party candidate as even more extreme than is warranted by the record (for evidence of this pattern, see Sood & Iyengar, 2018). In this sense, representation is more illusory than real; politicians are free to pursue their policy agendas knowing that voters' biased views of their positions immunize them from any electoral punishment.

The phenomenon of affective polarization—the tendency of Democrats and Republicans to treat each other as a stigmatized out-group and to exaggerate the ideological extremity of the opposing party—has far-reaching consequences for the behavior of politicians. For one thing, it creates incentives for politicians to use inflammatory rhetoric and demonize their opponents. The most frequent and enthusiastic chant at Republican rallies in 2016 was "lock her up." Illegal immigrants, in Trump's words, were "rapists and drug dealers." Earlier, during the debate over the passage of the Affordable Care Act, some Republicans likened the mandatory insurance requirement in the law to the forced deportation of Jews by the Nazis. In response, the liberal commentator Keith Olbermann declared that Republicans' opposition to the law was based on racism. Symptomatic of the pressures facing politicians to demonstrate their party colors, a study found that taunting of the opposition party is the most frequent theme in congressional press releases (Grimmer & King, 2011).

Of course, the same perverse incentives carry over to campaigns, where, as we documented in Chapter 6, candidates are in full attack mode when producing and airing their political ads. Partisan division and animus have become the driving forces of electoral politics and, in the aftermath of the 2016 election, was the principal governing strategy of the Trump administration.

Unless the rhetoric of partisan polarization can be contained, our fundamental democratic norms, such as the rule of law, may be in jeopardy. In such a political climate, politicians who engage in corrupt or illegal behavior won't be removed from office because their supporters will refuse to accept the evidence of wrongdoing. Moreover, partisans will distrust the actions and motives of the agencies charged with enforcing the law and investigating public officials, despite the organizational norms and incentives that commit these groups to telling the truth. As we will see in the next section, the problem of misinformation and distrust is compounded when the institution entrusted with keeping politicians honest and the public informed—that is, a free and independent press—loses its credibility and standing among large segments of the public.

COMMERCIALISM, INTERPRETIVE JOURNALISM, AND COMBAT STORIES

Under ideal conditions, the news media in democratic societies would invigorate the political process by providing a widely accessible forum, supplying a regular stream of quality news about the issues of the day, and keeping public officials constantly under the microscope. One of the reasons voters rely on party cues for evaluating leaders is that they typically lack information. As we argued in Chapter 2, voter ignorance (as opposed to misinformation) is attributable not only to unmotivated citizens but also to market forces that encourage news organizations to produce nonsubstantive news. When societies implement regulations that counter the market by requiring broadcast outlets to air news programs during peak viewing hours, relevant information can reach people who are uninterested in public affairs. Prudent regulations and significant financial subsidies for public broadcasters make it possible for democratic societies to maintain reasonably well-informed electorates. In the United States, by contrast, the absence of meaningful regulation and the dictates of the market ensure that broadcast outlets will strive to attract viewers by making their news reports more entertaining and thus more superficial. This is one area where the evidence is clear: societies with strong public broadcasters exhibit higher levels of public political awareness.

Market forces and the "dumbing down" of news programming are but one aspect of the private interests motivating the production of news. An equally significant distorting influence is the drive toward maximizing journalistic autonomy and voice. As we showed in Chapter 3, journalists have abandoned the old-fashioned descriptive paradigm that treated politicians and government officials as the principal newsmakers of the day. During campaigns, significant segments from the candidates' stump speeches would make their way into the daily stream of news. Present-day practice, however, is quite different. Journalists aspire to deliver more than mere descriptions of the candidates' words and deeds on the campaign trail. But by turning to analysis and interpretation and dwelling incessantly on the horse-race aspects of the campaign, journalists leave their audience uninformed and turned off.

The tendency toward interpretive journalism not only amplifies the journalist's voice but also allows the journalist to frame the news in terms of keeping politicians honest by turning to so-called experts and pundits who scrutinize the words and deeds of public officials. It is revealing that in the current era of interpretive journalism (post-1988), all presidents with one exception (Obama) received more critical than favorable coverage during their first months in office. In recent years, this built-in tension between the press and the White House has escalated into intermittent warfare. As noted in Chapter 9, President Obama temporarily denied reporters from Fox News access to briefings from high-level officials in retaliation for harshly critical coverage from that network. For his part, Donald Trump prevented reporters from several news organizations from attending his campaign rallies and later, some White House press briefings, on the grounds that they were biased against his candidacy and his administration.

Interpretive journalism is, by definition, journalism that is skeptical of officials' pronouncements. But in its initial incarnations, the interpreters featured in the news were either rival politicians or professional commentators (many of whom were ex-politicians). In this model, reporters merely relayed rather than initiated criticism from opponents of the president. More recently, however, journalists have taken on the role of opposition party. According to the Harvard study of media coverage of the first 100 days of the Trump presidency (Patterson, 2017), a striking finding was that only 6 percent of the sound bites concerning Trump came from elected Democrats, while the rest came from pundits and commentators. This is a clear departure from the predictions of indexing theory (discussed in Chapter 4) and signifies the extent to which conflict between the White House and the press has escalated.

The gradual escalation of the conflict between journalists and the White House does not bode well for the reputation of a free press that seeks to provide objective and unbiased news. When the press regularly critiques the performance of incumbent officials, it is only to be expected—given the level of polarization in the country—that supporters of these officials will cry foul. As noted in Chapter 3, assessments of media credibility have become closely associated with partisanship. Republicans view most mainstream news organizations as biased in an anti-conservative direction. Democrats are more measured in their assessments of source credibility, but it is likely that as coverage of the Biden presidency turns negative (as it did during the chaotic evacuation of Americans and Afghans from Kabul in August 2021), Democrats will also question the motives of reporters.

The politicization of the press is not healthy for the democratic process. Once the press loses its aura of objectivity and credibility, it can no longer be an effective watchdog, and it becomes possible for politicians to deny and deflect allegations of wrongdoing, even in the face of direct evidence. President Trump could claim that he did not make denigrating comments about immigrants from African nations—despite the presence of multiple witnesses—because he understood that his supporters would believe his version of events over journalists' accounts. He could count on conservative-leaning outlets to back up his version of events because polarization has set in motion a vicious circle. Partisans increasingly demand news with a slant; more news outlets abandon the "point-counterpoint" paradigm of journalism; and when news reports uncover corruption and wrongdoing, the watchdog is no longer taken seriously.

It is true that the tradition of a partisan press in and of itself is not antithetical to democracy (as witnessed by several European democracies), and it is also not foreign to the United States. In fact, American political campaigns originated in the late eighteenth century when activist newspaper editors allied themselves with the Democratic Republicans. The Federalists countered in 1798 by passing the Alien and Sedition Acts, but their attempts at censorship only accelerated politicization of the press. By the middle of the nineteenth century, most American newspapers were openly affiliated with a party:

> Partisan newspapers and loosely organized parties (aided by government subsidies) combined to create a hitherto unrecognized institution, the newspaper-based party, which dominated the American political scene in the antebellum years, remained strong in the late nineteenth century, and did not disappear completely until the twentieth century. (Pasley, 2001, p. 17)

The presence of a vigorous partisan press helped create a sense of common identity among party supporters. Urgent notices in the party newspaper were especially useful when it was time to get voters to the polls. The heyday of the partisan press and strong party organizations generated the highest levels of voter turnout in American history. In the presidential campaign of 1896, Democrat William Jennings Bryan traveled the entire breadth of the country delivering hundreds of speeches to enthusiastic supporters. Bryan's appeal was based entirely on issues, most notably his opposition to free trade and the gold standard. The Republican campaign, masterminded by Marc Hanna (the first paid political consultant), brought in thousands of supporters to Washington, where they listened to William McKinley rebut Bryan's populist positions on the issues. Both parties mobilized their supporters with brass-band parades and torchlight marches; on Election Day, nearly 80 percent of the electorate voted.

As the urban population grew and printing costs fell, newspaper publishers began to realize that they could more easily expand their circulation by shedding their partisan ties and appealing to readers on the basis of the everyday utility of their product rather than the correctness of their politics. Once mass-circulation media and professional journalism came of age, the die was cast for the current system of media politics. As outlined in Chapter 2, all it took was the advent of the direct primary and the weakening of the political party organizations for journalists to replace party leaders as the central players in the campaign.

In the current era of polarized politics, there is renewed demand for partisan journalism. The emergence of Fox News as the cable news ratings leader suggests that in a highly competitive market environment, a clear polit-ical slant allows a news organization to grow by creating a niche for itself. Theoretical work by economists corroborates this observation by showing that with competition and a diversity of opinion among readers, newspapers will provide content that is more biased: "Competition forces newspapers to cater to the prejudices of their readers, and greater competition typically results in more aggressive catering to such prejudices as competitors strive to divide the market" (Mullainathan & Shleifer, 2005, p. 1,042). Thus, in a congested market with multiple suppliers, rational owners of news organizations stand to gain by injecting more rather than less political slant or bias into their news. In the case of online news providers, the market leaders include several with a clear pro-Republican or pro-Democratic slant. The increased availability of news with a partisan slant only accelerates the vicious cycle of selective exposure and partisan animus.

A different challenge to the standing of the press is the increased ability of politicians to harness social media to engage in direct communication with their supporters. As strategic actors, candidates can be expected to take advantage of this relatively new mode of direct campaigning. In some cases, this might enable them to publicize their positions on the issues in more nuanced terms than conveyed by the typical sound bite. The fact that the internet is just as transparent a forum as televised advertising or candidate debates makes it unlikely that direct candidate-to-voter communication will be any more misleading or deceptive than standard campaign presentations. The presence of vigilant journalists and activist citizens, motivated to fact-check every utterance by politicians, can keep candidates close to the facts. However, when disagreement over the facts breaks down, as is the case in the current polarized environment, politicians can lie and mislead with impunity, knowing that their supporters will remain steadfast and that media fact-checkers will be ignored.

CONCLUSION

When politicians, journalists, and voters pursue their respective narrow interests or personal convenience with little regard for the public good, what institutions are left to represent shared democratic values, social cohesion, tolerance, and restraint? Elected officials have shown that they are willing participants in the game of media politics, all too eager to fan partisan antagonisms rather than promote civil discussions of important policy problems. Within the halls of Congress, classic compromises after meaningful debate on the issues rarely occur; instead policy makers resort to brinkmanship with unpredictable results. When the chief executive and his advisers actively provoke societal fault lines while disregarding established practices intended to protect the public against self-interest and corruption, pessimism about our system of media-based politics and concern over the strength of democratic institutions seems largely justified.

In terms of the public sphere, it is clear that the market rules. News reports focus on colorful accounts of embarrassing episodes rather than on the details of public policy formation. When issues are examined, the coverage is typically anecdotal, often accompanied by partisan slant. During campaigns, journalists mute the voices of the candidates in favor of pundits and commentators.

At the level of the electorate, lack of interest and information and intolerance for opposing views are commonplace. Voters seem content to act as partisan robots, blissfully unaware of the flaws of their favored candidates. Despite these limitations of public opinion, the real question at this point is whether enough has "gone wrong" that a reserve of shared democratic values will finally find expression to demand higher standards of behavior from public officials and more rational, responsive policy responses.

Despite his thorough skepticism about the role of public opinion in the democratic process, Walter Lippmann was convinced that the American public could act as a safety valve and turn against those who seek to undermine democratic institutions:

> Public opinion, in this theory, is a reserve of force brought into action during a crisis in public affairs. Though it is itself an irrational force, under favorable institutions, sound leadership, and decent training, the power of public opinion might be placed at the disposal of those who stood for workable law as against brute assertion. . . . By canceling lawless power, it may establish the condition under which law can be made. It does not reason, investigate, invent, persuade, bargain, or settle, but by holding the aggressive party in check, it may liberate intelligence. Public opinion in its highest ideal will defend those who are prepared to act on their reason against the interrupting force of those who merely assert their will. (Lippmann, 1925, p. 110)

Consistent with Lippmann's account above, we can only hope that when the behavior of those in office falls sufficiently below expectations, many Americans will be prepared to enforce the mechanism of electoral accountability. In the final analysis, therefore, we look to disgruntled public opinion as the restraining influence of last resort.

Summary

1. Media politics involves the interrelationships between three sets of players: politicians, voters, and journalists. All three pursue their own interests, often at the expense of the public good.
2. Politicians are motivated to win reelection; they campaign on policies that will boost their popularity, even when they know these policies to be less than effective. They also promote policies backed by their donor and activist base. Because donors and activists on either side typically have ideologically extreme preferences, compromise is difficult, and legislative gridlock occurs frequently.
3. Most voters are insufficiently interested in becoming informed about matters of public policy. In the current era of polarization, partisans are not only uninformed but also misinformed; they accept misleading or false claims made by party leaders as true. Misinformation makes it less likely that voters will hold incumbents accountable for their actions; politicians who engage in unethical or illegal behavior are able to remain in office because their supporters refuse to accept evidence of wrongdoing.

4. Journalists and publishers are preoccupied with economic survival; commercial pressures and consumer demand work against the delivery of substantive news. The drive toward journalistic autonomy and interpretive rather than descriptive news coverage has escalated the conflict between politicians and reporters. When reporters write stories critical of politicians, supporters of those politicians cry foul and allege journalistic bias. The lowered credibility of news organizations in the eyes of partisans makes it more difficult for the press to keep elected officials honest; politicians can deny and deflect allegations of corruption or wrongdoing.

FURTHER READINGS

Fiorina, M. P. (2017). *Unstable majorities: Polarization, party sorting, and political stalemate.* Stanford, CA: Hoover Institution Press.

Gottschalk, M. (2009). The long reach of the carceral state: The politics of crime, mass imprisonment, and penal reform in the US and abroad. *Law and Social Inquiry, 34,* 439–472.

Grimmer, J., & King, G. (2011). General purpose computer-assisted clustering and conceptualization. *Proceedings of the National Academy of Sciences USA, 108,* 2643–2650.

Hamilton, J. T. (2003). *All the news that's fit to sell: How the market transforms information into news.* Princeton, NJ: Princeton University Press.

Lippmann, W. (1925). *The phantom public.* New York: Transaction Publishers.

Parker, R. N. (2012). Why California's "three strikes" fails as crime and economic policy, and what to do. *California Journal of Politics and Policy, 5*(2), 206–231.

Pasley, J. L. (2001). *The tyranny of printers: Newspaper politics in the early American republic.* Charlottesville: University of Virginia Press.

Patterson, T. E. (2017). *News coverage of Donald Trump's first hundred days.* Unpublished paper, Kennedy School of Government, Harvard University, Cambridge, MA.

NOTES

1. The Andrade case was the basis for a prolonged legal challenge to the California three-strikes law on the grounds that the sentence constituted "cruel and unusual punishment." The US Court of Appeals for the Ninth Circuit upheld the challenge, but the California attorney general appealed the decision to the US Supreme Court. In a 5-to-4 vote, the Supreme Court overturned the appellate decision and reinstated the sentence.

REFERENCES

CHAPTER 1

Associated Press. (2021, January 13). Transcript of Trump's speech at rally before US Capitol riot. Retrieved August 24, 2021, from the AP website: https://apnews.com/article/election -2020-joe-biden-donald-trump-capitol-siege-media-e79eb5164613d6718e9f4502eb471f27.

Besley, T., & Prat, A. (2006). Handcuffs for the grabbing hand? Media capture and government accountability. *American Economic Review, 96,* 720–736.

Davis, R. (2014). Political and media factors in the evolution of the media's role in US Supreme Court nominations. *Oñati Socio-Legal Series, 4*(4).

Grimmer, J., & King, G. (2011). General purpose computer-assisted clustering and conceptualization. *Proceedings of the National Academy of Sciences, 108,* 2643–2650.

Mann, T. E., & Ornstein, N. J. (2016). *It's even worse than it looks: How the American constitutional system collided with the new politics of extremism.* New York: Basic Books.

CHAPTER 2

Besley, T., & Prat, A. (2006). Handcuffs for the grabbing hand? Media capture and government accountability. *American Economic Review, 96,* 720–736.

Bishop, R., & Hakanen, E. A. (2002). In the public interest? The state of local television programming fifteen years after deregulation. *Journal of Communication Inquiry, 26,* 261–276.

Brants, K. (1998). Who's afraid of infotainment? *European Journal of Communication, 13,* 315–335.

Goldmark, P. C., Jr. (2001). *Old values, new world: Harnessing the legacy of independent journalism for the future* (with a report of the Fourth Annual Aspen Institute Conference on Journalism and Society, *The evolution of journalism in a changing market economy,* by D. Bollier). Washington, DC: Aspen Institute.

Hallin, D. C., & Mancini, P. (2004). *Comparing media systems: Three models of media and politics.* Cambridge, England: Cambridge University Press.

Heinderyckx, F. (1993). Television news programmes in western Europe: A comparative study. *European Journal of Communication, 8,* 425–450.

Iyengar, S. (1997). Overview of media-based political campaigns. In S. Iyengar & R. Reeves (Eds.), *Do the media govern?* (pp. 143–148). Thousand Oaks, CA: Sage.

Iyengar, S., & Curran, J. (2009). Media systems, news delivery and citizens' knowledge of current affairs. Retrieved October 1, 2010, from the Social Science Research Council website: https://publicsphere.ssrc.org/iyengar-curran-media-systems-news-delivery-and-citizens-knowledge-of-current-affairs/.

Kaid, L. L., & Jones, C. A. (2004). United States of America. In B. Lange & D. Ward (Eds.), *The media and elections: A handbook and comparative study* (pp. 25–59). Mahwah, NJ: Erlbaum.

Krasnow, E. G. (1997). *The "public interest" standard: The elusive search for the Holy Grail.* Briefing paper prepared for the Advisory Committee on Public Interest Obligations of Digital Television Broadcasters. Retrieved from the National Telecommunications and Information Administration website: www.ntia.doc.gov/legacy/archives/pubintadvcom/octmtg/KRASNOW.htm.

Krüger, U. M. (1996). Boulevardisierung der Information im Privatfernsehen. *Media Perspektiven, 7,* 362–375.

Lacy, S., & Simon, T. F. (1993). *The economics and regulation of United States newspapers.* Norwood, NJ: Ablex.

Martin, G. J., & McCrain, J. (2019). Local news and national politics. *American Political Science Review, 113,* 372–384.

McNicholas, A., & Ward, D. (2004). United Kingdom. In B. Lange & D. Ward (Eds.), *The media and elections: A handbook and comparative study* (pp. 145–164). Mahwah, NJ: Erlbaum.

Pew Research Center (2017, May 11). Buying spree brings more local television stations to fewer big companies. Washington, DC: Pew Research Center. Retrieved October 18, 2017, from the Pew Research Center website: http://www.pewresearch.org/fact-tank/2017/05/11/buying-spree-brings-more-local-tv-stations-to-fewer-big-companies/.

Polsby, N. W. (1983). *Consequences of party reform.* New York: Oxford University Press.

Project for Excellence in Journalism. (2003, April 29). *Does ownership matter in local television news: A five-year study of ownership and quality.* Washington, DC: Pew Research Center. Retrieved from the Pew Research Center website: https://www.pewresearch.org/journalism/2003/04/29/does-ownership-matter-in-local-television-news/.

Project for Excellence in Journalism. (2004). *The state of the news media, 2004: Overview—ownership.* Washington, DC: Pew Research Center. Retrieved from the Pew Research Center website: http://assets.pewresearch.org/wp-content/uploads/sites/13/2017/05/24141554/State-of-the-News-Media-Report-2004-FINAL.pdf.

Williams, G. (2003). *European media ownership: Threats on the landscape—A survey of who owns what in Europe* (Upd. ed.). Brussels, Belgium: European Federation of Journalists. Retrieved from the University of Huddersfield website: http://eprints.hud.ac.uk/id/eprint/1644/.

Zechowski, S. (2013). Public interest, convenience, and necessity. In H. Newcomb (Ed.), *Encyclopedia of television* (2nd ed., pp. 1847–1849). New York: Routledge.

CHAPTER 3

American Society of News Editors. (2017). Newsroom diversity survey. Retrieved from the American Society of News Editors website: http://members.newsleaders.org/newsroom_diversitysurvey.

Arana, G. (2018, November 5). Decades of failure. *Columbia Journalism Review.* Retrieved from the *Columbia Journalism Review* website: https://www.cjr.org/special_report/race-ethnicity-newsrooms-data.php.

Baker, C. E. (2002). *Media, markets, and democracy.* New York: Cambridge University Press.

Crouse, T. (1972). *The boys on the bus.* New York: Random House.

Curran, J., Iyengar, S., Lund, A. B., & Salovaara-Moring, I. (2009). Media system, public knowledge, and democracy: A comparative study. *European Journal of Communication, 24,* 5–26.

D'Alessio, D., & Allen, M. (2000). Media bias in presidential elections: A meta-analysis. *Journal of Communication, 50,* 133–156.

Gilliam, F. D., Jr., & Iyengar, S. (2000). Prime suspects: The influence of local television news on the viewing public. *American Journal of Political Science, 44,* 560–573.

Goldman, S., & Mutz, D. (2011). The friendly media phenomenon: A cross-national analysis of cross-cutting exposure. *Political Communication, 28,* 42–66.

Hayes, D., & Lawless, J. L. (2015). As local news goes, so goes citizen engagement: Media, knowledge, and participation in US House Elections. *Journal of Politics, 77,* 447–462.

Hayes, D., & Lawless, J. L. (2018). The decline of local news and its effects: New evidence from longitudinal data. *Journal of Politics, 80,* 332–336.

Iyengar, S., Norpoth, H., & Hahn, K. (2004). Consumer demand for election news: The horserace sells. *Journal of Politics, 66,* 157–175.

Kernell, G., Lamberson, P. J., & Zaller, J. (2017). Market demand for civic affairs news. *Political Communication, 35,* 239–260.

Klite, P. K., Bardwell, R. A., & Salzman, J. (1997). Local TV news: Getting away with murder. *Harvard International Journal of Press/Politics, 2,* 102–112.

Kurtz, H. (1999). *Media meltdown.* Annual Carlos Kelly McClatchy Lecture, Stanford University, Stanford, CA.

McChesney, R. W. (1999). *Rich media, poor democracy: Communication politics in dubious times.* Urbana: University of Illinois Press.

Patterson, T. E. (2000). *Doing well and doing good: How soft news and critical journalism are shrinking the news audience and weakening democracy—and what news outlets can do about it.* Joan Shorenstein Center on the Press, Politics, and Public Policy, Kennedy School of Government, Harvard University, Cambridge, MA. Retrieved from the Shorenstein Center website: https://shorensteincenter.org/how-soft-news-critical-journalism-are-shrinking-news-audience/.

Patterson, T. E. (2007). *Young people and news.* Joan Shorenstein Center for the Press, Politics and Policy, Kennedy School of Government, Harvard University, Cambridge, MA. Retrieved from the Shorenstein Center website: https://shorensteincenter.org/wp-content/uploads/2012/03/young_people_and_news_2007.pdf.

Patterson, T. E. (2016). *News coverage of the 2016 general election: How the press failed voters.* Unpublished manuscript. Joan Shorenstein Center on the Press, Politics, and Public Policy, Kennedy School of Government, Harvard University, Cambridge, MA. Retrieved from the Shorenstein Center website: https://shorensteincenter.org/news-coverage-2016-general-election/.

Patterson, T. E. (2020). *A tale of two elections; CBS and Fox News' coverage of the 2020 presidential campaign.* Unpublished manuscript. Joan Shorenstein Center on the Press, Politics, and Public Policy, Kennedy School of Government, Harvard University, Cambridge, MA. Retrieved from the Shorenstein Center website: https://shorensteincenter.org/patterson-2020-election-coverage/.

Peterson, E. (2021). Paper cuts: How reporting resources affect political news coverage. *American Journal of Political Science, 65,* 443–459.

Pew Research Center (2007). *Two decades of American news preferences, Part 1: Analyzing what news the public follows—and doesn't follow.* Washington, DC: Pew Research Center. Retrieved from the Pew Research Center website: http://www.pewresearch .org/2007/08/15 /two-decades-of-american-news-preferences/.

Project for Excellence in Journalism. (2013). *The state of the news media 2013: An annual report on American journalism.* Washington, DC: Pew Research Center. Retrieved from the Pew Research Center website: http://assets.pewresearch.org.s3.amazonaws.com/files /journalism/State-of-the-News-Media-Report-2013-FINAL.pdf.

Sigal, L. (1973). *Reporters and officials: The organization and politics of newsmaking.* Lexington, MA: Heath.

Slattery, K. L., & Hakanen, E. A. (1994). Sensationalism versus public affairs content of local TV news: Pennsylvania revisited. *Journal of Broadcasting and Electronic Media, 538,* 205–216.

Stephens, M. (1994). History of newspapers. *Collier's encyclopedia.* Retrieved from www.nyu .edu/classes/stephens/Collier%27s%20page.htm.

CHAPTER 4

Althaus, S. (2003). When news norms collide, follow the lead: New evidence for press independence. *Political Communication, 20,* 381–414.

Althaus, S., Edy, J., Entman, R., & Phalen, P. (1996). Revising the indexing hypothesis: Officials, media and the Libya crisis. *Political Communication, 13,* 407–421.

Ansolabehere, S., Behr, R., & Iyengar, S. (1993). *The media game: American politics in the television age.* New York: Macmillan.

Arlen, M. J. (1969). *Living-room war: Writings about television.* New York: Viking.

Braestrup, P. (1977). *Big story: How the American press and television reported and interpreted the crisis of Tet 1968 in Vietnam and Washington.* Boulder, CO: Westview.

Center for Public Integrity. (2008). False pretenses. Retrieved from the Center for Public Integrity website: www.publicintegrity.org/2008/01/23/5641/false-pretenses.

Conetta, C. (2003, October 20). *The wages of war: Iraqi combatant and noncombatant fatalities in the 2003 conflict* (Project on Defense Alternatives Research Monograph No. 8). Retrieved July 26, 2005, from the Project on Defense Alternatives website: www.comw.org/pda /0310rm8.html.

Diamond, J. (2017, September 28). Trump administration projects confidence amid Puerto Rico crisis. CNN. Retrieved from the CNN website: www.cnn.com/2017/09/28/politics/elaine -duke-puerto-rico-response/index.html.

Dorman, W. A. (1997). Press theory and journalistic practice: The case of the Gulf War. In S. Iyengar & R. Reeves (Eds.), *Do the media govern? Politicians, voters and reporters in America* (pp. 118–125). Thousand Oaks, CA: Sage.

Entman, R. M. (2004). *Projections of power: Framing news, public opinion, and U.S. foreign policy.* Chicago: University of Chicago Press.

Frenznick, D. A. (1992). The First Amendment on the battlefield: A constitutional analysis of press access to military operations in Grenada, Panama and the Persian Gulf. *Pacific Law Journal, 23,* 315–359.

From the Editors. (2004, May 26). The *Times* and Iraq. *The New York Times,* p. A10.

Grynbaum, M. M. (2017, January 23). Sean Spicer, Trump's press secretary, reboots his relationship with the press. *The New York Times.* Retrieved from the *New York Times*

website: www.nytimes.com/2017/01/23/business/media/sean-spicer-trump-press
-secretary.html.

Hayes, D., & Guardino, M. (2013). *Influence from abroad: Foreign voices, the media, and U.S. public opinion.* New York: Cambridge University Press.

Karnow, S. (1997). *Vietnam: A history* (2nd ed.). New York: Penguin.

Krueger, A. B., & Laitin, D. (2004, May 17). Are we winning the war on terror? (Editorial). *The Washington Post*, p. A21.

Mermin, J. (1999). *Debating war and peace: Media coverage of U.S. intervention in the post-Vietnam era.* Princeton, NJ: Princeton University Press.

Mueller, J. (1973). *War, presidents and public opinion.* New York: Wiley.

Postol, T. A., & Lewis, G. N. (1993). Video evidence on the effectiveness of Patriot during the 1991 Gulf War. *Science and Global Security, 4,* 1–63.

Rutenberg, J. (2017). "Alternative facts" and the costs of Trump-branded reality. *The New York Times.* Retrieved from the *New York Times* website: www.nytimes.com/2017/01/22 /business/media/alternative-facts-trump-brand.html.

US Department of State. (2004, June 22). *Remarks on the release of the revised patterns of global terrorism 2003 annual report.* Retrieved from the US Department of State Archive website: https://2001-2009.state.gov/secretary/former/powell/remarks/33796.htm.

Zaller, J. R. (1994). Elite leadership of mass opinion: New evidence from the Gulf War. In W. L. Bennett & D. L. Paletz (Eds.), *Taken by storm: The media, public opinion, and U.S. foreign policy in the Gulf War* (pp. 186–209). Chicago: University of Chicago Press.

CHAPTER 5

Abramowitz, A. I., & Saunders, K. L. (2006). Exploring the bases of partisanship in the American electorate: Social identity vs. ideology. *Political Research Quarterly, 59,* 175–187.

Alcott, H., & Gentzkow, M. (2017). Social media and fake news in the 2016 election. *Journal of Economic Perspectives, 31,* 211–236.

Bakshy, E., Messing, S., & Adamic, L. (2015). Exposure to ideologically diverse news and opinion on Facebook. *Science, 348,* 1130–1132.

Bakshy, E., Rosenn, I., Marlow, C., & Adamic, L. (2012). The role of social networks in information diffusion. In A. Mille (Ed.), *Proceedings of the 21st International Conference on the World Wide Web* (pp. 519–528). New York: Association for Computing Machinery.

Barthel, M., & Mitchell, A. (2017). Americans' attitudes about the news media deeply divided along partisan lines. Washington, DC: Pew Research Center. Retrieved October 28, 2017, from the Pew Research Center website: https://www.pewresearch.org /journalism/2017/05/10/americans-attitudes-about-the-news-media-deeply-divided -along-partisan-lines/.

Bessi, A., & Ferrara, E. (2016, November 7). Social bots distort the 2016 presidential election online discussion. *First Monday, 21*(11).

Bimber, B., & Davis, R. (2003). *Campaigning online: The internet in U.S. elections.* New York: Oxford University Press.

Boulianne, S. (2009). Does internet use affect engagement? A meta-analysis of research. *Political Communication, 26,* 193–211.

Boulianne, S. (2018). Twenty years of digital media effects on civic and political participation. *Communications Research, 47,* 947–966.

Cilizza, C. (2016, May 11). This Donald Trump interview should set off all sorts of alarm bells for the GOP. *The Washington Post.* Retrieved from the *Washington Post* website: https://www.washingtonpost.com/news/the-fix/wp/2016/05/11/this-donald-trump -interview-should-set-off-all-sorts-of-alarm-bells-for-the-gop/.

Dalton, R. (2016, March 22). Why don't millennials vote? *The Washington Post.* Retrieved from the *Washington Post* website: www.washingtonpost.com/news/monkey-cage /wp/2016/03/22/why-dont-millennials-vote/.

Delli Carpini, M. X., & Keeter, S. (1996). *What Americans know about politics and why it matters.* New Haven, CT: Yale University Press.

Fiorina, M. (2017). *Unstable majorities polarization, party sorting, and political stalemate.* Stanford, CA: Hoover Institution Press.

Flaxman, S., Goel, S., & Rao, J. M. (2016). Filter bubbles, echo chambers, and online news consumption. *Public Opinion Quarterly, 80,* 298–320.

Gallup. (2021). Interactive presidential job approval center. Gallup.com. Retrieved from the Gallup website: https://news.gallup.com/interactives/185273/presidential-job-approval -center.aspx.

Gentzkow, M., & Shapiro, J. (2011). Ideological segregation online and offline. *Quarterly Journal of Economics, 126,* 1799–1839.

Gottfried, J., & Shearer, E. (2017, September 7). Americans' online news use is closing in on TV news use. Washington, DC: Pew Research Center. Retrieved November 29, 2021, from the Pew Research Center website: https://www.pewresearch.org/fact-tank/2017 /09/07/americans-online-news-use-vs-tv-news-use/.

Han, H. C. (2009). *Moved to action: Motivation, participation, and inequality in American politics.* Stanford, CA: Stanford University Press.

Hassanpour, N. (2014). Media disruption and revolutionary unrest: Evidence from Mubarak's quasi-experiment. *Political Communication, 31,* 1–24.

Hill, S. (2009). World wide webbed: The Obama campaign's masterful use of the internet. *Social Europe Journal, 4,* 9–15.

Ingram, M. (2015, August 18). Facebook has taken over from Google as a traffic source for news. *Fortune.* Retrieved from the *Fortune* website: http://fortune.com/2015/08/18 /facebook-google/.

International Telecommunications Union. (1994). Remarks prepared for delivery by US Vice President Al Gore. World Telecommunication Development Conference, Buenos Aires, March 21.

Iyengar, S. (1990). Shortcuts to political knowledge: Selective attention and the accessibility bias. In J. A. Ferejohn & J. H. Kuklinski (Eds.), *Information and the democratic process* (pp. 161–185). Champaign: University of Illinois Press.

Iyengar, S., & Hahn, K. (2009). Red media, blue media: Evidence of ideological polarization in media use. *Journal of Communication, 59,* 19–39.

Iyengar, S., Hahn, K. S., Krosnick, J. A., & Walker, J. (2008). Selective exposure to campaign communication: The role of anticipated agreement, interest in politics, and issue salience. *Journal of Politics, 70,* 186–200.

Jacobson, G. C. (2006). *A divider, not a uniter: George W. Bush and the American people.* New York: Pearson.

Jamieson, K. H. (2020). *Cyberwar: How Russian hackers and trolls helped elect a president—what we don't, can't, and do know.* New York: Oxford University Press.

Kang, C., Hsu, T., Roose, K., Singer, N., & Rosenberg, M. (2018, April 11). Mark Zuckerberg testimony: Day 2 brings tougher questioning. *The New York Times*. Retrieved from the *New York Times* website: www.nytimes.com/2018/04/11/us/politics/zuckerberg-facebook-cambridge-analytica.html.

King, G., Pan, J., & Roberts, M. E. (2013). How censorship in China allows government criticism but silences collective expression. *American Political Science Review, 107*, 1–18.

Kollanyi, B., Howard, P., & Wooley, S. (2016). Bots and automation over Twitter during the U.S. election. Data Memo 2016.4. Oxford, England: Project on Computational Propaganda. Retrieved November 9, 2017, from the University of Oxford website: http://comprop.oii.ox.ac.uk/publishing/working-papers/bots-and-automation-over-twitter-during-the-u-s-election/.

Kraut, R., Lundmark, V., Patterson, M., Kiesler, S., Mukopadhyay, T., & Scherlis, W. (1998). The internet paradox: A social technology that reduces social involvement and psychological well-being. *American Psychologist, 53*, 1017–1031.

Kreiss, D., & McGregor, S. (2018). Technology firms shape political communication: The work of Microsoft, Facebook, Twitter, and Google with campaigns during the 2016 U.S. presidential cycle. *Political Communication, 35*, 155–177.

Krosnick, J. A. (1990). Government policy and citizen passion: A study of issue publics in contemporary America. *Political Behavior, 12*, 59–92.

Lazarsfeld, P. F., Berelson, B. R., & Gaudet, H. (1948). *The people's choice.* New York: Columbia University Press.

Lelkes, Y., Sood, G., & Iyengar, S. (2017). The hostile audience: The effect of access to broadband internet on partisan affect. *American Journal of Political Science, 61*, 5–20.

Markoff, J. (2016, November 17). Automated pro-Trump bots overwhelmed pro-Clinton messages, researchers say. *The New York Times*. Retrieved from the *New York Times* website: www.nytimes.com/2016/11/18/technology/automated-pro-trump-bots-overwhelmed-pro-clinton-messages-researchers-say.html.

Messing, S. (2013). *Social influence in social media.* Unpublished doctoral dissertation, Stanford University, Stanford, CA.

Messing, S., & Westwood, S. J. (2014). Selective exposure in the age of social media: Endorsements trump partisan source affiliation when selecting news online. *Communication Research, 41*, 1042–1063.

Miller, C. C. (2008, November 7). How Obama's internet campaign changed politics. *The New York Times*. Retrieved from the *New York Times* blog website: https://bits.blogs.nytimes.com/2008/11/07/how-obamas-internet-campaign-changed-politics/.

Mitchell, A., Jurkowitz, M., Oliphant, J. B., & Shearer, E. (2020). *Americans who mainly get their news on social media are less engaged, less knowledgeable.* Washington, DC: Pew Research Center. Retrieved from the Pew Research Center website: https://www.pewresearch.org/journalism/2020/07/30/americans-who-mainly-get-their-news-on-social-media-are-less-engaged-less-knowledgeable/.

Mullainathan, S., & Shleifer, A. (2005). The market for news. *American Economic Review, 95*, 1031–1053.

Mummolo, J. (2017). News from the other side: How topic relevance limits the prevalence of partisan selective exposure. *Journal of Politics, 78*, 763–773.

National Intelligence Council (2021). *Foreign threats to the US 2020 federal elections.* Washington, DC: National Intelligence Council. Retrieved from the Office of the Director of National Intelligence website: https://www.dni.gov/files/ODNI/documents/assessments/ICA-declass-16MAR21.pdf.

Pennycook, G., Cannon, T., & Rand, D. G. (2018). Prior exposure increases perceived accuracy of fake news. *Journal of Experimental Psychology: General, 147*(12), 1865–1880.

Peterson, E., Goel, S., & Iyengar, S. (2017). Echo chambers and partisan polarization: Evidence from the 2016 presidential campaign. Unpublished paper, Stanford University, Stanford, CA.

Pew Research Center (2005). The Dean activists: Their profile and prospects. Washington, DC: Pew Research Center. Retrieved from the Pew Research Center website: https://www .pewresearch.org/politics/2005/04/06/the-dean-activists-their-profile-and-prospects/.

Pew Research Center (2011). Internet gains on television as public's main news source. Washington, DC: Pew Research Center. Retrieved November 29, 2021, from the Pew Research Center website: https://assets.pewresearch.org/wp-content/uploads/sites/5 /legacy-pdf/689.pdf.

Pew Research Center (2011). Press widely criticized, but trusted more than other information sources. Washington, DC: Pew Research Center. Retrieved December 10, 2014, from the Pew Research Center website: https://www.pewresearch.org/politics/2011/09/22/press -widely-criticized-but-trusted-more-than-other-institutions/.

Price, V., & Zaller, J. (1993). Who gets the news? Alternative measures of news reception and their implications for research. *Public Opinion Quarterly, 57*, 133–164.

Rheingold, H. (2002). *Smart mobs: The next social revolution.* Cambridge, MA: Basic Books.

Rhoads, C. (2008, October 18). Web data offer new slant on traditional horse race. *The Wall Street Journal*, p. A5.

Robinson, M. J., & Sheehan, M. (1983). *Over the wire and on TV: CBS and UPI in campaign '80.* New York: Basic Books.

Rosen, G. (2018). Facebook publishes enforcement numbers for the first time. Meta Newsroom. Retrieved from the Meta website: https://about.fb.com/news/2018/05/enforcement-numbers/.

Sears, D. O., & Freedman, J. L. (1967). Selective exposure to information: A critical review. *Public Opinion Quarterly, 31*, 194–213.

Seetharaman, D. (2016, November 10). Zuckerberg defends Facebook against charges it harmed political discourse. *The Wall Street Journal.* Retrieved from the *Wall Street Journal* website: www.wsj.com/articles/zuckerberg-defends-facebook-against-charges-it-harmed -political-discourse-1478833876.

Shambaugh, D. (2007). China's propaganda system: Institutions, processes, and efficacy. *China Journal, 57*, 25–58.

Smith, A., Schlozman, K. L., Verba, S., & Brady, H. (2009). *The internet and civic engagement.* Washington, DC: Pew Research Center.

Smith, T. J., III, Lichter, S. R., & Harris, T. (1997). *What the people want from the press.* Washington, DC: Center for Media and Public Affairs.

Subramaniam, S. (2017, February 15). Inside the Macedonian fake-news complex. *Wired.* Retrieved from the *Wired* website: www.wired.com/2017/02/veles-macedonia-fake-news/.

Sunstein, C. (2001). *Republic.com.* Princeton, NJ: Princeton University Press.

Timberg, C., Shaban, H., & Dwoskin, E. (2017, November 1). Fiery exchanges on Capitol Hill. *The Washington Post.* Retrieved from the *Washington Post* website: www.washingtonpost .com/news/the-switch/wp/2017/11/01/fiery-exchanges-on-capitol-hill-as-lawmakers -scold-facebook-google-and-twitter/.

Townsend, T. (2016). Meet the Romanian Trump fan behind a major fake news site. *Inc.* Retrieved from the *Inc.* website: http://www.inc.com/tess-townsend/ending-fed-trump -facebook.html.

Tyler, M., Grimmer, J., & Iyengar, S. (2022). Partisan enclaves and information bazaars: Mapping selective exposure to online news. *Journal of Politics*, forthcoming.

Valkenburg, P. M., & Peter, J. (2007). Online communication and adolescent well-being: Testing the stimulation versus the displacement hypothesis. *Journal of Computer-Mediated Communication, 12*, 1169–1182.

Valkenburg, P. M., & Peter, J. (2009). Social consequences of the internet for adolescents: A decade of research. *Current Directions in Psychological Science, 18*, 1–5.

VanNest, A. (2016). Facebook is the referral traffic story of 2016. MediaShift. Retrieved October 30, 2017, from the MediaShift website: http://mediashift.org/2016/12/facebook -referral-traffic-story-2016/.

CHAPTER 6

American National Election Studies. (2020). 2020 time series study. Retrieved September 13, 2021, from the American National Elections Study website: https://electionstudies.org /data-center/2020-time-series-study/.

Ansolabehere, S., & Iyengar, S. (1995). *Going negative: How attack ads shrink and polarize the electorate.* New York: Free Press.

Ayson, J. (2020). *Campaigning in the Tower of Babel: A functional analysis of multilingual political ads in Los Angeles elections.* Unpublished master's thesis, Stanford University, Stanford, CA.

Buckley v. Valeo, 424 U.S. 1 (1976).

Citizens United v. Federal Election Commission, 558 U.S. 50 (2010).

CNN. (2008, September 29). Obama-Biden camp hype Palin's debating skills. CNN, *Political Ticker* (blog). Retrieved from the CNN website: https://politicalticker.blogs.cnn.com /2008/09/29/obama-biden-camp-hype-palin%E2%80%99s-debating-skills/.

Condon, S. (2010, August 16). Ground Zero mosque debate becomes a campaign issue. CBS News. Retrieved from the CBS News website: http://www.cbsnews.com/news/ground -zero-mosque-debate-becomes-a-campaign-issue/.

Diamond, E., & Bates, S. (1992). *The spot: The rise of political advertising on television.* Cambridge, MA: MIT Press.

Fowler, E. F., Franz, M. M., Martin, G. J., Peskowitz, Z., & Ridout, T. N. (2021). Political advertising online and offline. *American Political Science Review, 115*, 130–149.

Fowler, E. F., Ridout, T N., & Franz, M. M. (2016). Political advertising in 2016: The presidential election as outlier? *The Forum, 14*, 445–469.

Graham, D. A. (2016, September 26). How Trump lowered expectations for the first debate. *The Atlantic.* Retrieved from *The Atlantic* website: https://www.theatlantic.com/politics /archive/2016/09/trumps-expectation-setting/501605/.

Grynbaum, M. (2016, June 13). *Washington Post* is latest news outlet barred by Trump. *The New York Times.* Retrieved from the *New York Times* website: www.nytimes.com /2016/06/14/business/media/trump-kicks-phony-and-dishonest-washington-post-off -his-campaign.html.

Lioz, A., Navarro-Rivera, J., & McElwee, S. (2017). Court cash: Election money resulting directly from Supreme Court rulings. Demos.org. Retrieved from the Demos website: http://www.demos.org/publication/court-cash-2016-election-money-resulting-directly -supreme-court-rulings.

McCutcheon v. Federal Election Commission, 572 U.S. 185 (2014).

Mellman, M. (2004, November 9). The 2004 American presidential election: Voter decision-making in a complex world (Conference remarks). Institute for Research in the Social Sciences, Stanford University, Stanford, CA.

Nielsen (2020). 2020 election hub. Retrieved on September 28, 2021, from the Nielsen website: nielsen.com/us/en/insights/article/2020/2020-election-hub/.

Peoples, S., Miller, Z., and Barrow, B. (2020, September 27). Biden, Trump take differing approaches to debate preparation. ABC News. Retrieved from ABC News website: https://abcnews.go.com/Politics/wireStory/biden-trump-differing-approaches-debate -preparation-73281602.

Pew Research Center. (2016). 2016 campaign: Strong interest, widespread dissatisfaction. Washington, DC: Pew Research Center. Retrieved from the Pew Research Center website: http://www.people-press.org/2016/07/07/1-campaign-engagement-and-interest/.

Rucker, P., & Fahrenthold, D. (2016, July 22). Donald Trump positions himself as the voice of "the forgotten men and women." The Washington Post. Retrieved from the Washington Post website: www.washingtonpost.com/politics/in-speech-at-republican-national-convention -trump-to-paint-dire-picture-of-america/2016/07/21/418f9ae6-4fad-11e6-aa14-e0c1087f7583 _story.html?utm _term=.04de210dd826.

Sonmez, F., and DeBonis, M. (2019, July 14). Trump tells four liberal congresswomen to "go back" to their countries, prompting Pelosi to defend them. The Washington Post. Retrieved from the Washington Post website: https://www.washingtonpost.com/politics/trump-says -four-liberal-congresswomen-should-go-back-to-the-crime-infested-places-from-which -they-came/2019/07/14/b8bf140e-a638-11e9-a3a6-ab670962db05_story.html.

Stahl, L. (2017, October 8). Facebook "embeds," Russia and the Trump campaign's secret weapon. Interview with Brad Parscale. 60 Minutes, CBS News. Retrieved from the CBS News website: www.cbsnews.com/news/facebook-embeds-russia-and-the-trump -campaigns-secret-weapon/.

Wesleyan Media Project (2021). Political ads in 2020: Fast and furious. Wesleyan Media Project, Wesleyan University. Retrieved September 28, 2021, from the Wesleyan Media Project website: https://mediaproject.wesleyan.edu/2020-summary-032321/.

CHAPTER 7

Ansolabehere, S. (2009). Effects of identification requirements on voting: Evidence from the experiences of voters on Election Day. *PS: Political Science & Politics, 42*, 127–130.

Ansolabehere, S., & Iyengar, S. (1995). *Going negative: How attack ads shrink and polarize the electorate.* New York: Free Press.

Bartels, L. M., & Zaller, J. (2001). Presidential vote models: A recount. *PS: Political Science & Politics, 33*, 9–20.

Brady, H. E., & Johnston, R. (1987). What's the primary message: Horse race or issue journalism? In G. R. Orren & N. W. Polsby (Eds.), *Media and momentum: The New Hampshire primary and nomination politics* (pp. 127–186). Chatham, NJ: Chatham House.

Buchanan, B. (1991). *Electing a president: The Markle Commission research on Campaign '88.* Austin: University of Texas Press.

Cantoni, E. & Pons, V. (2021). Strict ID laws don't stop voters: Evidence from a U.S. nationwide panel, 2008–2018. *Quarterly Journal of Economics, 136*(4), 2615–2660.

364 References

De Pinto, J., Salvanto, A., Backus, F., Khanna, K., & Cox, E. (2020, September 30). Debate-watchers say Biden won first debate, but most felt "annoyed." CBS News poll. Retrieved from the CBS News website: https://www.cbsnews.com/news/who-won-debate-first-presidential-biden-trump/.

Druckman, J. (2003). The power of television images: The first Kennedy–Nixon debate revisited. *Journal of Politics, 65,* 559–571.

Enos, R. D., & Fowler, A. (2018, October). Aggregate effects of large-scale campaigns on voter turnout. *Political Science Research and Methods, 6,* 733–751 (preview published online May 18, 2016, by Cambridge University Press).

Enos, R. D., Fowler, A., & Vavreck, L. (2014). Increasing inequality: The effect of GOTV mobilization on the composition of the electorate. *Journal of Politics, 76,* 273–288.

Frey, W. H. (2021, May 5). Turnout in 2020 election spiked among both Democratic and Republican voting groups, new census data shows. Brookings Institution report, Washington, DC. Retrieved from the Brookings Institution website: https://www.brookings.edu/research/turnout-in-2020-spiked-among-both-democratic-and-republican-voting-groups-new-census-data-shows/.

Gallup Poll. (2020, October 9). Americans view Biden as likable, honest; Trump, as strong. Retrieved from the Gallup website: https://news.gallup.com/poll/321695/americans-view-biden-likable-honest-trump-strong.aspx.

Gerber, A. S., & Green, D. P. (2008). *Get out the vote.* Washington, DC: Brookings Institution Press.

Gerber, A. S., Green, D. P., & Nickerson, D. W. (2002, May 7). *Getting out the youth vote in local elections: Results from six door-to-door canvassing experiments.* Unpublished report, Center for Information and Research on Civic Learning and Engagement, University of Maryland, College Park, MD.

Kalla, J. R., & Broockman, D. E. (2017). The minimal persuasive effects of campaign contact in general elections: Evidence from 47 experiments. *American Political Science Review, 112,* 148–166.

Lau, R. R., Sigelman, L., Heldman, C., & Babbitt, P. (1999). The effects of negative political advertisements: A meta-analytic assessment. *American Political Science Review, 93,* 851–875.

Liptak, A. (2013, June 25). Supreme Court invalidates key part of Voting Rights Act. *The New York Times.* Retrieved from the *New York Times* website: www.nytimes.com/2013/06/26/us/supreme-court-ruling.html.

Merry, R. (1996, September 1). Ed Rollins and the end of honor. *Weekly Standard.* Retrieved from the *Weekly Standard* website: www.weeklystandard.com/ed-rollins-and-the-end-of-honor/article/8455.

Mycoff, J. D., Wagner, M., & Wilson, D. C. (2009). The empirical effect of voter-ID laws: Present or absent? *PS: Political Science & Politics, 42,* 121–126.

Neiheisel, J. R., & Horner, R. (2019). Voter identification requirements and aggregate turnout in the U.S.: How campaigns offset the costs of turning out when voting is made more difficult. *Election Law Journal: Rules, Politics, and Policy 18,* 3, 227–242.

Parker, B., Brady, D., & Iyengar, S. (2021). *Do issues still matter? Examining the effects of candidate positioning on partisan voting.* Unpublished paper, Stanford University, Stanford, CA.

Pastor, R. A., Santos, R., Prevost, A., & Stoilov. V. (2010). Voting and ID requirements: A survey of registered voters in three states. *American Review of Public Administration, 40,* 461–481.

Valentino, N. A., & Neuner, F. G. (2017). Why the sky didn't fall: Mobilizing anger in response to voter identification laws. *Political Psychology, 38,* 331–350.

Yoder, J., Thompson, D., Handan-Nader, C., Wu, J., Yorgason, C., Nowacki, A., & Hall, A. (2021). *How did absentee voting affect the US 2020 election?* (Working Paper No. 21-011). Stanford, CA: Stanford Institute for Economic Policy Research, Stanford University.

CHAPTER 8

Alcott, H., Braghieri, L., Eichmeyer, S., & Gentzkow, M. (2020). The welfare effects of social media. *American Economic Review, 110,* 629–676.

Alcott, H., & Gentzkow, M. (2017). Social media and fake news in the 2016 election. *Journal of Economic Perspectives, 31,* 211–236.

Almond, G. A., & Verba, S. (1963). *The civic culture: Political attitudes and democracy in five nations.* Princeton, NJ: Princeton University Press.

Annenberg Public Policy Center. (2016, September 13). Americans' knowledge of the branches of government is declining. Retrieved from Annenberg Public Policy Center, University of Pennsylvania, website: https://www.annenbergpublicpolicycenter.org /americans-knowledge-of-the-branches-of-government-is-declining/.

Ansolabehere, S., Behr, R., & Iyengar, S. (1993). *The media game: American politics in the television age.* New York: Macmillan.

Ansolabehere, S., & Iyengar, S. (1995). *Going negative: How attack ads shrink and polarize the electorate.* New York: Free Press.

Ansolabehere, S., & Iyengar, S. (1998). *Message forgotten: Misreporting in surveys and the bias towards minimal effects.* Unpublished manuscript, Department of Political Science, Massachusetts Institute of Technology, Cambridge, MA.

Ansolabehere, S., Iyengar, S., & Simon, A. (1999). Replicating experiments using aggregate and survey data: The case of negative advertising and turnout. *American Political Science Review, 93,* 901–910.

Arceneaux, K., & Johnson, M. (2013). *Changing minds or changing channels: Partisan news in an age of choice.* Chicago: University of Chicago Press.

Bailenson, J., Iyengar, S., Yee, N., & Collins, N. (2009). Facial similarity between voters and candidates causes influence. *Public Opinion Quarterly, 72,* 935–961.

Baumgartner, F. R., & Jones, B. D. (1993). *Agendas and instability in American politics.* Chicago: University of Chicago Press.

Behr, R. L., & Iyengar, S. (1985). Television news, real-world cues, and changes in the public agenda. *Public Opinion Quarterly, 49,* 38–57.

Benen, S. (2015, September 1). GOP base: Obama wasn't born in US, but Cruz was. MSNBC News. Retrieved from the MSNBC News website: https://www.msnbc.com/rachel -maddow-show/gop-base-obama-wasnt-born-us-cruz-was-msna673571.

Bennett, W. L., & Iyengar, S. (2008). A new era of minimal effects? The changing foundations of political communication. *Journal of Communication, 58,* 707–731.

Berinsky, A. J. (2017). Rumors and health care reform: Experiments in political misinformation. *British Journal of Political Science, 47,* 241–262.

Berry, J. M., & Sobieraj, S. (2014). *The outrage industry: Political opinion media and the new incivility.* New York, NY: Oxford University Press.

Bullock, J. G., Gerber, A. S., Hill, S. J., & Huber, G. A. (2015). Partisan bias in factual beliefs about politics. *Quarterly Journal of Political Science, 10,* 519–578.

Campbell, A., Converse, P., Miller, W., & Stokes, D. (1960). *The American voter*. New York: Wiley.

Clinton, J., & Roush, C. (2016, August 10). Poll: Persistent partisan divide over "birther" question. NBC News. Retrieved from the NBC News website: https://www.nbcnews.com/politics /2016-election/poll-persistent-partisan-divide-over-birther-question-n627446.

Cohen, B. E. (1963). *The press and foreign policy*. Princeton, NJ: Princeton University Press.

Converse, P. (1962). Information flow and the stability of partisan attitudes. *Public Opinion Quarterly, 26*, 578–599.

Dearing, J. W., & Rogers, E. M. (1996). *Agenda-setting*. Thousand Oaks, CA: Sage.

Dias, N., & Lelkes, Y. (2021). The nature of affective polarization: Disentangling policy disagreement from partisan identity. *American Journal of Political Science*. https://doi .org/10.1111/ajps.12628.

Druckman, J. N. (2001). The implications of framing effects for citizen competence. *Political Behavior, 23*, 225–256.

Druckman, J. N., & Holmes, J. W. (2004). Does presidential rhetoric matter? Priming and presidential approval. *Presidential Studies Quarterly, 34*, 755–778.

Edwards, G. C., III., & Wood, B. D. (1999). Who influences whom? The president, Congress, and the media. *American Political Science Review, 93*, 327–344.

Eshbaugh-Soha, M., & Peake, J. S. (2005). Presidents and the economic agenda. *Political Research Quarterly, 58*, 128–137.

Eshbaugh-Soha, M., & Peake, J. S. (2008). The agenda-setting impact of major presidential TV addresses. *Political Communication, 25*, 113–137.

Eshbaugh-Soha, M., & Peake, J. S. (2011). *Breaking through the noise: Presidential leadership, public opinion, and the news media*. Stanford, CA: Stanford University Press.

Geer, J. G. (2012). The news media and the rise of negativity in presidential campaigns. *PS: Political Science & Politics, 45*(3), 422–427.

Gilliam, F. D., Jr., & Iyengar, S. (2000). Prime suspects: The influence of local television news on the viewing public. *American Journal of Political Science, 44*, 560–573.

Grimmer, J., & King, G. (2011). General purpose computer-assisted clustering and conceptualization. *Proceedings of the National Academy of Sciences, 108*, 2643–2650.

Hart, A., & Middleton, J. A. (2014). Priming under fire: Reverse causality and the classic media priming hypothesis. *Journal of Politics, 76*, 581–592.

Hart, P. S., & Nisbet, E. C. (2012). Boomerang effects in science communication: How motivated reasoning and identity cues amplify opinion polarization about climate mitigation policies. *Communication Research, 39*, 701–723.

Hayes, D. (2005). Candidate qualities through a partisan lens: A theory of trait ownership. *American Journal of Political Science, 49*, 908–923.

Hetey, R. C., & Eberhardt, J. L. (2014). Racial disparities in incarceration increase acceptance of punitive policies. *Psychological Science, 25*, 1949–1954.

Hovland, C. I. (1959). Reconciling conflicting results derived from experimental and survey studies of attitude change. *American Psychologist, 14*, 8–17.

Hovland, C. I., Janis, I. L., & Kelley, H. H. (1953). *Communications and persuasion: Psychological studies in opinion change*. New Haven, CT: Yale University Press.

Hovland, C. I., Lumsdaine, A. A., & Sheffield, F. D. (1949). A baseline for measurement of percentage change. In C. I. Hovland, A. A. Lumsdaine, & F. D. Sheffield (Eds.), *Experiments on mass communication* (pp. 284–289). Princeton, NJ: Princeton University Press.

Huber, G. A., & Malhotra, N. (2017). Political homophily in social relationships: Evidence from online dating behavior. *Journal of Politics, 79*, 269–283.

Iyengar, S., & Kinder, D. R. (1987). *News that matters: Television and American opinion.* Chicago: University of Chicago Press.

Iyengar, S., Konitzer, T., & Tedin, K. (2018). The home as a political fortress: Family agreement in an era of polarization. *Journal of Politics, 80.* 1326–1338.

Iyengar, S., Lelkes, Y., Levendusky, M., Malhotra, N., & Westwood. S. (2019). The origins and consequences of affective polarization in the United States. *Annual Review of Political Science, 22*, 129–146.

Iyengar, S., Sood, G., & Lelkes, Y. (2012). Affect not ideology: A social identity perspective on polarization. *Public Opinion Quarterly, 78*, 405–431.

Iyengar, S., & Valentino, N. A. (2000). Who says what? Source credibility as a mediator of campaign advertising. In A. Lupia, M. D. McCubbins, & S. L. Popkin (Eds.), *Elements of reason: Cognition, choice and the bounds of rationality* (pp. 108–129). Cambridge, England: Cambridge University Press.

Iyengar, S., & Westwood, S. (2015). Fear and loathing across party lines: New evidence on group polarization. *American Journal of Political Science, 59*, 690–707.

Johnston, R., Hagen, M. G., & Jamieson, K. H. (2004). *The 2000 presidential election and the foundations of party politics.* New York: Cambridge University Press.

Kahn, K. F. (1994). The distorted mirror: Press coverage of women candidates for statewide office. *Journal of Politics, 56*, 154–174.

King, G., Schneer, B., & White, A. (2017). How the news media activate public expression and influence national agendas. *Science, 358*, 776–780.

Klapper, J. T. (1960). *The effects of mass communications.* New York: Free Press.

Knox, D., Yamamoto, T., Baum, M. A., & Berinsky, A. (2019). Design, identification, and sensitivity analysis for patient preference trials. *Journal of the American Statistical Association, 114*, 1532–1546.

Krosnick, J. A., & Kinder, D. R. (1990). Altering the foundations of support for the president through priming. *American Political Science Review, 84*, 497–512.

Kull, S., Ramsay, C., & Lewis, E. (2003). Misperceptions, the media, and the Iraq war. *Political Science Quarterly, 118*, 569–598.

Lazarsfeld, P., Berelson, B., & Gaudet, H. (1948). The people's choice: How the voter makes up his mind in a presidential campaign. New York: Columbia University Press.

Lenz, G. S. (2012). *Follow the leader: How voters respond to politicians' performance and policies.* Chicago: University of Chicago Press.

Levendusky, M. (2009). *The partisan sort: How liberals became Democrats and conservatives became Republicans.* Chicago: University of Chicago Press.

Levendusky, M., & Malhotra, N. 2016. (Mis)perceptions of partisan polarization in the American public. *Public Opinion Quarterly, 80*, S1, 378–391.

Lippmann, W. (1922). *Public opinion.* New York: Harcourt Brace.

Lippmann, W. (1925). *The phantom public.* New York: Macmillan.

Luskin, R. L., Iyengar S., & Fishkin, J. (2005). *The deliberative citizen.* Paper presented at the 101st annual meeting of the American Political Science Association, Washington, DC, September 1–4.

Mason, L. (2014). "I respectfully disagree": The differential effects of partisan sorting on social and issue polarization. *American Journal of Political Science, 58*, 1–18.

Mason, L. (2018). *Uncivil agreement: How politics became our identity*. Chicago: Chicago University Press.

McCarty, N., Poole, K. T., & Rosenthal, H. (2006). *Polarized America: The dance of ideology and unequal riches*. Cambridge, MA: MIT Press.

McCombs, M. C., & Shaw, D. L. (1972). The agenda-setting function of mass media. *Public Opinion Quarterly, 36*, 176–187.

Mendelberg, T. (1997). Executing Hortons: Racial crime in the 1988 presidential campaign. *Public Opinion Quarterly, 61*, 134–157.

Mendelsohn, N. (1996). The media and interpersonal communications: The priming of issues, leaders, and party identification. *Journal of Politics, 58*, 112–125.

Messing, S., Jabon, M., & Plaut, E. (2016). Bias in the flesh: Skin complexion and stereotype consistency in political campaigns. *Public Opinion Quarterly, 80*, 44–65.

Miller, J. M., & Krosnick, J. A. (2000). News media impact on the ingredients of presidential evaluations: Politically knowledgeable citizens are guided by a trusted source. *American Journal of Political Science, 44*, 295–309.

Mutz, D. C., & Reeves, B. (2005). The new videomalaise: Effects of televised incivility on political trust. *American Political Science Review, 99*, 1–15.

Nelson, T. E., & Kinder, D. R. (1996). Issue frames and group-centrism in American public opinion. *Journal of Politics, 58*, 1055–1078.

Orr, L. V. & Huber, G. A. (2020). The policy basis of measured partisan animosity in the United States. *American Journal of Political Science, 64*, 569–586.

Patterson, T. (2016). *News coverage of the 2016 general election: How the press failed, the voters*. Unpublished report, Joan Shorenstein Center for the Press, Politics and Policy, Kennedy School of Government, Harvard University, Cambridge, MA. Retrieved from the Shorenstein Center website: https://shorensteincenter.org/news-coverage-2016-general-election/.

Peterson, E., Goel, S., & Iyengar, S. (2017). *Echo chambers and partisan polarization: Evidence from the 2016 campaign*. Political Communication Lab, Stanford University, Stanford, CA. Retrieved from https://pcl.sites.stanford.edu/sites/g/files/sbiybj22066/files/media/file/peterson-echo-chambers.pdf.

Pew Research Center. (2014, June 12). Political polarization in the American public: How increasing ideological uniformity and partisan antipathy affect politics, compromise and everyday life. Washington, DC: Pew Research Center. Retrieved March 4, 2015, from the Pew Research Center website: http://www.people-press.org/2014/06/12/political-polarization-in-the-american-public/.

Pew Research Center (2021, January 28). Economy and Covid-19 top the public's policy agenda for 2021. Washington, DC: Pew Research Center. Retrieved July 7, 2021 from the Pew Research Center website: https://www.pewresearch.org/politics/2021/01/28/economy-and-covid-19-top-the-publics-policy-agenda-for-2021/.

Price, V., & Zaller, J. (1993). Who gets the news? Alternative measures of news reception and their implications for research. *Public Opinion Quarterly, 57*, 133–164.

Prior, M. (2009). The immensely inflated news audience: Assessing bias in self-reported news exposure. *Public Opinion Quarterly, 73*, 130–143.

Prior, M., Sood, G., & Khanna, K. (2015). You cannot be serious: The impact of accuracy incentives on partisan bias in reports of economic perceptions. *Quarterly Journal of Political Science, 10*, 489–518.

Rogowski, J., & Sutherland, J. (2016). How ideology fuels affective polarization. *Political Behavior, 38*, 485–508.

Saad, L. (2017). Concerns about sexual harassment higher than in 1998. Gallup.com. Retrieved from the Gallup News website: https://news.gallup.com/poll/221216/concerns-sexual-harassment-higher-1998.aspx.

Sood, G., & S. Iyengar, S. (2018). All in the eye of the beholder: Asymmetry in ideological accountability. In Howard Lavine & Charles Taber (Eds.), *The feeling, thinking citizen: Essays in honor of Milton Lodge* (pp. 195–228). New York: Routledge.

Swire, B., Berinsky, A. J., Lewandowsky, S., & Ecker, U. K. (2017). Processing political misinformation: Comprehending the Trump phenomenon. *Royal Society Open Science, 4*, 160–180.

Tversky, A., & Kahneman, D. (1981). The framing of decisions and the psychology of choice. *Science, 211*, 453–458.

Vavreck, L. (2007). The exaggerated effects of advertising on turnout: The dangers of self-reports. *Quarterly Journal of Political Science, 2*, 325–343.

Wattenberg, M. P., & Brians, C. L. (1999). Negative campaign advertising: Mobilizer or demobilizer? *American Political Science Review, 93*, 891–899.

CHAPTER 9

Ansolabehere, S., Behr, R., & Iyengar, S. (1991). Mass media and elections: An overview. *American Politics Quarterly, 19*, 109–139.

Ansolabehere, S., Behr, R., & Iyengar, S. (1993). *The media game: American politics in the television age.* New York: Macmillan.

Apple, R. W. (1990, September 20). Confrontation in the Gulf: Criticism of U.S. Gulf policy growing louder in Congress. *New York Times*, p. A10.

Arnold, R. D. (2004). *Congress, the press, and political accountability.* Princeton, NJ: Princeton University Press.

Auletta, K. (2004, January 19). Fortress Bush: How the White House keeps the press under control. *The New Yorker.* Retrieved from the *New Yorker* website: www.newyorker.com /magazine/2004/01/19/fortress-bush.

Brody, R. A. (1991). *Assessing the president: The media, elite opinion and public support.* Stanford, CA: Stanford University Press.

Canes-Wrone, B. (2001). The president's legislative influence from public appeals. *American Journal of Political Science, 45*, 313–329.

Clayman, S. E., Elliot, M., Heritage, J., & Beckett, M. (2010). A watershed in White House journalism: Explaining the post-1986 rise of aggressive presidential news. *Political Communication, 27*, 229–247.

Clayman, S. E., Elliot, M., Heritage, J., & McDonald, L. (2007). When does the watchdog bark? Conditions of aggressive questioning in presidential press conferences. *American Sociological Review, 72*, 23–41.

CNBC. (2009, June 16). *Obama on the economy, Iran.* John Harwood interview with Barack Obama. Retrieved December 8, 2014, from the CNBC website: www.cnbc.com /id/31393724.

CNN. (2005, January 27). Bush expounds on theme of freedom: President says, "I firmly planted the flag of liberty." Transcript of the January 26, 2005, presidential press conference. Retrieved July 20, 2005, from CNN's website: www.cnn.com/2005 /ALLPOLITICS/01/26/bush/.

Cook, T. E. (1998). *Governing with the news: The news media as a political institution.* Chicago: University of Chicago Press.

Golbeck, J., Grimes, J. M., & Rogers, A. (2010). Twitter use by the US Congress. *Journal of the Association for Information Science and Technology, 61,* 1612–1621.

Grimmer, J., Messing, S., & Westwood, S. J. (2012). How words and money cultivate a personal vote: The effect of legislator credit claiming on constituent credit allocation. *American Political Science Review, 106,* 703–719.

Grossman, M. B., & Kumar, M. J. (1981). *Portraying the president.* Baltimore: Johns Hopkins University Press.

Hahn, K., & Iyengar, S. (2007). History versus media management as determinants of presidential popularity. In D. Lacorne & J. Vasse (Eds.), *La Presidence Imperiale: De Franklin D. Roosevelt a George W. Bush* (pp. 144–160). Paris: Odile Jacob.

Hertsgaard, M. (1988). *On bended knee: The press and the Reagan presidency.* New York: Farrar, Straus & Giroux.

Jacobson, G. (2008). *A divider, not a uniter: George W. Bush and the American people.* New York: Longmans.

Kernell, S. (1986). *Going public: New strategies of presidential leadership.* Washington, DC: Congressional Quarterly Press.

Kernell, S., & Rice, L. R. (2011). Cable and the partisan polarization of the president's audience. *Presidential Studies Quarterly, 41,* 696–711.

Kumar, M. J. (2003). The contemporary presidency: Communications operations in the White House of President George W. Bush—Making news on his terms. *Presidential Studies Quarterly, 33,* 366–393.

Lowi, T. J. (1981). *Incomplete conquest: Governing America.* New York: Holt, Rinehart & Winston.

NASA (National Aeronautics and Space Agency). (1986, January 28). Explosion of the space shuttle *Challenger*, President Reagan's address to the nation. Retrieved from the NASA History Office website: https://history.nasa.gov/reagan12886.html.Neustadt, R. (1960). *Presidential power: The politics of leadership.* New York: Wiley.

Patterson, T. E. (2017). *News coverage of Trump's first 100 days.* Unpublished paper, Joan Shorenstein Center on the Press, Politics, and Public Policy, Kennedy School of Government, Harvard University, Cambridge, MA. Retrieved from the Shorenstein Center website: https://shorensteincenter.org /news-coverage-donald-trumps-first-100-days/.

Peters, J. W., Plott, E., & Haberman, M. (2020, April 26). 260,000 words, full of self-praise, from Trump on the virus. *New York Times.* Retrieved from the *New York Times* website: https://www.nytimes.com/interactive/2020/04/26/us/politics/trump-coronavirus -briefings-analyzed.html.

Pew Research Center. (2009, March 19). *The state of the news media 2009: An annual report on American journalism.* Washington, DC: Pew Research Center. Retrieved from the Pew Research Center website: https://assets.pewreseach.org/files/journalism/State-of-the -News-Media-Report-2009-final.pdf.

Pew Research Center. (2017). Covering President Trump in a Polarized Environment. Washington, DC: Pew Research Center. Retrieved from the Pew Research Center website: https://www.pewresearch.org/journalism/2017/10/02/covering-president-trump -in-a-polarized-media-environment/.

Stelter, B. (2009, October 11). Fox's volley with Obama intensifying. *The New York Times.* Retrieved January 20, 2011, from the *New York Times* website: www.nytimes.com /2009/10/12/business/media/12fox.html.

Straus, J., Glassman, M., Shogan, C., & Smelcer, S. (2013). Communicating in 140 characters or less: Congressional adoption of Twitter in the 111th Congress. *PS: Political Science & Politics, 46*, 60–66.

Tulis, J. K. (1987). *The rhetorical presidency.* Chatham, NJ: Chatham House.

Vinson, D. C. (2003). *Through local eyes: Local media coverage of Congress and its members.* Cresskill, NJ: Hampton.

Washington Post. (2005, September 15). President Bush delivers remarks on Hurricane Katrina. Retrieved from the *Washington Post* website: www.washingtonpost.com/wp-dyn/content/article/2005/09/15/AR2005091502252.html.

White House Press Office. (2017, January 21). Statement by Press Secretary Sean Spicer. Retrieved from the White House Archives website: www.trumpwhitehouse.archives.gov/briefings-statements/statement-press-secretary-sean-spicer/.

CHAPTER 10

Canes-Wrone, B., & K. W. Shotts. (2004). The conditional nature of presidential responsiveness to public opinion. *American Journal of Political Science, 48*, 690–706.

Davis, J., & Stolberg, S. (2018, January 9). Trump appears to endorse path to citizenship for millions of immigrants. *The New York Times.* Retrieved from the *New York Times* website: www.nytimes.com/2018/01/09/us/politics/trump-daca-immigration.html.

Domanick, J. (2004). *Cruel justice.* Berkeley: University of California Press.

Fiorina, M. P (2017). *Unstable majorities: Polarization, party sorting, and political stalemate.* Stanford, CA: Hoover Institution Press.

Gottschalk, M. (2009). The long reach of the carceral state: The politics of crime, mass imprisonment, and penal reform in the US and abroad. *Law and Social Inquiry, 34*, 439–472.

Gramlich, J. (2020). *Black imprisonment rate in the U.S. has fallen by a third since 2006.* Washington DC: Pew Research Center. Retrieved from the Pew Research Center website: https://www.pewresearch.org/fact-tank/2020/05/06/share-of-black-white-hispanic-americans-in-prison-2018-vs-2006/.

Grimmer, J., & King, G. (2011). General purpose computer-assisted clustering and conceptualization. *Proceedings of the National Academy of Sciences of the USA, 108*, 2643–2650.

Lippmann, W. (1925). *The phantom public.* New York: Transaction Publishers.

Mullainathan, S., & Shleifer, A. (2005). The market for news. *American Economic Review, 95*, 1031–1053.

Parker, R. (2012). Why California's "three strikes" fails as crime and economic policy, and what to do. *California Journal of Politics and Policy, 5*, 206–231.

Pasley, J. L. (2001). *The tyranny of printers: Newspaper politics in the early American republic.* Charlottesville: University of Virginia Press.

Patterson, T. E. (2017). News coverage of Donald Trump's first hundred days. Unpublished paper, Kennedy School of Government, Harvard University, Cambridge, MA.

Sood, G., & Iyengar, S. (2018). All in the eye of the beholder: Asymmetry in ideological accountability. In H. Lavine & C. Taber (Eds.), *The feeling, thinking citizen: Essays in honor of Milton Lodge* (pp. 195–228). New York: Routledge.

Weaver, V. M., & Lerman, A. E. (2010). Political consequences of the carceral state. *American Political Science Review, 104*, 817–833.

CREDITS

TEXT

Ch. 9: Mike McCurry, "A Day in the Life of the Presidential Press Secretary," Speech at Stanford University, May 8, 2001. Reprinted with permission of the author.

FIGURES

Figure 5.2: Reprinted with permission from "More than eight-in-ten Americans get news from digital devices," FactTank. Pew Research Center, Washington, D.C. (January 12, 2021), https://www.pewresearch.org/fact-tank/2021/01/12/more-than-eight-in-ten-americans-get-news-from-digital-devices/.

Figure 6.2: Kantar/CMAG with analysis by the Wesleyan Media Project. (2020, October 29). "Presidential general election and spending tops $1.5 billion." Retrieved September 13, 2021, from the Wesleyan Media Project website: https://mediaproject.wesleyan.edu/releases-102920/. Adapted with permission from the Wesleyan Media Project.

Figure 6.3: Republished with permission of Walter du Gruyter and Company, from "Political advertising in 2016: The presidential election as outlier?", E. Franklin Fowler, T. N. Ridout, and M. M. Franz, *The Forum*, Vol. 14, No. 4, 2016; permission conveyed through Copyright Clearance Center, Inc.

PHOTOS

Page 1: Pacific Press Media Production Corp./Alamy Stock Photo; **p. 97:** AP Photo/Pablo Martinez Monsivais; **p. 116:** AP Photo/Keith Srakocic; **p. 276:** Photo courtesy of Shanto Iyengar, J. Bailenson, S. Iyengar, N. Yee, & N. Collins (2009). Facial similarity between voters and candidates causes influence. Public Opinion Quarterly, 72, 935-961; **p. 305:** Cynthia Johnson/Getty Images

INDEX

Affordable Care Act (2010), 15, 179, 227, 256, 291, 307–8, 340, 341, 346
Afghanistan, 100, 178–79, 254, 327
African Americans
    Barack Obama, misinformation about, 255–56
    Black Lives Matter, 141
    diversity in journalism, 81–82
    framing and stereotypes, 273–74
    group identity, voting behavior and, 276
    pandering on law and order, 273–74, 339
    policy issue public, 135
    support for African American candidates, 223
    voter turnout and, 236
    voting behavior 2020 elections, 232
    "Willie Horton" ad, 74–75, 181, 188, 247–48, 274
African nations, news coverage of, 35
age
    attentive public hypothesis, 129
    civic engagement demographics, 129
    issue public hypothesis, 135–37
    online political engagement and, 125–26
    voter turnout and, 235, 236
agenda setting, 14
    defined, 258
    going public and, 15–17
    media effects, research on, 246, 257–65
    psychological accounts of, 264–65
agenda-setting effect, defined, 259–60
aggregators of news, 120, 133–34
Agnew, Spiro, 88
Ahmed, Saladin, 115
Ailes, Roger, 156
Alabama, 182
Albuquerque Tribune, 44
Alcindor, Yamiche, 161
Alcott, Hunt, 143
Alexa.com, 56, 120
Alien and Sedition Acts (1798), 349
Allen, Thad, 294
Almond, Gabriel, 281
Al Qaeda, 94–95
"alternative facts," 96
Amazon Prime Video, subscriber data, 62–63
American National Election Study, 219, 251, 280–81
American Society of Newspaper Editors, 81–82
America Rescue Plan Act (2021), 3
analytic frame of reference, 272
analytic journalism. *See* interpretive journalism
Ansolabehere, Stephen, 188–89, 216–17, 248, 249, 251, 265, 279
antitrust legislation, print media regulation, 43
AOL, 134
Apple, R. W. (Johnny), 81, 85
approval ratings. *See* public opinion

Arab Spring, 147
Arbitron, 40
ARD, public financing of, 6
Arizona, 182, 211
Arlen, Michael, 101
Armitage, Richard, 99–100
Army-McCarthy hearings, 315
Arnett, Peter, 59
Arsenio Hall Show, The, 165
assault rifles, 342
"A Tale of Two Mitts" ad, 186
attentive public hypothesis, 127, 128–29
attitude change. *See* persuasion
audience. *See also* media effects; media marketplace; specific media type
    advertising, campaign strategies for, 169–74
    for Clarence Thomas nomination, 316
    debates, campaign strategy and, 198–203
    fragmentation of, 10
    internet, effects of, 118
    issue public hypothesis, 135–37
    micro targeting, 173
    narrowcasting, 308
    for news media, 56–63
    partisan polarization hypothesis, 127, 128, 130–34
    for presidential speeches, 306–8
    social media and selective exposure, 137–44
Audit Bureau of Circulations, 56
Australia, 29
authoritarian governments, 147
authoritative sources, 8
autonomy, 74–75
Axelrod, David, 161, 294
Axios, 55

bandwagon effects, 212
Bannon, Steve, 294
Bartels, Larry, 210
base voter, holding of, 214–21
battleground states, 211–12
Baumgartner, Frank, 263
BBC (British Broadcasting Company). *See also* United Kingdom
    coverage of African nations on, 35
    Ethiopia famine (1980s), 22
    partisan polarization hypothesis, 132
    public financing of, 6, 33, 37
    public *vs.* commercial ownership, 30–37
    regulation of broadcast media, 42
BCRA (Bipartisan Campaign Reform Act, 2002), 13, 196–97
"Bear in the Woods" ad, 178
beat system, 84–85
Behr, Roy, 265
Belgium, 33–34, 46–48
Benghazi, 159, 189, 321

Cain, Herman, 157, 221
California
    campaign advertising strategy and,
        169–71, 217
    designated media areas (DMAs), 58
    direct mail, use in, 190–91
    gubernatorial race 1990, 248
    gubernatorial race 1994, 180, 182, 184–85
    gubernatorial race 2002, 183
    gubernatorial race 2010, 156, 184–85, 186
    immigration as wedge issue, 180–81, 182,
        184–85, 236
    Latino electorate, 185, 236
    media market, presidential elections,
        169, 171
    national news coverage of, 83
    pandering on law and order, 338
    population of, 24
    primary ballot qualifications, 27
    Proposition 66, 338–39
    Proposition 209, 182
    Propositions 184 and 187, 184–85
    voter demographics in, 236
Cambridge Analytica, 149
campaign finance
    advertising and, 13, 156, 172–73, 192
    Bipartisan Campaign Reform Act
        (BCRA, 2002), 13, 196–97
    Buckley v. Valeo, 193–94
    Citizens United v. Federal Election
        Commission (2010), 197–98
    direct mail, costs for, 190–92
    McCutcheon v. Federal Election Commission
        (2013), 198
    media campaign costs, 28
    reform efforts, 193–98
    social media, reduced costs from, 116–17
    soft money and issue finance, 194–95
campaigns, for public office. *See also*
        media effects
    advertising costs, 156, 172–73, 190–92
    advertising strategy, 167–82
    campaign financing reforms, 193–98
    candidate debates, 198–203
    candidate viability, 212, 230
    debates, impact on voters, 219–21
    debate strategy, 198–203
    direct mail, use of, 190–92
    holding the base, 214–21
    influence of, 211–12
    internet, impact on political organizations,
        144–50
    issue ownership, 176–79
    managing events, 161–63
    media use, history of, 155–57
    negative advertising, 183–90, 237–38
    political context *vs.* campaign effects,
        207–12

    primaries, learning and momentum,
        228–33
    regulating access to candidates, 163–65
    reinforcement effect, 220
    rise of television media campaigns, 26–30
    strategies for managing the press, 157–67
    swing voters, attracting of, 221–23
    voter dynamics, forecasting elections and,
        209–11
    voter education strategies, 224–28
    voter turnout and, 233–39
    voting as expression of partisanship,
        213–28
campaign staff, media professionals on, 293–95
Canada, 6, 29, 270
candidates
    advertising strategies of, 12–13
    campaign coverage, regulation of, 45–48
    candidate-based voting, 214
    character issues (*See* character issues)
    going public, 14–17
    horse race reporting (*See* horse race
        reporting)
    incumbents, advantages of, 197, 208–11,
        224–28
    internet, impact on political campaigns,
        144–50
    personality impression, 225–26
    physical attributes, voter perception
        and, 223
    policy positions, voter knowledge of,
        226–27
    primary elections, campaign strategies,
        228–33
    selection process, outside of U.S., 28–30
    selection process, U.S., 7, 23–30
    shaping the news, 11–13
    viability of, 212, 230, 269–70
    voice of, in news coverage, 78
Canes-Wrone, Brandice, 293, 341
capital punishment, 338
carceral state, 339
Carson, Ben, 225
Carter, Jimmy, 201–2, 221
    1976 debate with Ford, 219
    1976 primary elections, 232–33
    Iran hostage issue, 266, 327
    press conferences, 309
CBC (Canadian Broadcast Company), 6
CBS
    coverage of invasion of Iraq (2003),
        108
    as daily news source, 54, 59–60
    horse race reporting, 76–77
    local outlets for, 57
    MoveOn.org ad, 2004 Super Bowl, 42
    news coverage of presidents, 301, 302
CBS Evening News, 59, 69

CBS *Nightly News,* 60
censorship
    Alien and Sedition Acts (1798),
        349–50
    Chinese government and, 147
    FEMA efforts during Hurricane Katrina
        response, 4
    Grenada, military action in, 103–5
    media pools, 106
Center for Public Integrity, 108–9
Challenger explosion, 307, 328
Chappaquiddick incident, 221
character issues
    biographical advertising and, 174
    campaigns and voter education strategies,
        224–28
    character assassination, negative ads,
        183–89
    playing one source against another,
        165–66
    priming, effects of, 269–70
    reporting on, 79–82, 157–59
    "Soldiers and Sailors" ad, 186–87
    swing voters, attracting of, 221–23
Charlottesville, VA, 310–11
Cheney, Liz, 291
China, internet censorship and, 147
Citizens United v. Federal Election Commission
    (2010), 197–98
civic engagement, internet use and, 123–27.
    See also informed citizenry
    attentive public hypothesis, 128–29
    issue public hypothesis, 135–37
    partisan polarization hypothesis, 130–34
civil rights legislation, 289
Clark, Wesley, 230–32
Clear Channel, 40
Clinton, Hillary, 85
    advertising strategy in 2016, 168–69, 178, 189
    "basket of deplorables" comment, 159
    Benghazi and, 159, 189, 321
    campaign advertising strategy, 171–72, 173
    debates in 2016 election, 161, 202, 220
    dueling press releases, 2016 campaign,
        166–67
    election forecasts and, 209, 210
    election of 2008, 160, 232
    election of 2016, 28, 41, 76, 79–80, 139–41,
        160, 162, 232
    on LGBTQIA+ rights, 181
    NAFTA and, 159–60
    name recognition of, 225–26
    policy positions of, 227
    political identity of, 214
    as presumptive nominee, 160
    private e-mail server, 79, 158
    Russian use of social media misinformation
        and, 139

    strategies for managing the press, 158–59
    swing voters, attracting of, 222
    use of internet in campaign, 149
    wedge issue appeals, 181
Clinton, William (Bill), 17, 79–80
    character flaws, media coverage and,
        165–66
    election of 1992, 13–14, 175, 266, 340
    election of 1996, 210, 279
    impeachment of, 2, 320–21
    "It's the economy stupid," effect of, 208
    Monica Lewinsky and, 80–81, 85, 88, 94,
        298, 307, 320–21, 323–24
    news coverage of presidents, 302
    pool sprays and, 313
    as "Slick Willie," 166, 175
    "Soldiers and Sailors" ad, 186–87
    swing voters, attracting of, 222
    use of military force by, 17
    White House media operations, 298
Clinton Foundation, 139, 159, 222, 290
closed party list, 29
CloutHub, 123
CNBC, 41, 54–55, 302
CNN
    coverage of African nations on, 35
    as daily news source, 54–55
    debates in 2012, 202
    Hurricane Katrina coverage, 4
    media credibility, views on, 64, 65–66, 89
    online user data, 121
    Operation Desert Storm (1991), 59
    partisan polarization hypothesis, 132
    on *Patterns of Global Terrorism* report,
        99–100
    point-counterpoint journalism of, 136
    Trump, coverage of, 165
    Trump, refusal of interviews, 314
    Trump's suspension of journalist
        credentials, 303
    use of social media for viewer engagement,
        123
cognitive dissonance, theory of, 130–34
Cohen, B. E., 259–60
Cold War, 98–99
    Ford-Carter debate 1976, 219
    restricted press access, Grenada, 103–5
    Vietnam War, case study, 100–103
Collins, Susan, 17
Columbia University, 245
Comcast, 40, 41, 57
Comey, James, 139, 298
commercial broadcast media. *See* broadcast media
Committee for the Study of the American
    Electorate, 203
communication, forms of, 116
computers. *See* digital devices
ComScore, 56, 62, 120

Franken, Al, 258, 318
free-agent candidates, 7
Freedman, Jonathan, 135
freedom of the press, 18
free media
        campaign use of, 156
        defined, 11
        incumbents, advantages of, 197
        presidential speechmaking and, 307–8
        shaping the news, 12
free speech rights, 38
friendly media phenomenon, 65
fundamental attribution error, 225
fundraising
        campaign finance reform and,
            193–98
        internet and, 6–7, 144–50
        press criticism, effects of, 132
        strategy frame and fundraising tactics, 76

Gaetz, Matt, 318
gaffes, 201–2
        Ford-Carter debate, 219
Gallup Polls
        Barack Obama, approval ratings,
            268, 321
        Biden-Trump personal attributes poll, 2020
            election, 222
        concern about crime, over time, 261
        concern about sexual harassment, over
            time, 259, 265
        Donald Trump, approval ratings, 322,
            325, 330
        George H. W. Bush, approval ratings,
            327–28
        George W. Bush, approval ratings, 267
        name recognition poll, 2016 election,
            225, 226
        name recognition poll, 2020 election, 225
        Trump approval ratings, 131, 186
Gannett, 53, 54
Gannon, Jeff, 310
Gantt, Harvey, 181–82
GateHouse Media, 54
gatekeeping, 66–71
        media effects, research on, 246
        for online news content, 122
gender
        issue public hypothesis, 135–37
        stereotypes, issue ownership and, 178
        stereotypes, persuasion and, 279
General Electric, 41
generalizability, surveys and, 250–53
General Social Survey, 63–64
Gentzkow, Matthew, 133, 143
Georgia, 211
Gerber, Alan, 235

Gergen, David, 293
Germany, 34
        candidate selection process, 29
        public financing of news media, 6
        regulation of broadcast media, 42
Gibson, Charles, 60
Gilliam, Franklin, 273–74
Gingrich, Newt, 180, 202
Giuliani, Rudy, 70, 84, 174
going public, politician's use of, 14–17, 289–95
        congressional committee hearings,
            315–17
        defined, 292
        media management, importance of,
            325–27
        news coverage, 299–303
        policy *vs.* electoral goals, 317–19
        presidential popularity and, 319–31
        press conferences, 308–13
        press conferences, alternatives to, 313–14
        rally effect, 327–31
        speechmaking, 303–8
        White House media operations,
            organization and roles, 295–99
Golden Triangle, 85
Goldman, Seth, 65
Goldmark, Peter, 21
Goldwater, Barry, 214, 345
Google, at congressional hearings, 315
Google News, 121
Gore, Al, 122, 133, 202, 210, 232
"gotcha" journalism, 79
government shutdowns, 290
government sources, 8
Gray (media company), 39
Green, Donald, 235
Greene, Marjorie Taylor, 7, 132, 219
Grenada, invasion of, 17, 103–5, 326
Grisham, Stephanie, 297
Grossman, Michael, 301–2
gross rating points (GRPs), 57–63
        campaign advertising strategy, 172–73
group identity, voters and, 218–19, 274–75
        affective polarization, 4, 131, 282–84,
            346–47
Guardian, The
        Edward Snowden and, 95
        online user data, 121
guilt by association ads, 186
Gulf of Tonkin, 100–105
gun control, 271, 342
Gun Owners of America, 140

Hanna, Marc, 350
Hannity, 12
Hannity, Sean, 167, 314
Harding, Warren G., 308

media pools
defined, 106
Operation Desert Storm, 105–7
media professionals, White House appointment
of, 293–95
mediated messages, 20
Meetup.com, 146
Mellman, Mark, 188
Mendelberg, Tali, 274
Mendelsohn, Matthew, 270
message learning theory, 245
messages. *See* media effects
Michigan, 170, 171–72, 211
micro targeting, 173
military conflicts. *See also* Iraq war (1991);
Iraq war (2003)
Afghanistan, 100, 178–79, 254, 327
embedded journalists, Iraq invasion (2003),
9, 107–9
Grenada, press access, 17, 103–5, 326
indexing the news and, 109–12
Iraq and weapons of mass destruction, 94–95
issue ownership, 178–79
Libya, 147
media pools, Operation Desert Storm,
105–7
official sources, dependence on, 8–9
presidential popularity and, 321, 323, 326
rally effect, 327–31
Vietnam War, case study, 100–105
Miller, Joanne, 270
Minnesota, Jesse Ventura and, 145–46
misinformation. *See also* fact-checking
affective polarization and, 4, 131, 282–84,
346–47
democratic process, effect on, 18
fact-checking of online information, 122
financial incentives for, 138
media effects, becoming informed, 254–57
in negative attack ads, 189
rise of, 4
social media and selective exposure,
137–44
social media content moderation, 138–44
Trump and spreading of misinformation, 343
Trump White House media operations, 298
uninformed voters, effects of, 343–47
voters ability to recognize, 143–44
mobile devices, as daily news source, 55
modified primaries, 27
Mondale, Walter, 233, 339–40
Monroe Doctrine, 103
Moore, Michael, 42
Moore, Roy, 167, 188, 219, 344
mosques, building of, 180
motivated reasoning, 214
MoveOn.org, 42

MSN
internet traffic, measuring of, 62
portal sites with non-news content, 134
MSNBC
2016 presidential debates, 161
Comcast and, 41
as daily news source, 54–55
media credibility, views on, 65–66, 89–90
news coverage of presidents, 303
as partisan news provider, 136
partisan polarization hypothesis, 131, 133
point of view, promotion of, 7
use of social media for viewer engagement,
123
Mubarak, Hosni, 147
Mueller, Robert, 88, 186, 292, 298
Muir, David, 60
multimember-district representation, 29
multistage systems, candidate selection, 29
Mummolo, Jonathan, 136
mundane realism, 249
Murdoch, Rupert, 39–40, 57
Murkowski, Lisa, 17
Murrow, Edward R., 59
Mutz, Diana, 65

name recognition, 224, 225
narrowcasting, 308
National Annenberg Election Study, 252
national conventions, political parties, 24–26
National Enquirer, 85, 157
National Intelligence Council, 140
National Opinion Research Center, 63–64
National Rifle Association, 140, 189, 342
national security
indexing the news, 100–112
issue ownership, 178–79
presidential popularity and, 326
rally effect, 327–31
reporting on, 96–100
National Security Agency (NSA), 95
natural disasters, 3–4, 294
NBC
coverage of invasion of Iraq (2003), 108
as daily news source, 54, 60
Ethiopia famine coverage (1980s), 22
Harvey Weinstein coverage, 88
local outlets for, 57
NBC News, online user data, 121
NBC Nightly News, 60
NBC Universal, 41
negative advertising, use of, 168–69, 183–90,
212, 237–38, 252
Nelson, Thomas, 274
Netflix, subscriber data, 62–63
Netherlands, 33–34
net neutrality, 48

New Hampshire primary, 160, 229, 230, 232–33
New Jersey, 237–38
new media. *See* internet / internet service
    providers (ISPs)
New Orleans, 294
news adjacencies, 172
news aggregators, 120, 133–34
News Corporation, 39–40, 57
news coverage. *See also* media effects
    Access Hollywood tape, Trump and, 79–80
    agenda setting, 246
    autonomy and objectivity, 74–75
    campaign strategies for managing the
        press, 157–67, 212
    candidates playing one source against
        another, 165–66
    of Congress and the president, 299–303
    congressional media operations, 317–19
    of controversial ads, 187–89
    decisions about, 66–71
    diversity of journalists and, 81–82
    dumbing down of news programming,
        347–51
    horse race reporting, 76–78, 90, 160–61,
        229–30, 269–70
    interpretive journalism, 75–82
    issue public hypothesis, 135–37
    issues-based coverage, 77–78
    of national party conventions, 162–63
    new media, effects on consumers, 121–44
    objectivity imperative, 159–60
    pack journalism, 85–86
    partisan polarization hypothesis, 130–34
    of presidential elections, 156–57
    of primary elections, 229–33
    regulating access to candidates, 163–65
    routines and procedures, 84–86
    selective exposure to online news, 127–37
    social media and selective exposure, 137–44
    sources, 86–87
news media. *See also* media, effects of; media
        marketplace
    audience fragmentation, 10
    behavior and performance of, 7–11
    broadcast media, regulation of, 38–43
    campaign coverage, regulation of, 45–48
    democratic process, effect on, 17–19, 20–24
    in Europe, 5
    free *vs.* paid media, 11
    hard *vs.* soft news, 36–37
    media ownership and regulation, 30–37
    point of view, promotion of, 7–8
    print media, regulation of, 43–45
    private ownership of, 5–6, 20, 23
    public services of, 5
    regulation of, 6
    shaping of, 11–13
    technology, effect on marketplace, 9
    watchdog function of, 5
news organizations
    autonomy and objectivity, 74–75
    diversity of journalists and, 81–82
    horse race reporting, 76–78
    interpretive journalism, 75–82
    issues-based coverage, 77–78
    news coverage, decisions about, 66–71
    processes and routines, 73–87
    routines and procedures, 84–86
    sources and, 86–87
newspapers
    Alien and Sedition Acts (1798), 349
    audience size and, 56–63
    circulation data, 53–54
    decline in daily papers, 44
    internet, effects of, 118–19
    market pressures, 68, 70–71
    print media regulation, 43–45
    user demographics, 118–19, 120
Newsweek, 101
New Yorker, 88
    on Eric Schneiderman, 117
    on Harvey Weinstein, 258
New York Post, 39–40
New York Times
    on 2016 presidential debates, 161
    circulation data, 56
    congressional media operations, 317
    coverage of Congress and the president,
        300–302
    coverage of John Kennedy, 81
    on Harvey Weinstein, 258
    on Iraq and weapons of mass destruction,
        94–95, 109
    market pressures, 68, 70–71
    media credibility, views on, 65–66, 89
    online audience, 120, 121
    pack journalism, 85–86
    on Trump's COVID daily briefings, 299
Nexstar, 39
NHK, public financing of, 6
Nicaragua, Iran-Contra scandal, 307, 310, 320
Nicholas, Henry III, 339
Nielsen Company, 56, 57
    debate audience data over time, 200–201
    national party convention ratings, 163
    online streaming audience, measuring of, 62
Niger, 97
Nigeria, 35
9/11 terror attacks, 163, 266, 326–27
Nixon, Richard
    credibility after Watergate, 292
    debates with Kennedy, 9, 155–56, 198, 223
    election of 1960, 9, 155–56, 198
    election of 1972, 210

media credibility, views on, 63–66
media effects, becoming informed, 254–57
media effects, implications for, 279–84
news coverage of presidents, 302–3
online news sources, 122–23
partisan polarization hypothesis, 130–34
persuasion, media effects, 277–82
playing one source against another, 166
selective exposure to online news, 127–37
shaping the news, 11–13
Sinclair Broadcasting, 40
social media and selective exposure, 137–44
source credibility, 276
partisan polarization hypothesis, 127, 128, 130–34
partisanship
    affective polarization, 4, 131, 282–84, 346–47
    audience fragmentation, 10
    candidate selection and, 23–24
    COVID-19, presidential approval and, 329–31
    debates, impressions of performance and, 219–21
    democratic process, effect on, 17–19
    effects of, 343–47
    group identity and, 218–19
    holding the base, 214–21
    issue ownership and, 176–79
    media credibility, views on, 63–66
    media effects, implications for, 279–84
    persuasion, media effects, 277–82
    presidential popularity and, 17
    primary elections, campaign strategies, 228–33
    rally effect, 327–31
    reinforcement effect, 220
    swing voters, attracting of, 221–23
    voter turnout and, 14, 233–39
    voting as expression of partisanship, 213–28
    wedge issue appeals, 179–82, 185, 208, 236, 342–43
Patriot missile system, 107
Patterns of Global Terrorism, 99–100
paywalls, 56–57
PBS (Public Broadcasting Service), 6
    coverage of invasion of Iraq (2003), 108
    embedded journalists, Iraq invasion (2003), 108
    market pressures and, 68
    public *vs.* commercial media ownership, 32–33
Pelley, Scott, 60
Pence, Mike, 162

Pennsylvania, 170, 171–72, 211
Pentagon
    embedded journalists, Iraq invasion (2003), 107–9
    journalist beat and, 84–85
    media pools, Operation Desert Storm, 105–7
    as news source, 8
    Niger, investigation of military deaths, 97
    restricted press access, Grenada, 103–5
    Vietnam War, case study, 100–105
Perot, Ross, 79
Perry, Rick, 202
personality, voter impressions of, 225–26
persuasion, 14
    attitude change, 245
    going public and, 15–17
    media effects, 277–82
    polarized politics and, 279–84
    receiver-related contingencies, 277–78
    source- and message-related contingencies, 278–79
Pew Project of Excellence in Journalism
    news coverage of presidents, 302
Pew Research Center
    civic engagement by education and income, 124
    civic engagement online and offline, 128
    Facebook as news source, 137
    hard news *vs.* soft news, viewer recall and, 69
    Howard Dean's internet campaign, 146–47
    internet use surveys, 117–20
    local news revenue, 73
    local TV station ownership, 39
    media bias, 132, 303
    network news ratings, 60
    news coverage of presidents, 303
    newspapers, status of, 58
    news source use by age, 120
    online political engagement by age and education, 126
    on partisan animus, 280–81
    presidential debates 2016, viewer response to, 199
    time spent following news, 119
    on use of social media for news content, 137
    on voter's top issues 2021, 265
Philadelphia, PA, 38
photography and eyewitness accounts, smartphones and, 111
photo ID, for voters, 238–39
pizzagate, 139
Plame, Valerie, 87
planting reporter, press conferences and, 309–10
Point Salines Airport, 103
point-to-point communication, 116
polarized politics, implications for media effects, 279–84